Readings in
VOCATIONAL TRAINING FOR THE MENTALLY RETARDED

Special Learning Corporation
42 Boston Post Rd. Guilford, Connecticut 06437

Special Learning Corporation

Publisher's Message:

The Special Education Series is the first comprehensive series designed for special education courses of study. It is also the first series to offer such a wide variety of high quality books. In addition, the series will be expanded and up-dated each year. No other publications in the area of special education can equal this. We stress high quality content, a superb advisory and consulting group, and special features that help in understanding the course of study. In addition we believe we must also publish in very small enrollment areas in order to establish the credibility and strength of our series. We realize the enrollments in courses of study such as Autism, Visually Handicapped Education, or Diagnosis and Placement are not large. Nevertheless, we believe there is a need for course books in these areas and books that are kept up-to-date on an annual basis! Special Learning Corporation's goal is to publish the highest quality materials for the college and university courses of study. With your comments and support we will continue to do this.

John P. Quirk

SPECIAL EDUCATION SERIES

- ● Autism
- * ● Behavior Modification
  Biological Bases of Learning Disabilities
  Brain Impairments
- ● Career and Vocational Education
  Child Abuse
  Child Development
  Child Psychology
  Cognitive and Communication Skills
- * ● Counseling Parents of Exceptional
  Children
  Creative Arts
  Curriculum and Materials
- * ● Deaf Education
  Developmental Disabilities
- * ● Diagnosis and Placement
  Down's Syndrome
- ● Dyslexia
  Early Learning
  Educational Technology
- * ● Emotional and Behavioral Disorders
  Exceptional Parents
- * ● Gifted and Talented Education
- * ● Human Growth and Development of
  the Exceptional Individual
  Hyperactivity
- * ● Individualized Educational Programs

- ● Language & Writing Disorders
- * ● Learning Disabilities
  Learning Theory
- * ● Mainstreaming
- * ● Mental Retardation
- ● Motor Disorders
  Multiple Handicapped Education
  Occupational Therapy
- ● Perception and Memory Disorders
- * ● Physically Handicapped Education
- * ● Pre-School Education for the
  Handicapped
- * ● Psychology of Exceptional Children
- ● Reading Disorders
  Reading Skill Development
  Research and Development
- * ● Severely and Profoundly Handicapped
  Education
  Slow Learner Education
  Social Learning
- * ● Special Education
- * ● Speech and Hearing
  Testing and Diagnosis
- ● Three Models of Learning Disabilities
- * ● Visually Handicapped Education
- * ● Vocational Training for the Mentally
  Retarded

● Published Titles   * Major Course Areas

Readings in
Human Growth And
Development of the
Exceptional Individual

Readings in
Pre-School Education
For The Handicapped

Readings in
Vocational Training For
The Mentally Retarded

Readings in
Career And Vocational
Education For
The Handicapped

CONTENTS

3. Special Education's Responsibility

4. Manpower Development and Utilization

GLOSSARY OF TERMS

Adaptive Behavior How well the individual solves problems and how well he adapts to the behavioral expectations and standards of society.

Assessment Considerd to be a battery of tests (formal and informal) to evaluate a person's performance.

Career Education The entire educational curriculum, coordinating all school, family and community components together to develop each individual's potential for economic, social and personal success.

Cognition The process or act of knowing. Thinking skills and processes are often considered cognitive skills.

Cue Redundancy Color to facilitate the acquisition of a complete assembly task. Color Coding.

Education Team The group of professional individuals, classroom teachers, supportive service teachers (resource room, speech therapist, etc.) psychologist, school nurse principals who are involved in diag nosing and supervising a child's educational program.

Employability Possessing a "marketable skill," one that enables a person to be attractive as an employee in a work setting appropriate to that person's potential.

Feedback The process of recognizing or receiving notice for a behavior or performance.

Fine motor Most frequently relates to use of the hands to perform manipulation and writing tasks.

Function Level Ability level at which a person can perform for a given task.

Gross Motor Most frequently relates to use of the large muscles of the body to perform acts of motion such as turning, jumping, running. Gross motor also involves the ability to coordinate large muscle movements.

Habilitation Improvement in a skill or level of adjustment, as with respect to an increase in the ability to maintain satisfactory employment.

Intelligence Quotient (I.Q.) An intelligence-test score; also the relationship between chronological age and mental age.

Job samples Mock work situations set up within the school to provide practice applicable to a job in the community.

Mental age The mental age a person functions based upon a specific diagnostic or achievement test.

Mental deficiency A synonym for mental retardation. Sometimes used in a more restricted sense to refer to those whose mental retardation is attributable to structural defect.

Normalization The opportunity of an individual to function in as normal a setting as possible, to realize his potential, and to maintain behaviors and characteristics which are as culturally normal as possible.

Perception The attachment of meaning to the reception of a stimulus. Understanding that which is received by the sense organs.

Rehabilitation Restoration of a skill or restoration of efficiency to a level compatible with partial or complete vocational and social independence.

Resident The general term used to refer to mentally retarded persons who receive services from a residential facility.

Sensori-motor A term which relates to the combination of the input of sensations and the output of a motor activity. The motor activity indicates what is happening to the sensory organs such as sight, hearing, tactual and kinesthetic sensations.

Sheltered workshops A facility which provides occupational training and/or protective employment.

Special class A class, usually in a school setting, that provides special instruction for mentally retarded children as well as for other types of students with special needs.

Task analysis In depth examination of tasks before assigning to a client. Involves analysis for: ease of movement, economy, method (s) easiest to teach and to learn, and process analysis for format and type of feedback.

Token reward In a behavior modification program a reward is usually given for correct response or appropriate behavior. A reward is usually withheld if the person fails to respond or perform within previously established guidelines.

Vocational education That part of the curriculum concerned with the competencies involved in successful employment and vocational choice.

Work study program School curriculum set up so student can work part of the time in the school dealing with academics and job related subject matters, and part of the time in the community on the job.

PREFACE

The United States is just beginning to utilize an important manpower resource, the mentally retarded. Recognition and acceptance is long overdue. In order to lead normal lives they must be given the right to work. Many employers still need to overcome fears and prejudices towards this group and support the development of the skills and abilities to fit the demands of a job.

There are a number of programs today to assist in the training and placement process. Advances are continuing to be made in *assessment* techniques to learn and define abilities and appropriate methods for realization of full potential. *Special Education* is being directed towards work-study programs and vocational preparation on all levels. The National Association for Retarded Citizen's (NARC) *On the Job Training* Project (OJT) encourages employers to hire and train mentally retarded workers and alleviate manpower shortages. Exciting progress is being made in *Sheltered Workshops* and *Residential* programs where the opportunity to develop and increase vocational skills, and provide for one's self in a real work/living environment is provided. "Elwyn" is changing the definition of *Institutions*, although the movement is to get the mentally retarded out of the institution and into the *Community*.

Lifetime care for an institutionalized individual can cost as much as $400,000. Vocational training is a positive alternative. Recent studies show that 75% of all mentally retarded children in the United States could become self-supporting adults. Another 10-15%, with proper attention and training, could become partially self-supporting. The average mentally retarded individual working in a community contributes $10.00 in income taxes for every dollar spent on his/her education and vocational training. Instead of a drain on the economy and a burden to their family, the mentally retarded can become contributing members of their community.

Photographs by Ann Rivellini

THE LAST MINORITY: AN INTRODUCTION

The mentally retarded know about job discrimination, both when applying for a job and after (if) they are hired. It is frustrating to be denied the right to participate fully and make a meaningful contribution to society.

The many barriers that exist range from written tests to the "token" quotas companies have for hiring a handicapped. They are treated like "children in grown-up bodies." Negative reactions and stereotyping give a limited chance for performance and are obstacles to success.

There is an increasing problem with employee disatisfaction in the lesser skilled jobs. Many of these are services that the mentally retarded can and will eagerly do. Employers who hesitate because they feel "such people can't handle regular employment" are mistaken. The odds favor the mentally retarded. On the job surveys show that they are above the average in punctuality, attendance and tenure. They are usually better than their "normal" co-workers for the same position in motivation, task performance and fatigue resistance. They have a higher potential for job satisfaction and reward their employer with loyalty and hard work.

Studies show that even severely and profoundly retarded individuals can learn to care for their basic needs and perform useful activities. They can, and should be allowed to live outside institutions and contribute to their community.

In spite of their positive work records, many employers still believe that the mentally retarded have no business in the working world. While the National Association for Retarded Citizens, government agencies and other organizations are helping to increase knowledge and understanding, legislation is necessary for protection against job prejudice.

The Rehabilitation Act of 1973, sections 503 and 504 insure protection. All federal agencies and contractors must employ and advance qualified handicapped. The law insures the right to file complaints of alleged discrimination. The Rehabilitation Act of 1974 includes state rehabilitation agencies. Many states have passed supporting laws.

The mentally retarded are asking for a chance to make good on the job. They are asking for the opportunity to learn, to perform as well as they can, and to gain the acceptance and respect of their co-workers and employers. Employers need to be urged to replace "unselective rejection" hiring practices with "selective placement." The right person must be given the right job, regardless of his/her handicap.

"Can the applicant do the job?" should be the basis for hiring all persons.

THE LAST MINORITY

A handicap gives some people, like golfers, an even chance.

Other people aren't so lucky, like prospective employes — especially ones who are mentally retarded.

"But the last minority is being heard," said Bernard Posner, executive secretary of the President's Committee on Employment of the Handicapped. "The mentally retarded have finally started acting like any other nasty minority."

A slow turn of events in favor of mentally retarded people who want jobs has happened, but not simply because "America saw fit to pass Affirmative Action legislation," Posner said.

However, this legislation does help mentally re-

tarded people. It is an amendment to the 1973 Rehabilitation Act which mandates hiring qualified handicapped, including mentally retarded citizens, by government contractors with contracts of more than $2,500.

"Before Affirmative Action, hiring the handicapped was a nice, good, well-meaning, voluntary effort on the part of some employers," Posner said.

"Interlarded with some kind of subtle charity, hiring the handicapped in general manifested itself in some crumby ways over the years," he said. "In the last few years, it's become a whole new ball game. Gone are the days when I'd hear employers ask where they could 'find some of those people' because they thought they could pay them less and lower their payroll figures."

Affirmative Action helped, but increased awareness of the civil rights of everyone, including mentally retarded citizens, was the impetus for the change.

"The handicapped were not a big priority with the government until the civil and human rights movement of the '60s," said Dr. Allen Phelps, of HEW's Bureau of Education for the Handicapped. "The result is a general change in the country's attitude toward educating and employing the handicapped."

The attitudes started changing toward mentally handicapped citizens when significant public figures, like President John F. Kennedy and Senator Hubert H. Humphrey, revealed their personal relationship to this handicap. Senator and Mrs. Humphrey's daughter is retarded.

In 1962 President Kennedy revealed his sister's condition and wrote a memo which allowed, in effect, mentally handicapped persons to compete for civil service jobs by eliminating the written examination.

In 1966 the President's Committee on Mental Retardation was formed under Executive Order. President Kennedy was an example of how most

Subcontract work keeps rehabilitation centers in the business of training and offering paying jobs to their clients. Putting automobile owner manuals into pouches and working a drill press are among the jobs they do.

people become involved in the struggle of the mentally retarded. The Kennedy family was able to do more than most to help. The Joseph P. Kennedy Jr. Foundation was set up by the family for that purpose. It sponsors the annual Special Olympics designed for mentally retarded participants.

Approximately three percent of the population of the United States is mentally retarded to some degree. That's about 6.5 million persons. About 80 percent of that number are identified as being moderately retarded. This group is classified as "educable" with an intelligence quotient which would permit them to learn social science, some mathematics, reading and writing.

"Though IQ is not the best measure, it does provide some indication of the educational potential of mentally retarded individuals," said Fred J. Krause, executive director of the President's Committee on Mental Retardation.

Over the years many tests for determining degrees of retardation, as well as assessing vocational skills and aptitudes and other abilities and interests, have been standardized.

Other clues to the needs and desires of mentally retarded persons have recently been provided by the individuals themselves.

"Traditionally, we sought information only from professionals and parents, but now we are beginning to hear from the mentally retarded themselves," Krause said. "Soon we will begin polling them on a small scale to develop a questionnaire to poll a larger group later."

The poll will ask such things as what kind of housing and jobs mentally retarded people want; whether or not they think they get enough recreation and social activity opportunities and what their general life attitudes are.

"These preferences could affect policy on all levels," Krause said.

Reflecting the goal of finding out from the mentally retarded about themselves, two of his staff consultants are formerly institutionalized retarded individuals.

The polling will be done through three research and training centers set up by HEW and the President's Committee on Mental Retardation. The three centers are at Texas Tech in Lubbock, the University of Wisconsin at Madison, and the University of Oregon at Eugene.

"Retarded people are just like anyone else. They want a part in determining their own destinies," Posner said.

The polls are only one way mentally retarded people will be heard.

One group has started its own newspaper called *The Milwaukee Citizen*. The paper is produced entirely by mentally retarded persons with help from a University of Wisconsin student advisor. It began in August of 1975 and is published bi-monthly.

"The idea for starting the paper was to allow mentally retarded people to express themselves for themselves," explained Laura Falbo, a member of a group of Milwaukee parents of mentally retarded persons which sponsors the paper. "Self-advocacy is a real trend. The publication is usually four pages and consists of a calendar of events, recipes, editorials and a big issue story. Some of the issues the paper has tackled have been the opening of group homes for retarded citizens and discussion of the city's transit system."

A staff of ten, plus several contributing writers, produces the publication.

People First, a group of retarded citizens in

Mastering the art of silk screen printing and constructing portable scientific laboratories are two activities in which employes participate at New Horizons, a Michigan rehabilitation organization which also places clients in outside jobs.

Photos courtesy of NEW HORIZONS

Oregon, held its third convention last October in Portland. About 850 people attended.

"People First is a chance for retarded people to speak for themselves. There is nothing else like it in the U.S. as far as I know," said Dennis Heath, a social worker and advisor to the organization.

"The goal is self-sufficiency. The convention helps them to see what others like them can do. They have learned to get up and speak in front of a group, use a microphone, and organize a convention," Heath said. "My purpose is to be helpful without leading. I call myself a friend and advisor."

Through these self-assertive efforts as well as awareness programs of government and parent organizations, prospective employers are beginning to recognize retarded people as not only possible but desirable employes.

They are wrestling with how and where to find qualified employes for the jobs they have open. Mainstream, a Washington, D.C.-based nonprofit organization, founded to promote the cause of all handicapped people, has an infant offshoot called HIRE (Handicapped Information Resource for Employment).

The program is designed to provide computerized information on available prospective employes, offer seminars in facility accommodation for handicapped people and explain where handicapped persons can fit into a company's work force. HIRE will start in New York City in June to gather information about what agencies exist and what training programs they provide for handicapped people.

This information will then be made available to subscribing companies (who will pay $100 for the service). Eventually, HIRE wants to cover the entire nation in this way. Fifty more cities' agencies will be covered within the year, officials hope.

A special hiring program, designed and run by the National Association of Retarded Citizens (NARC), has yielded 20,000 new jobs since it began in 1967.

"This on-the-job training project has worked

very well," said Mike Stumbaugh, director of the project. "We have placed about 5,000 people each year for the past three years. The program is designed to match employable men and women with specific jobs in industrial and service organizations.

"The employer provides the trainee with a job and 320 hours of intensive on-the-job training. To offset the additional cost of training the employe, NARC pays 50 percent of the wage for the first 160 hours and 25 percent for the second 160 hours," Stumbaugh explained.

NARC also sends promotion material to prospective employers and publishes a monthly newsletter called "OTJ [on-the-job] Information." It describes what a mentally retarded man or woman can bring to a job. It is being sent to the 2,000 largest employers in the United States.

According to some authorities, corporations are generally doing a good job. And NARC recognizes those who do an especially good job of hiring mentally retarded people. Last year's award winner was the Bally Manufacturing Co., a Chicago-based manufacturer of pinball and slot machines. Other winners have been American Motors and the Marriott Corporation, which was the first profit-making company to win the award.

"The on-the-job training project has opened a lot of doors because it's been in existence for a long while. It has also assisted in breaking down some employment barriers," Stumbaugh said.

But the program places individuals who are ready to work. How do they become "ready"?

"There are approximately 3,000 sheltered workshops in the U.S.," Bernard Posner said. "About half of the 450,000 people in these workshops are retarded. Half the workshops are designed exclusively for mentally retarded people."

The nonprofit workshops provide opportunities for handicapped persons to improve their job potential. Participants are taught specific skills as well as social behavior and workday procedures.

HEW provides monetary incentive for some of the workshops to train and find employment for their participants. The workshops can receive 18 months' worth of funds to study, evaluate and rehabilitate handicapped, including mentally retarded, individuals. After this period the individual must be placed in some kind of a job — which could continue to be at the workshop.

"There's hardly a community in the U.S. that doesn't have a sheltered workshop of some kind," said Fred Krause. "The number of them has grown beyond my wildest imagination."

The workshops are quasi-commercial establishments which do subcontract work for companies in their areas. Some assemble soft-drink cartons; others sort nuts and bolts; still others collate printed material and kits or stuff envelopes.

But Dr. Phelps of HEW maintains that the public school systems must accept more of the responsibility for training handicapped people.

"We are trying to put these kids in the mainstream of schooling," he said. "Because of the human rights movement, we have gotten away from labeling students as to their capabilities, but we have seen few retarded kids in special vocational education classes at the secondary level. The whole attitude is changing, but there is also the problem of finding teachers who are equipped to train these youngsters in salable job skills."

'Before Affirmative Action, hiring the handicapped was a nice, well-meaning, voluntary effort on the part of some employers.'
Bernard Posner

Reports from the federal General Accounting Office showed that the Bureau of Education wasn't "doing a darn thing" to train teachers of the handicapped.

"And the reports are correct," Dr. Phelps admitted. "As a result, we are spending a significant part of our budget now for teacher training programs."

Thirty-six projects of this type are being funded by the Bureau. They are university based programs where the professors go to the public school teachers at their own schools and teach them skills which will improve their ability to identify retarded youngsters and develop specific instructional techniques for teaching them.

"In the long run, I hope, these programs will have some effect on education curricula at the university level. But for now we are trying to reach as many teachers as possible who are already teaching," Phelps said.

Such courses, he said, had never been developed because there was little consciousness of the handicapped as potential workers.

"In light of the Affirmative Action legislation, we better start preparing more teachers so they can provide job skill training for these people before they leave public school," Phelps insisted. "The mechanism is there to do it. We have to realize that being handicapped doesn't mean you can't be employed."

Some school systems reimburse teachers who participate in such programs. The teachers are often given credit which would help to keep up

1. MINORITY

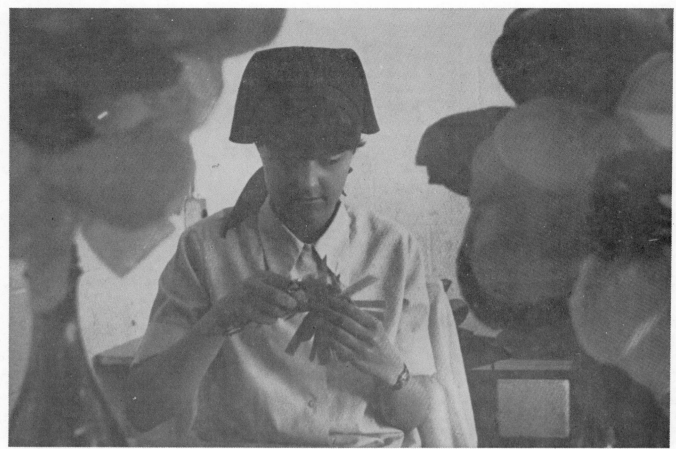

Photo by EDWARD J. SPERKO

Some rehabilitation centers custom make products such as art pedestals, ceramic mirrors, wind chimes, mailboxes and tissue flowers such as the young woman is assembling.

their state certification, as well.

"We've found we can't get the job done by asking teachers to stay after school to train in their spare time. It has to be made worth their while," Phelps said.

All of HEW's vocational education programs have to relate specifically to community job possibilities. One Pennsylvania school system shop teacher found some of those possibilities, and he designed his own training program around them.

A number of homes in the area were badly in need of refurbishing. This teacher, who had carpentry skills, convinced the school system to purchase the homes. The students then went into the homes and were taught, by doing, to gut the homes and redo them.

As the homes were rebuilt they were sold. Proceeds were used to buy more homes, train and employ more youngsters.

The unions in the area then considered these students as possible apprentices. This idea is also used in California.

Carpentry may not be a skill most people would consider retarded people able to develop, but it is. This pessimistic opinion of what retarded people can do is another employment problem.

"We've got to stop stereotyping people. Almost any of our facilities could employ mentally retarded people in some capacity," said Don Werner, an assistant director in the employment relations department of General Motors and a member of the President's Committee on Employment of the Handicapped. "Our toughest problem is selling management on the fact that the retarded can do a good job.

"We know we have to employ handicapped people if they are qualified and the corporation is committed to this project."

"The cue came long ago — to hire the protected classes," said Norman A. Houle, an employment supervisor in General Motors' Technical Center Personnel Administration. "Our approach is reflected in our willingness to hire people (like the retarded) as we can accommodate them. This is the kind of commitment necessary to get the program going."

"The biggest problem in employing the mentally retarded is inertia among ourselves," said Burt Sparhawk, manager of personnel placement at GM's Technical Center Personnel Administration.

"The training being provided for them in the sheltered workshops is excellent. These employes are dedicated, loyal and devoted, and there are very few problems with them. All of us are becoming more enlightened than we were 10-15 years ago."

Sparhawk is the father of a retarded son. He said that at the Tech Center, GM is starting to hire retarded persons on a contingency basis as cafeteria workers and general maintenance personnel, and "we think we can convince other department heads, too," he said.

GM became involved in hiring retarded people through a county rehabilitation organization. Personnel Staff members visited it over a two-year period to become more familiar with its programs and to investigate the job potential of some of its participants.

The rehabilitation organization has provided information for preparing supervisors to deal with retarded employes and has worked closely in selecting, supervising and follow-up of employes GM has hired.

"Involving such an organization is something I would have to insist on as an employer. If a problem arises, as it can with any employe, there is someone who can help, when the employe has been referred by a rehab organization. They are familiar with the employe they nurtured for the job, and they have analyzed the person's situation so they can probably deal better with any problem than we could," Houle said. "If you hire someone off the street who is mentally retarded and something happens, you have no recourse for evaluating the problem," Houle said. "These workshop personnel can provide orientation for both the employe and the employer . . . they know the individual, and they have experience dealing with retarded people that even parents cannot provide."

Many businesses have a use for workers who may not be skilled but who are dependable. The important thing is to look at the whole person, not just the handicap.

"We are beginning to look at specific aptitudes of people, rather than jobs that would avoid their handicap specifically," Phelps.said.

Posner said big business is surprised that handicapped people don't fit the traditional stereotypes in job placement.

Kenneth Muenk, human resources management coordinator at GM's Technical Center, said GM has hired people on ability regardless of any handicap "for years." Actually there are places where mentally retarded people excel. Many of these jobs would bore the average person.

"Retarded employes are very good at repetitive assignments. Once they learn a task they do it

very well and love that sort of thing," Sparhawk said. "Repetitive jobs command all their attention. They have limited faculties, so they have to put their whole minds to the one task they're doing."

A manufacturer of puzzles and other toys said he could not keep any so-called "normal" employes in his plant because they went "bananas" trying to assemble the brightly colored parts. However, when he started employing mentally retarded people, he found they did the work with

---

'The training being provided for them [the mentally retarded] in the sheltered workshops is excellent. These employes are dedicated, loyal and devoted, and there are very few problems with them. All of us are becoming more enlightened than we were 10 to 15 years ago.'

Burt Sparhawk, GM Tech Center

---

fervor and never became frustrated. By employing mentally retarded workers, he built a dependable and stable work force.

A man who ran a cleaning establishment in the West found that he was employing workers who would stay with his operation long enough to get a little money then quit. They also quit because the work was too boring.

The President's Committee on Mental Retardation advised the man to hire mentally handicapped workers. The new employes didn't get bored with the same ironing job day after day.

"Mentally retarded employes won't get 'down' because of a routine job," Krause said. "Automation will not take care of all the jobs in the world. Service organizations are still going to need a lot of people. The job market, according to the futurists, will be open there. We know that people with impaired learning development are very capable in those occupations."

Many government programs are focusing on which service jobs are most applicable to mentally retarded workers. Are these government programs worth the money?

"It is much cheaper than paying for these people through a variety of social programs," Krause said. "One economist who worked for us figured the government was losing $6 billion every year in lost productivity as long as institutionalized people stayed where they were and didn't have jobs.

"For decades we were staffing and building

more and larger institutions as the number of retarded people to fill them grew to about 200,000 in 1968. The average cost per person per year was around $15,000 and that did not include new construction costs, maintenance or remodeling of older institutions. The overall cost each year was about $3 billion," Krause said.

About 154,000 mentally retarded people are now institutionalized in public facilities. Krause said that, at considerably less cost, the government could provide rehabilitation for a large number of these people.

Dr. Phelps feels the government could do even more despite the fact it already employs 20,000 mentally handicapped persons. He said there is a wide-ranging concern in government, but it's a matter of translating that concern to people who are going to monitor or respond to it in terms of funding programs, getting budget allocations and the like.

The government, like most institutions of soci-ety, he said, responds very slowly to changing needs and attitudes. "But maybe in the years ahead you'll see this bureau spending more money to provide vocational education for the handicapped at the secondary school level," Phelps said.

We no longer see work as Bob Cratchit did. No longer do people go to work, sit in a corner with an eyeshade and never converse with fellow workers through the day. Nor would Bob's Tiny Tim be viewed as someone to pity, someone who'd never be able to work.

Instead, work is a very social function of our lives. And mentally retarded workers are becoming, and will become even more, important to the work and social scheme of life.

Progressive parents no longer hide their trainable mentally handicapped children in institutions. They realize these children have the potential — indeed the right — to lead active and productive lives.

New Roles, New Hope For Mentally Retarded

*Interview With Fred J. Krause, Executive Director,
President's Committee on Mental Retardation*

**It's an optimistic prospect laid out by
a leading authority—progress in preventing
retardation, success in educating
and employing many of those afflicted,
bringing them back into the home community.**

Q Mr. Krause, how are retarded Americans faring today compared with their situation a few years ago?

A The overall progress has been significant.

Mental retardation has been far more on the minds of the public, and this has brought much of the progress and local community services which we've been striving for. We've made important gains in bringing the retarded back into the mainstream of the community. And we've been broadening their legal and human rights.

Q How many Americans today are classified as retarded?

A There have been no exact census figures, but we calculate approximately 6 million Americans who, as a result of inadequately developed intelligence, are significantly impaired in their ability to learn and to adapt to the demands of society.

At least 85 percent of these represent a moderate form of retardation, and a good portion of these children could be taught to function effectively if acted on early. Some 88 percent suffer from additional handicapping conditions, such as poor hearing or eyesight, that could slow their progress if not detected.

Q Do you classify the retarded on the basis of their IQ's?

A No. The intelligence quotient by itself can be misleading in determining the capability of a person. It must be used with other measurements of the individual's abilities and potential.

Q How many retarded persons need institutional care?

A The vast majority can be cared for in the community, if not in their own homes. A few will need some care and supervision all their lives, but the numbers may be less than 3 percent of the mentally retarded population: those who may need medical and nursing supervision 24 hours a day.

Q What progress is being made in preventing or correcting mental retardation?

A There have been a number of important biomedical and behavioral research studies which could point to a significant reduction—possibly as much as 50 percent—in mental retardation through improved health care and education. In the longer range, brain and other basic research can help correct prenatal defects.

At present, however, the best prospects are in preventive measures by parents to make sure they will not bear a physically or mentally defective child.

Q What seems to be the single biggest factor that contributes to retardation?

A A deprived environment and lack of public understanding of the causes and a lack of prenatal care are some factors.

For example, researchers have learned that mothers with a history of chronic alcoholism, extremely heavy smoking or serious drug problems run more risk of premature delivery, low birth weight and similar problems that often go with mental retardation and other developmental disabilities.

Q Are any clues coming out of the growing research on the workings of the human brain?

A The brain is still one of the organs we really know very little about.

The federal-government spending in this area is about 38 million dollars. By stepping up our research efforts, we can learn not only more on the causes of mental retardation but how we can prevent it.

Q How many Americans are victims of what is called Mongolism, or Down's syndrome?

A There are over 200 causes related to mental retardation. Down's syndrome—a chromosomal abnormality occurring in 1 out of 600 to 700 live births—can be prevented if there is genetic counseling and if women, especially over the age of 35, consult their physician and determine the risk if they conceive.

One test during pregnancy is called amniocentesis, which extracts amniotic fluid from a pregnant woman and can determine if the fetus has a chromosomal abnormality.

Q What other causes of mental retardation are preventable?

A Many metabolic disorders which contribute to retardation could be prevented. There's the Rh factor and the phenylketonuria—or PKU—group.

We know one blood sample can detect at least 11 metabolic disorders; yet there are few medical clinics in the country that are applying this known knowledge. In fact, there are only a few states, such as Massachusetts, Oregon and Pennsylvania, that require the testing for hypothyroidism, and this condition is found in three times as many cases as PKU, for which 44 states—at last count—require testing.

Q Can the embryo be treated if tests show up positive?

A A certain amount of research is going on to find the answer—in drugs and/or surgery—of correcting such a condition. We think research is on the threshold of some major advances in that area.

Q Does fear of producing a retarded child contribute to the growing number of abortions in this country?

A We have little information, but there's another side to the relationship between retardation fears and abortion: Often mothers are fearful that because of genetics or some incident during pregnancy they will have an abnormal child and therefore should consider alternatives.

Studies in this country and England suggest that the embryo is normal more often than not. In such cases, and when parents are reassured by tests and counseling, they often abandon plans for an abortion.

Q What are the most important preventive measures?

A They fall into four basic categories:

First, prior to conception, we find that many women seem unaware of the need for good nutrition, medical care and health services. Then, during pregnancy, the emphasis is on better health care, testing for defects and avoiding excessive amounts of drugs or alcohol. At birth, we urge testing for metabolic disorders. And, finally, early-intervention programs in infancy can detect and bring some correction in what otherwise could be a serious and disabling degree of retardation.

Q Do you mean retardation sometimes can be corrected?

A Definitely. Studies that have been made, such as one in Milwaukee, have shown that we can significantly improve upon the intelligence and the developmental and cognitive learning of the child through stimulation of the infant's physical, emotional and mental growth.

Q How many retarded children altogether would you say are educable to some degree?

A Of all those who are mildly or moderately retarded, from 90 to 95 percent can participate in regular educational programs with individualized educational planning. About 5 percent need special training or residential living.

Q Are you saying that most of the educable can be "mainstreamed" into classrooms alongside other pupils?

A In most cases, this will become prevalent as states and local districts meet the requirements of Public Law 94-142, which requires an individualized educational plan for each handicapped child so that he or she would only go to a special class as needed.

For instance, a mentally retarded youngster would not be guided to algebra but would take studies that enhance his or her economic usefulness and place in community life.

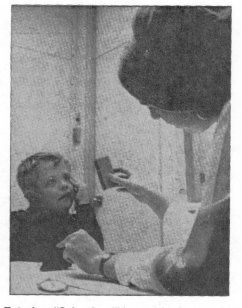

Tutoring. "Schools will be required to provide education for all—including the retarded."

Q What kind of treatment do retarded children generally get from other pupils and teachers in public schools?

A Their difficulties in some subjects can and do sometimes make them the object of criticism or jeers. But teachers who are familiar with the special problems of the mentally retarded children can help make them accepted. Moreover, school officials can help by providing more emphasis on vocational education as an alternative to difficult academic subjects.

Q Are we training enough teachers in working with the special problems of the retarded?

A Not yet. Many universities are increasing their output of special-education teachers, but the effect is felt mainly in large cities where teaching salaries are higher.

Q Can school districts afford the costs to carry out the mandate for educating retarded youngsters?

A I think they will be able to do so. The law requires a steady escalation of the federal contribution up to 40 percent of the actual cost of educating a child in a special-education program. This is now estimated at about $2,800 per pupil a year for those who need separate special instruction.

The schools can and will be required to provide education for all their handicapped children including the retarded.

Q For what ages?

A The age range is from 3 to 21, according to the overall programs policy provided by the individual school district.

Q How will tax-supported help for the handicapped fare in the pressure to cut property and other taxes?

A The passage of Proposition 13 in California shouldn't necessarily raise any serious problem for an established special-educational program for the handicapped any more than it does for standard classes in geography or mathematics. California has mandated special education for its handicapped, and the substantial support it's getting from the federal government should allow the program to remain without any interference.

Q What are you doing to get more mentally retarded Americans into paying jobs?

A First, we're trying to promote a better understanding of the fact that the retarded worker can undertake a wide range of jobs. Second, the government is training vocational counselors to help place the retarded persons and other handicapped in jobs. Third, we're subsidizing part of the salary paid to them in job-training programs.

All this has helped remedy a lack of understanding among employers. In fact, 31,800 mentally retarded were habilitated and placed in jobs last year.

Q How well do mentally retarded persons do on the job?

A The fact is that employers find them often more conscientious than other workers because of their concentration on details and their low level of frustration with routine jobs.

Q What kind of work do they do best?

A Routine work and assignments that give them some satisfaction in what they're doing.

For example, we have found that their manual dexterity can be quite good in handling the sometimes tedious details of assembling or disassembling products.

They also like to work out of doors if possible. We have some very successful horticultural programs where they do gardening and agricultural work that is now very much needed: potting small plants, helping with garden supplies, and so on.

Q Do many reach the point of being able to support themselves, marry and find a place in the community?

A Approximately two thirds or more of the mentally retarded are living a fairly normal life. Many can take part in social activities, marry and have families. Some of the more severely retarded need guidance in their social, sexual and economic life.

The federal government is supporting a protection-and-advocacy office in each state to meet needs of the mentally retarded as well as other developmentally disabled persons.

Q In what ways?

A By training both citizen advocates and professionals to protect the rights of retarded people and consulting and guiding them on such matters as entering into a contract or purchasing an appliance. The mentally retarded person can go to an advocate and ask: "Is this a good arrangement?" or "How can I handle this matter?"

Q Do many neighborhoods still try to bar retarded people?

A Unfortunately, yes. Local communities control various types of housing programs through zoning ordinances that sometimes close off housing for the mentally retarded. We are getting at this problem in two ways: first, by having laws amended or changed to prevent discrimination; second, by persuading the public that there's no serious economic or social consequences from having mentally retarded persons in their neighborhoods.

Q Can retarded people drive cars?

A Yes, but this raises a serious problem in many parts of the country where their right to get a driver's license—as well as other rights—is denied because of community pressures or the ignorance of those who have a measure of authority over them.

Q Do underwriters insure the retarded?

A A few years ago this was a serious problem, especially with health-insurance companies—even in group plans—which would often cancel the family's policy on the grounds that a mentally retarded child might require certain unusual or expensive medical treatment. This was brought to the attention of legislators in some states, and they upheld the view of parents that they were entitled to insurance.

While this problem is by no means resolved among all insurance companies, public notice is apparently prompting more and more companies to insure the retarded.

Q How many parents institutionalize children?

A Very few. Most parents of a mentally retarded child want to care for him or her in their own home. But they need moral support and financial assistance as well as community understanding.

Of course, they also have to look at long-term needs when they can no longer look after a severely retarded person, and this may entail consideration not only of guardianship arrangements but the possibility of residential care.

On the job. "Employers find the retarded often more conscientious than others because of their concentration on details."

Q Can such a person legally reject institutionalization if parents or guardians propose it?

A There's a lawsuit now before the Supreme Court which deals with this question, and we're hoping for a clear answer.

My own feeling is that there is enough legal precedent for a ruling that retarded individuals should have the freedom of choice where to live. At least in the case of adult persons, parents should not always be the ones to make the decision.

Q What kind of care is being given to those mentally retarded persons who are in institutions?

A Unfortunately, we have 153,000 mentally retarded in the 237 public institutions in the country. We know that abuse or neglect occurs in some of these facilities.

This has brought emotional distress to many parents who are joining the fight for larger appropriations and better programs and living conditions in public facilities. When that fails, they are asking the courts to intercede. This has resulted in rulings of judges that where institutional environment prohibits the full educational and training potential of the individual, either the environment must be changed or, failing that, the institution should be phased out.

Some facilities in this country are trying to live up to a better standard of care and services for the mentally retarded. But some of the older institutions are overcrowded, underfinanced, and with insufficient numbers and quality of staff to meet proper standards.

Q Where does the parent of a mentally retarded child turn for help—money or services—in the community?

A Many communities unfortunately have little to offer. At the President's Committee on Mental Retardation office, letters arrive daily from distressed and frustrated parents who know that money is being made available for help but see no positive evidence of it in their communities.

In most big communities there are some resources for directing parents to the services they need.

One important volunteer agency that is available in all 50 states—and, I understand, in over 1,200 localities—is the National Association for Retarded Citizens, which has its headquarters in Arlington, Tex.

I would recommend that they seek information from the schools on the rights of their child for special education—even in rural areas, where school, transportation and classes should be available.

Q What's the impact of the assistance that you've gotten from such persons as the late Senator Hubert Humphrey and the Kennedy family, who have had retarded individuals in their families?

A The impact has been considerable.

The Kennedy Foundation helped in organizing the Special Olympics, which serves over 400,000 mentally retarded throughout the country annually, while in addition bringing together sports celebrities, public officials and others to be aware of the needs of retarded persons.

Q Do retarded children have the same life expectancy that others do?

A We are completing a study on this issue, and the preliminary information is that there is little difference in life expectancy for the general population and the mentally retarded. More retarded children, however, are born with severe chronic problems. In such cases, life expectancy is probably less due to these medical complications.

Q How prevalent are these types of complications among the retarded?

A About 88 percent of the mentally retarded have some additional handicap: a speech difficulty, a hearing loss, deficient vision and sometimes motor defects. I might add that such problems are far less frequent among those with mild or moderate retardation.

Q How much more change is needed to bring care and help for the mentally retarded to a satisfactory level?

A We're probably at the midway point in public acceptance. Earlier in the 1970s, I would have put it at much less than that, and the difference lies in public awareness of the problems of the mentally retarded and acceptance of them as individual Americans with abilities and rights.

At last, a complaint procedure for the disabled

Ellen Bollert

Disabled people who believe they have been discriminated against by Federal departments and agencies now have a complaint procedure available for seeking redress. It is set forth in a set of regulations which finally implement a 1948 law making it illegal for Federal departments and agencies to discriminate against disabled people in employment. The regulations will allow disabled people to use the same Equal Employment Opportunity procedures that are available to women and minorities under the Civil Rights Act of 1964. The following summary of the procedures was prepared by the Disability Rights Center of Washington, D.C.

The regulations prohibit discrimination against anyone who:

1. has a physical or mental impairment which substantially limits one or more of that person's major life activities (such as caring for one's self, performing manual tasks, walking, seeing, hearing, speaking, breathing, learning and working); or

2. has a record of that kind of impairment; or

3. is regarded as having that kind of impairment.

The regulations provide the following rights for disabled people and create the following obligations on Federal agencies:

"Agencies shall give full consideration to the hiring, placement, and advancement of qualified mentally and physically handicapped persons. The Federal Government shall become a model employer of handicapped individuals. An agency shall not discriminate against a qualified physically or mentally handicapped person."

Agencies are required to make reasonable accommodations to the limitations of disabled applicants and employees unless to do so would impose an undue hardship on the agency. Reasonable accommodations include making facilities accessible, job restructuring, part-time or modified work schedules, acquisition or modification of equipment or devices, modification of examinations, provision of readers and interpreters and other actions.

Agencies may not use tests or selection procedures that screen out disabled people unless they are job-related and alternatives that do not screen out disabled people are shown not to be available.

Agencies may not conduct pre-employment medical examinations or make pre-employment inquiries about a person's disability. However, the agency may ask about a person's ability to meet medical qualifications for the job. The Civil Service Commission may ask about a person's disability in order to modify a test to make it accessible. Pre-employment medical information may be gathered for the purpose of using special appointing procedures for disabled people.

Agencies may not discriminate because of facility inaccessibility. However, an agency will be deemed accessible if it complies with the Architectural Barriers Act of 1968. (This means that facilities built before 1968 do not have to be accessible.)

The complaint procedure may be used by anyone who was discriminated against after April 10, 1977, well as anyone experiencing discrimination after the

"At Last, A Complaint Procedure for the Disabled," *Arise* Vol. 1, No. 9, July 1978. ©1978 by American Research Institute in Special Education.

regulations' effective date, April 10, 1978. To be able to file a complaint alleging discrimination which occurred after April 10, 1977, and before April 10, 1978, the following conditions must be met:

1. The complaint of discrimination was brought to the attention of the agency within 30 days after the discrimination occurred. This is satisfied if the disabled person complained to the EEO officer, the administrator of the agency, the personnel officer, or another official of the agency.

2. The complaint has not been decided under another grievance procedure.

3. The complaint must be filed with an EEO officer of the agency before Oct. 6, 1978.

This procedure is available for complaints of discrimination involving failure to hire a qualified handicapped applicant and unfair treatment of handicapped employees. It may be used by Schedule A and 700-hour appointees.

Questions about this procedure should be addressed to:

> The Office of Selective Placement
> Bureau of Recruiting and Examining
> Civil Service Commission
> 1900 E Street N.W.
> Washington, D.C. 20415
> (202) 632-4437

Or write to the Disability Rights Center, 1346 Connecticut Ave., N.W., Washington, D.C. 20036. The center does not handle individual complaints and would not be able to help solve a particular problem but is compiling letters to see which areas pose the greatest number of problems.

Disability Rights Center serves as advocate for all the handicapped

The Disability Rights Center of Washington, D.C., has been working to strengthen the rights of disabled people since September, 1976. Established with the help of Ralph Nader, it is an advocate for the rights of all disabled people which operates with a limited staff and budget on the principle that you don't have to be big to be effective.

The center strongly believes that disabled persons and their parents, who are directly affected by Federal policy decisions and activities, must become involved in monitoring the Federal Government's effectiveness in implementing legislation, managing programs, and drafting regulations and guidelines.

The center is a tax-exempt, non-profit corporation. Its board of directors is made up of disabled persons with a background of involvement in the rights of all disabled people. Center director Debby Kaplan is a disabled attorney whose specialty is disability law.

The center will not accept any Federal funds, since a large part of its work involves monitoring the Federal Government. Contributions from individuals and non-governmental organizations are its sole means of support.

Among the projects being conducted by the center are these:

Research on the implementation of Federal affirmative action, as required by Sec. 501 of the Rehabilitation Act of 1973;

Dissemination of materials to disabled people across the country on how to enforce their employment rights with respect to the federal government;

Publication of reports and testimony on the results of the center's research and its recommendations for change;

Legal resource guides on the rights of disabled people as consumers of medical devices and equipment;

Representing disabled people as co-counsel with other disability rights attorneys in major legal cases;

Testifying before Congressional committees and Federal agencies on major issues involving the rights of disabled people.

For further information: Disability Rights Center, 1346 Connecticut Ave. NW, Washington, D.C. 20036.

America's Needs in Habilitation and Employment of the Mentally Retarded

These, Too, Must Be Equal

The Approach

This report does not take the easy way of merely asking for new laws, new money, new government involvement.

There already are many laws on the books that can serve the vocational needs of the retarded. These must be implemented. The retarded must be kept in mind in their implementation.

The answer to the vocational needs of the retarded—if there is a single answer—lies in everybody's involvement.

This report, then, stresses the roll of *all* the citizens of America in meeting the employment problems of the mentally retarded.

Building A Highway

Properly preparing the mentally retarded for the world of work is like building a highway. Each mile of the way leads us closer to our goal. On the way we pass these guideposts:

Early preparation

Education and training

Medical habilitation

Employment

Independent or sheltered living

Vital to the entire journey, public promotion and education, to build acceptance of the retarded.

What follows is a discussion of each guidepost with some proposals for future action.

Early Preparation

What does it take to hold a job in the world of work? Ability to perform certain tasks, yes; but far more. It takes certain attitudes: appreciation of, and respect for, a job; willingness to accept responsibility (even if it is for mopping floors or loading trucks); ability to get along with others; capacity to manage the details of life (getting places, being on time, handling money, etc.).

Also, parents of the retarded must impart to them a concept of dignity of all work, regardless of its nature, as well as a sense of dignity of self.

Too often, positive attitudes and work habits are not taught early enough to the retarded. They usually are added as afterthoughts to a curriculum. Rather, they should weave their way through the education of the retarded, from his earliest days onward.

Proposals for Action

1 President Nixon recently called for national action to serve the needs of young people in America up to age 6. Such a national program should include in its charge a specific plan of action for the mentally retarded.

As a beginning in this direction,

A "Head Start," a child development program, should contain specific provisions for the enrichment of mentally retarded children; only through specific provisions can the retarded be assured of equal consideration.

B All "Model Cities" programs should include provision of services for the mentally retarded, to assure earliest possible development of their potential.

2 Parents should be encouraged to accept realistic vocational objectives for their retarded children. To do this, it is necessary to inform not only parents, but also persons to whom parents might turn for counsel (physicians, teachers, vocational rehabilitation counselors, ministers, psychologists, others). These professions should be provided with material dealing with training and employment of the mentally retarded, with the stress placed on the innate value of all work, skilled or unskilled.

The American Association on Mental Deficiency, the American Personnel and Guidance Association, the National Rehabilitation Association, the National Education Association, and the American Psychological Association are among the many professional organizations whose assistance would be essential to carry out this type of program.

3 The Handicapped Children's Early Education Assistance Act (Public Law 90-538) calls for model programs to develop new ways of assisting preschool handicapped children, including the mentally retarded. Preschool years are most critical for the retarded. Therefore, local planning is needed now, to build effective model programs under this Act.

Education and Training

Realism must be the key to the education and training of the mentally retarded. The retarded are going to have to enter a real world not truly made for them; get a real job that may be alien to their concepts of work; face up to real social and interpersonal situations that may not always be pleasant; handle real personal problems (money, transportation, living quarters, the like) that for us might be routine but for them are crisis-sized.

Early in life, education and training must prepare them for the world of useful work. And it must prepare them for the world of useful living outside of work.

The education and training resources in the United States are vast, mighty, and innovative. But they have not fully been brought to bear in the lives of the mentally retarded.

Proposals for Action

4 A set of curriculum guidelines should be prepared for every level of education of the mentally retarded, from earliest years onward. Guidelines should include stress on vocational and social preparation for work and for life.

Individual communities could develop their own curricula, based on these guides, to meet local employment conditions.

Preparation of the community guides should be a joint responsibility of private organizations concerned with the retarded, vocational rehabilitation, public employment service and education.

5 More materials on vocational and job-related subjects should be simply written for the mentally retarded themselves. Teachers' guides also should be prepared so that these booklets can be introduced into special education classrooms.

The booklets might contain realistic material dealing with work attitudes, job habits, problems of daily living, etc.

6 New concepts of vocational education that bring students out of the classroom into work-a-day situations should be encouraged. This can come about by increased use of voluntary

"America's Needs in Habitation and Employment of the Mentally Retarded," The President's Committee on Mental Retardation and The President's Committee on Employment of the Handicapped.

organizations in arranging of out-of-classroom instruction.

7 There is a need for many more work experience centers with living facilities. The Social and Rehabilitation Service should give special emphasis to the development of such facilities.

8 The "Job Opportunities in the Business Sector" program of the National Alliance of Businessmen should be broadened somewhat to state specifically that mentally retarded applicants are to be included. Also, special realistic entrance requirements should be established for the mentally retarded.

At present, many unidentified retarded persons undoubtedly are entering the JOBS program. With proper identification and proper consideration, many more might benefit from this program.

9 Centralized contract procurement systems should be encouraged fro sheltered workshops, either within individual communities or within regional areas. Centralized contracting can funnel contracts to workshops best equipped to handle them, and can properly assign contracts too large for any single workshop.

10 Many sheltered workshops for the retarded face problems of operations, productivity, safety, and management. There should be strong cooperative efforts among these workshops themselves to meet their common problems and to work together to solve them.

Standards for workshop operations are essential and should be considered in all phases of planning.[1]

11 Vocational education should play a far more meaningful role in meeting the educational and employment needs of the mentally retarded.

A report by the Office of Education shows that 10 percent of America's school population needs special education services. Yet less than 1 percent of vocational education funds have been used in behalf of those with special needs.

Vocational education should be a right to which every American student is entitled, retarded or not retarded, so long as he may reasonably benefit. Funds are needed to extend this right to all. The vocational education amendments of 1968 opened

the door to extensive, quality vocational education for the handicapped and the retarded— but full and immediate implementation is necessary, otherwise the amendments are but empty promises.

Meaningful cooperative agreements must be developed among vocational education, vocational rehabilitation, the public employment service, and special education.

12 At least 600 new sheltered workshops that include the mentally retarded are needed today, according to state facility plans. These should be located not only in nonprofit workshop facilities as we know them today, but also within private industrial plants.

13 Special attention must be given to the needs of the mentally retarded in rural communities. Special attention should be given the mentally retarded in families of migrant workers and American Indians. They are often found living in sparsely settled areas. It may be necessary to bring retarded persons quite some distance from home for services. No matter where they are sent, their rural backgrounds and interests should be considered.

County agents should be given material to acquaint them with mental retardation, so they can advise families of the retarded about sources of assistance.

14 More professional and supportive manpower is needed in the entire field of education and training of the mentally retarded, so that greater

numbers of retarded persons can be made ready for employment. Careers in retardation should be promoted in all ways possible, including subsidies for needy students.

The Medical Profession

It is not enough to consider only the vocational rehabilitation needs of the mentally retarded. For them to reach their highest aspirations and lead the fullest lives possible, their medical rehabilitation needs must be met as well.

Yet America has largely overlooked these needs.

There are some 79 medical schools in the United States with grants ranging from $30,000 to

$100,000 a year for training in rehabilitation medicine. However, there is but little opportunity for medical trainees to be exposed to concepts of medical rehabilitation of the mentally retarded.

Medical rehabilitation of the retarded must keep pace with advances in other fields. Otherwise the retarded can never hope to share fully in their America.

Proposals for Action

15 Rehabilitation Services Administration must make strong efforts to encourage medical schools

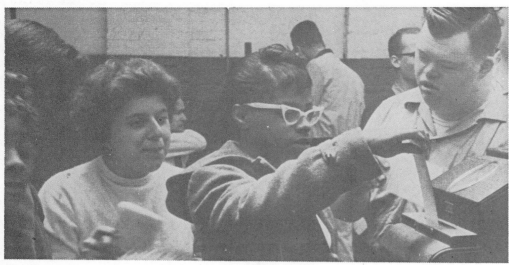

after work will be as full and meaningful as their lives during work.

A recent study by John Hopkins University, sponsored by the President's Committee on Mental Retardation, covered the economic side of preparing the retarded for work. Although the benefits and costs varied widely, many situations were found showing that the benefits greatly exceeded the costs. We know, for example, that when a retarded person is unable to work, he will, in many cases, eventually be institutionalized. Institutional care costs taxpayers about $40,000 per bed in construction costs and the yearly maintenance of the retarded may range from $2,000 to $10,000. In contrast, even at the minimum wage of $1.60 an hour, a retarded person will earn over $3,000 per year and instead of becoming a burden to taxpayers, he will actually lessen their tax burden since about $600 of his earnings will be paid to the community in the form of state and local taxes. The total cost of providing vocational training to the retarded so that they might become employable will probably range between $1,000 and $9,000 in the great majority of cases. It appears that the average cost to taxpayers of preparing the retarded for employment will be about the cost that they would incur for the provision of only 1 year of institutional care for the retarded. (A copy of this study may be obtained from The Johns Hopkins University Press, Charles & 34th Sts., Baltimore, Md. 21218.)

Proposals for Action

29 Living facilities for the mentally retarded should be established in the vicinities where they work. These facilities can include hotels, group homes, halfway houses, cooperative apartments, community homes or farms.

30 Independent living facilities in institutions should be encouraged when possible. These facilities go hand-in-hand with the development of sheltered workshops on the premises.

31 There are some retarded persons for whom competitive employment is not feasible; yet they are fully able to perform in sheltered workshops. Everything possible should be done to encourage more workshops to serve their needs—including financial assistance when necessary.

For example, up to $1,500 per year should be provided for each retarded person in such workshops operated by nonprofit organizations.

Also, retarded workers in these workshops should be subsidized, if need be, to make it possible for them to remain in the community and at work. Workshop employment for the retarded has two advantages: it is more economical than institutionalization, and it is better for the retarded than institutionalization, and it is better for the retarded than institutional life.

32 Retarded persons in institutions, with employment potential as determined by rehabilitation counselors assigned there, should be given every possible service to "graduate" them into jobs and independent living in the community. They should be referred to a vocational rehabilitation counselor no later than their 18th birthday.

33 All living facilities for the mentally retarded should provide for full recreational, medical, vocational, and social needs. Facilities never should be mere living shells; they should offer total living environments.

Promotion and Education

It is not enough to stop short with the preparation of the mentally retarded for employment. America must be told, and told again, of their abilities. We must constantly emphasize their capacity to work, their assets, what they can do rather than what they cannot do.

There can be no end to mass promotion and education. America's memory is short. Unless we repeat ourselves constantly, she is likely to forget.

Proposals for Action

34 The President's Committee on Employment of the Handicapped, the President's Committee on Mental Retardation and the National Association for Retarded Children, the Manpower Administration of the Department of Labor and the Social and Rehabilitation Service of the Department of Health, Education, and Welfare, should continue to work closely to promote jobs for the retarded. It is realized that all three organizations also have other programs to promote, but employment of the retarded should retain a position of high priority.

35 Labor unions should be encouraged to exampt low echelon jobs from ususal "career-ladders," so that the mentally retarded might fill them—without having to face upward steps to jobs beyond their capabilities.

36 State and local governments should be encouraged to establish special hiring procedures for the mentally retarded similar to those of the federal government. Only a dozen states have such procedures at present.

37 An information center should be established to gather data on training and employment of the retarded and to serve·as a national focal point for its dissemination. This could be a joint venture of the President's Committees on Mental Retardation and on Employment of the Handicapped.

38 Promotional efforts should be directed to top management to encourage written policy statements favoring jobs for the retarded; to middle-management to encourage implementation of these policies; to rank-and-file workers to gain their acceptance of the retarded as fellow workers.

39 There should be more employer conferences on utilization of lesser-skilled manpower in the labor force, with special reference to the retarded.

Prototype for such conferences might be one held recently by New York University and the President's Committee on Employment of the Handicapped, attended by some 200 leading employers in New York City.

OPENING MORE DOORS FOR THE NATION'S RETARDED

A new world is at hand for many retarded persons as they learn to live and work in the broad community—and earn some of its rewards.

More and more of the nation's 6.4 million mentally retarded—children and adults—are moving into an outside world that, until recently, largely shunned them.

Waning is the old practice of segregating the retarded in institutions "for their own good." Today the emphasis is on keeping them in the mainstream of community life and enabling them, with appropriate help, to lead as normal and useful an existence as possible.

Experts in the field say that the new approach is opening new vistas to the retarded and their families. Comments Dr. Louis Brown of the University of Wisconsin:

"We have proven that when we isolate the retarded in institutions, they do not improve. When we allow them to be members of a complex, heterogeneous society, using public rest rooms, crossing streets and going to school along with the rest of us, they do improve—often remarkably."

From 1970 to 1975, the number of retarded who were confined in public institutions dropped from 187,000 to 168,000. The goal, according to Fred J. Krause, executive director of the President's Committee on Mental Retardation, is to cut that number by another 50,000 by 1980.

Reformation paying off. In California, the number of hospitalized retarded is down to 1 in every 60, from an earlier peak of 1 in every 30. The other 59 are obtaining services of some kind in their communities.

In New York City, thousands of mentally retarded inmates at the Willowbrook Developmental Center are being relocated gradually into homes that are operated by private agencies or by foster parents.

Throughout the country, mentally retarded children are being assisted in leading normal lives in schools with other children, while group homes and sheltered workshops are providing opportunities for retarded adults to live and work in the community.

Institutions themselves are being reformed with the purpose of releasing inmates for reintegration into the community as soon as possible.

Coming into wide use is an "early intervention" technique. As typified by the Daytime Development Center in Fairfax, Va., run by the county health department, mentally retarded infants are diagnosed at birth and undergo training, together with their mothers, from the age of 6 weeks onward.

"We begin the socialization process far earlier than textbooks say," remarks co-ordinator Joy Chance. "There are 2-year-olds here who are more independent than my normal 2-year-old."

Also in Fairfax County, a private organization provides specialists who will baby-sit mentally retarded children at either their own homes or at the homes of the parents.

In Arlington, Va., another organization provides emergency help for the parents of mentally retarded children on a 24-hour basis.

The trend of recent court decisions and State laws has been to affirm the right of handicapped children—including the mentally retarded—to equal educational opportunities. Most of the States have laws that require education of the handicapped, and 20 States include the preschool handicapped in this provision.

The Federal Government is assisting the States in providing education for the handicapped by making annual grants that may escalate to more than 3 billion dollars by 1982.

Already, 90 per cent of the country's 1,057,000 mentally retarded children are being served by public schools, according to the U.S. Office of Education.

In New York State, for example, public schools were ordered in 1973 to educate all children, including the severely retarded and those with multiple handicaps who had previously been left to private agencies to care for.

Three public schools in New York City have early-childhood programs for 5 to 7-year-olds. One Manhattan school has a "hot line" over which parents of the retarded can discuss their problems among themselves.

Public schools in the city are operating a retrieval and redirection program aimed at the retarded, aged 15 to 17, who have quit school. These teen-agers are given training in workshops, aid in locating jobs and a $1-an-hour stipend.

School officials in Madison, Wis., have set up the Zero Reject Plan, designed to educate all developmentally disabled children from birth to age 21.

Under this plan, children whose

ALAN PEARLMAN

Zero Reject Plan at Madison, Wis. public schools provides instruction for all developmentally disabled children.

handicaps are judged not to be excessively severe attend regular schools. They go to normal classes for subjects they can handle, such as art or physical education, and attend special classes for subjects that they cannot cope with. The other retarded go to a special school for the mentally handicapped.

The University of Oregon's Center on Human Development in Eugene is instructing mixed classes of 10 retarded and 30 normal preschool children. The Oregon experiment is reported to be so successful that there is a waiting list for the Center's services.

Springing up everywhere are group homes where mentally retarded persons of different ages are living together under the supervision of specially trained "house parents" and staff.

In Georgia, for example, the first group home was opened in 1972; the present total is 29. "We have about 1,500 persons currently in institutions whom we would like to move into a community-living situation," reports Budd Hughes, in charge of the State's mental-retardation program.

One such home is in Marietta and

"Opening More Doors for the Nation's Retarded," *U.S. News and World Report,* Vol. LXXXI No. 9, August 30, 1976. ©1976 U.S. News and World Report.

1. MINORITY

ARDEN MUNKRES

University of Oregon conducts mixed classes for retarded, normal children. Retarded child wears protective helmet.

houses eight men aged 20 to 36, who between them had previously spent 102 years at institutions. The oldest had been an inmate for 28 years.

In most cases, points out social worker Maggie Smith, the men were institutionalized only because they had nowhere else to go.

"These people are more like us than unlike us," says Mrs. William D. McSwain, the housemother, who lives in the Marietta home with her husband and two sons.

The men participate in making the home's rules, such as lights out at 11 p.m. and restriction of smoking to certain hours. They pitch in with the chores on an informal basis. They go to movies or shopping or church on their own.

Churches and civic groups in the community are helping to organize trips and other activities for them.

Seven of the eight attend workshops where they are taught such basic skills as counting change.

One works full time as a dishwasher in a cafeteria. Some also contract for such jobs as packaging fishing tackle and making planters for sale through nurseries. Pay, based on proficiency, averages $10 a week. They spend their earnings as they please.

Only one man has had to leave the Marietta home to return to an institution because of adjustment problems.

Mr. Hughes's hope is that after further progress is made, some of the men will be able, with some assistance, to take apartments, or live with families on a more or less independent basis.

Wisconsin has about 100 group homes housing 800 individuals, of whom 600 would otherwise be in large institutions. According to Gerald Dymond, director of the State's bureau of mental health, it costs only $450 a month to keep one person at such a home, as opposed to $1,500 a month at a full-care institution.

The Federal Government is contributing not only money but incentives in this trend.

Finding them jobs. Federal regulations require any company having Government contracts of $2,500 or more to take "affirmative action" to secure employment for handicapped individuals, including the mentally retarded.

Under modified examination procedures, more than 7,400 mentally retarded persons have been hired for minor positions by the Federal Government itself since 1964.

An on-the-job training program, funded at about 2 million dollars a year by the Federal Government and administered by the National Association for Retarded Citizens, has placed some 14,000 retarded in competitive jobs at private firms since 1967.

Many others find employment in sheltered workshops. For example:

At workshops run by the Chicago Association for Retarded Citizens, 500 individuals make lamps and candles for department stores and pillowcases for airlines, fill tubes with glue, stuff envelopes and shred polyester. They are supervised by employes of the companies who have hired them and earn a minimum wage based on piecework.

Otto Whitehall, executive director of the association, makes the observation that these people are being returned to communities where "they feel productive and worthwhile."

Within institutions, increased efforts are being made to train retarded inmates so they can eventually return to the community.

One example is Stockton State Hospital near Sacramento, Calif., where student volunteers from the University of the Pacific are teaching retarded children simple behavioral skills that may enable them eventually to return home.

California officials estimate that, for each youngster between the ages of 5 and 18 who can be trained and released to his home, the State would save in the neighborhood of $14,000.

Experts point out that all this does not mean that every retarded person in institutions can, or should, be released.

"Some very handicapped people have more freedom in a hospital than they can have in the community," observes Harold Schmitz of Pacific State Hospital in Pomona, Calif. He reports that some parents are fighting legal battles to keep their children hospitalized because they want to be sure that they are getting good care.

Problems of budgeting. At the same time, in one community after another, officials are reporting money and other shortages that make it impossible for them to provide all the retarded on the outside with the supportive services they need to lead near-normal lives in their communities.

In New York City, public-school programs for the retarded suffered budget cuts during the city's fiscal crisis, and there are not enough small community residences for retarded adults.

In Montgomery County, Md., a critical shortage of trained and specialized staff is reported to be making it difficult to comply with a State law which mandates special educational programs for all mentally retarded from birth to age 20.

North Dakota, officials say, has only eight group homes for the mentally retarded, whereas 150 are needed.

Another major obstacle to the mainstreaming of the retarded, according to experts, is the persistence of adverse community attitudes. Some instances:

Near Washington, D.C., a major bank until recently refused to allow the residents of a home for the mentally retarded to open savings accounts.

Notes Thomas T. Crowner, director of special services at the Madison, Wis., public schools: "We have had people ask us why we spend money on kids whom they call 'wet noodles.'"

Says Samih Ismir, assistant director of Mental Health and Retardation Services for North Dakota: "Our main problem is neighborhood resistance. People are afraid to have the retarded living next door to them."

Increasingly, however, officials and ordinary citizens are pushing ahead to offer America's mentally retarded the kind of "normal" life in the broad community that many of them are capable of leading.

Instructors at workshop in Chicago teach retarded to make pillowcases for airlines.

WIDE WORLD

CAREERS OF MENTALLY RETARDED YOUNG PERSONS: SERVICE, JOBS, AND INTERPERSONAL RELATIONS

Albert Einstein College of Medicine of Yeshiva University

Life histories and follow-up data at age 22 were obtained for a total city population of children classified as mentally retarded (index cases). Histories were also obtained at age 22 from matched comparisons who at no time had been classified as retarded. Matching was on age, sex, and social background. Placement at school-leaving age and major occupation at age 22 were reported for the index population. Those 22-year-old index cases not receiving mental retardation services and their matched comparisons were examined on objective and subjective measures of the jobs they held and selected indicators of interpersonal relationships.

This is the initial report of a study designed to describe the life courses from age 10 to 22 of a total population of young people in a city who were administratively defined during childhood as mentally retarded. My purpose in this report is to give a summary of the life courses of the total population and to examine the postschool careers of the subpopulation of young adults who cease to be officially considered as mentally retarded after leaving school.

Since 1910, there have been a number of reports of studies that follow-up into adulthood young people who had been classified as mentally retarded. The earliest and most numerous studies dealt with people who had been in residential institutions for retarded persons and were released or had escaped. The results showed that these persons, in many cases, were able to function in the community, find and hold jobs, and marry and raise families. They did not exhibit the social-pathological behavior ex-

pected of retarded persons and those who had children did not produce large numbers of retarded children (Cobb, 1972; Goldstein, 1964; Tizard, 1965). The studies were valuable in that they challenged the conventional wisdom of the early 20th century that genetic factors were dominant in the etiology of mental retardation. It was a time of segregating mentally retarded persons into large isolated institutions, a time when legislation was passed permitting sterilization of retarded persons, and a time when there seemed little point in social habilitation. Major difficulties in interpreting these studies are the absence of data on the level of functioning of the individuals when they were children and knowledge about whether they were in any way representative of the populations in residential institutions. Placement in institutions occurred for many reasons other than clear evidence of severe mental retardation, including placement of people who were judged to be nuisances or troublemakers by families, courts, or influential members of the community; some were orphans or persons for whom no other placement could be found. Although it might be expected that studies of residents and ex-residents of mental retardation institutions would focus on severely retarded persons for whom placement in residential facilities has some rationale, the focus has been largely on adults with mild degrees of mental retardation, for

This study was supported by the Foundation for Child Development, the Grant Foundation, the National Institute of Child Health and Human Development Grant No. HD 07907, and the Social Science Research Council of the United Kingdom. The author thanks Helene Koller, Janice McLaren, and other members of the project who participated in the study and Raymond Illsley, Gordon Horobin, and Barbara Thompson who provided scientific consultation and administrative support.

whom institutional care was probably inappropriate.

A second kind of study has been the follow-up into adulthood of young people who were placed in special classes for mentally handicapped individuals (Ferguson & Kerr, 1955, 1958; Tizard, 1974; Kennedy, Note 1; Saenger, Note 2). These researchers have shown that many of these young people were able, as young adults, to live in the community away from their parents' homes, a proportion found employment, and some married, raised families, and were able to function as adults in the society. Others experienced real problems in achieving satisfactory living conditions.

These investigators have focused attention on neglected problems and have challenged dogmatic and limited conceptualizations of mental retardation. There are, however, a number of methodological and substantive limitations that make it difficult to generalize about the studies or apply them to some of the contemporary issues in the field of mental subnormality:

1. The studies are largely retrospective, with limited information on the adults when they were of school age.
2. The criterion for inclusion in the studies has predominantly been placement in special facilities for mentally handicapped persons and sometimes the availability of an IQ score.
3. Often, the study populations in the United States included a heavy representation of individuals from minority groups or recent immigrants.
4. The nature of the selection process for special educational placement is not known.
5. Few of the studies have any comparison group matched on age, sex, and similar social background, so it is not possible to interpret the extent to which the functioning of mentally retarded persons at later ages is a consequence of their intellectual impairment.
6. Because total populations of mentally retarded young persons have not been followed up, it has not been possible to examine the subsequent life histories of people with different subtypes of mental retardation living in the same community.
7. There have been no longitudinal studies of mental retardation in which investigators examined the experiences of young people as they progress from childhood to adulthood. Neither has there been emphasis on the influence of parents, relatives, neighbors, and friends who are significant to the young people, and of the influences of various agencies of the community, e.g., education, health, social work, vocational, and residential services.

Little is known about the life course after leaving school of those who are no longer classified as mentally retarded. The rise in the prevalence of mental retardation to a peak in the late school years, followed by a rapid decline was first reported by Penrose (1963) using data from the Lewis (1929) survey. Gruenberg (1964), in a review of seven epidemiological studies, estimated that the prevalence of mental retardation among young adults is only half as high as the peak rate reached around the age of 14. It is clear from several studies that those persons who disappear from official note are mildly retarded (Innes, 1975; Kushlick & Blunden, 1974; Susser, 1968). These findings pose critical questions for understanding the nature of mental retardation and for decision making in public policy. Gruenberg (1964), e.g., suggested that:

For this drop in prevalence to occur, a large group of people regarded as retarded at fourteen must improve in their functioning to the point where people no longer regard them as retarded and also must succeed in escaping their history of earlier unsatisfactory performance. (p. 274)

Either these individuals are continuing to be extremely handicapped in later life and are unknown because the services they need are unavailable to them (in which case society is failing to do its duty toward them and ought to learn how to find and help them), or they have stopped being retarded in any real sense at all and do not need any special protection, help or services, in which case one had better change one's concept of what "real" retardation "really" is. . . . The phenomenon cries out for investigation. (p. 274)

To examine this issue requires identifying all children in a community who at any time during schooling have been administratively classified as mentally retarded and then following them into adulthood to determine who are and are not receiving services related to mental retardation after leaving school. In addition to obvious questions such as whether they are employed, it is important to examine the quality of their lives compared to lives of peers from comparable social backgrounds who went to regular schools. Clearly, a major research challenge is to work out objective indicators of what constitutes quality of life.

Method

A city in the United Kingdom was selected that met the following requirements of the study design: (a) a relatively stable population in order to make possible a follow-up study over a 14-year period; (b) a comprehensive administrative structure for the careful identification of the total population of children in the community who are mentally retarded, based on a clinical judgment taking into account IQ, school performance, social competence, and a medical evaluation; (c) in order to have an adequate number of cases for study, a community that has a minimum of 30 children in each birth year who are administratively defined as mentally retarded when at school; (d) standardized information on the level of functioning and the health and social environments of the young adults when they were children; (e) as a basis for selecting a comparison set of cases who are not mentally retarded, adequate data on children in the community who were not mentally retarded; and (f) a high degree of cooperation from the study population; the authorities responsible for health, education, and welfare services; and other scientists working in the community.

Data used in this report were derived from a standardized interview with the young adults when they were 22 years old. Whenever possible, an interview with parents was used as a cross-check on the basic outlines of the young adult career. The parent interview was the primary source in cases where the young adult had severe communication limitations and cases where we were unable to interview the young adult. Records from a variety of institutions provided further independent data sources. The data necessary for the selection of the mentally retarded subjects and the matched comparisons were obtained in 1962 in a program of research in the same community (Birch, Richardson, Baird, Horobin, & Illsley, 1970).

To examine the level of skill, training, and responsibility of the jobs held, we developed an occupational classification in conjunction with the Director of Youth Employment Services in the city, who has an intimate knowledge of the various jobs held by young adults. This special classification was developed only after finding that the widely used national occupational classification of the Registrar General did not discriminate sufficiently for 22 year olds who came predominately from the lower end of the socioeconomic scale. A 6-point scale was used: professional, highly skilled, skilled, semi-skilled, limited skill, and unskilled. The classification was developed from job descriptions without the classifier knowing whether the job was held by a young person who had or had not been considered mentally retarded as a child.

To obtain some indication of how the young adults felt about their social relationships, they were asked, "On the whole how do you feel you have got along with other people since you left school? Would you say you got along well or not well?" If the response were "well," a follow-up question was asked, "Would you say you got along very well or well?" If the response was "not well," the follow-up was, "Would you say you got along not well or badly?" These questions provided four categories of response, but young adults only had to choose between two alternatives. This procedure was adopted to simplify the task for young adults who had difficulty in thinking in conceptual terms.

The study population for the present report was selected from all persons who were born in the years 1951 and 1952 and resided in the city in 1962. The index cases were children who were administratively classified as mentally retarded and placed in special education facilities or residential care at any time during their school years. For each index case a matched comparison was selected who had at no time during schooling been administratively defined as mentally retarded. The matching variables were age, sex, occupation of head of the household, where the child lived at age 8 to 10, and the type of housing at this time. Comparison children did not include any child who at age 7 and 9 had scored less than 75 and 80, respectively, in group intelligence tests given to all children in the city and might therefore on psychometric grounds alone be considered as borderline retarded, even though they had not been administratively defined as mentally retarded.

Where an index case migrated away from the city before the age of 18, no comparison was selected. This was done because had a comparison been selected, differences found between the index case and matched comparison could be due to differences in the communities (e.g., different employment opportunities or differences in the availability of mental retardation services) rather than differences due to mental impairment.

In presenting results, index cases who moved away from Aberdeen before the age of 18 and for whom no comparisons were selected were omitted from analyses involving index and comparison cases. In addition, where index and comparisons were not both engaged in the activity being examined they were excluded from analysis.

Results

There were 97 cases born in 1951 and 1952 who met the definition of an index case. Two had died, leaving 95 survivors at age 22. Data were obtained on 88 (93 percent) of the survivors (50 males, 38 females). Of the 7 index cases for whom data were not obtained, 6 refused to be interviewed and 1 had migrated away from Aberdeen and has not yet been interviewed.

Seventy-six of the 88 index cases were matched. Twelve comparisons are missing for the following reasons: comparisons were not selected for the 8 index cases who had left Aberdeen before 18 years of age, interviews with 3 comparisons have not yet been completed, and 1 index case could not be properly matched because he had been in various forms of foster and institutional care since birth.

A brief summary of the life careers of all the index cases (their last school placement at the minimum school-leaving age of 15 and their major occupation at age 22) is given in Tables 1 and 2. It is noteworthy that 14 percent of the index cases returned to regular schools after spending a period of time at the school for the educationally subnormal (Table 1). Of those who remained in special facilities for mentally retarded persons until school-leaving age, three-quarters were at the school for the educationally subnormal, with the remaining quarter in a junior training center or in a residential institution for total care.

TABLE 1

PLACEMENT OF INDEX CASES ($N=88$) AT SCHOOL-LEAVING AGE (15 YEARS)

Placement	Male	Female	Total
Regular school following period at ESN[a] school	7 (14)	5 (13)	12 (14)
ESN school	32 (66)	23 (61)	55 (63)
Junior training center[b]	5 (10)	7 (18)	12 (14)
Residential institution for total care	5 (10)	3 (8)	8 (9)
Approved school[c]	1 (2)	0 —	1 (1)

Note. Percentages in parentheses.
[a] Educationally subnormal (educable mentally retarded in U.S. terminology).
[b] For trainable mentally retarded persons in U.S. terminology.
[c] In U.S. classification, residential facility for juvenile delinquents.

At age 22, two-thirds of the index cases were not receiving any special mental retardation services (Table 2). Of this subpopulation, 89 percent of the males were in full-time jobs, with the remaining 11 percent unemployed. With one exception, all the index cases not receiving mental retardation services at age 22 had attended the school for the educationally subnormal. There was a tendency for more males (73 percent) than females (58 percent) to function without mental retardation services at age 22, but the difference was not statistically significant. For those index cases receiving mental retardation services at age 22, there was a tendency for more females (75 percent) than males (38 percent) to be in

day care rather than residential total care facilities (Table 2).

The histories of the index cases between school leaving and age 22 were examined

TABLE 2

MAJOR OCCUPATION OF INDEX CASES AT AGE 22

Occupation	Male[a]	Female
Cases not receiving MR[b] services		
Full-time job	27	10
Full-time plus part-time job	4	0
Full-time job plus further education	1	1
Unemployed	4	1
Housewife	—	7
Housewife plus part-time job	—	3
Total of cases not receiving MR services	36	22
Cases receiving MR services		
In day care at senior occupation centers	5	12
In total care at residential institutions	8	3
Special placement by social services, living with elderly couple and receiving disability pension	0	1
Total of cases receiving MR services	13	16

[a] For one male case information was not obtained on major occupation at age 22.
[b] Mental retardation.

by grouping them into subsets based on their placement at school-leaving age. Of the 12 young people who returned to regular schools after a period at the special school, 11 have received no subsequent mental retardation services. The remaining individual, a female, worked at a senior occupational center. Of the index cases who stayed at the special school until they left school, 80 percent received no subsequent services, and there was no difference in this percentage between males and females (Table 3). Nine percent were in a daytime senior occupational center and living at home, and 9 percent were or had been in residential facilities for mentally retarded persons. The primary reason for institutional placement for all cases was behavioral disturbance or antisocial behavior. The remaining 1 case (2 percent) was placed with an elderly couple. She received social security and helped around the house. Of the remaining index cases who were at the junior training center or in residential care at school-leaving age, all were receiving mental retardation services with the exception of 1 male who presently had a full-time job but who earlier was receiving mental retardation services.

TABLE 3

POST SCHOOL SERVICES RECEIVED BY INDEX CASES WHOSE LAST SCHOOL WAS THE EDUCATIONALLY SUBNORMAL SCHOOL

Services	Males[a]	Females
No mental retardation (MR) services at any time since leaving school	25 (80.5)	18 (78)
No MR services at present but some services between ages 16 and 22		
Stay in MR institution because of behavior problems	2 (6.5)	0 —
Receiving MR services at age 22		
At a senior occupational center	2 (6.5)	3 (14)
At MR institution because of behavioral problems	2 (6.5)	1 (4)
Living with elderly couple, receives social security and does some housework	0 —	1 (4)

Note. Percentages in parentheses.
[a] In addition, there is one male case for whom this information is not known.

There was little interchange between the day-care senior occupation center and residential treatment in an institution. One case from the senior occupation center spent a brief period in the residential facility because of psychiatric problems, and another case from the center received brief respite care to enable her parents to have a holiday.

Careers after Leaving School of Those Index Cases not Receiving Mental Retardation Services at Age 22

To examine the issue discussed by Gruenberg in the introduction to this paper, we investigated the extent to which the careers of the subset of index cases who have not received mental retardation services after leaving school were similar or different from their comparisons. The overall study encompassed many aspects of the young people's lives—their vocational careers; spare-time interests and activities; the institutions of society that impinge on their lives; their social relationships with family, relatives, neighbors, and fellow workers; and their subjective evaluations of their lives and themselves. In this paper we will give results illustrating examples of objective and subjective indicators of the young peoples' job histories and their social relationships.

Table 4 shows the current major occupations of the subset of index cases not currently receiving mental retardation services and their matched comparisons. There were no significant differences between the index cases and their comparisons. There was somewhat higher unemployment and no full-time further education among the index cases.

Three measures were used to examine the kinds of jobs held by the index cases who were in open employment and their comparisons: (a) a classification of the degree of skill, training, and responsibility the job requires; (b) take-home pay; and (c) whether the job deals with objects only or persons as well.

Job classification. The results are shown for the subset of matched pairs where both index and comparisons were working (Table 5). For those unemployed, their most recent jobs were used for purposes of classification. Those in full-time education were excluded. For both males and females, the index cases had a higher fre-

TABLE 4

CURRENT OCCUPATIONS OF INDEX CASES NOT CURRENTLY RECEIVING MENTAL RETARDATION SERVICES AND THEIR MATCHED COMPARISONS

Occupation	Male[a]		Female	
	Index	Comparison	Index	Comparison
Full-time job	21 (73)	22 (76)	9 (43)	7 (33)
Full-time plus part-time job	4 (14)	1 (4)	0 (0)	0 (0)
Full-time job plus further education	1 (4)	0 (0)	1 (5)	0 (0)
Full-time job plus housewife	0 (0)	0 (0)	0 (0)	2 (10)
Part-time job plus housewife	0 (0)	0 (0)	3 (14)	4 (19)
Unemployed	3 (10)	1 (4)	1 (5)	0 (0)
Full-time housewife	0 (0)	0 (0)	7 (33)	7 (33)
Full-time further education (FTE)	0 (0)	4 (14)	0 (0)	0 (0)
FTE plus casual job	0 (0)	1 (4)	0 (0)	0 (0)
FTE plus housewife	0 (0)	0 (0)	0 (0)	1 (5)

Note. Percentages in parentheses.
[a] n = 29 in each male group and 21 in each female group.

TABLE 5
KINDS OF JOBS HELD AND FEELINGS ABOUT JOBS FOR INDEX AND COMPARISON CASES

Job information	Males		Females	
	Index	Comparison	Index	Comparison
Job classification by level of skill[a]				
Semi-skilled & skilled	5	15	4	10
Limited skill and unskilled	14	4	6	0
Weekly take-home pay[b]				
Greater than 32 pounds	2	9	—	—
23–32 pounds	5	6	—	—
22 pounds & less	9	1	—	—
Proportion of cases whose job requires interpersonal skills[c]				
Skilled	0/1	2/6	0/4	6/6
Semi-skilled	0/4	2/9	0/4	3/4
Limited skill and unskilled	0/14	0/4	2/6	—
Response to Question 1[d]				
Yes	9	12	3	8
No	13	10	8	3
Response to Question 2[e]				
Yes	7	15	3	5
No	15	7	8	6

Note. Data for subset of index cases who were not receiving mental retardation services at age 22.
[a] Full-time students excluded.
[b] For females, too few cases for analysis.
[c] Controlled for level of skill. For the comparison group holding skilled jobs, 33 percent of the males and 100 percent of the females required interpersonal skills; for the semi-skilled comparison group, 22 percent of the males and 75 percent of the females required such skills.
[d] "Is there any other work you would rather have done?"
[e] "Is there anything you would change about your working life?"

quency of less-skilled jobs ($\chi^2 = 8.55, p < .01$ and Fisher's exact test $p = .005$ for males and females, respectively.)

Take-home pay. The amount a person is paid is indicative of community values about the worth of a job. Weekly take-home pay was ascertained. The male index cases received, on the average, two-thirds the income of the comparisons. As can be seen in Table 5, the distribution of the amount of take-home pay shows that the index males received significantly less pay than comparisons ($\chi^2 = 10.95, p < .01$). There was an insufficient number of females for analysis where index and comparison matched pairs both worked.

Person- and object-oriented jobs. Because social competence is a criterion used in the assessment of mental retardation, all the jobs held by the study population were evaluated to determine whether they involved skills related primarily to objects or to persons as well. The evaluation was done without knowing who held the jobs. Because it is reasonable to expect that jobs requiring higher levels of occupational skill will more often require interpersonal skills, level of occupational skills was used as a control variable (Table 5). The results support this expectation. Fewer index males and females held jobs that required personal skills. For both index and comparisons, women had a higher proportion of

jobs requiring interpersonal skills than did men. The number of cases was so small that statistical tests were inappropriate.

In addition to considering objective indicators of the young adults, it is important to learn something about their subjective reactions to their job experiences. Responses to two questions are illustrations. "Is there any other work you would rather have done?" and "Is there anything you would change about your working life?" Although the index cases had jobs requiring less skill and received less take-home pay, they did not more often feel there was other work they would rather have done (Table 5). In fact, the trend was in the opposite direction ($\chi^2 = 2.91, p < .10$ for females). Again, the index cases less often said that there were changes they would like to make in their working lives and for the males the difference was significant ($\chi^2 = 4.45, p < .05$).

Interpersonal Relationships

An important potential source of personal satisfaction is the network of interpersonal relationships that individuals develop and use. Within this network there will be others who will probably be of particular significance, e.g., parents, siblings, spouse, and close friends. In addition to whether these relationships do or do not exist, individuals' feelings about their

TABLE 6
INTERPERSONAL RELATIONS FOR INDEX AND COMPARISON CASES

Interpersonal relations	Male		Female	
	Index	Comparison	Index	Comparison
Cases able to name two best friends	13/21 (62)	18/21 (86)	9/17 (53)	16/17 (94)
Cases who said they had special opposite sex friends[a]	3/16 (19)	10/16 (63)	5/8 (63)	6/8 (75)
Marital status				
Single	27/29 (76)	12/29 (41)	10/21 (48)	6/21 (29)
Cohabiting	0 —	0 —	1/21 (4)	0 —
Married	7/29 (24)	15/29 (52)	10/21 (48)	15/21 (71)
Separated	0 —	1/29 (3)	0 —	0 —
Divorced	0 —	1/29 (3)	0 —	0 —
Answers to relationship question[b]				
Very well	9/26 (35)	21/26 (81)	6/17 (35)	12/17 (71)
Well	12/26 (46)	5/26 (19)	11/17 (65)	5/17 (29)
Not well	4/26 (15)	0 —	0 —	0 —
Badly	1/26 (4)	0 —	0 —	0 —

Note. Data from subset of index cases not receiving mental retardation services at age 22.

[a] Question, "Do you have any special boy/girl friend now?" Only asked of single, separated, and divorced persons.

[b] Question, "How well have you got along with other people since you left school?"

interpersonal relationships also need to be considered. In this study the interpersonal network of each young adult was examined. A few examples appear below.

Young adults were asked to name their two best friends. The index cases were less often able than their comparisons to name as many as two friends (Table 6). For the females, the difference was significant ($\chi^2 = 5.44$, $p < .05$). The male response was in the same direction but was not significant. The young adults who were not married or cohabiting were asked, "Do you have any special (opposite sex) friend now?" The index males answered in the affirmative less often than did the comparison males ($\chi^2 = 4.66$, $p < .05$). Examination of Table 6 shows that, for the males, a higher proportion of index cases were single than were married or cohabiting ($\chi^2 = 4.5$, $p < .05$). The difference was not significant for the females. As might be expected at 22 years of age, more females than males were married. Of the young adults who were married, there was no difference between the male and female index and comparison cases on how many children they had. The numbers of children ranged from one to three.

The answers to the subjective question, "On the whole how do you feel you have got along with other people since you left school?" show that the index males less often than their comparisons responded "very well" ($\chi^2 = 9.53$, $p < .01$). For the females the trend was in the same direction ($\chi^2 = 2.95$, $p < .10$).

Discussion

The summary of the life courses from 10 to 22 years of the total population of chil-

dren who at any time had been placed in special facilities for mentally retarded persons during their school years shows that the classification does not have to be a one-way irrevocable process. Fear has been expressed that once a child is classified or labeled as mentally retarded, declassification will not occur either because educational authorities feel that it will be regarded as an admission of a mistaken earlier judgment or that once classified the initial judgment is never revised. Another fear is that the rate of educational progress is so much slower in the educationally subnormal (special) than in the regular classroom that with increasing length of stay in a special classroom, the more difficult it becomes for a child to return to a regular class. Of the index children who were at the special school, 18 percent returned to regular schools, indicating that at the time and place of this study, placement in special education was not a one-way process.

Lewis (1929) and O'Connor and Tizard (1956) found that approximately 25 percent of the administratively classified cases of mental retardation had IQs below 50. The present investigator found a similar percentage. Twenty-seven percent of those index cases who remained in mental retardation placement until school-leaving age and whose IQs were predominantly below 50 were in a junior training center or in residential care.

Gruenberg (1964) estimated that about one-half of those classified as mentally retarded as children disappear from administrative note after leaving school. At age 22, in the present study, two-thirds were not receiving any mental retardation service and were not administratively considered as mentally retarded. This is a higher proportion than that given by Gruenberg.

Eighty percent of the index cases who finished schooling in special classes received no subsequent mental retardation services. This suggests that the term "educationally subnormal" used in Britain as a description of a current functional level is more appropriate than the American term "educable mentally retarded," which has the connotation of a more permanent state.

Of the index cases not receiving any mental retardation services at age 22, 8 percent were unemployed as opposed to 2 percent of the comparisons. It is important to know that most of those who were considered mildly mentally retarded at school obtained jobs under conditions where there is virtually full employment in their age group.

My second purpose in this paper was to determine to what extent the index cases who disappeared from administrative note after leaving school had careers that were similar or different from the comparisons. The evidence considered in light of the two alternatives suggested by Gruenberg (see p. 350 of this article) is that they are not "continuing to be extremely handicapped" (p. 274). Whether "they have stopped being retarded in any sense at all" (p. 274) depends on the meaning of "retarded" and the point of view that is adopted. From the viewpoint of whether those index cases would stand out as different when encountered by strangers in public places, they are probably indistinguishable. But when their lives are compared with those who are of the same age, sex, and general socioeconomic background in childhood and who were at no time classified as mentally retarded, there are important distinguishable differences. Of jobs held at the age of 22, the index cases, as a group, differed in holding positions requiring lower levels of skill, with less take-home pay, and requiring fewer dealings with people as compared to objects. When, however, subjective reactions to their work were elicited, the index cases appeared to have a lesser degree of discontent. This suggestion should be treated with caution because the index cases may be limited in their ability to envisage other work they would rather have done or ways in which they would have changed their working lives.

The findings about jobs should not be generalized beyond the age of 22. If there is differential advancement in the kinds of jobs held by the index and comparison young people, the differences early in their careers may be far less noticeable than, e.g., at the mid-point of their job careers. While the index cases may not perceive invidious comparisons between their own jobs and other people's at age 22, they may become aware of differences in another 10 to 20 years. Later, as job careers draw to a close and retirement begins and when society's expectations for an individual's work performance diminishes and ends, then the index and comparison cases may again appear more alike.

The discrepancy found between the objective and subjective measures related to jobs does not occur in the results related to interpersonal relations. The objective indicators suggest that the index young adults have a more restricted set of interpersonal relations than do the comparisons. But here the index cases assess how they get along with other people less favorably than do the comparisons. It should be noted, however, that the subjective questions related to interpersonal relations probably require less conceptual ability than the subjective questions about jobs.

Further analysis will broaden the picture of ways in which the index cases who disappear from administrative note after leaving school do and do not differ from comparisons in their past and present daily lives. It will also show the variation that exists in this subset of index cases and how these variations are related to their social and biological histories.

The present report is restricted to two birth cohorts while the overall study will include five birth cohorts. The research design requires the young adults to be interviewed at age 22. Data-gathering must therefore span 5 years. The total number of cases will provide larger numbers and, consequently, opportunities for more wide-ranging analysis. We felt it important, however, not to delay the presentation of any results until data gathering was complete.

Department of Pediatrics
Albert Einstein College of Medicine
of Yeshiva University
1300 Morris Park Ave.
Bronx, NY 10461

Reference Notes

1. Kennedy, R. J. *A Connecticut community revisited: A study of the social adjustment of a group of mentally deficient adults in 1948 and 1960.* Hartford: Connecticut State Department of Health, Office of Mental Retardation, 1966.
2. Saenger, G. *The adjustment of severely retarded adults in the community* (Report). Albany: NY State Interdepartmental Health Resources Board, 1957.

TIME AND MONEY FOR VOCATIONAL REHABILITATION OF CLIENTS WITH MILD, MODERATE AND SEVERE MENTAL RETARDATION

RICHARD T. WALLS, M. S. TSENG, AND HAROLD N. ZARIN
West Virginia University

Mildly, moderately, and severely mentally retarded vocational rehabilitation clients comprised a random national sample of 600 clients. One-half of the sample had been closed (services completed) "rehabilitated," and half had been closed "nonrehabilitated." Variables selected for analyses were time in referral, training, and rehabilitation process; dollars in evaluation, facilities, all services, and earnings. Rehabilitated clients tended to require more time in referral, less moneys for extended evaluation and rehabilitation facilities, and earned more per week than the nonrehabilitated clients. Severely mentally retarded clients required more time in training and higher costs for extended evaluation, rehabilitation facilities, and all services than the moderately or mildly retarded groups. A consistent interaction across five variables indicated that the greatest amounts of service in time and money went to the nonrehabilitated severely retarded group.

In the 1973 Rehabilitation Act (Public Law 93-112, 93rd Congress, H.R. 8070, September 26, 1973), services were specifically mandated to severely handicapped individuals, ". . . provid[ing] such [vocational rehabilitation] services for the benefit of such [handicapped] individuals, serving first those with the most severe handicaps, so that they may prepare for and engage in gainful employment" (p. 2). Further, Section 401, Title IV, concerning program evaluation includes reference to the severely handicapped client, requiring ". . . [a] reassess[ment of] priorities to which such activities [research, demonstration, etc.] should be directed; and review [of] present research, demonstration, and related activities to determine . . . whether and on what basis such activities should be continued, revised, or terminated" (p. 31).

One of the primary target groups for vocational rehabilitation thus becomes the clients whose disability is classed "mental retardation, severe." Although the vocational rehabilitation system has always dealt with such clients, their number has been disproportionately low. Many more clients assessed as "moderately" or "mildly" retarded have traditionally been accepted for and provided with vocational rehabilitation services.

Cobb (1972) noted similarly that the overwhelming majority of studies of community adaptation have involved individuals classified as mildly retarded. Recent emphasis toward decentralization of residential services has prompted increased interest in the rehabilitation potential associated with moderate and severe mental disability. Deinstitutionalization has become a watchword, and predictive characteristics in union with innovative effective intervention curricula are widely sought.

From a noninstitutional setting, Saenger (Note 1) reported a high frequency of moderately retarded adults who were former special-education students in New York City achieving stable social and occupational adaptation on a semi-independent basis. Katz (1968) emphasized the importance of social, educational, and occupational community services. While several investigators have reported that mildly retarded pupils can function in adult society with little or no postschool intervention (e.g., Cobb, 1972; Deno, Note 2), those with moderately and severely retarded intellec-

This investigation was supported in part by the Rehabilitation Services Administration (U.S. Department of Health, Education, and Welfare) through the West Virginia Regional Rehabilitation Research and Training Center (West Virginia University and West Virginia Division of Vocational Rehabilitation).

tual capacity often require much more in the way of rehabilitative aid.

Researchers continue to extend and document the inadequacy of simple demographic or unidimensional predictors of vocational "success." Students' IQ and cognitive behavior are integrally related to maturational and cultural factors and provide poor prognostication of adult adaptation (Baller, Charles, & Miller, 1966; Charles, 1966). Such factors have proven to be substantially malleable via skillful programs of rehabilitation or changes in environmental constraints. Brolin (1972) found retarded clients, judged to have received "adequate services" in accordance with the diagnostic evaluation, were more likely to attain a favorable vocational outcome than those receiving "inadequate services."

Elo and Hendel (1972) compared mildly retarded, moderately–severely retarded, and nonretarded clients on a number of outcome dimensions. These vocational rehabilitation clients were from a single state. The moderate and severe disability classifications were combined with no report of the respective numbers of clients composing that group. As might be expected, when the retarded clients (mild and moderate–severe) were compared with nonretarded clients, the retarded clients had greater cost of rehabilitation, lower earnings at closure, more time in referral and applicant statuses, and were more likely to be placed in a sheltered workshop or service occupation. When the mildly retarded group and moderately–severely retarded group were compared, few salient differences were identified. The only major finding Elo and Hendel reported was, "Moderately–severely retarded clients earned less than the mildly retarded clients in professional and clerical, farming, and blue collar occupations but earned slightly more in service occupations" ·

The present investigation was directed toward possible differentiation by monetary and duration variables of clients classified as mildly, moderately, and severely retarded within the framework of the intake, process, and outcomes system of vocational rehabilitation. In the present comparisons of these three groups of retarded clients via a rehabilitated–not rehabilitated criterion, the subjects were from all 50 states representing a national sample of vocational rehabilitation clients with mental retardation.

Method
Subjects

The subjects were 600 vocational rehabilitation clients closed in fiscal year 1971.

From the national records of approximately 750,000 clients whose services were completed or terminated in that year, the 600 clients were randomly sampled to meet the following requirements of mental retardation and outcome. One-half of the sample (300 clients) had been closed "rehabilitated" (vocational rehabilitation status 26) and half (300 clients) "nonrehabilitated" (vocational rehabilitation status 28 or 30). The Rehabilitation Services Administration definition in the former case required the client to have completed several steps in the rehabilitation process and to "be suitably employed *for a minimum of 30 days* [our italics]." Nonrehabilitated clients did not successfully achieve this criterion.

These two groups were further subdivided into three groups: (a) mild, (b) moderate, and (c) severe, as defined in the *Rehabilitation Service Administration Service Manual* based on recommendations by the American Association on Mental Deficiency. The primary design was thus a 2 (rehabilitated, nonrehabilitated) × 3 (mild, moderate, severe) format with 100 clients in each cell.

Procedure

Time and money variables were selected to represent evaluative and pragmatic concerns. Finite time and resources constitute major rehabilitation process variables of historic significance in the selection of clients for services. Many false-negatives relative to accepting clients for services have undoubtedly been created within the moderate and to an even greater extent within the severe retardation classification because of such cost/benefit concerns in the system. Specifically, the variables selected for analyses were:

1. Time in the referral status—the number of months (rounded to the nearest month) from the first referral to completion of the referral process
2. Time in training—the number of months (rounded) in occupational training
3. Time in the vocational rehabilitation process—the number of months (rounded) from acceptance to closure
4. Money in extended evaluation—the dollars spent by vocational rehabilitation for extended evaluation of the client
5. Money in facilities—the dollars spent by vocational rehabilitation for services within a center, workshop, or other facility
6. Money for all services—the dollars spent by vocational rehabilitation for all services combined
7. Money earned at closure—the weekly earnings by the client in dollars

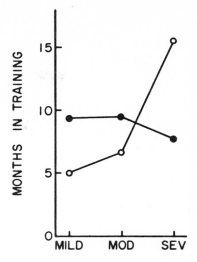

FIGURE 2.   Number of months in training.

Results

Separate 2 (rehabilitated, nonrehabilitated) × 3 (mild, moderate, severe) factorial analyses of variance were computed for each of the variables listed above. Missing data were excluded from the analyses. Results of these analyses are summarized below. Figures 1 through 7 depict these findings:

1. Months in referral did not differ among the three retardation classifications, but the main effect for outcome was significant with rehabilitated clients spending more months in referral than nonrehabilitated clients ($F = 10.8$, $1/587$ df, $p < .01$). The interaction of these factors was nonsignificant.

2. A significant main effect for retardation and multiple comparisons by the Duncan procedure revealed more months in training for severely than either moderately or mildly retarded clients ($F = 4.9$, $2/536$ df, $p < .01$). Moderately and mildly retarded clients did not differ. The main effect for

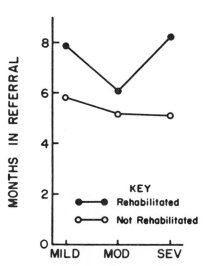

FIGURE 1.   Number of months in referral status.

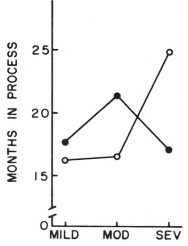

FIGURE 3.   Number of months from acceptance to closure.

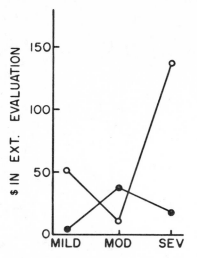

FIGURE 4. Dollars spent for extended evaluation.

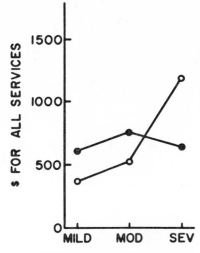

FIGURE 6. Dollars spent for all services.

outcome was nonsignificant; however, the interaction yielded a significant effect ($F = 10.4$, 2/536 df, $p < .01$). Multiple comparisons to interpret this interaction revealed a marked increment in training time for severely retarded clients who were not rehabilitated as compared to nonrehabilitated moderately retarded or rehabilitated severely retarded clients.

3. The main effects of retardation and outcome did not yield differences in total time from acceptance to closure. However, the same pattern of interaction was disclosed ($F = 5.7$, 2/480 df, $p < .01$). That is, severely retarded nonrehabilitated clients spent more time in the process than moderately retarded nonrehabilitated clients or severely retarded rehabilitated clients.

4. Analysis of funds expended for extended evaluation yielded a significant main effect for outcome ($F = 5.3$, 1/519 df, $p < .01$), with less expended for rehabilitated than for nonrehabilitated clients. The retardation main effect was significant, with more spent in extended evaluation for severely than for mildly or moderately re-

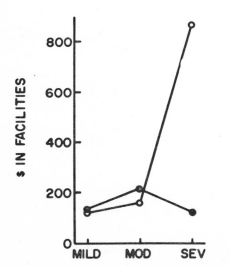

FIGURE 5. Dollars spent for services in facilities.

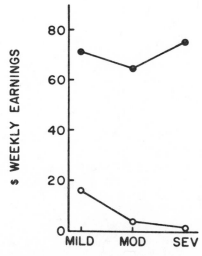

FIGURE 7. Dollars earned per week by client at closure.

tarded clients ($F = 3.3$, 2/519 df, $p < .05$). Again, the interaction produced a similar picture ($F = 4.0$, 2/519 df, $p < .01$). Severely retarded nonrehabilitated clients required more funds than moderately retarded nonrehabilitated or the severely retarded rehabilitated group.

5. The analysis of variance for money spent by vocational rehabilitation facilities yielded a significant effect for outcome with fewer dollars expended for rehabilitated than for nonrehabilitated clients ($F = 9.4$, 1/539 df, $p < .01$). The main effect for retardation revealed more funds for severe than for moderate or mild retardation ($F = 9.4$, 2/539 df, $p < .01$). Again, the same pattern emerged in the interaction. Severely retarded nonrehabilitated clients utilized more funds than moderately retarded nonrehabilitated or severely retarded rehabilitated clients. Other salient findings within that interaction were more facility funds for rehabilitated moderately retarded than rehabilitated mildly, rehabilitated severely, or nonrehabilitated moderately retarded clients. Finally, more funds were spent for the nonrehabilitated moderately retarded than nonrehabilitated mildly retarded group.

6. Cost of all services yielded a significant main effect for retardation ($F = 6.3$, 2/590 df, $p < .01$). Cost was greater for severely retarded than moderately or mildly retarded clients. Once again, the same relationship emerged, noted in 2, 3, 4, and 5 above for the significant interaction ($F = 6.9$, 2/590 df, $p < .01$). Severely retarded clients who were not rehabilitated had greater total service cost than the moderately retarded nonrehabilitated or the severely retarded rehabilitated group.

7. As would be expected, those clients who were rehabilitated earned much more per week than nonrehabilitated clients ($F = 100.4$, 1/512 df, $p < .01$). Perhaps a more interesting finding here was that there was no difference among the mildly, moderately, and severely retarded rehabilitated groups with respect to earnings at closure. This relationship is readily apparent in Figure 7.

Could the finding that severely retarded rehabilitated clients earn as much as the mildly and moderately retarded clients be accounted for by some unique pattern of occupations in which they were placed? To answer this question, we further analyzed the data set relative to the three rehabilitated groups, especially in reference to (a) work status and (b) occupation at closure. Results are summarized in Table 1. As can be seen, there were no appreciable differences among the frequency distributions for the

three client groups (mildly, moderately, severely retarded) in terms of their work statuses as characterized by competitive, sheltered workshop, self-employed, state-agency-managed business enterprises, homemaker, and unpaid family worker. In addition, there were no distinctive differences in the frequency distribution of occupational fields as represented by the first digit of the DOT (*Dictionary of Occupational Titles*) code (see Table 1). We should point out, however, that the criterion of rehabilitation used here is that of 30 days gainful employment as defined by the vocational rehabilitation agencies for case closure and that this circumscribed criterion could be responsible for the findings. Therefore, inferences should be drawn within this particular context.

It should also be noted that the severely retarded group represented only 8 percent of the mentally retarded persons who were accepted for vocational rehabilitation services. The mildly and moderately retarded group constituted 62 and 30 percent, respectively. Further, of these clients who were accepted for services, this vastly underrepresented severely retarded group achieved the rehabilitation criterion slightly less frequently than the other two groups (mildly retarded, 81 percent; moderately retarded, 78 percent; and severely retarded, 74 percent). Thus, the equal cell sizes chosen for analysis in this investigation must not be misinterpreted as representing the actual frequencies in the vocational rehabilitation system.

It should be noted in the above discussion of interactions relative to Variables 2, 3, 4, 5, and 6 that of the 15 possible multiple comparisons, only a selected number of significant mean differences were presented to reflect the more important aspects of the relationship. Figures 2 through 6 are further explications of these interactions.[1]

Discussion

Using a national sample of mentally retarded clients, we investigated three time variables (months in referral, months in training, and months from acceptance to closure) and four money variables (dollars for extended evaluation, facilities, all services, and weekly earnings) in the vocational rehabilitation process. It was assumed that such variables might reflect significant main effects of mental retardation (mild vs. moderate vs. severe) and rehabilitation out-

---

[1] A complete summary is available upon request from the authors.

TABLE 1
NUMBER OF CLIENTS FROM EACH GROUP ACCORDING TO WORK STATUS AND OCCUPATION

	Group		
Variable	Mildly retarded	Moderately retarded	Severely retarded
Work status at closure			
Competitive	76	74	74
Sheltered workshop	3	7	4
Self-employed	4	6	3
BEP[a]	0	0	0
Homemaker	8	5	14
Unpaid family worker	3	1	3
Dot code (first digit)			
0 Professional, technical, and managerial	8	9	7
1 Professional, technical, and managerial	3	6	5
2 Clerical & Sales	13	14	13
3 Service occupations	26	26	23
4 Farming & related	4	4	8
5 Processing occupations	11	8	18
6 Machine trades	15	2	9
7 Bench work occupations	12	8	6
8 Structural work	4	7	7
9 Miscellaneous	4	12	4

[a] State-agency-managed small business enterprises.

come (rehabilitated vs. nonrehabilitated) and the Retardation × Outcome interaction effect.

When clients were classified on the basis of rehabilitation outcomes (as defined by vocational rehabilitation agencies) and compared, rehabilitated clients (those who were closed on the criterion of 30 days gainful employment) tended to require more time in the referral status, less moneys for extended evaluation and rehabilitation facilities, and to earn more per week at closure than nonrehabilitated clients. It is of interest to note that, on the average, about the same amounts of rehabilitation services were rendered to both the rehabilitated and nonrehabilitated groups in terms of months in training, months from acceptance to closure, and dollars for all services.

Multiple comparisons among the combinations or rehabilitation outcomes and disabling conditions revealed that the largest amounts of service time (months in training and months from acceptance to closure) and money (costs for extended evaluation, rehabilitation facilities, and all services) went to the nonrehabilitated severely retarded group. The amounts of service rendered to this group were significantly greater than those given to the rehabilitated severely and nonrehabilitated moderately retarded groups. This, together with the finding that on the whole the rehabilitated severely retarded group did not require more rehabilita-

tion time or cost as compared to the rehabilitated moderately, rehabilitated mildly, nonrehabilitated moderately, or nonrehabilitated mildly retarded groups, would suggest the following. Given the existing intervention, placement practices, and closure criteria in vocational rehabilitation, an appreciably large investment is being made by the rehabilitation agency (in terms of time and money) for assisting the severely retarded clients until they are closed as nonrehabilitated cases. Post hoc examination of demographic characteristics revealed no apparent differences between the severely retarded clients achieving successful rehabilitation and their nonrehabilitated counterparts.

In light of the growing emphasis that is being placed on serving severely handicapped individuals as mandated by the 1973 Rehabilitation Act, the findings of this study concerning time and money for serving severely retarded clients (both rehabilitated and nonrehabilitated) can be used as baseline data. Any refined and/or new intervention strategies, job development and placement schemes, and rehabilitation outcome criteria contemplated and implemented in the future may eventually yield the kind of data which can be systematically related to the baseline. Thus, effectiveness of such services may be assessed in a data-based fashion.

A Vocational Delivery System For The Mildly Retarded

HARRY P. BLUHM
University of Utah

It is estimated that there are 6.1 million retarded persons in the United States. Approximately 2.4 million of these individuals are children and young people under 21 years of age. According to conservative estimates, three-fourths of these individuals could become self-supporting and another 10% to 15% partially self-supporting as adults if appropriate education and training are given to them.

To attain these expectations, delivery systems must be implemented to enable the retarded citizen to become employed either competitively or under sheltered conditions. My purpose is to discuss a vocational delivery system that is aimed primarily at the competitive employment market. This system consists of two phases, a prevocational or educational phase and a vocational or work-oriented phase. The components of each phase are diagrammed in Fig. 1.

THE PREVOCATIONAL PHASE

The prevocational phase is educationally based and incorporates several fundamental aspects of occupational training. This phase generally commences at the junior high school level and is maintained in the initial senior high curriculum. It precedes the vocational phase, which begins in the upper grades of high school and may continue at the postsecondary school level. Curriculum considerations provide for the development of functional academic skills, exploratory experiences pertaining to the world of work, and the attainment of personal-social and home-living skills needed to function in society.

Functional academic skills

The purpose of academics, according to Syden (1962), is to provide retarded individuals with information and experiences that should assist them in meeting daily problems, finding their place in the economic world, and giving them an understanding of their responsibilities as citizens. Basic skills would be taught in reading, language, and number concepts during the elementary years with the emphasis taking a decidedly vocational direction during the junior and senior high school years.

Reading. Baroff (1974) suggests that a secondary reading skills program with the primary focus on protection and information is necessary. The ability to read safety and warning signs are primary examples of the protection emphasis. Reading for information includes the functional use of catalogs, telephone directories, maps, classified ads, magazines, television and movie listings, etc.

Language. The primary focus of language instruction is oral expression or the effective use of expressive language (Martens, 1950). Listening for comprehension, carrying on conversations, talking on the telephone, and being able to ask and answer questions are all critical to the development of basic communication structures. A degree of writing proficiency should also be attained by retarded individuals, permitting them to write legibly and accurately in either print or cursive form. They should develop experience in completing various printed forms and in writing personal and business letters.

Number skills. The basic skills in arithmetic would essentially be delimited to addition and subtraction, although multiplication, short division, and simple fractions are also relevant concepts of the arithmetic curricula for this population. The ability to read time

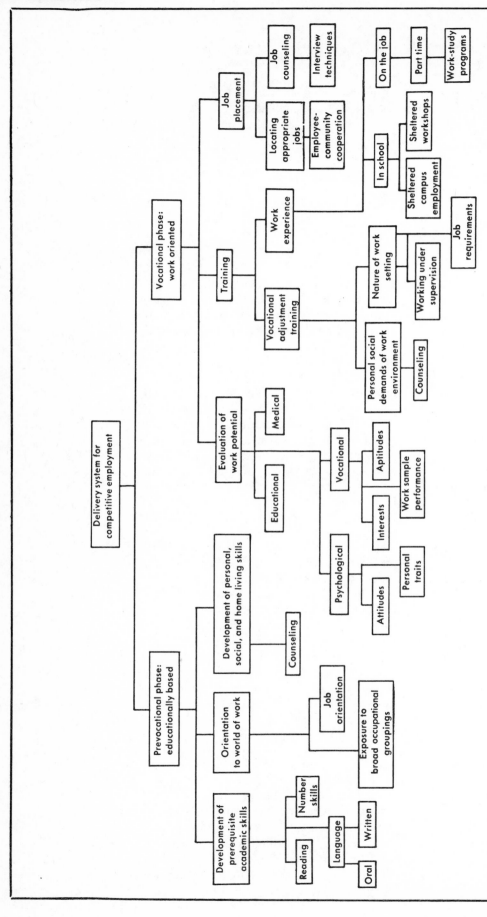

Fig. 1. A vocational delivery system for the mildly retarded individual.

tables and schedules and to employ common units of measures must be emphasized in order to ensure job survival.

The application of number skills to the activities of daily living becomes essential. Thus retarded individuals must develop the skill of using coins and bills of all denominations and must learn about budgeting, banking, credit buying, insurance, taxes, and wage and payroll deductions.

Summary. Although functional academic skills are accented in the retarded individual's educational program, literature in this area has suggested that the absence of functional reading and number skills does not seriously limit the employment of retarded individuals in unskilled work. Dinger (1961) indicates that almost one-half (47%) of the jobs engaged in by employed retarded individuals required no more than counting, and 10% of the jobs required no number skills at all. Approximately 69% of the jobs required no more writing than signing a paycheck or application form. Additionally, 67% of the jobs required only the reading of single words (word recognition), and 33% required no reading at all. These findings suggest that at the junior and senior high school levels the educational experience should not be limited totally to academic training but should also include prevocational and vocational experiences as well (Baroff, 1974).

Orientation to the world of work

Special education teachers and/or school counselors have the responsibility of orienting retarded individuals to the world of work. Vocational guidance deals with the matters of occupational choice, preparation, placement, and adjustment on the job (London, 1973). Typically, vocational guidance regarding career choice is initiated during the latter part of the adolescent years. However, during junior high school retarded individuals are generally introduced to the world of work through simulated and on-the-job exploratory experiences. They learn about various occupations, participate in industrial tours or field trips, and experience certain jobs through in-school work situations.

Specifically, classroom experiences for the retarded individual would involve learning about the opportunities and requirements of service, clerical, agricultural, skilled, semiskilled, and unskilled occupations. These seem to be the job areas in which most retarded persons find employment. The percentage of retarded individuals employed in given job areas is reported to be: service (30%), clerical (12%), agricultural (5.9%), skilled (5.4%), semiskilled (19.3%), unskilled (21.2%), and family worker (6.2%) (President's Committee on Employment of the Handicapped, 1963).

It is also highly recommended that parents of the retarded be involved in this orientation. This permits both parties to obtain information regarding the opportunities available, facts about entry requirements, working conditions, duties performed, health hazards encountered, and the rate of pay for each of the studied occupations.

Field trips. The field trip experience provides the retarded individual with firsthand information regarding alternative career choices. The individual becomes aware of working conditions and worker requirements through this direct observation method (London, 1973). These field trips, organized as part of the orientation process, include visits to laundries, medical centers, hotels, restaurants, large retail stores, meat packing plants, and large farms or dairies. It is important to note that the use of audiovisual media and specialized guest speakers is an effective alternative when personal direct observation is not possible.

Simulated work experiences. The in-school simulated work experience provides another means of orienting retarded individuals to occupational alternatives. These simulated experiences coordinate the interests and capabilities of the retarded individual to the requirements of the work setting. Common junior high experiences include school lunch, custodial, shop, school office, and library clerical jobs. The in-school work placement program at the senior high level provides specific preparatory training experiences prior to on-the-job training.

Personal-social and home-living skills. The retarded individual must possess the requisite personal-social and home-living skills in order to function independently in society and become engaged in productive work experiences. Throughout the junior and senior high school levels, instructional objectives should focus on assisting retarded individuals to: (1) become aware of themselves, their strengths, and their limitations; (2) develop good health and nutritional practices; (3) become aware of and maintain appropriate dress and grooming; (4) get along with others—adults, the opposite sex, and the same sex peers; and (5) develop home economic skills (Baroff, 1974).

Retarded individuals who are experiencing poor peer relationships, feeling of inadequacy, and a tendency toward self-deprecation may need counseling services. When a counseling service is available the counselor should seek to provide a much more friendly, accepting, and supportive learning situation than would be required for nonretarded individuals with these same feelings (Thorne, 1960).

THE VOCATIONAL PHASE

The primary purpose of the vocational phase is preparation of the retarded individual for placement in the world of work. The components of this phase, including the evaluation of work potential, job training, and placement, have their roots in the trait and factor vocational theory (Shertzer and Stone, 1968; Zaccaria, 1970). This theory provides for the following steps:

1. The traits of the retarded individual are to be assessed by psychological tests and other evaluative tools. This permits the retarded individual and those who work with him or her to obtain a clear understanding of the individual's attitudes, abilities, interests, ambitions, resources, and limitations.
2. An assessment is obtained regarding the requirements and conditions for success, advantages, compensation, and the prospects of alternative occupational opportunities as they relate to the retarded individual.
3. The counselor (school and/or rehabilitation), the special education teacher, or the vocational coordinator seeks to match the retarded individual to the job with the greatest opportunity for success.

The relationship between the components of the vocational phase and the steps associated with the trait and factor theory is shown in Fig. 2. Burrow (1964) suggests that the match between the job and the individual is the culmination of the entire job development process. The retarded individual's prospects for job stability are not good if the match is not made on a completely selective basis.

Evaluation of work potential

The purpose of evaluating the work potential of retarded individuals is to determine what type of work they can do or can be trained to do. This requires identifying the specific abilities or assets they may possess. The evaluation should be comprehensive in order to examine the retarded individual's intellectual abilities, academic achievement, manual skills, personality traits, vocational interests, etc. (Patterson, 1964; Katz, 1968; Kolstoe, 1960).

Instruments used to collect these data include standardized tests, attitude scales, vocational adjustment scales, checklists, rating scales, personal-social inventories, performance scales, interest inventories, and work samples. A basic concern regarding the use of these instruments is their reliability and validity. One problem with standardized tests is that they have not been normed on mentally retarded individuals, thus making their reliability and validity questionable with this population (Walthall and Love, 1974; Katz, 1968).

Personality inventories have been of little use with the retarded since it is unclear whether they tap the characteristics important to job success. The utilization of work samples for evaluative purposes has also been questioned because of the lack of a specified criteria and a low correlation with job requirements (Patterson, 1964). However, direct observations by trained personnel are essential. They are useful in providing information on the retarded individual's vocational interests, attitudes, and work habits.

It is essential that only skilled personnel be included in the comprehensive evaluation. The team approach involving psychologists, physicians, social workers, educational specialists, and rehabilitation counselors is highly recommended (Katz, 1968). The evaluation may be conducted by public

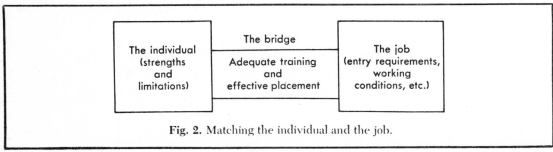

Fig. 2. Matching the individual and the job.

schools, sheltered workshops, or rehabilitation agencies. It may last from several weeks to 1 or 2 years, depending upon the problems presented by the retarded individual (Bolanovich, 1972). The evaluation of the retarded individual's work potential should be considered as a process of gathering, interpreting, analyzing, and synthesizing all vocationally significant data (Malikin and Rusalem, 1969).

Training

The employability of the retarded individual is dependent upon the successful development of vocational skills in combination with desired personal-social skills. This goal is attained through vocational adjustment training and work experiences. Personal-social factors have been recognized as the most important determinant of the retarded individual's employability (Syden, 1962; Deno, 1966). Vocational adjustment training serves to assist the individual in becoming dependable and emotionally mature. Additionally, work experiences enable the retarded individual to practice job skills in a protective environment under the supervision of an employer and school official.

Work adjustment training. Work adjustment training is work rather than education oriented (Daniels, 1974). It may be given without any specific job in mind, but generally occurs when the retarded individual is obtaining job training in an on-campus or community job.

The purpose of work adjustment training is for the retarded individual to experience actual work situations under the guidance of a work supervisor and counselor. During such training retarded individuals are oriented to the personal-social demands of the work environment and to the nature of work settings. They are taught courteousness, cleanliness, punctuality, cooperation, tolerance toward pressures of meetings and deadlines, and the need to work harmoniously with other employees, to stick to given work tasks, and to take responsibility for work assigned (Davis, 1959; Stahlecker, 1964; Daniels, 1974; Bolanovich, 1972).

The counselor conducting the training can assist the retarded individual in learning appropriate behaviors and eliminating those that are undesirable. Individual or group counseling may be utilized depending upon the situation or problem that exists. Two techniques, role playing and behavior modification, have been found to be very ef-

fective in a variety of these counseling situations. Role playing is effective in providing retarded individuals the opportunity of confronting interpersonal problems in a simulated and sheltered environment. Behavior modification focuses upon specific behaviorally defined problems incorporated within a system of consistent feedback. This facilitates the monitoring of client progress within a designated program structure (Halpern and Berard, 1974).

Counselors and sheltered workshop foremen may monitor or assess the work adjustment behavior by using one of several vocational adjustment scales (Daniels, 1972; Bitter and Bolanovich, 1970). The scales purport to measure job readiness but may be limited by interrater variations and the lack of empirical data correlating measured behavior to rehabilitation needs (Bitter and Bolanovich, 1970).

Work experience. Erickson (1947) defines work experience as

. . . a means and method in the program of the school by which the learner actually produces goods or renders useful service through participation in socially desirable activities in the community under real conditions. [p. 355]

Successful in-school work experiences should precede out-of-school vocational encounters. These in-school work experiences may be obtained through sheltered campus employment and sheltered workshops. Out-of-school experiences result from student participation in work-study programs.

Work experience serves as a valuable testing ground for practicing related job skills under the supervision of school officials. The retarded individuals are in a protective environment where they may learn by trial and error with no fear of losing the job. The practical experience they obtain serves to help them develop work confidence (Stahlecker, 1964; Kokaska, 1964; Burdett, 1963). Additionally, school officials have the advantage of observing the retarded individual's work attitude and response to supervision. Deficits that are noted can be incorporated into the vocational adjustment program. A disadvantage of sheltered on-campus work experiences is that the supervising personnel, including custodians and cafeteria workers, may look at the retarded individual as merely a helper and thus fail to instruct or supervise (Hickman, 1967).

The sheltered workshop program has two basic functions: (1) to train retarded individuals for employment in competitive jobs, and

(2) to provide a terminal employment opportunity for retarded adults who cannot succeed in competitive employment conditions (Wallin, 1960; Bolanovich, 1972). As a rehabilitative facility, the sheltered workshop seeks to prepare mildly retarded individuals for unsheltered employment through the molding of attitudes, vocational training, and achievement of social skills (Zaetz, 1971; Conley, 1973).

On-the-job training of retarded individuals between the ages of 17 and 21 years is facilitated through the establishment of work-study programs. Generally, individuals participating in work-study programs are considered to be emotionally stable and socially mature. Physically, they should be able to perform the job requirements and not represent a danger to themselves or their fellow workers (Shawn, 1964).

The responsibility for work-study programs is shared by the local school district and community agencies. School officials must identify employers within the community that have jobs suited to the needs and limitations of the retarded client. Vocational rehabilitation offices and state employment agencies should assist in this process. Once identified, employers must be willing to assume responsibility for training the retarded individual and orienting current employees to the exceptional needs of the retarded client. Retarded individuals must also accept responsibility. They must be willing to work cooperatively with their fellow employees and supervisory personnel. Retarded individuals who participate in work study programs profit by (1) learning the characteristics of a particular job, (2) knowing what the job requirements are, (3) receiving assistance in job interviewing, (4) understanding the purpose of wage deductions and various fringe benefits, and (5) acquiring an identity as responsible and productive workers (Daniels, 1974).

Job placement. Job placement is the culminating activity of the delivery system for competitive employment. It consists of matching the right person to the right job. Job placement brings the employer, school or rehabilitative counselor, and the retarded client together. Burrow (1964) outlines several steps a counselor should follow in securing employment for the retarded individual in a competitive labor market. First, the counselor seeks to identify employers with jobs available that meet the skill requirements of the retarded client. The counselor then discusses with the employer the needs, capabilities, and limitations of the retarded client. When the employer and counselor are reasonably sure that the client matches the job, the retarded individual is brought in for a formal job interview. Role playing of the job interview should have been previously conducted in order to prepare the retarded individual for this situation. Once the job has been secured the counselor is obligated to conduct follow-up assessment on the retarded individual's job performance. The previously discussed delivery system will be successful if the retarded individual, through continual employment in the labor force, attains the expected goal of self-sufficiency.

REFERENCES

Baroff, G. A.: Mental retardation: nature, cause, and management, New York, 1974, Halsted Press.

Bitter, J. A., and Bolanovich, D. J.: WARF: a scale for measuring job readiness behaviors, Am. J. Ment. Defic. 74: 616-621, 1970.

Bolanovich, D. J., Drought, N. E., and Stewart, D. A.: Full employment for the mentally retarded, St. Louis, 1972, The Jewish Employment and Vocational Service.

Burdett, A. D.: An examination of selected prevocational techniques utilized in programs for the mentally retarded, Ment. Retard. 1: 230-237, 1963.

Burrow, W. H.: Job development: a problem in interpersonal dynamics training, Training School Bull. 61: 12-20, 1964.

Conley, R. W.: The economics of mental retardation, Baltimore, 1973, The Johns Hopkins University Press.

Daniels, L. K.: An experimental edition of a rating scale of vocational adjustment for the mentally retarded, Training School Bull. 69: 92-98, 1972.

Daniels, L. K., editor: Vocational rehabilitation of the mentally retarded, Springfield, Ill., 1974, Charles C Thomas, Publisher.

Davis, D. A.: Counseling the mentally retarded, Vocational Guidance Quarterly 7: 184-188, 1959.

Deno, E.: Vocational preparation of the retarded during school years. In Michael, S. G. D., editor: New vocational pathways for the mentally retarded, Washington, D.C., 1966, American Personnel and Guidance Association, pp. 20-29.

Dinger, J. C.: Post-school adjustment of former educable retarded pupils, Except. Child. 27: 353-356, 1961.

Erickson, C. E.: A basic text for guidance workers, New York, 1947, Prentice-Hall, Inc.

Halpern, A. S., and Berard, W. R.: Counseling the mentally retarded: a review for practice. In Browning, P. L., editor: Mental retardation: rehabilitation and counseling, Springfield, Ill., 1974, Charles C Thomas, Publisher, pp. 269-289.

Hickman, L. H., Jr.: A foundation for the preparation of the educable child for the world of work, Training School Bull. 64: 39-44, 1967.

Katz, E.: The retarded adult in the community, Springfield, Ill., 1968, Charles C Thomas, Publisher.

HIRING AND SUPERVISING MENTALLY RETARDED WORKERS

A Handbook for Supervisors

Larry Kovnat, Sherri LaPointe,
Walter Pieczkolon and Shayne Style

Placement Specialists

There are approximately 6 million people in the United States who are mentally retarded—about 3 percent of the total population. All but a small percentage can achieve a degree of independence when provided with training and the opportunity to work.

As more mentally retarded people enter the workforce in an increasing variety of jobs, you may be faced with hiring and supervising a mentally retarded worker. Will you be effective? Yes—by knowing the answers to the following questions:

1. Who are "mentally retarded" people?
2. What qualifies a mentally retarded person as work-ready?
3. How do companies recruit, interview and select mentally retarded applicants?
4. How do you instruct and supervise mentally retarded workers?
5. Where can further advice and assistance be obtained?

The answers to these and other questions appear in the following pages. In this handbook, we present successful practices of supervisors who have employed mentally retarded workers in business, industry and government.

WHO ARE "MENTALLY RETARDED" PEOPLE?

The mentally retarded people to whom we refer in this handbook are those with the capacity to be trained for work and to hold productive jobs when selectively placed. They learn more slowly than others and are limited in what they can learn.

"Mental Retardation" does not mean that the person's total being is retarded. His intellectual capacity is limited but he may have other skills and aptitudes which enable him to perform better than other workers, thus making him or her a valued employee.

When properly placed, like everyone else, retarded workers can do a job well.

WHAT QUALIFIES A MENTALLY RETARDED PERSON AS WORK-READY?

TRAINING. Work training programs stress practical job experiences as well as dependability, punctuality and personal appearance. In most cases, mentally retarded individuals have received more work related training than many high school graduates.

Training programs are conducted by specialists in accredited facilities providing work experiences in such areas as building maintenance and custodial care, food service, machine operations, assembly and packaging, to name a few. Throughout training, good work attitudes and motivation are positively reinforced through evaluation and feedback of work habits and accomplishments.

ATTITUDE. Because attitude plays such an important part in job success, it is stressed throughout training. Desire to work, cooperation and pride in a job well done make the difference.

A mentally retarded worker with these attitudes will pay more attention to his work, have lower lateness and absentee rates and make fewer job changes—all are indicators of job satisfaction.

SOURCES FOR RECRUITING MENTALLY RETARDED WORKERS

The major sources for recruiting mentally retarded workers are agencies and facilities which can be found in the telephone listings under the titles:

> Rehabilitation Services;
>
> Social Service Organizations;
>
> State (e.g., Pennsylvania) Bureau of Vocational Rehabilitation;
>
> (Local County) Association for Retarded Citizens.

When you call, a placement counselor will discuss your job openings with you, provide applications or resumes describing applicants' education, training, abilities and accomplishments and refer individuals to you for interviews.

> You make the decision.
>
> You make the selection.
>
> You do the hiring.

BEFORE THE INTERVIEW

The first step in hiring is to give the placement coordinator complete information about the job including specific duties, equipment to be used and working conditions. A job site visit is often used to determine exactly what the job entails. Only then can the proper referrals be made.

The second step in hiring is to obtain background information about the mentally retarded applicants. This is the key to effective interviewing. The job placement coordinator who recommends applicants will give you all the available facts: education, training, abilities and work experiences. Having this information prior to the actual face-to-face interview will enable you to ask specific job-related questions of the applicants, and to discover personal qualities and positive work attitudes.

After completing these basic steps, you will be closer to deciding if a particular applicant is suitable for the job.

THE INTERVIEW

The purpose of the interview is to get to know the applicant and to determine whether or not he is able to perform a given job. This is also true of interviewing a mentally retarded applicant. Conduct the interview as you would with any potential employee. Do not prejudge the applicant before the interview. Avoid the tendency to talk down to a mentally retarded person as though he were a child. Speak directly to the applicant and choose commonly-used words.

Explain the duties and working conditions of the job, describing precisely what is to be done. Basing your questions on the information provided in the application, ask the applicant questions concerning his previous job training and work experience. Ask questions that require more than a simple "yes" or "no" answer. Be specific. Be concrete. Be job-related.

For example:

Where were you trained?

What were you trained to do?

What tools or equipment did you use?

Where have you worked before and what did you do?

What did you like about your job?

What did you do best?

Take particular note of the applicant's attitude and desire to work. Be objective. Remember not to judge the ability of the mentally retarded applicant by how well he talks during the interview; not everyone verbalizes well. If possible, show the applicant the job site and explain or demonstrate the duties to be performed. Allow the applicant to explain or demonstrate what he can do.

Now that you have met the applicant and assessed his strengths and capabilities, and if you have any questions about the applicant's ability, discuss the outcome of the interview with the job placement coordinator.

ONE STEP AT A TIME

All new employees go through a "breaking in" period. Introduce the worker to his co-workers. The acceptance by co-workers is vital to the success of the mentally retarded worker. It will be easier for everyone if fellow employees are cordial but not overfriendly. Because the mentally retarded worker may be shy the first few days on the job and not always initiate conversation, you could assign a co-worker to "break the ice."

Any new worker must learn company rules and the specific duties of the job. The following check-lists cover both kinds of information.

Company Rules

Explain General Procedures:

☐ Hours and wages;

☐ To whom he reports and his work station;

☐ Procedure for calling-in if absent (give worker written copy of company phone number and name of supervisor);

☐ Proper clothing on the job;

☐ Show him the timeclock, lockers, restroom, cafeteria and supply room as you would for any new employee.

Explain Working Conditions:

☐ Plant safety rules;

☐ Hazardous areas and the signs;

☐ Safety clothing and equipment required.

Now you can start instructing the worker, asking questions as you progress to check his understanding.

On The Job Instruction

☐ Give one direction at a time and be specific. Post copy of directions at work station.

☐ Explain briefly what needs to be done, clearly stating what to do first and showing where to locate supplies to be used.

☐ Show worker how to do each task. Let him repeat it for you. ("Now show me what you're supposed to do.") Make any corrections in the way the worker performs each step.

☐ Establish a routine. Give instructions in a sequence of steps in order of priority. ("When you come in each morning, do - - - first. Next do - - -.")

☐ Ask questions to verify his grasp of instructions, making sure he is keeping up with you. Take nothing for granted; because no questions are asked, does not mean he understands. ("What will you do next? What do you do with - - - ?")

☐ Regular feedback to the new employee regarding his job performance will improve his efficiency. ("This is done right, but do - - - better.") A sincere compliment when a task is completed satisfactorily will build confidence and reduce initial anxiety.

☐ If you want the worker to improve one specific area of performance, show him again exactly how he should do that task.

☐ Once a worker learns a method of completing a task, if you want that method changed, you will have to repeat the above steps and establish a new routine.

☐ Follow-up and evaluation should be informal and continuous. Check often to follow progress and taper off as work is done correctly.

☐ Before leaving the worker on his own, make sure he knows these two basic items:

> What he should do when he is finished with the present task;

> To whom he should report if there is a question or a problem and where to find that person.

☐ Keep the job placement coordinator informed of the worker's progress and if necessary the coordinator will come to the job site to assist you with on-the-job instruction.

IN SUMMARY:

Job Instruction = Explanation + Demonstration

Job Instruction = Routine + Repetition

Any method of job instruction takes time, but it is worth your efforts if it results in a quality worker instead of another turnover statistic.

©HVAS

TYPICAL SITUATIONS ON THE JOB

Generally an individual becomes adjusted to the duties and environment of a new job within the first few weeks. This adjustment period is two-sided. The worker is becoming accustomed to his job and co-workers; at the same time, the supervisor and co-workers are becoming accustomed to the mentally retarded worker. He fits in with the daily routines and everything proceeds smoothly. This is the way things usually are but occasionally there might be a rough spot or two in need of smoothing out. What do you do? Examples of situations which other supervisors have handled effectively follow.

Starting On Time

Larry has been arriving an hour too early. What should you do?

Ask him why he is arriving too early. Is it because of his transportation arrangements? Is he overanxious to please and afraid of losing his job? Is he leaving home too early? Explain again the correct working hours and tell him he is not expected to arrive before starting time. Give him a written copy of his schedule. If Larry keeps arriving too early, call the placement coordinator for assistance.

Following Instructions

Linda has been shown her daily routine several times. She is doing her tasks in the wrong order. What should you do?

Tell her she is not doing her job in the right order. Linda is not trying to change the routine or do things her own way, but may be forgetting the sequence of steps. The supervisor decides to write down the list of tasks including simple illustrations and places it near her work station. The supervisor continues to spot check Linda's work and reminds her to look at her list when she finishes each task. As she masters her routine, he tapers off his supervision.

Doing The Whole Job

Carol has many duties, one of which is to count and wrap twelve necklaces per package. She cannot count to twelve except with a structure. What should you do?

The supervisor prepares a piece of paper with twelve lines. Carol lays one necklace on each of the twelve lines and then packages the twelve necklaces for shipment. A simple modification enables her to do the whole job. If you doubt that an individual can perform a certain task, check with the placement coordinator. It can usually be solved very simply.

Speeding It Up

George assembles belts and buckles in a factory. After having George use the usual method of assembling for a few days, the supervisor feels that George's speed is not acceptable. What should you do?

The supervisor contacts the placement coordinator and asks him to come to the job site to try to assess the difficulty. The coordinator observes that the usual method suits right-handed people and that George is left-handed. The coordinator works with George to develop a routine of assembling that is easier for a left-handed worker and increases his speed to an above average rate.

Promoting A Good Worker

Jose operates microfilm machines and is being considered for a promotion because of his excellent work record. Will he be able to perform the extra duties? How do you decide?

Explain to Jose why you wish to promote him and what promotion means, asking him whether he is willing. Explain the duties and responsibilities of the new position to him. The supervisor orients Jose to the new duties which include checking the work of others and keeping new records. If he is the most qualified for the new position, and if he can handle it satisfactorily, then promote him. If not, keep him in his present position.

FOLLOW-UP SERVICES

Throughout the process of hiring and supervising mentally retarded workers, the job placement coordinator provides continual assistance. Should the need arise, talk with the coordinator *before* a serious problem or disciplinary action occurs. Often difficulties can be attributed to a break in communication which can be identified and solved by the placement coordinator. Since most problems can be averted or solved, follow-up services are available as needed.

The follow-up services are based on your feedback, both oral and written. Periodic evaluations give you the opportunity to assess the worker in comparison with other workers and to notify the coordinator of any area in which improvement is needed.

The coordinator keeps in touch with the worker to discuss his feelings and reactions which might affect his job performance. This counseling with the worker may be necessary to help him adjust to major job changes, such as promotion, or more routine matters like determining a better or new route to work.

If you wish, the coordinator will provide these follow-up services to any other handicapped employees in your company. You may also contact the placement coordinator for up-to-date information about:

1. Supervisory Training Programs;
2. Job Restructuring;
3. Barrier-Free Architecture;
4. Employer Seminars;
5. Affirmative Action Programs;
6. Equal Opportunity Employment.

SUMMARY

Today and in the future, employment of mentally retarded workers will be due to the cooperation and determination of many individuals and groups. Whether in business, industry or government, employers expect "a full day's work for a full day's pay." Job-ready mentally retarded workers can measure up to that basic standard, and usually beyond, when properly placed and supervised.

Hopefully this handbook has met its goal of informing you about an untapped, valuable source of dependable employees for your present and future workforce. Whether you are hiring your first mentally retarded employee or are already employing mentally retarded workers, this handbook will reassure you and guide you through the essential initial period of instruction and supervision.

Evaluation and Recommendations of the Second International Seminar on Vocational Rehabilitation for Mentally Retarded Persons

Introduction

The participants in the Second International Seminar on Vocational Rehabilitation for Mentally Retarded Persons acknowledge with gratitude the help we have received from the Rehabilitation Services Administration, Office of Human Development, United States Department of Health, Education and Welfare; and the American Association on Mental Deficiency.

As advocates of the cause of mentally retarded citizens, we feel that this Seminar will do much to strengthen the common bond among those affected by the problems of mental handicap throughout the world.

Our hosts have encouraged us to make recommendations which will be useful to practitioners in the field of mental retardation and we offer the following suggestions in the spirit which inspired the participants of the Seminar — a spirit of constructive appraisal.

While we hope that our recommendations are valid and relevant, we recognize that they can only be provisional and account must be taken of the cultural context where they may be implemented.

The participants in the Seminar are in accord that the target population of retarded persons served by vocational rehabilitation includes all levels of retardation, including the most severely involved non-communicative, non-ambulatory, multiply-handicapped individuals, who may never achieve economically productive careers.

Similarly we are in accord with the projected goal of rehabilitation for mentally retarded individuals which is normalization. By normalization of handicapped persons it is understood that their way of life shall differ as little as possible from that of the non-handicapped. In other words, the handicapped person shall live a life which is as normal and integrated as possible.

This is an urgent need to develop more opportunities for consumer involvement and participation in decisions about their individual vocational futures. Just as we have tended to underestimate the potential of the handicapped for work, we have likewise tended to neglect their capacity for meaningful interventions in the shaping of their own lives.

The participants in the Seminar do not make fine distinctions between habilitation and rehabilitation. It is clearly understood that early intervention attempts at the habilitation of the mentally retarded are most likely to prevent secondary problems requiring *re*habilitation efforts. Also understood is that primary prevention of mental retardation eliminates the need for vocational rehabilitation.

Listening to our colleagues from other lands has heightened our perception of the problems facing those dealing with the assessment, care, education, and vocational rehabilitation of mentally retarded citizens. While the magnitude of the problem may not, at times, engender a great sense of optimism, the advances which have been made recently in the United States of America and which we have been privileged to observe in the past three weeks will be a source of inspiration and hope for all of us. We feel that our shared experience has expanded our philosophy of vocational rehabilitation and we hope that the new ideas which we have absorbed will be the springs of actions, helping us to initiate similar advances in our own countries.

The sincere attempts to work toward a more dignified and satisfying life for mentally retarded persons which we have witnessed in the United States of America in the past three weeks have been helped, we feel, by focusing attention on certain key issues which we now propose to consider in some detail.

Legislation

The Declaration of Rights of Mentally Retarded Persons was adopted by the United Nations in 1971. The members of the Seminar, without exception, agree that this is a specific example of the application of human rights and that impressive steps have been taken in many countries towards the realization of these rights. It has become more apparent that the first essential steps in procuring the rights of mentally retarded citizens is through legislation.

One of the most comprehensive legal documents which exemplifies this first step is the compilation of the United States of America Rehabilitation and Development Disabilities Legislation (Public Law 93-112, P.L. 93-516, P.L. 88-164, and P.L. 94-103). It is encouraging to witness the zeal which this has inspired in many professionals and in families whose common goal is the improvement of opportunities for mentally retarded persons.

We feel, however, that without encouragement and guidance, declarations of rights without the intention to implement them, or even with the best intentions but without the skills of implementation, will accomplish little for mentally retarded citizens. Subsequent litigation may be a necessary follow-up to ensure implementation.

We recommend that the following specific steps should be taken to help mentally retarded people in all our countries to gain from our shared experience:

1. The rights of the mentally retarded shall be secured by legislation which designates a responsible local authority and outlines the procedures for monitoring of the services and programs.

2. International governmental agencies (UNESCO, WHO, ILO) should be required to follow the Declaration of Rights by a detailed analysis of the extent to which these rights are being implemented in member states and applied for the benefit of handicapped persons in every country.

3. International non-governmental agencies, including the International League of Societies for the Mentally Handicapped (ILSMH), International Association for the Scientific Study of Mental Deficiency (IASSMD), Rehabilitation International, etc., should be invited to monitor programs and services and to advise on the details of such analyses.

4. National societies should be helped to examine the feasibility of models being transferred from one system to another and to see how far legislation, successfully implemented in one country, may be promoted in other countries. This should be effected by a data bank set up by one of the specialist organizations of the United Nations or any other appropriate international organization.

5. While the United Nations should be required to ensure that mandatory laws to procure the rights of mentally retarded persons will be enacted in all member states, voluntary non-governmental agencies should accept it as an obligation to press for enabling legislation in all countries to ensure that programs for handicapped persons will have parity with those which are appropriate for ordinary citizens.

6. We also recommend that the above mentioned Rehabilitation and Developmental Disabilities legislation be circulated to all national societies concerned with mentally handicapped citizens throughout the world.

7. We recommend that all legislation regarding the mentally retarded be broadly transmitted to parents and consumer groups so that they may promote its application.

8. Legislation which is designed to protect the mentally retarded may sometimes have a negative effect, such as maintaining an adult retarded person in a perpetual child-like status. It is advisable that all laws be reviewed and amended, if necessary, so that rights of mentally retarded are *not* restricted.

9. Every government department dealing with handicapped persons should be required to set up advisory boards composed of parents and professionals who would monitor professional practice ethics, undertaking such tasks as ensuring the confidentiality and proper disposal of records of mentally retarded persons. We recommend a policy which includes a percentage of clients (consumers) on all such advisory boards.

Funding

Concern for the protection of handicapped persons is highlighted by the growth of voluntary societies and of advocacy, by the development of techniques for monitoring improvement in facilities and by the general acceptance of the principle that our obligations to the handicapped are fulfilled only by delivery of services appropriate to their needs. The realization of these ideals is often hampered by lack of funds, by inertia, and by self-interest.

In the course of the past three weeks, we have had frequent demonstrations of the advantages of community-based programs over institutions. It is apparent that such community programs contribute more to the personality development and well-being of mentally retarded persons than do institutionally-based programs. We are assured that in the long term such community programs will be much more economical and although the case for this been partially demonstrated, we feel the need for additional evidence which would accelerate the acceptance of mentally retarded persons in community-based programs.

We make the following recommendations:

1. Cost effectiveness studies of the advantages of community-based programs and long-term service delivery for mentally retarded citizens must form an integral part of planning for regional service systems.

2. Since modes of funding and availability of funds must vary from region to region and from country to country, we cannot make any specific recommendations which would be universally applicable. We feel, however, that the principle of equity should apply and that funds should be made available not only for the basic minimal needs but also adequate financial assistance to support normative living in the mentally retarded citizen's own community.

3. Funds should be set aside for higher education, universities and community agencies to support training and research programs for personnel and to initiate planning and development programs.

4. Funding should be utilized to prevent the need for institutionalization, to encourage community-based facilities, and to facilitate the return of mentally handicapped persons from institutional to community care programs.

5. To encourage international cooperation and to aid regional planning and programming around the world, funds should be made available to international organizations and agencies. Such funds should secure at least basic support staff salaries and administrative overheads and should be paid through international organizations and agencies. This would ensure that more time would be given to work towards the primary objectives of improving the lot of mentally retarded persons and their families, and less time taken up by fund-raising, at present so necessary to support agency activities.

Family Involvement

More comprehensive community-based service delivery systems are evolving; however, the extent to which the family can contribute to the development of retarded persons has not yet been fully developed. Attitudes which stemmed directly from the "incurable illness" model of mental retardation still persist. It must be stressed that with appropriate care, training, and education of mentally retarded individuals, attainment of normative or near normative state of functioning is possible.

All service delivery systems should recognize the important role of the family in promoting and sustaining developmental processes in the retarded member of the family.

Families with appropriate guidance and help may be in the best position to utilize the individual's spontaneous mental development and to maintain programs of systematic stimulation for growth and development.

Resources are needed to initiate programs which will increase the family's competency in dealing with all the problems of mental retardation. The following proposals would do much to implement such a policy:

1. The creation of new professional roles, e.g., an early child care worker with an educational/social work/nursing orientation competent in the evaluation, support, and education of parents with handicapped children.

2. The improvement of teacher training programs to include a greater working knowledge of handicaps and methods of dealing with the problems of handicapped pupils and their families.

3. A more balanced partnership between parents and professional people in assuming responsibility for their children's future and in public advocacy roles.

4. Work with families of mentally retarded persons to form an integral part of training of all those professional people who come in contact with mentally retarded persons.

5. The funding and setting up of family resource programs with a view to helping families in times of crises, such as illness, bereavement, and transportation problems.

6. The family's need for rest and recreation should not be overlooked in order to sustain the family's desire to keep the mentally retarded individual in the community.

7. Families wishing to create a trusteeship as an agency to care for the mentally retarded family member should be assisted by the establishment of a follow-through guardianship system.

Assessment

Assessment and training of mentally retarded persons can no longer be regarded as two separate processes but as

1. MINORITY

essentially inter-related activities. A number of difficulties may be traced to the separation of these concepts. For example, "assessment" has frequently been carried out for the purpose of selection (or screening out) of individuals who are being considered for training. A predictive function has been given to such testing — even though research has shown predictions to have much less reliability than hitherto supposed. There has been the emergence of specialists in testing: psychologists and more recently psychometrists, with access to tests which others, such as teachers, are unable to use. The design of many tests leads the tester to focus more on what the testee *cannot* do than on what he/she can do. The time spent in administering certain tests is not warranted in light of the inadequacy of educational and training programs subsequently available.

We believe that many of these difficulties may be resolved by an affirmation that the best way of assessing a person's ability to perform a task is by trying to teach him to do it. A more balanced use of testing is necessary, that is, less time spent testing and more time teaching. We recommend:

1. Models which stress the nature of a deficit and seek to remediate it should be replaced by the (re)habilitative model which seeks to discover also the individual's assets in order to build on them. This change in emphasis, widely evidenced in the U.S.A., is more likely to lead to the development of individualized programs of training and to challenge assumptions which have been traditionally made about individuals carrying a common diagnostic label.

2. Most of the offensive labels once used to classify mentally retarded individuals have been discarded. Nevertheless, unprecise terminology detrimental to the chances of mentally retarded individuals is still in common use. We feel that professionals should exercise their minds in finding an improved classification system which would stress the potential of mentally retarded individuals rather than serve as an excuse for inaction (e.g. ineducable, untrainable).

3. A select, annotated bibliography should be produced by one of the specialist organizations of the United Nations or any other appropriate international organization concerning those assessment techniques which have achieved recognition in the field of vocational rehabilitation of the mentally retarded and which are both widely used and culturally valid in the context in which they are used.

4. Funds should be made available for the standardization of tests and for the training of people in assessment techniques, particularly in developing countries.

5. By assessment we imply continuous *re*assessment of the client in terms of social skills, vocational skills, etc. Assessment, which is often conducted by professionals, should serve as an opportunity for dialogue with the client and also should serve as a link to other professionals providing care to the retarded individual.

6. Results of assessment should be adequately transmitted to both the client and his family.

7. Informed consent for assessment should be obtained.

Manpower Development and Utilization

Because of the ever-widening spectrum of services to mentally retarded individuals and their families, and because of the changing patterns of service delivery dictated by the normalization-integration principle (e.g., from the custodial institution to community-based services), attention to manpower development and utilization is vitally important. Future services depend on an increasing supply of appropriately trained and skilled personnel to fill staff and related positions. Manpower needs will *not* always be met by relying exclusively on persons trained and credentialed in traditional human service professions. A more rational approach

to manpower development will also place increasing emphasis on the contributions of other appropriately qualified and trained personnel, both employed and volunteer, who can make major contributions to the habilitation and rehabilitation of mentally retarded persons.

One approach to this area which is gaining increasing attention on an international level and which is being studied by the International League of Societies for the Mentally Handicapped (ILSMH) is the four-level Manpower Model developed in Canada by the National Institute of Mental Retardation (NIMR). Other approaches to meeting manpower needs which merit study are the utilization of short-term "in-service" types of staff training and retraining, and the adoption of competency-based systems of training.

It is recognized that remarkable achievements can result from the efforts of a well trained, enthusiastic and committed staff even when facilities available may be less than satisfactory. We would therefore recommend that:

1. Where limited resources exist, priority should be given to staff training and development — a policy of investing in people.

2. Recognizing that many of those classified as retarded may need assistance throughout their lives, attempts should be made to improve the coordination of all services dealing with mentally retarded persons. To this end, we recommend that agencies at national and local levels should be established to plan and coordinate services for mentally retarded persons and their families at early stimulation pre-school, school, pre-vocational and vocational training levels. Staff training schemes for all personnel engaged in the field of mental retardation should be a structured element in any program of change.

Evaluation of Service Quality: Accountability and Self-Renewal

Human services in general, and mental retardation services in particular, have always been oriented toward evaluation and the measurement of outcomes and results. However, much of what has gone on in the past under the name of "evaluation" has tended to make the "quantifiable important rather than the important quantifiable." In recent years this situation has changed as a result of increasing client and consumer input into service planning and operation, demands for greater programmatic and fiscal accountability by service consumers and by funders, and the development of new approaches and tools for evaluating service programs and entire systems.

The members of the Seminar believe that services to mentally retarded people can be made more accountable and can be elevated to increasingly higher levels of service quality through a systematic, ongoing and rigorous approach to program evaluation. With respect to the evaluation of mental retardation services, we would make the following recommendations:

1. That evaluation be both *internal* (conducted by staff and people involved in the program) and *external* (conducted by outside consultants and experts).

2. That evaluation be *multi-level*, i.e., different means and methods of evaluation be utilized to assess:

   a. client progress,

   b. staff performance,

   c. operation of the total program, and

   d. functioning of the overall organization or system (in a multi-component agency or system).

3. That accountability be judged in both fiscal and programmatic terms:

   a. fiscal — cost-benefit ratios, etc.

   b. programmatic — adherence to up-to-date human management principles such as normalization-integration and to various systems for program analysis, standards for accreditation, etc.

4. That programs allocate human (staff time) and financial resources (5-10% of yearly operating budget) to carry out such evaluation.

A second and related aspect is *self-renewal*. This is another key to adaptive service delivery and quality assurance. The members of the Seminar recommend attention to this area and the adoption by services of means and mechanisms which will promote internal communication, self-criticism, non-defensiveness, innovation and an inner-orientation to increased flexibility.

Pre-Vocational and Vocational Training Programs

Recognition should be accorded to the substantial evidence available from both research and practice that mentally retarded adults of all ages and levels of retardation are able to benefit from opportunities to improve and develop their abilities, provided that they are given systematic and structured help to enable them to reach a level of skill. The absence of such opportunities for personal development of work skills on the other hand leads to apathy and under-expectation which in turn produces under-achievement.

As society becomes more industrialized, changing concepts should be reflected in the vocational rehabilitation programs provided for mentally retarded individuals. Work should be a way for the mentally retarded to feel useful in society — to be contributing members, not just to "get paid." Work must have a meaningful purpose and provide intrinsic satisfaction.

A key aspect of developing as a successful worker and a productive member of society is to also develop skills necessary to be a totally functionally individual. This means that all of the social skills, e.g. dressing, toileting, communication, social interaction, mobility and travel skills, money and banking skills, use of leisure time, and survival skills should be an integral part of the training program.

For many individuals who are being trained and those who are being deinstitutionalized and entering the delivery system for the first time there may be skills that are needed for the world of work in a sheltered or vocational shop. The activities and program in a pre-vocational component should be of a nature to prepare the individual in these vital skills.

Work can take place in a variety of settings including comprehensive training centers, specific work experience groups, sheltered work groups, seasonal/temporary periods of employment, trial periods of employment, on-job training in industry, innovative training centers such as one specializing in horticulture, and/or permanent employment.

It should also be considered that if a workshop model is being developed, the workshop should be not only for the retarded but may serve individuals with a variety of handicaps and normal individuals. It should also provide a variety of work experiences so that the workers can experience choice and a degree of responsibility. We therefore recommend that:

1. The administration of work programs should be governed by rehabilitation that is client oriented rather than by administrative convenience.

2. Staff should be recruited from a variety of occupations, both of professional and vocational orientations. It is essential that the workshop manager be a team leader, exploring individual staff interests and skills to provide staff with every opportunity to apply their skills to their work.

3. The concept of normalization will differ in those countries where job opportunities are plentiful and the work ethic prevails from those developing where job opportunities are few. Even in highly industrialized countries, the pace of change is so rapid and technological progress is transforming

normal work patterns in such radical ways that what is normal now will have changed within the next decade. Plans for mentally retarded people must reflect similar patterns of change. We recommend that the normalization principle be reviewed so as to adapt it to developing countries when appropriate.

4. In countries where the pace of industry is rapid and where technological progress is transforming normal work patterns, a system should be developed to review the job markets available on a timely basis to evaluate which jobs would be suitable for the mentally retarded.

5. A frequently neglected area of vocational rehabilitation of the mentally retarded is recognition of the need for pre-vocational training. Needed is directed research to develop further structured objectively measurable criteria for facilitating reasonable success for on-the-job vocational training. Utilization of extant special education and behavioral shaping techniques that are responsibly monitored and have appropriate consumer input should facilitate this development.

6. Employment of mentally retarded persons should be preceded by vocational training and preparation for community living within the educational services common to all others.

7. Follow-up services or "outcome evaluations" should be an integral part of vocational rehabilitation programs.

Attitudes and Change Effectors

Although there has been considerable attention and progress with regard to improving vocational and social skills of the mentally retarded, the fact remains that without compensatory attention to the reaction of society at the community level, the rehabilitation and integration of the retarded will not be successfully achieved or maintained. It is recommended therefore that more work must be done in the area of attitudes and behavior and that experts in the field of communication, sociology, and behavioral change be mobilized to that end as part of an interdisciplinary team. We recommend the following specific steps:

1. A basic comprehensive review of all literature with regard to attitudes to the retarded (including an analysis of the implications of such research) should be carried out and widely published.

2. A study of the impact of movies and other mass communication approaches should be carried out. Strategies for better use of the communication media so as to create a better image of the retarded and his abilities need to be worked out.

3. Demonstration projects of a long-term nature, based on a socio-psychological approach in the community should be carried out. This should also include studies of possible conflicting images created in the minds of people by communications delivered by charitable fund-raising organizations as compared to rehabilitation-oriented agencies.

4. Further work (basic applied research) is called for, with regard to the relationship between attitudes and behavior, placing greater emphasis on behavioral change as compared to attitudinal change as far as the social and professional public is concerned.

5. National and international societies should be conscious of the impact their organizational names have on community attitudes. Many of the names of these organizations and societies reflect a philosophy based on pity or an unconscious deprecation of the mentally retarded clients being served.

6. Efforts should be concentrated on improving the self-concept of the mentally retarded individual so that his enhanced self-image can influence the public image.

1. MINORITY

Research

Research, broadly defined as designing an activity to provide an answer to a question, establishes that the aims of research in the field of vocational rehabilitation of the mentally retarded are:

1. research in prevention methodologies,
2. research in early diagnosis and intervention, and
3. research in service delivery.

We recognize that in the achievement of these aims, universities will play an important part. At the same time we realize that research, teaching, and manpower development in the field of mental handicap cannot take place divorced from service delivery. This sometimes raises questions as to whether service delivery should take place in institutions which are primarily oriented to research and teaching or should research and development of personnel take place in service systems. We agree that research and training cannot take place in the absence of practical experience and interaction with mentally handicapped persons.

It is possible that there may be dangers associated with the placement of mentally handicapped persons in locations which are not primarily designed to meet their needs, but, since practical experience and interaction with mentally handicapped persons are essential in the formation of professional personnel, we make the following recommendations:

1. Where research and training programs are closely associated with service delivery systems for the handicapped, objective evaluative procedures should be set up to ensure that the needs of the consumers are carefully considered and always assume primacy.

2. Research and training programs should take place within the service systems as well as in the universities. The "laboratory" for field action research should be as normative as possible rather than in an artificially created situation.

3. Time should be set apart for researchers to develop effective strategies for implementation. Trained researchers should be encouraged to utilize practitioners.

There appear to be five important stages in this:

a. There should be research carried out that is relevant to practice, e.g., in areas where practitioners report problems.

b. The research findings should be communicated to practitioners in clear, precise and unambiguous language.

c. Research workers should demonstrate the applications of results to practitioners in the natural field setting.

d. Practitioners should be given a chance to try these methods out for themselves, under guidance of the researchers.

e. Research workers should collaborate with practitioners and those with administrative responsibility for the service(s) concerned in devising ways of ensuring that fruitful applications are built into long-term practice. This means that thorough evaluation of the applications, and their feasibility of continuation after the research team have left, must be demonstrated by the research team.

FOCUS...

Rehabilitations Per 10,000 Disabled Population, by State, FY 1977

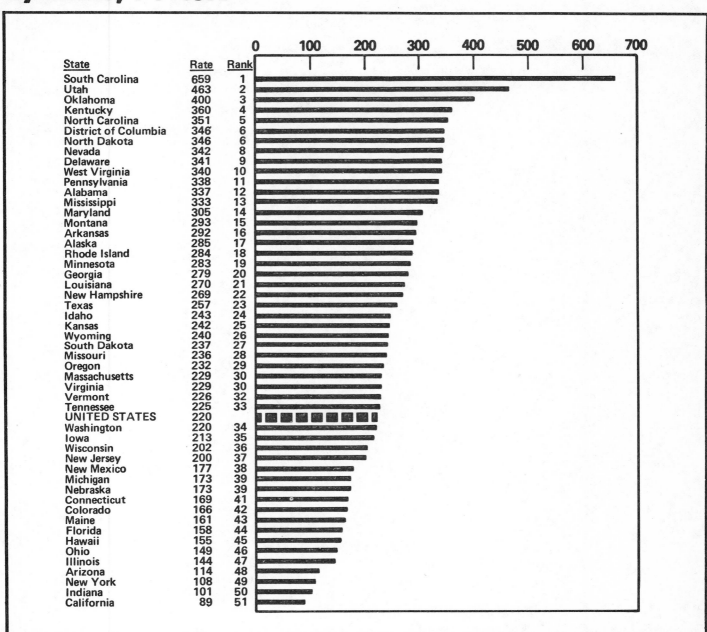

State	Rate	Rank
South Carolina	659	1
Utah	463	2
Oklahoma	400	3
Kentucky	360	4
North Carolina	351	5
District of Columbia	346	6
North Dakota	346	6
Nevada	342	8
Delaware	341	9
West Virginia	340	10
Pennsylvania	338	11
Alabama	337	12
Mississippi	333	13
Maryland	305	14
Montana	293	15
Arkansas	292	16
Alaska	285	17
Rhode Island	284	18
Minnesota	283	19
Georgia	279	20
Louisiana	270	21
New Hampshire	269	22
Texas	257	23
Idaho	243	24
Kansas	242	25
Wyoming	240	26
South Dakota	237	27
Missouri	236	28
Oregon	232	29
Massachusetts	229	30
Virginia	229	30
Vermont	226	32
Tennessee	225	33
UNITED STATES	220	
Washington	220	34
Iowa	213	35
Wisconsin	202	36
New Jersey	200	37
New Mexico	177	38
Michigan	173	39
Nebraska	173	39
Connecticut	169	41
Colorado	166	42
Maine	161	43
Florida	158	44
Hawaii	155	45
Ohio	149	46
Illinois	144	47
Arizona	114	48
New York	108	49
Indiana	101	50
California	89	51

Nationally, there were 220 people rehabilitated in the State-Federal Program in Fiscal Year 1977 for every 10,000 disabled people of working age. This rate has declined in each of the 4 years in which it has been measured. Interestingly, as many as 32 states plus the District of Columbia had rates which exceeded the national level. This inequality occurred because some of the largest states, notably California, New York, Illinois and Ohio, all with very large populations, produced relatively few rehabilitations per 10,000 disabled population.

South Carolina led the state rankings with a rate of 659 rehabilitations per 10,000 disabled population. California was last (51st) in the rankings, the only state with a rate below 100 (89).

(The basis for the rates is the state disability information found in the 1970 Census of Population, Series PC (1)-C, *General Social and Economic Characteristics*, which has been updated to reflect the total population growth to July 1 of each year. Census disability data are not available for Puerto Rico, Virgin Islands, Guam, and the Trust Territories of the Pacific Islands).

"Rehabilitations Per 10,000 Disabled Population by State, FY 1977," *American Rehabilitation*, Vol. 4, No. 2, November-December 1978. ©1978 Rehabilitation Services Administration.

ASSESSMENT

Section two is an introduction to a number of assessment materials and research used to develop vocational skills for the mentally retarded. The necessary elements for a useful study are careful observation, strict baseline conditions, and standardized measurements. There is a great need for further research involving continual followup. It is necessary to evaluate the progress of those receiving services,as well as the service itself to decide future direction of skills.

Evaluation should involve all members of the clients training community, the classroom teacher, physical therapist, occupational therapist, speech and language therapist, psychologist and community trainer. A team carefully trained in observation techniques can better determine function level, rehabilitation goals and family expectations. Results help to identify factors affecting future development, the type and level of training required by each individual and predict rehabilitative outcome.

It is important for the mentally retarded to meet with success on their first job. Assessment and training enables placement matching occupational capabilities with job requirements. The non-reading method assists the client in finding an occupation consistent with his/her interests. The chances for higher job satisfaction and success are increased.

The concluding articles are involved with the evaluation of the programs themselves. Just as important as the study of client's endurance, rate and quality of performance is the study of services. Standardized results make it possible to compare facilities and make transdisciplinary exchanges of information. The study becomes a checklist for developing new programs and improving those already in existence.

OCCUPATIONAL EDUCATION FOR SEVERELY HANDICAPPED STUDENTS: ASSESSMENT AND IMPLEMENTATION

Tim Crowner

Recent thinking regarding occupational programming for severely handicapped persons appears to follow two lines of thought. First, if occupational education-special education programs are to be successful they must become more community based. A second line of thought involves the use of applied behavioral analysis to the occupational needs of severely handicapped persons. Unfortunately, community programming advocates and advocates of applied behavioral analysis have not collaborated as well as they might have. The Individual Educational Plan (IEP) may furnish the ground upon which this communication will begin to occur. A systematic application of the available technical concepts underlying both lines of thought may be reflected in IEP's for the severely handicapped. Such plans would include descriptions of the various contexts in which work might be performed in a given community. A delineation of specific skills required to operate within various contexts would follow. Finally, task analysis would be applied to components of these contexts and instructional sequences, leading to the student's acquisition of specific relevant skills.

A useful organization of information on occupational evaluation and instruction will be set forth in this chapter. Discussion will be based upon an operating program in Madison, Wisconsin. It is felt that the Madison program exemplifies the kind of marriage between the two schools of thought about occupational education for the severely handicapped. Emphasis will be placed on three key themes: (a) precision, (b) completeness, and (c) cooperation. Precision refers to how well an IEP details strategies for goal attainment, measurement, evaluation, and delineation of roles and responsibilities for parent, staff, and related agencies. Completeness refers to how thoroughly the IEP deals with those contingencies affecting the environmental context in which the vocational goals must be performed. Cooperation refers to evidence that the plan has been well coordinated across all individuals and relevant agencies.

The phrase "severely and profoundly handicapped" is meant as a functional term to encompass a population of students who require extraordinary medical, therapeutic, and educational prescription in order to compensate for, or habilitate presenting handicaps. It would be unrealistic to assume that one day, all severely and profoundly handicapped persons will be competitively employed. It is therefore necessary to operationally define what is meant by occupational goals for this population. Writers of IEP's must be able to discriminate the aspects of occupational training which are important across all children of any age or degree of handicap.

Occupational education is being used in this paper to convey a broad view of prevocational and vocational education ranging across age and ability. An occupational goal continuum must be established as a conceptual guide in planning for severely and profoundly handicapped persons. This continuum is based on the concept of community effort required to sustain the handicapped individual. It is assumed that, for some handicapped individuals, self-maintenance is a reasonable occupational goal. The economic contributions to society gained by a handicapped person's maintenance are only different in degree from those gained through competitive employment. Certainly, the human dignity a profoundly handicapped individual achieves through self-maintenance is as significant as economic self-support achieved by a mildly handicapped person.

There are obviously many degrees of economic self-support, and self-maintenance. Figure 1 represents a continuum leading from complete reliance on others to complete economic self-support.

Figure 1
Occupational Continuum
Complete Reliance on Others
Self Maintenance
Sheltered Work
Complete Economic Self Support

There is no dichotomy in this continuum. Individual educational plans for occupational goals should identify jobs for severely and profoundly handicapped persons regardless of placement on the occupational continuum. For example, a job may be serving food to oneself. Many

"Occupational Education for Severely Handicapped Students – Assessment and Implementation," Tim Crowner, *Developing Effective Individual Educational Programs for Severely Handicapped Children and Youth*, Topical Working Conference Sponsored by BEH, Washington, D.C., August 1977.

skills needed and developed for competitive employment by the handicapped are the same as those necessary for self-maintenance. Following directions, being socially appropriate, and self-discipline are examples of such common skills. In particular, rate, endurance, and quality of performance are essential to holding down a competitive job. Enhancing these skills even in a pre-schooler has direct connection to occupational success in later life. Each of these skills will be discussed in more detail later. They are brought up at this point to imply that IEP's should address occupational goals even for the most profoundly handicapped.

Writers of IEP's should also bear in mind that existing occupational programs often fail. The U.S. Department of Health, Education, and Welfare commissioned a study of occupational preparation programs for the handicapped in 1972. The report of this study, *Improving Occupational Programs for the Handicapped,* cites three basic ways in which existing programs fail:

> They fail to prepare the environment for the student as well as they prepare the student for the work environment. Secondly, they fail to take advantage of or solicit assistance from services or groups outside of the immediate administration of the program. Thirdly, they do not assure the relevance of program content to the job market and environment in which the students will live when they graduate. (HEW, 1972, p.6)

In addition to the above observations, occupational education is too often treated as an isolated goal. It is seen as task oriented. A narrow view of sheltered workshop tasks prevails for the severely handicapped. However, well designed IEP's may help the student avoid many of the deficiencies which have been identified in the past with vocational preparation of the handicapped. Especially as IEP writers recognize the advantages of combining applied behavioral analysis to community based occupational preparation. IEP's can force focus upon long and short range goals for each child and provide parents and advocates with a blueprint from which to check progress. Well written IEP's will, with precision, completeness and coordination, set forth goals to which professionals will be held accountable.

In summary, the literature reviewed indicates that severely handicapped persons can learn complex and sophisticated behaviors. However, service delivery models that assure generalization of learned behaviors are underdeveloped. Diagnostic services have been characterized as overdeveloped and irrelevant. The solution proposed to alleviate service deficiencies involves more active involvement with the community on the part of service purveyors.

Literature addressing the occupational needs of the

profoundly retarded is nonexistant. This is maybe due to a narrow definition of what constitutes occupational preparation. Yet, many of the efforts designed to lead a severely handicapped person to gainful employment are applicable to the needs of the profoundly handicapped person.

Before discussing the specific aspects of assessment, prescription, and implementation, an overview of an operating program may prove useful. In an article tracing the evolution of a community-based vocational preparation program, Certo, Brown, Belmore, and Crowner (1977) review the facts that led the Madison Metropolitan School District (MMSD) away from the school house and into the community. Essentially, MMSD found that:

1. A model which prescribed a single teacher and single class (the traditional elementary school model) had administrative convenience as its greatest advantage. That is, the number of variables needing attention by the service purveyors was smallest in this model. Small groups attached to a single teacher were easy to monitor. However, the structures evolved in such environments tended to be static. Thus, students tended to become stimulus-bound to a given teacher and classroom.
2. A departmentalized model – the traditional secondary school model where teachers specialize in a specific subject and students rotate from teacher to teacher – tended to provide for better student generalization. It also allowed for the rapid development of a specialized curriculum because the teacher could attempt to teach the same concepts to a variety of students. This model, however, led to a disjointed program where various skills become isolated.
2. MMSD finally moved to a model which combined the self-contained class with community-based experiences. A brief description of this model will assist the reader in understanding the context from which positions taken in this paper arise. In the community-based training model students spend about a fifth of their instructional time out of the classroom. Certain teachers operate as community-based instructors, and they have flexible schedules which allow them to operate during the evening hours with days free when appropriate. Community-based instructors have six functions: (1) to identify community environments in which students will ultimately function; (2) to analyze the elements of a given environment to determine criteria for survival in that environment; (3) to work with classroom teachers to evolve instructional strategies leading to survival skills; (4) to aggressively prepare the environment for the eventual presence of the severely and profoundly handicapped individual; (5) to implement an instructional program directly within that environment with targeted students; (6) to follow-up into post secondary placement – transition to the Division of Vocational Rehabilitation (DVR).

Community-based instructors, support staff, and classroom teachers work with parents and outside agencies to identify skills which are immediately meaningful to a given student. Activities are then designed for skill development and are executed in the classroom, home and community. Skills immediately meaningful to the student are related to skills ultimately needed. In the classroom, for example, the teacher may work with students on simple meal preparation as a desired skill while stressing work-site preparation and clean-up duties. At home, the parents are instructed to work with their child in table setting and cleaning skills. In the community the trainer stresses proper arrangement of tools before work is begun.

Cognitive, affective, sensory, motor and language goals are identified for each student, as are ways in which these goals may be achieved through functional activities. For example, language may involve indicating a student's need to use a public bathroom. Cognition for the student may involve learning that soap works better if water is applied to the hands first. Affective learning may involve learning to act unobtrusively, and sensory goals may relate to desired water temperature while washing, while motor goals may relate to the zipping and buttoning of clothing.

One can see the importance of using the precise, complete, and coordinated IEP as a document to guide parents and professionals through the complexity of such interrelated and comprehensive programming. MMSD has observed two great advantages in this community based approach. There has been rapid skill acquisition and retention by students, and the community is becoming increasingly sensitized to the presence and needs of severely and profoundly handicapped persons. However, a main disadvantage to the community based model is that it is administratively inconvenient. Scheduling becomes a horrendous problem; monitoring staff time is very difficult, and liability related to safety factors increases. Of course, our moral obligation does not involve the development of administratively convenient models. Yet, any model should produce individual programs which can be clearly understood and held to account. Thus the significance of IEP's as blueprints or even contracts becomes clear.

Initial Assessment

Initial assessment for occupational skills should occur across the occupational continuum described earlier. Thus, all students should be assessed for functional occupational level. Focus for occupational assessment of a given student will be drawn from information regarding the student's age, ability and need. Age will dictate the amount of time left in school. The shorter the time in school available, the greater the focus on specific occupational goals will be. Ability will dictate the kinds of environments in which occupational information will be collected. That is, will information on student performance occur in a community-based work site, or would a room in a small group treatment facility be a more appropriate site to observe the student's performance? It may be appropriate, for some students, to observe dressing or feeding in the student's home. Need may dictate both emphasis and choice of work site. For example, a seriously behavior disordered student may be 20 years old but have such bizarre behavior that self discipline as a self care objective may dominate his needs. A multihandicapped/hearing impaired student may need a work site where very little verbal direction occurs.

Recent Research

Perhaps the most striking aspect of the literature concerning vocational preparation of severely handicapped persons is that it illustrates the range of complex skills which such persons can acquire. Crosson (1969),

Schoreder and Yarbrough (1972), Bellamy, Peterson, and Close (1975), Gold (1976), among others, have demonstrated that the severely handicapped can learn complex assembly skills through the use of task analysis strategies and chained instructional sequences. Furthermore, Huddle (1967), Brown and Pearce (1970), and Schroeder and Yarbrough (1972), have demonstrated that arrangement of environmental contingencies can enhance the productivity of severely handicapped persons.

Researchers have been successful in proving that severely handicapped individuals can learn rather sophisticated behaviors. However, a number of unresolved issues remain which concern the ability of handicapped individuals to generalize these learned skills. Williams (1975), contends that trainers must determine whether or not these skills can be performed across persons, places, instructional materials, and language cues. In short, are many of the behaviors performed by severely handicapped persons stimulus Bound? If learned behaviors are in fact bound to a specific set of circumstances then there is a danger that skills being taught later in time will be more difficult to teach because of earlier learning. This phenomenon, proactive inhibition, is discussed by Underwood (1964). Underwood has found that habits learned earlier in time will tend to interfere with newly acquired skills, increasing the probability that these new skills will be forgotten.

Furthermore, retention of a given skill may be affected by the importance of that skill to the student. For years, general educators have been calling for "relevant curriculum" in public schools. Ferrara (1975) observes that behaviors learned earlier in time were not retained by a group of severely and profoundly handicapped students. However, when skills were taught which had immediate application to a student's needs, these skills tended to be retained. For example, if a severely handicapped person is taught to go to a refrigerator, and to pour a glass of milk, this behavior has great utility to that individual. Ferrara notes that such behaviors are more readily generalized by severely handicapped students from the classroom to the home setting. Examining educational structures may help explain this phenomena.

Crowner (1977) suggests that there is a relationship between restriction and structures developed to instruct students. A structure is defined as an element constructed in the learner's environment which is designed to direct, guide, or inhibit the learner's behavior. Structures may be physical or behavioral in nature. Physical structures include room arrangements, degree of isolation from normalized environment, or some prosthetic device such as a jig used in an assembly task. Behavioral structures encompass all personal interactions such as social reinforcement, language cues, and home-school relationships. The degree to which such structures are available or natural in many different settings is directly related to how easily a behavior being taught in one environment will be generalized and retained across settings. Thus, structures must be constructed that are available in naturalized environments if the trainer wishes the learner to generalize behaviors.

In an extensive review of the literature on sheltered workshops, Pomerantz and Markolin (1977) state:

In general, sheltered workshops are not now using available instructional technology in ways that lead to job placement of severely handicapped clients. Workshop programs rely on production and adjustment training within the workshop, in the hope that a general upgrading of client skills may lead to future placement. (p. 131)

These authors call for more aggressive job placement activities. They suggest a more active involvement with the community. The HEW study of occupational programs for the handicapped (cited earlier) draws this same conclusion.

Wolfensberger (1975) voices disatisfaction with another aspect of services provided to handicapped individuals — diagnosis. He cites a number of "embarrassments in the diagnostic process" (p. 181-185). His observations that are particularly relevant to this discussion are:

1. Diagnosis for the family is quite often a dead end, frequently resulting in a frustrating series of cross referrals instead of leading to a meaningful service assignment.
2. Many diagnostic centers do not provide adequate feedback counseling and consider their duty done when the diagnostic process is satisfactorily completed.
3. Diagnostic services are often overdeveloped in comparison to other available resources.

Occupational assessment should be an integrated part of a general assessment strategy. This is particularly important because much guiding information on ability arises from a general assessment process. Assessment for severely and profoundly handicapped persons is a very complex process because of the multiple needs of the child. Occupational assessment is then a component of a transdisciplinary based evaluation. To clarify, Crowner (1977) makes the following distinction regarding a transdisciplinary model:

There are three across-discipline service delivery models. Multidisciplinary models join a number of separate disciplines so they are available for evaluation and prescription. Interdisciplinary models enforce interrelationships among each of the disciplines so that there is coordination of effort. Transdisciplinary models not only enforce interdisciplinary cooperation but encourage interchangeability across disciplines. This process can be referred to as a "skills swap", where each discipline must inservice all other disciplines so that all disciplines acquire many "traded" skills. (p.6)

Often a primary professional is designated to carry out the recommendations made by other members of the transdisciplinary team.

Depending on specific circumstances, the community based trainer may be the most logical choice as primary professional. As a specialist, the community based trainer often is involved in making program recommendations to the primary professional (generally a class-

room teacher). The IEP can act as a transdisciplinary guide for the primary professional and, if well written, can hold supportive disciplines accountable for their specific responsibilities.

General Assessment Strategies

Severely and profoundly handicapped individuals are usually assessed by the classroom teacher, physical therapist, occupational therapist, speech and language therapist, and the psychologist. If the initial assessment calls for observation in the community environment, the community-based trainer becomes involved. This always occurs with students over 14 years of age. A good assessment is the primary basis for a good IEP. Clear, complete and well coordinated assessment strategies are essential in individual program development. Four assessment strategies are followed within the context of a transdisciplinary model using applied behavioral analysis designs:

1. When assessing a severely and profoundly handicapped student, it is advised that specific activities for the student be created to provide a standard of observation for each discipline.
2. It should also be made clear, initially, who will collect what information so that duplication of duties does not occur. Each discipline should focus upon specific areas for assessment purposes.
3. It is important to determine how information will be collected. For example, it might be decided that the classroom teacher will engage the student in certain activities while the other professionals observe unobtrusively. Or perhaps the occupational therapist will visit the home during mealtime. Some standardized measures associated with psychology or therapy may be deemed appropriate.
4. There must be interdisciplinary agreement. That is, a behavior, or lack of a behavior, must be considered absent or present by two or more disciplines. Often, the parent fills the role of a reliability checker. This strategy is continued throughout the student's schooling.

Use of these strategies will produce guiding information which may be used in developing the initial IEP. Information should be generated regarding cognitive, effective, motor, language, medical, and physical stamina. This information should be based on functional examples such as rate, endurance, and quality of performance in a given environment and across different environments.

Occupational Assessment Strategies

Once again depending on age and ability and need of a given student occupational assessment may be the focus for the general assessment of a student. That is, if age, ability, and need imply it then the transdisciplinary team may decide to make their assessment in a community based site. This would be in accordance with the first assessment strategy discussed earlier. For purposes of this discussion it will be assumed that occupational assessment was chosen as a primary focus.

Applied behavioral analysis comes into play very heavily once the decision on assessment focus has been made. Staff must bring to bear task analysis and observational technique. Measurement will focus on rate, endurance, and quality. Observations must be made under strict baseline conditions. Baseline conditions

2. ASSESSMENT

means that precise objectivity is used in assessments. Information gathered at this point must be standardized in a way which will allow it to be compared with information gathered later in time. Precision then is a key because precision implies detail. Detail which can communicate clear and concise information about the student. Information which can be validated by more than one person. Information which not only verifies the presence of a behavior but also specifies rate and endurance and quality of behavior.

Task analysis is essential. It forms the cornerstone of assessment for severely and profoundly handicapped persons. Task analysis provides information on a task that can be matched against pupil skills. Thus, a pupil's location on a given task at a given level of the occupational continuum can be pinpointed.

Applied behavioral analysis may be overly task oriented but it provides the tightest information on students one can achieve. Its importance to precise IEP's and ultimately to accountability is obvious. Within the context in which it is being applied here, there is far less need for concern over becoming task orientated. Because of the community based and transdisciplinary nature of the program it is important that precision be maintained. Skill transfer, generalization, and reliability of information are enhanced by the community based transdisciplinary approach.

For example, understanding student motivation is of major concern to the trainer. The trainer is interested in why a student performs well in a given work environment. What is reinforcing the student's behavior, and are the reinforcers natural to a given work environment? For example, some severely handicapped students perform only to please a trainer, or because the task is novel and seems fun. These reinforcers are not likely to sustain the learner once the trainer withdraws from the work site. After determining what the natural work site reinforcers are, existing student reinforcers may be paired with natural reinforcers in the environment using basic operant strategies. The probability of a student's sustained performance will then be enhanced. The trainer's understanding of student motivation is essential to other members of the transdisciplinary team. Basically this information is used to form many of the programs for a child. In the example just used, a natural reinforcer would likely be money. Thus, the classroom teacher, acting on this information, will initiate educational programs related to money and its usage.

Assessment Tools

A primary tool for occupational assessment is the check list. Check lists are used extensively in assessing the severely handicapped. Unfortunately, few efforts to publish generalizable check lists have been made to date. Often check lists are location specific and would have little meaning across different communities. This is why understanding how to conduct a task analysis is an

important competency for professionals working with severely and profoundly handicapped persons. Not only is it necessary for professionals to develop their own complete check lists through task analysis, but often, existing check lists must be broken down considerably in order to be applied to the severely handicapped. Some task analysis are generalizable across settings.

Understanding the student's potential within a given work site is founded upon a thorough understanding of that work site. In addition, information about community based sites influence curriculum at all levels. Belmore and Brown (1976) describe an analysis format for work sites. An outline of that format appears on the next page. This detailed analysis provides information on related work skills, transportation, legal considerations as well as simple job site descriptions. It is an excellent format with which to collect precise information for IEP's. Also it helps delineate where coordination among disciplines and agencies should logically occur. Teachers of even very young or profoundly handicapped persons may use the information gathered by this tool in developing occupational orientated sections of IEP's for their students. Schwartz (1976) has developed a complete job site and skill analysis for a dishwashing work site. Schwartz's study is an excellent example of the use of the job skills inventory developed by Belmore and Brown.

An Outline of the Madison Job Skill Inventory

A. General Information
   1. Reasons why severely handicapped students are considered for this job.
   2. A general description of the job.
   3. A general description of the work setting.
   4. A general description of the social environment:
      a) Information related to fellow workers.
      b) Information related to supervision.
      c) Information related to special contingencies.
B. Specific Skill Requirements of the Job Under Analysis
   1. A List of the basic physical-sensory motor skills required.
   2. A list of the basic interpersonal skills required.
   3. A list of the basic language skills (verbal and nonverbal) required.
   4. A list of the basic functional academic skills required
   5. A list of the basic machine and tool skills.
   6. A list of the basic hygienic skills required.
C. Supportive Skills and Other Information Required
   1. Transportation skills required.

2. Skills related to work preparation.
3. Basic money management skills required.
4. Time-telling and time-judgment skills required.
5. Health code requirements.
6. Informed consent and legal requirements.

Rating scales are another method for gaining information on occupational needs of the severely handicapped. Ferrara (1977) has designed a rating scale for community survival screening. This scale rates performance across transportation, general behavior, clothing, direction following, staying in a group, frustration level, toilet needs, waiting, walking, locating destinations, and amount of supervisors needed.

Individual Educational Plans

Goals and Objectives

Once occupational information is gathered it must be integrated with general information in order to form a complete and coordinated IEP. Long and short range goals must be stated in the IEP. Because of the functional nature of occupation, many of the goals relating to it are very pragmatic. To begin, a general goal relating to work site should be established. Goals may be evolved by asking key questions. For this first general goal one might answer the following two questions.

1) Was performance in the work site used for initial assessment such that the student is ready for placement in that particular environment? If question one is answered no, then the primary goals may involve reaching criteria for entrance into some particular environment. If question one is answered yes, then goals should be developed which are based on criterion for complete success in the chosen site. Criterion will be set for rate, endurance, and quality of performance as well as affective behavior.

2) How much time does the student have left in school? The answers to this question will relate to emphasis on occupational goals and will dictate the long or short range nature of occupational goals. For instance, should emphasis be on specific job training or on surveys across many work sites, and how much instructional time should be spent in occupational preparation as compared to other activities.

In some regards setting occupational goals is a process of moving from the general (guiding information) to the specific. Once goals related to criterion for rate, endurance, quality and affective behaviors have been determined then relationships between occupational activities and other goals need to be examined. Specifically, what are the general goals in language, cognition, motor, medical, and affective areas and what specific subgoals in each of these areas can be set for occupational preparation? For example, what is the language goal in the work environment?

Writing the IEP

This paper has taken the position that individual educational plans for severely handicapped students should include occupational goals as part of precise, complete, and coordinated statements about pupil needs and programming. Rate, endurance, quality, and affective behavior are seen as relevant occupational goals which may be connected to general educational goals for children. Because of the number and complexity of goals for this population, the IEP becomes an essential blueprint for parents and professionals. The IEP can marry applied behavioral analysis to realistic community based occupational training. It can provide a format for transdisciplinary and interagency planning and cooperation. Individual Educational Plans appear as formal written documents. The IEP document should be a record of past events, and of events which should occur in the future of a student's life. Specifically, the information that must by law, appear in the student's current level of functioning, expectations (goals) for immediate and long range future functioning, and "precisely" how and when the student's goals will be achieved. Writing an IEP provides an opportunity for interested parties to organize and verify information about a student.

Information about a student's occupational functioning both presently and in the future, should be an integrated part of an IEP. A separate IEP dealing with occupational information would encourage discontinuity in a student's program. If there are separate IEP's for general and occupational information, it might be reasoned that the programming implied will occur as distinct and separate. In fact, certain information regarding occupational expectations should be stated in all IEP's. The student's age and time left in school should influence the focus of information, and specifically of information relating to occupational programming. If, for example, a student is graduating at the end of the school year, then general educational and therapeutic activities would all be designated to support occupational goals. This fact would reflect itself in the IEP.

Complete IEP's will contain answers to many occupational related issues which are arrived at through the strategies outlined in this paper. Specifically the complete IEP will address at least these questions:
1. How much time is available before graduation?
2. Where is this student in terms of the occupational continuum?
3. What things may the student be able to do with prosthetic support?
4. What is currently reinforcing this student?
5. Of those behaviors a student has, what are his

rates, levels of endurance, and quality of performance? The well coordinated IEP will spell out how persons will work together to achieve the occupational goals which have been set. For example, with proper coordination desirable recreation could become contingent upon work performance. However, if agencies responsible for recreation have not been involved, it is not likely that such a plan could be worked out. In short, the educational services being provided should be supported and reinforced by as many persons and agencies as possible.

The precise IEP will spell out specifically who will do what by when. It will be based on sound behavioral orientated objective data. It will specify how available instructional sequences will be used to achieve goals. It will delineate measurement strategies, objective criteria, a schedule for examining progress, and dates by which goal achievement might realistically be expected.

Evaluating the IEP

It should be obvious by this point that IEP's should be evaluated on the basis of precision, completeness, and coordination. However, there is a final consideration which is crucial to the evaluation of an IEP. That is, does the IEP reflect a realistic plan for the student? What information will help answer this question? First of all, judgments about precision, completeness, and coordination will help the consumer in assessing the relevancy of a plan. The consumer/evaluator of IEP's must look at the structures that are implied by instructional strategies. Are the structures natural or contrived? Have the educators provided for continued progress to a higher level on the occupational continuum once the most immediate next level is reached (good long range goals)? Does the plan reflect the skills needed for survival in the local community?

A Mental Retardation Rehabilitation Research and Training Center Program in the United States of America

Joseph Fenton

Abstract. Three Research and Training Centers of the Rehabilitation Services Administration in HEW are directed to the rehabilitation of mentally retarded children, youth and adults. They are affiliated with the University of Oregon, Texas Tech University and the University of Wisconsin. Although the other 16 Research and Training Centers are primarily concerned with the areas of Medical Rehabilitation (12), Vocational Rehabilitation (3), and Deafness (1), some have also conducted investigations on the multi-handicapping and related aspects of mental retardation.

The Mental Retardation Research and Training (RT) Center concept is an outgrowth of Congress' response to recommendations made by the President's Panel on Mental Retardation in 1962. Emphasis was placed on the urgency for new knowledge and trained personnel to make major strides in assisting mentally retarded persons to reach their fullest levels of social, emotional, educational and vocational competencies.

The RT Centers are designed (a) to undertake research targeted toward the production of new knowledge which will improve rehabilitation methodology and service delivery systems, alleviate or stabilize handicapping conditions, and promote maximum social and economic independence; and (b) to institute related teaching and training programs, to disseminate and promote the utilization of the research findings, thereby reducing the usual long intervening delay between the discovery of the new knowledge and its wide application in practice.

Additional training responsibilities include increasing the numbers of rehabilitation personnel in fields where acute manpower shortages exist; training rehabilitation research and service personnel; incorporating rehabilitation education into all rehabilitation-related university curricula; and improving skills of rehabilitation students, professionals, para-professionals, volunteers, consumers, parents and other personnel participating in the rehabilitation process. These objectives are achieved through short- and long-term in-service and continuing education programs including seminars, workshops, courses of study, conferences and demonstrations — all for the ultimate purpose of favorably impacting and improving the effectiveness of those services that are assisting handicapped citizens to achieve the most productive life possible.

The Mental Retardation RT Centers are concerned with psycho-social-educational-vocational and behavioral studies to learn how best to help mentally retarded persons to develop and utilize all their potential abilities to the maximum, achieve independent living competencies, work skills, employment, and social acceptance at home, at work, and in the community.

Each Center has a Regional RT Center Advisory Council whose membership consists of representatives from the Rehabilitation Services Administration Regional and State Vocational Rehabilitation Offices in which the Center is located; also from professional and voluntary rehabilitation agencies, labor and industry, consumers and other related Departments within the University. These Councils not only serve as a mechanism for ongoing communication between the RT Centers and the regional and state rehabilitation program, but also for assurance that the research and training activities are responsive to priority areas of need.

The following briefly describes the research and training activities of the three RT Centers in Mental Retardation.

2. ASSESSMENT

University of Oregon RT Center in Mental Retardation

The Center at first completed a number of successful basic research projects in learning characteristics and the application of behavior modification principles to the vocational training needs of severely retarded adults. These were followed by applied programs of community adjustment problems. The long-term training program objectives were implemented through the development of graduate level courses and a sponsored doctoral fellowship program. The short-term training program consists of campus seminars and field workshops addressed to ongoing in-service needs of multi-disciplinary practitioners who work with mentally retarded clients in a variety of service agencies.

Research Activities. One of the Center's cores is concerned with the identification and measurement of social and prevocational competencies that are critical to post high school community adjustment of mildly retarded young adults. The Social and Prevocational Information Battery (SPIB) tests were developed to assess the knowledge of skills and competencies needed for employability, economic self-sufficiency, family living, personal habits, and communication. Because these are regarded as important for the community adjustment, the SPIB tests are now frequently used in high school curriculum of work-study programs for educable mentally retarded (EMR) pupils.

Another major research project was a national survey of community residential facilities for developmentally disabled people. The study responded to the issue of the prevention of institutionalization and the reduction of the population in state institutions; it also identified over 600 facilities and gathered basic information regarding source of referrals, program development, resident population, and major problems. Altogether 105 facilities are being studied in depth for an understanding of the operations of community residential facilities and the problems they must overcome to function effectively as an alternative to institutionalization.

The Oregon Center also developed and implemented a planning and evaluation strategy for use by State Developmental Disabilities Councils. In this project, three cyclical activities of planning, influencing, and evaluating were identified, each requiring the collection and management of information. The other components of the strategy — influencing and evaluating — were also outlined, and training materials developed to assist Council members in understanding and implementing their roles. Included among these materials is a 15-minute slide-tape presentation which provides an overview of the entire strategy.

Other listings of this RT Center's studies include, "Community Group Homes for Developmental Disabled;" "The Development and Prescriptive Criterion Measure for Assessing Community Adaption of Mildly Retarded Adults;" "Multi-Media Depiction of the Implementation of Concept of Normalization in Community Residential Facilities;" "Recreational Activities and Opportunities of Deinstitutionalized Retarded Adults;" and "Predicting Rates of Acquisition and Production of Complex Institutionalized Moderately and Severely Retarded Adults."

Training and Information Dissemination Activities. Doctoral fellows from a variety of mental retardation professions participated in a 2-year multi-disciplinary fellowship program which included didactic and practicum experiences as well as an active role in the Center's research and training projects. The major thrust of the training resides in the short-term campus seminars and field workshops. These bring participants to the University for 3 to 5 days of intensive training in a variety of mental retardation related rehabilitation areas. The field workshops, on the other hand, are designed to serve those in-service personnel training needs requested by state agencies at locations of their choice.

Also of significance is the Center's concern for developing methods of evaluating short-term training.

In keeping with the charge to all RT Centers to disseminate rehabilitation information and findings, the Oregon Center staff have produced 85 working papers, 7 monographs, and one book. Approximately 9,500 copies of Center publications were distributed.

Texas Tech University RT Center in Mental Retardation

This Center works productively with its University departments of Psychology, Special Education, Engineering, Business Administration, Speech, and Home Economics, as well as with many agencies in the region and nation.

Research Activities. The Center's research focuses on the development of an empirically-based training program in mental retardation, the rehabilitation of the multiply handicapped, vocational evaluation, and community adjustment and training.

The Empirically-Based Curriculum in Mental Retardation Forms aims to develop better orientation and in-service programs for rehabilitation counsellors through a systematic attempt to determine the job function of rehabilitation personnel in mental retardation, current levels of proficiency, and the content now provided in training programs. Rationale for this activity stems from a study of existing training programs for new counsellors and a literature analysis which indicated that more than 50% of the general field counsellors felt their professional training was inadequate and much of their in-service training related to policies and procedures rather than to substantive content. With this information, training priorities were established and materials developed which included such areas as problems in parent counselling, level of aspiration among the retarded, employers' orientation to the retarded, and special problems related to minority groups.

In addition to a completed project demonstrating that blind multiply handicapped persons can be trained for productive work, the Center undertook a descriptive incidence study of deafness among the retarded in state and private residential facilities, in cooperation with Gallaudet College and the American Speech and Hearing Association. Preliminary findings revealed (with only 17% of the private facilities responding), that the total population of retarded living in the responding private facilities is 2,372, with 3.2% of this number being classified as deaf and 6.3% as hard-of-hearing. The 81% response from state facilities revealed that they served a total of 104,603 retarded, with 2.4% being classified as deaf and 5.4% as hard-of-hearing; most reevaluate their deaf and hard-of-hearing residents on an annual basis; approximately two-thirds provide a speech and hearing evaluation upon admission: and hard-of-hearing and deaf residents seem to be distributed equally over the age range, except among children under six and adults over 60 where a lower percentage were identified. This probably reflects the difficulty of accurately testing hearing acuity in the very young and among elderly residents. Also, there was not a great variation in the incidence of hearing impairment among the retarded of different mental levels.

The third core area relates to the Development of an Automated Vocational Assessment Battery to provide work skill information in rapidly-prepared and concise reports to vocational counsellors. The instrument is proposed to give the counsellor an overview of the skills usually required, or inquired about, in obtaining employment for the retarded rather than assessments of the social and interpersonal skills usually considered more important in maintaining employment.

The retarded have historically been prepared for jobs requiring large amounts of physical energy expenditure (e.g., lifting, carrying, and pushing) on the basis they they enjoy and have the capacity to perform physical instead of intellectual tasks. Another Center project, therefore, studied the physical work capacities of the mentally retarded. The preliminary results indicate that the retarded have less physical endurance and capacity than average age-mates in the working society.

Several Community Adjustment and Training deinstitutionalization studies were undertaken in which dynamic aspects of the normalization process and the community living alternatives of halfway houses and group homes have and are being thoroughly investigated. In the past 2 years, "The Management of Behavior in Extended Living Facilities for the Retarded" and "Life Patterns of Residents and Houseparents in Group Homes for the Retarded" projects have been completed. Other studies included, "The Evaluatcon of Halfway House Training Programs for the Mentally Retarded," "Factors Underlying Successful Adjustment of Retarded Released from Institutions," "Group Homes for the Mentally Retarded in the Rehabilitation Process," "Group Living for Retardates in the Community: Investigation through Participant Observation," "The Vocational Adjustment Process of Halfway House and Cooperative Work-Study Clients," and "Community Acceptance of Retardate-as-Neighbor: Development of Measurement Techniques and Attitude Change Procedures."

The many observations and findings resulting from the studies are being utilized in the development and testing of guidelines for pre-discharge programs, readiness for community living, placement considerations, needed types of community support and all other elements involved in the deinstitutionalization process.

Training and Information Dissemination Activities. The training effort has been devoted to the area of deinstitutionalization. Conferences attended by rehabilitation and mental retardation staff were held to strengthen the skills of leadership personnel, to enable them to work more effectively with the retarded, and to develop community programs to provide necessary support systems for maintaining the retarded in the community. The conference themes were: Extended Living (Group Homes); Interdisciplinary Programming for the Multiply Handicapped; Developing Social Skills in the Developmentally Handicapped; Protective Services for the Developmentally Handicapped; and Structured and Unstructured Employment of the Mentally Retarded.

Three short-term workshops involved state rehabilitation agency staff development directors who developed a set of RT Center training priorities and the program content for two following conferences. One, oriented toward staff development and supervisory personnel, dealt with cooperative work-study programs. Also, dissemination conferences were held dealing with research underway in sheltered living and vocational evaluation.

As part of its long-term training activities, a group credit rehabilitation research seminar for doctoral level students was initiated to promote competencies and career interests in applied mental retardation rehabilitation research. Staff from nine University departments donate time as guest faculty on a voluntary basis to present up-to-date information on law, architecture, management, food and nutrition, as well as the traditional topics of psychology, education, speech and hearing and other services needed by the developmentally disabled population.

University of Wisconsin RT Center in Mental Retardation

A major emphasis of the Center has been cultural-familial mental retardation within the disadvantaged population group. This was established as a unique focus before

the relationship of poverty to mental retardation became a national concern.

Research Activities. A High-Risk Population Laboratory for studies and surveys was established in a city characterized as having the lowest median income, highest population density, highest dilapidated housing rate and according to the school system, the highest number of educable mentally retarded children. This survey research served as a basis for studying the cultural-familial mentally retarded in a large number of disadvantaged families located in an area having the highest known rate of mental retardation. A longitudinal pool of generated data is being continually updated for research to refine the relationship of poverty to mental retardation and the effects of comprehensive family intervention (a) on vocationally rehabilitating slum dwelling retarded adults who generally have not been motivated to seek out, participate in, or profit from the usual rehabilitation resources in the community and (b) to determine whether family intervention is an effective means of preventing consequent rehabilitation problems presented by children who have been reared in high-risk families.

The results from the surveys show that the very high prevalence of mental retardation occurring in the slums of American cities is not randomly distributed but it is contained within a small proportion of families who can be identified on the basis of maternal intelligence. Also, that the probability of a child's IQ falling within a range of 52-67 is 14.2 times more likely if the mother's IQ is in this range than if the mother's IQ is at or above 100. There was a striking concurrence of maternal and paternal IQ supporting the original survey's finding that declining intelligence as age increases is restricted to offspring of less bright mothers. The data showing the concentration of mental retardation among those disadvantaged families where there were many siblings and where maternal intelligence was depressed suggested the need for a total family approach to rehabilitation and prevention of retardation.

Adult women (with a newborn child) with intelligence scores below 75 were randomly assigned to a Control Group or the Experimental (the comprehensive family stimulation) Group. This total stimulation program involved parents and all children residing in the home. The mother received rehabilitation training including (a) remedial academic education, (b) vocational information and counselling, and (c) occupational training as nurses aides, including such areas as housekeeping, janitorial work, food preparation, etc., and (d) general counselling. The infants in the Experimental Group were in a preventive program which included an individualized prescribed curriculum to facilitate intellectual, academic, and social development.

The Experimental children, now averaging over 8 years, show superiority in all measures of development compared to the Control Group. The acceleration of the Experimental Group is in marked contrast to both the test norms and to the progress of Control Group. They have maintained a 30 IQ differential (112 vs 82) and vast advantage on various learning and language measures. The underlying hypothesis of the experimental program was of infant stimulation and prevention of a decline from the norm in rate of development, rather than an acceleration in the rate of development. The Control infants of retarded mothers in contrast appear to be following the expected pattern of development with a gradual decline in measured intelligence as age increases.

The most significant posttreatment performance measure of the Experimental children was in the form of regular class placement for all the children — such placements were previously not typical for groups so socio-economically disposed with measured retardation existing in the family.

The project demonstrated that intervention is effective in the prevention of cultural-familial mental retardation. In

2. ASSESSMENT

the efforts directed toward developing job or employment skills in the mothers and improving home management skills, a number became gainfully employed and others have shown improved homemaking skills; sensitivity to personal and family needs (including nutrition and health); increased receptivity to suggestions from responsible outsiders; and changes in the motivation to seek out, participate in and profit from the rehabilitation resources in the community.

The Laboratory of Applied Behavioral Analysis and Modification is organized around five research and development sections and related supportive services. The section of Instrumentation and Environmental Design maintains the equipment utilized in research and field training projects as well as providing consultation services to rehabilitation agencies in the design and construction of various instruments and systems for use as training or prosthetic components in workshop settings. The section on Remediation of Basic Behavioral Deficits studies evaluating procedures for developing and maintaining high-rate behavior over extended periods of time in the highly distractible, low-motivated retarded adult. The section on development of Work Related Behaviors is concerned with procedures for managing the intra-and interpersonal behaviors of the retarded functioning in a group setting. The section on Behavior Change, Cognitive, Social, Affective, evaluates the effectiveness of various behavior therapy procedures in remediating maladaptive social and emotional behavior patterns in the mentally retarded adult. The section on Utilization of Laboratory Findings in Applied Settings provides consultation to private and public agencies in the design and implementation of rehabilitation programs based on behavior modification concepts.

In addition, a Laboratory of Client, Family, School and Community Variables Related to the Education-Rehabilitation Needs of the Mildly Retarded has been inaugurated to investigate programming processes and practices for the adolescent retarded who are potential rehabilitation clients. Individuals diagnosed as mildly retarded are being assessed in the form of a long-term follow-up study during the phase of client lives which are critical to the vocational outcome variables, i.e., securing a job.

Training and Information Dissemination Activities. Campus Short-Term Training Programs are conducted at regular intervals and during the summer. The field institutes assist state rehabilitation agencies in developing and implementing state-wide institutes dealing with basic information or specialized rehabilitation process topics. The Center Leadership Training program provides indepth interdisciplinary training or full time graduate students in any of the rehabilitation disciplines. Students completing this program qualify for leadership roles in federal, state and local rehabilitation programs for the retarded.

A course, Introduction and/or Orientation to Mental Retardation was conducted on state-wide educational television channels utilizing input primarily from the Center's ongoing research project. It was also used for a series of six field seminars conducted in rehabilitation districts throughout the state and attended by 1,300 professionals and non-professionals on a graduate, undergraduate or audit status.

JOSEPH FENTON, Ed.D., is Chief, Division of Special Centers, Office of Research and Evaluation — Rehabilitation Services Administration, Department of Health, Education and Welfare, Washington, D.C. He received his doctorate from Columbia University and has served in the faculties of the University of Virginia, Syracuse University and Columbia University. Prior to assuming his present position, Dr. Fenton served as Special Assistant to Governor Nelson Rockerfeller's New York State Advisory Council on Rehabilitation and the New York State Interdepartmental Health and Hospital Council. He also served in the capacities of Superintendent of a residential and day rehabilitation and educational center for multiply handicapped persons in Santa Barbara, California, and Associate in the Bureau for Handicapped Children, New York State Education Department. Dr. Fenton has been principal investigator for numerous research projects and has authored 27 articles and publication.

Vocational Assessment and Training of the Mentally Retarded--A Review of the Program Developed at the B.M. Institute of Mental Health in India

M. R. Kulkarni

Abstract. The paper describes the vocational assessment and training program developed by the Research and Demonstration Project for Rehabilitative Assistance to Mentally Retarded Youth, jointly sponsored by the B.M. Institute and the Rehabilitation Service Administration (RSA) of the United States Department of Health, Education and Welfare. The method of vocational assessment evolved by the project is presented. A detailed description of the four-phase vocational training program based on the Work Personality Development approach is given. Benefits accruing to the clients undergoing the training program are discussed. A brief picture of the mental retardation movement in India is provided as background information.

This paper describes the vocational assessment and training program for severely mentally retarded youths who need development and assessment of psycho-social skills required for different work situations, development and assessment of work skills, work tolerance, work habits and attitudes, and total evaluation of work potential for future employment. Though designed to provide overall development of the mentally retarded in essential life skills, the program is specifically aimed at vocational development leading to employability through the process of work adjustment training. This program was developed as a part of the B.M. Institute-RSA Demonstration Project for Rehabilitation Assistance to Mentally Retarded Youth which was in operation in Ahmedabad from July 3, 1972 to January 2, 1976.

Before presenting the details of the program, it would be appropriate to present background information about the mental retardation movement in India and a general description of the services for the mentally retarded at the B.M. Institute. This information will give an idea of the state of affairs and put into proper perspective the program developed by the project and its usefulness to and utilization by other agencies.

The Mental Retardation Movement in India

The mental retardation movement in India is of very recent origin. In 1941, the first school for the mentally retarded, known as "The School for the Mentally Deficient Children," was established in Bombay. In the next two dec-

ades, there was slow progress in the mental retardation movement; only about 25 institutions were established, largely by interested parents and some voluntary organizations. However, the major breakthrough in this regard came in 1963, when the Indian Society for the Rehabilitation of the Handicapped celebrated the first All Indian Day for the Mentally Retarded on December 8, 1963. This was followed by the organization of a number of Seminars/Conferences in Bombay, Ahmedabad, Delhi and other parts of the country. In 1964, the Social Welfare Department of the Government of India took a major step by establishing a "Model School for the Mentally Retarded" at Delhi. Due to increasing interest on the part of the government and because of efforts of some professionals and parents, the first All India Conference on Mental Retardation was held in Delhi in 1965, which resulted in the establishment of the Federation for the Welfare of the Mentally Retarded. Such seminars, conferences, and the efforts of the voluntary organizations for the mentally retarded brought about more awareness of the needs of the mentally retarded. The Social Welfare Department of India and many of the state governments made more funds available through their grants-in-aid to voluntary agencies. The liberal grant-in-aid policy of the government and increased public awareness has resulted in the establishment of more than 100 institutions for the retarded throughout the country. Even though there has been a substantial rise in the number of institutions for the retarded, compared to the needs of the country as a whole it is far from satisfactory. Presently there are no available data which permit a precise statement of the prevalance of mental retardation in India. However, an estimate of 14-16,000,000 can be made on the basis of the generally accepted estimate that approximately 2.5% of the general population consists of the mentally retarded. There are approximately 120 institutions in India, largely developed by voluntary organizations, which provide various ranges of services to nearly 4,000 mentally retarded. It is obvious that there is a need for a great organizational effort in order to provide even minimum services for the retarded in the country.

As far as vocational training programs for the retarded are concerned, these are still in early stages of development. In a survey conducted by the B.M. Institute in 1972, out of

2. ASSESSMENT

the total of 91 institutions covered, 33 were reported as having some kind of pre-vocational and vocational training programs, largely of the arts and crafts variety. Of these, five institutions were in the process of organizing sheltered workshops for the retarded.

Services for the Mentally Retarded at the B.M. Institute

The B.M. Institute of Mental Health began in 1951 as an institution devoted to the study of child development. It has gradually evolved over the period of 25 years into a comprehensive mental health facility for emotionally disturbed and mentally retarded children and adults, and runs an experimental pre-primary school program for normal children.

The Institute offered token services for the middle-aged mentally retarded as a part of the child guidance clinic of the Institute. From these small beginnings, facilities for the retarded at the Institute have gradually expanded over the years and presently we are in the process of establishing a semi-autonomous center within the Institute. The first of these services to be exclusively established for the mentally retarded was the Clinic for the Mentally Retarded Children. This school was the first to be organized in the city of Ahmedabad. The 'Sharada' school, which started with only three children, mainly as a primary educational program for children ages of 6-16, increased to 30 children by 1967. The services included diagnostic evaluation, training in the three R's and parental counselling. Since most of the children had speech problems, a speech and audiology service was provided in 1967. The occupational therapy program was added in 1970, as increasing need was felt by the Institute for starting vocational training programs for children who had reached adolescence. Soon after the pre-vocational occupational therapy program started, we were fortunate enough to be granted a three and one-half year research demonstration grant by RSA for developing a vocational assessment and training program for mentally retarded adolescents. The project became operational in July of 1972, providing much needed impetus for developing new operations towards a vocational assessment and training program for the retarded and serving as a pilot project to demonstrate the efficacy of vocational training in the rehabilitation of the mentally retarded. The Institution formally established a vocational training program for the mentally retarded based on the experience gained from the project. Currently, the Institute is in the process of developing a sheltered workshop for the mentally retarded under a grant from the Department of Social Welfare, Government of India. It is to be noted that in 1972 the Institute started the first one-year University diploma course in India for training special teachers in the field of mental retardation. The graduate teachers from this program have helped establish more schools in Ahmedabad and other parts of the state with the result that the total number of programs in Gusant State has increased to nine. Also this year, in joint collaboration with the Federation for the Welfare of the Mentally Retarded and the Guyastat University, the B.M. Institute is providing the first one-year all India postgraduate course for scientific study of the developmentally handicapped for teachers, social workers, psychologists, occupational therapists, speech therapists and psychiatrists. The B.M. Institute has pioneered developing services for the mentally retarded in India. Presently the Institute is planning to establish a separate semi-autonomous unit known as the "Center for the Developmentally Handicapped." This center will provide diagnostic evaluation, treatment, education and training and vocational rehabilitation services for approximately 150 mentally retarded individuals from birth to adulthood in day programs.

The Institute, which is financed by private charities and government grants, has made provisions for quality care one

of its cornerstones in providing services to its clients. Because of this approach, our service programs have remained small in size, client-oriented and are closely monitored. The Institute has been psychodynamically-oriented from its inception and this approach forms the core of all the services provided for the mentally retarded at the Institute. All the programs are serviced through a multi-disciplinary team approach. The Institute has always encouraged experimentation and incorporation of new techniques in the service programs. This process is facilitated through case conferences, seminars and continuous in-service training programs which form a regular part of a working week at the Institute. Involvement of parents in the various educational and service programs is actively promoted through parental counseling, staff-parent meetings and other such programs. As a matter of policy, the Institute provides only the day care program for the mentally retarded, as it is felt that separation of the child from his parents would adversely affect the development of the child. Though normally responsive to the needs of the community because of the above stated policy, the Institute has refrained from starting a residential center for the retarded, in spite of pressure from parents.

The B.M.-RSA Project for Rehabilitative Assistance to Mentally Retarded Youth

As already stated, the B.M.I.-RSA project became operational on July 2, 1972. The project had an evaluation and training staff of nine people, which included a clinical psychologist, a social worker, a special teacher, a senior occupational therapist, a junior occupational therapist, three full-time occupational instructors, and a research officer who was a psychologist by training. In addition to these people, services of the Director of Occupational Therapy and Rehabilitation and the Senior Psychologist were provided to the project on a part-time basis. Other specialist services were made available to the project when necessary. Except for the Senior Occupational Therapist, none of the staff had any experience in working with the mentally retarded; therefore the staff was exposed to a three-month intensive orientation and in-service training program in the area of evaluation, training, and treatment of the mentally retarded. At the end of this training, the staff started working with clients admitted to the project. The criteria for admission to the project was as follows:

1. Only mentally retarded clients between ages 14-21 referred from the Sharada Special School for the Mentally Retarded and the Clinic for the Mentally Retarded will be admitted to the program.

2. Mentally retarded cases of all classification and categories below the IQ level of 75 will be admitted.

3. Clients having problems such as respiratory disease and cardiac disease, etc., will be admitted only after obtaining a fitness certificate from the consulting physician.

4. Only clients who do not have severe physical handicaps which might interfere with the participation in the program are admitted.

5. Clients who are adequately self-sufficient in certain basic personal care needs are admitted.

The first batch of five clients from the Sharada School were admitted to the program in the middle of October and every quarter thereafter a fresh group of five clients were admitted to the program. It was decided by the authorities that the maximum number of clients in training in the program should not exceed 30 at any one time. In all, 37 clients were admitted to the project.

Through a policy decision, the project staff was encouraged to experiment and innovate in the area of evaluation and training of the retarded clients. The evaluation and the training program described in the paper were effectively used only in the third year of the project. Also, during the first two years, considerable effort was put into training the staff in the evaluation and training techniques.

Approach

The project program was based on the synthesis of the understanding of mental retardation developed at the Institution based on experience gained over the years, and the vocational developmental approach advocated by Dr. William Gellmam and his associates at the Jewish Vocational Service in Chicago. Dr. Gellman, the Director of Jewish Vocational Service in Chicago, was a consultant to our project and influenced our thinking to a great extent.

Over the period of years, we have come to understand mental retardation as a condition in which we come across delay in the overall developmental process. In the process of development, the human organism expects and is expected to achieve specific adaptive behaviors which equip him to cope with life. Meeting societal demands requires adaptive skills and the mastery of self and environment. In the course of his development, an individual is expected to grow and develop along a longitudinal continuum into adulthood. The tasks of adulthood include holding a job, learning to manage a home, developing congenial social relationships, and meeting social obligations. In the process of human development, should the individual experience physical or psychological traumas related to disease, injury, environmental factors or interpersonal relationships, the natural developmental process is interrupted or delayed, leading to deficiency in growth and development of basic life skills and the ability to cope with the environmental demands. The definition of mental retardation given by the American Association on Mental Deficiency in 1961, in *A Manual on Terminology and Classification in Mental Retardation* was used as the operational definition for this project. "Mental Retardation refers to subaverage general intellectual functioning, which originates during the developmental period and is associated with impairment in adaptive behavior." We conceptualize that the mentally retarded individual is affected by the developmental delay in the areas of neuro-physiological, physical, and psycho-social growth which impede his intellectual functioning and impair the development of social language, daily living skills, academic skills and social-cultural skills. In order to habilitate the mentally retarded person into normal community living and his assumption of the adult role, it is essential to facilitate his continued growth in the above-mentioned areas.

We have viewed the (re)habilitation of the mentally retarded as the process of change induced by the modality of the vocational development and adjustment. Gellman and Friedman (1965) state: "The Vocational development program is designed for persons who have never achieved an adequate level of functioning in achievement-demanding situations or who lack a positive orientation and are characterized by paralysis of achievement, e.g., schizophrenic or retarded. It is directed towards the formation of work personality for persons who because of congenital or early disability have deviated from the normal process of vocational development."

The process of vocational development "sets the framework" for future productive life. It has to be initiated quite early in childhood and extended well into adulthood. "The process of learning to work and vocational development leads to the formation of work personality which enables the individual to assume a work role and adjust to work." (Gellman, 1973). The vocational developmental process brings about change in the retarded person as he grows from childhood into adolescence and adulthood. This change is brought about through the family, the social groups, the peers, co-workers, work supervisors and the work environment of the rehabilitation workshop, who function as agents of change. This process of change has to be goal-oriented. While, in the initial phases of (re)habilitation, the goals are directed toward developing psycho-social abilities in the retarded individual, in the later stages the goals are development of adequate work behavior. The rehabilitation workshop uses work as a situational tool to assess and modify work behaviors. The work environment of the workshop provides the psycho-social pressure on the retarded client in terms of participation in work groups, conformity to the role of a worker, an achievement orientation, anticipated production, etc. Workshop counselling, individual counselling, placement in work stations, on-the-job assistance, and follow-up work all help in adjustment and adaptation to a "workday world."

The vocational development process was conceptualized as the movement towards formation and modification of work personality in the mentally retarded individual. Gellman (1973) has defined "work personality" as an integrated, semi-autonomous part of the total personality which functions as a constellation of work behavior, attitudes, and values manifested in typical achievement or work-demanding situations. It is defined operationally as the set of work behavior patterns exhibited in a work situation, or the manner in which the individual enacts the work role. The project conceptualized that the work personality is the product of developmental processes occurring from infancy to old age, the interplay of such forces as culture, social values, nurturing and the acquisition of habits and the effects of man's interaction with the socio-cultural environment. The development of the work personality is considered synonymous with development of employability in the individual. The term "employability" or "work personality" has three components — workability, adjustability, and placeability:

Workability — the possession of background knowledge and skill to perform a task, or number of tasks, singly, in sequence, or simultaneously, within a work setting.

Adjustability — the ability to adjust to changing situations and to new situations within the work setting.

Placeability — the possession of maximum workability, along with work tolerance and social and personal ability useful in obtaining gainful occupation.

The three components of work personality develop in stages over a period of years through vocational developmental processes. They grow parallel to each other until the individual reaches employability in a given work situation. Each stage represents a stage in the development of work personality and ability to adjust to a vocation. The following are the stages of vocational development in the mentally retarded individual:

1. Personal and social adjustment phase-development of adequate skills in personal social functional area;

2. Work skills training phase-development of work skills related to particular tasks;

3. Job adjustment phase — development of job specific skills along with development of work behavior essential for successful vocational adjustment;

4. Employment phase — preparation for employment by developing an adaptable, well-motivated and work-ready person who is capable of performing entry level jobs.

To develop the above-mentioned required abilities in the mentally retarded person requires sensitivity on the part of the teaching staff in understanding the disadvantages that the client has suffered because of his retardation and the ability to understand the client's needs and aspirations. Besides, the individual client belongs to a family which has its own expectations and aspirations for the client. Any program for the vocational (re)habilitation of the mentally retarded must be based on thorough evaluation of work personality and training leading to the development of work personality as previously conceptualized. As a result the project staff developed the 5-phased Vocational Evaluation and Training Program.

Five-Phased Vocational Evaluation and Training Program

The emphasis of the program was to first evaluate the needs, abilities and potentialities of the mentally retarded client, so that on the basis of this evaluation the client can be put through phase-wise, dynamically oriented, sequential work adjustment training programs. The client functioning below a given level was provided extensive service programs, so that following training he could move up to the next level of the training program. Thus initial evaluation, training, re-evaluation pattern was put into use at all phases of training program. Details of the evaluation and training program follow:

Phase I: Initial Evaluation Phase

A detailed evaluation program was worked out as part of the project to assess the needs of the client and his family at the time of his admission in addition to the work evaluation. The primary areas for evaluation were:

1. Initial evaluation to identify the level of the function of the client along with other relevant factors such as (re)habilitation goals, family expectations, periodical evaluation, etc.

2. To provide interim assessment of the client's performance as he moves from one phase of training to the next phase of training. This interim evaluation helped in locating areas in which client had not progressed sufficiently and indicated the direction of training or treatment to be provided.

3. The terminal evaluation to determine the final level of functioning when the client left the training program. The terminal evaluation helped in identifying the attainments of the client during his training.

The evaluative program at the initial evaluation phase usually required a period of six to seven weeks, out of which the first three weeks were spent in individual detailed evaluation by the psychiatrist, psychiatric social worker, the clinical psychologist, the educational specialist and the occupational therapist, before he was exposed to a three-week detailed work evaluation program within the workshop situation. The psychiatric social worker prepared a detailed case study by interviewing the parents and the client, and through home visits, so that sufficient information and the psycho-social background of the client were available for the use of all clinical staff. The psychological testing primarily assessed the cognitive abilities and the emotional development of the client. The special teacher evaluated the reading, writing and arithmetic abilities of the client and the client's capacity to learn through a formal teaching program. The occupational therapist provided information on perceptual motor functions, neuromuscular co-ordination, and evaluation of any other functional disabilities associated with primary diagnosis. He also evaluated the problem areas in the Activities of Daily Living.

The work evaluation was conducted by the occupational therapist, along with the help of workshop instructors and other clinical staff. This involved three weeks of intensive observation of the client within the workshop in realistic work situations. This helped in preparing the profile of client's work performance. It also provided us with dynamic analytical information regarding client's vocational potential, his capacity for change, and his potential for emotional and social adjustment to the demands of work. The work sample testing was done to evaluate work abilities of the client. The following evaluation tools were used:

1. A modified version of the *Adaptive Behavior Scale*, developed originally by the American Association on Mental Deficiency;

2. Workshop observation scale, which was modified from Goodwill Industries' "Supervisors Observation Guide" (*Employability Scale*);

3. Seven work-sample tests developed by the project staff.

These tools provided information on personal and social adaptation and the present level of function of the client along with identification of maladaptive behaviors. This information then helped us in organizing a program which was specifically aimed at overcoming the problems revealed by the evaluation process. This evaluation answered the following basic questions:

1. What type of background does the client come from, and what are his personal assets and liabilities in terms of social, emotional and economic functioning?

2. What are the factors that are affecting the client's future development?

3. What type and level of training program is to be provided to the client and does he need other therapeutic intervention?

4. What predictions can be made about the rehabilitation outcome of the client?

The following is the detailed analysis of the attributes of the clients admitted at the B.M.I.-RSA project at the initial evaluation Phase (total 37):

1. All except one were below an IQ level of 50. The highest level of IQ was 59 and lowest level of IQ was 19. The majority fell in the IQ 35-50 category.

2. All had problems in communication. Most of the clients had speech problems. In 30% of the clients, poor development of language was hindering the verbal communication process.

2. All clients had difficulty in social relationships.

4. All clients had motor problems.

5. Sixty percent of the clients had perceptual motor problems.

6. All clients showed poor self-esteem.

7. Forty percent of the clients had never been to school.

8. All the clients had problems in adjustment at home.

9. In all cases, either parents or siblings accompanied the client when he went out; he was never allowed to go out alone.

10. Except for clients from Sharada Special School, none had friends.

11. Almost all of them were reported as sulking, crying or having temper tantrums when they could not have their own way.

12. About 75% of the clients could not participate meaningfully in the social life of the program.

13. All the trainees perceived staff as parents or teachers and tended to act child-like.

14. All parents had guilt feelings about having a mentally retarded child.

15. Only 30% of clients had prevocational experience and only one client had any work experience.

16. All clients were toilet-trained and were able to locomote without assistance.

17. Among the clients, 18.8% belonged to the upper income group (annual income: above Rs $18,000), 59.6% belonged to the middle income group (annual income: between Rs $6,000 and $18,000), and 21.6% belonged to the lower income group (annual income: below Rs $6,000).

Phase II: Personal and Social Adjustment Phase

Though work activity is the primary means through which the retarded person is to be adjusted to work, since many of the clients had little or sometimes even no experience of situations outside the home and had poor psycho-social skills, it was essential to put them through a program for the development of psycho-social skills. Besides, nearly 70% of the clients had no work experience; it was essential to provide them with a non-threatening supportive environment which helped them to deal with the demands of new situations such as the workshop. The utilization of non-threatening work experience and the interpersonal relationship to satisfy the clients' personal needs, and to develop adequate adjustment proved to be an absorbing developmental process. Judicious use of supportive attitudes, discipline, and environmental structure based on therapeutically indicated flexibility provided the means for adaptation and adjustment to the work situation. The programs in the personal-social adjustment phase were introduced at the existing level of functioning of the client and were linked up with his earlier life experiences. Since most of the clients lacked skills in the area of Activities of Daily Living, personal-social hygiene, utilization of public transport, and verbal communication, special programs were set up in these areas. Because all of them required training in reading, writing and simple arithmetic work, a special education program was organized to develop a work-oriented classroom program, which attempted to train the clients in the areas of time-telling, weights and measures, and recognition of street signs, workshop tools, etc. Recreational activities were organized in the lunch recess to help in socialization and learning of the use of leisure time. Many of the maladaptive behaviors were handled through use of behavior modification strategies, environmental manipulation, workshop counselling and individual counselling. The peer group pressures and fear of rejection from the colleagues were an important influence in extinction of maladaptive behavior. All these approaches were organized within a work-oriented program in the workshop situation. Clients were introduced to simple tasks first, which later increased in complexity. Work experiences were provided in the area of maintenance tasks, simple workshop practice, simple food preparation and handling, and kitchen gardening. Basic operations like cleaning, dusting, and mopping were emphasized from the beginning.

Since the family plays a major role in (re)habilitation of a retarded person, parental counselling was provided to all the parents in addition to providing information about the etiology of mental retardation in general terms. Parents were encouraged to discuss their problems related to the handling of the clients at home. Both individual and group counselling methods were used.

It was observed that the clients became well-adjusted to the program within a period ranging from 3-6 months. When they reached this phase, they were observed to be well-adjusted to the workshop routine, and the training program had become a part of their living system. They showed no specific interest in learning new tasks and were able to sustain themselves for longer periods in the work situation.

Phase III: Work Skills Training Phase

The ability to work in different work situations is an important component of vocational development aimed at the development of maximum employability. Since the majority of our clients had limited work skills, we developed a work skills training program which provided for a wide spectrum of work experience. The work orientation program initiated in the second phase was extended to provide specific work experience in tasks such as woodwork, metal work, weaving, book binding, box mailing, printing, tailoring, needlework, laundrying, maintenance work, gardening, kitchen craft, etc. The clients were rotated from one task to another in order to provide them with a wide variety of experience. The program emphasized development of neuro-muscular skills, work tolerance, improvement in speed, quality and consistency in performance. The workshop environment was used to teach the retarded client to deal with the demands of a work-a-day world. The supervisors used interpersonal relationships, the work pressure and the demands of production to change the behavior of the client and for development of good work habits, as well as positive attitudes towards supervisors and co-workers. In the later stages of the work-skills training programs, the clients were placed on a part-time basis in the work situations like the canteen (cafeteria), the administrative offices, the library, the Day Care Unit and the telephone switchboard, providing reality-based work experience for the mentally retarded client. They learned the rules of the work place, and the social behavior appropriate to the work situation. The female clients were provided with intensive training in activities related to homemaker training, such as simple cooking, purchasing of groceries, stitching and mending of clothes. The special educationist worked in close cooperation with other workshop staff to relate classroom education to the training in the workshop. This was the core of the vocational-oriented educational program.

By this time the staff had begun to clearly understand the needs of the individual clients and also had been able to pinpoint various maladaptive behaviors which were hindering the progress of individual clients. Besides workshop counselling and group counselling, individual counselling was provided to those clients who needed such an approach. The work with the family at this stage was aimed at the values and the behavior patterns conducive to the work training of the retarded clients.

Phase IV: The Job Adjustment Phase

When the clients had achieved sufficient degrees of work skills, demonstrated good work habits and positive attitudes towards work, and interacted appropriately with co-workers and supervisors, they were put into a job-specific training phase. Each area of work was assigned as a work station and the client was put on full-time work in each work station. By the time the client reached job adjustment phase, he usually showed interest in the particular job area and he was assigned for intensive training in that job area. Due consideration was given to the cultural values of the family in deciding the areas in which the client was to be trained. For girls, the program emphasized training in operations related to kitchen and maintenance work at home with the intention of improving placeability of the client. Emphasis was given on punctuality in work, obedience, personal habits, social manners, appropriate communication, etc. In the later stages of job adjustment phase, clients were put on part-time work experience in work stations outside the Institute to provide them with real work experience. The other half of the day was utilized in providing additional training and guidance within the rehabilitation workshop, aimed at overcoming the shortcomings which the client had shown while working at the work stations outside. Such transitional work placements helped in making the client "work ready."

The vocational counselling of the client at this stage proved to be very important in preparing him for employment in the community. Individual counselling was provided to all the clients to deal with their problems and anxieties related to taking up a job outside. Families had to be prepared for accepting the retarded client as a worker who

2. ASSESSMENT

has his own place within the family system. Often, siblings had to be counselled, as they had not accepted the changed role of the client. In a few cases, intensive work with the family had to be initiated by the social worker.

Phase V: Employment Phase

The real test of growth of employability in a retarded client is his placement in community employment. Since it was not easy to get open employment in industry, we made efforts to secure employment for our clients through friends and relatives of the client's family. The help of the National Society for Equal Opportunities for the Handicapped (Gujarat Chapter) was utilized in locating jobs and securing jobs in industry. We also made attempts to place clients in self-employment with support from family.

In spite of our efforts, jobs were difficult to come by. Therefore, we decided to organize a sheltered workshop on a limited basis. Sub-contracts were secured for office file-making and lock assembly from local firms. Production-oriented work was started in woodwork and metal work sections and orders were solicited. The clients are paid wages on a piece-work basis. Currently, the plans are under way to organize a regular sheltered workshop within the premises of the Institute.

Those clients who are placed in community employment are being provided with follow-up services to deal with any problems which may arise consequent to their placement.

A Brief Summary of the Outcome of the Project

Seventy-four clients were called for admission to the programs, 44 turned up for registration, and six dropped out during evaluation. In addition, 37 clients were admitted to training, three dropped out during training due to domestic reasons, four clients were transferred to Shanada Special School as they were considered unsuitable for the program, and one client died while in training. Twenty-nine clients completed the training or were in different phases of training. By the end of the project, on January 7, 1976, 12 clients had been placed in employment, five were placed in sheltered employment, and the 12 were still in training. By August 1976, 14 clients had been placed in employment, eight were in sheltered employment and seven were in work-skills and job adjustment training phase. (Those interested can obtain detailed analysis of data from the author).

The project proved to be a useful demonstration to those working in the field of mental retardation. The project staff presented the vocational developmental model in the "All India Seminar on Developmental Approach in Occupational Therapy" in December of 1976, and at the "Second All India Refresher Course for Workers in Mental Retardation" held in February of 1976 at the B.M. Institute.

In summary, a mentally retarded adolescent is deprived or disadvantaged from early childhood. Disadvantages result in parental neglect, lack of opportunity, low self-esteem, depression, aggression, and many other maladaptive behavioral problems. The lack of opportunity to have normal psycho-social adjustment from early childhood hampers development and when he reaches adolescence, the retarded person is far behind other normal adolescents in social and economic competence. His ability to cope with environmental demands is poor, and he is unable to adapt to varying environments. Left by himself, he is not able to cope with the demands of the adult work-a-day world. For the adolescent retarded person, (re)habilation is a developmental process, which provides the necessary input of experiences to halt and, if possible, reverse the process of disadvantagement. The experiences provided in the *milieu* of a rehabilita-

tion workshop bring about vocational development in the mentally retarded as he grows from adolescence into adulthood. The three components of employability are: workability, adjustability, and placeability. Developed simultaneously in the retarded person, they lead to a growth of employability. This growth takes place by exposure of the retarded person to a work environment of the (re)habilitation workshop, wherein the workshop supervisors, the co-workers, the social group and the family are used to bring about the desired change. The agents of change work towards development of adequate psycho-social ability and work behavior in the retarded. As the retarded person develops in his workability due to exposure to the work training program, his placement in different work stations and counselling improve his ability to adjust to different work situations. The training in interpersonal abilities improves his ability to meet the demands of community employment. The work with the family is of great importance for the success of the program. The outcome of the project has proven that if the mentally retarded is provided with orderly sequential vocational preparation from early adolescence, this will lead to an orderly outcome of gainful employment in the community by the time he reaches adulthood.

References

Gellman, W. & Friedman, S. B. The workshop as a clinical tool. *Rehabilitation Literature*, 1965, 26(2).

Gellman, W. Adolescent and adult mentally retarded. Vaper presented at the All India Conference on Mental Retardation, B.M. Institute, January, 1973.

Kramer, J. Work adjustment, training, and evaluation for teenage retardates. In W. L. West (Ed.), *Occupational therapy for multiply handicapped child.* University of Illinois, 1965.

Kulkarni, M. R. Vocational development of the mentally retarded. Paper presented at the 5th Conference of Federation for the Welfare of the Mentally Retarded, New Delhi, February, 1976.

Kulkarni, M. R. *Second annual report of the B.M.I-RSA project for rehabilitation assistance to mentally retarded youth.* Ahmedabad, India: B.M. Institute, 1975.

Llorens, L. A. Facilitating growth and development: The promise of occupational therapy. Paper presented at the 52nd conference of American Occupational Therapy Association, November, 1969.

Shrivastarg, A. C. Vocational growth and development of work personality in mentally retarded youth. Paper presented at the 5th Pan-Pacific Conference on Rehabilitation, Singapore, November, 1975.

M. R. KULKARNI joined the Occupational Therapy Department, Indian Mental Hospital, Ranchi Biha State (after graduating with a diploma in Occupational Therapy in 1956) where he established the Occupational Therapy Department. He joined the staff of Occupational Therapy Training School and Centre, Government Medical College and Hospital, Nagpur Maharashtr State in 1958. In 1962, he became Director of The Occupational Therapy School and initiated the first Bachelors of Science program in Occupational Therapy. He joined the B.M. Institute of Mental Health Ahmedabad in August of 1969 to establish and develop an occupational therapy and rehabilitation unit for the rehabilitation of the mentally ill and the mentally retarded. Mr. Kulkarni conducted the B.M.I.-RSA project for Rehabilitative Assistance to mentally retarded youth as the Principal Investigator from 1972 to 1976. He has been conducting the postgrauduate training programs in Occupational Therapy affiliated to Gujarat University since 1972. He is the president of All India Occupational Therapists Association, Vice-President of the Federation for the Welfare of the Mentally Retarded (India), and is associated with many organizations concerned with rehabilitation of handicapped in India and abroad.

WARF: A SCALE FOR MEASURING JOB-READINESS BEHAVIORS

James A. Bitter [2] and D. J. Bolanovich
St. Louis Jewish Employment and Vocational Service

A rating scale (Work Adjustment Rating Form) to predict job readiness of retardates is described relative to the criteria of (a) systematic observation, (b) relevance, (c) reliability of observations, and (d) identification of behavior patterns. Results demonstrate that a simple scale can predict job adjustment with fairly high interrater agreement and holds promise for identifying meaningful behavior patterns. The main shortcoming of rating scale appoaches is that they are judgmental. Though these results do not provide conclusive information they illustrate that development of such a measure is feasible. Needed research includes the identification of more specific behaviors, attainment of observer consistency, and the development of normative information relative to predictive behaviors.

To ascertain "job readiness" necessitates identification of behaviors prior to employment which are predictive of job adjustment after employment (Bitter, 1968). In most entry-level jobs where skill requirements are minimal, such personal work behaviors are difficult to identify objectively; yet entry-level jobs are of concern to all rehabilitation counselors working with the retarded.

Reviews by Windle (1962) and Wolfensberger (1967) indicate that studies numbering in the hundreds have attempted to identify variables predictive of vocational success of the mentally retarded. It is not the intention of this report to add to the long list of measures which purport to predict employment success. Rather, the report attempts to (a) outline the requirements for a measure of job-readiness behaviors, (b) analyze experience with one instrument used in a rehabilitation program, (c) evaluate this experience in terms of the requirements, and (d) suggest direction for research to develop more suitable measures.

Requirements of the Measure

An effective instrument for measuring job-readiness behaviors would need to meet the following criteria:

1. The instrument should provide a systematic method for recording observations in a form that can be summarized and scaled.

2. The recorded behavior should be relevant to desired rehabilitation outcomes.

3. The instrument should be objective, and should provide consistent measurement from observer to observer.

4. The instrument should yield a description of behavior patterns which aid training decisions.

Experience with the Work Adjustment Rating Form

During the 1964–1966 school years the Work Experience Center staff of the St. Louis Jewish Employment and Vocational Service explored the feasibility of the Work Adjustment Rating Form (WARF). The WARF is a rating scale constructed primarily for use by counselors and workshop foremen working with the mentally retarded to assess areas of workshop strengths for purposes of training and to assess workshop adjustment progress. Available data from the 1965–66 school year were analyzed to determine the degree to which the form met the above requirements. It was then used to predict future success or failure of retardates between 16 and 21 years old in community employment.

The WARF forms were completed for 40 clients, 23 males and 17 females, after 3 and 16 weeks of training by three counselors and

[1] This study was supported in part by research grant No. RD-2197G from the Social and Rehabilitation Service, U.S. Department of Health, Education, and Welfare.
[2] Presently a Social and Rehabilitation Service Postdoctoral Rehabilitation Research Fellow at the University of Missouri, Columbia. Grateful acknowledgement is made to Oliver P. Kolstoe for his helpful suggestions in the writing of this paper.

"WARF: A Scale for Measuring Job-Readiness Behaviors," J.H. Bitter, D.J. Bolanovich, *American Journal of Mental Deficiency*, Vol. 74, No. 5, 1970. ©1970 American Journal of Mental Deficiency.

73

2. ASSESSMENT

TABLE 1

CORRELATIONS (BISERIAL) OF WARF RATINGS WITH JOB ADJUSTMENT CRITERIA

		Criterion			
		Job success		Pooled judgment	
Rater	N	3 Weeks	16 Weeks	3 Weeks	16 Weeks
Counselor A	26	.72**		.93**	
	19		.73**		1.00**
Counselor B	39	.43*		.47**	
	13		.51		.55
Counselor C	39	.76**		.77**	
Counselor D	13	.94**		.58	
	8		1.23**		.68
Foreman	39	.76**		.89**	
	40		.70**		.79**

Note.—The maximum value of a computed biserial correlation coefficient is 1.25 (DuBois, 1965).
* $p < .05$.
** $p < .01$.

one foreman. One additional counselor completed forms during the third week.

The mean age for the 40 clients was 17.41 years (17.40 and 17.42, respectively, for males and females) with a range of 15.92 to 19.83 years as determined upon entrance into the Center. The mean IQ from the Wechsler Adult Intelligence Scale or the Binet was 59.25 (58.83 and 59.71, respectively, for males and females) with a range of 39 to 84. Eight of the 40 clients were returnees from the 1964–65 school year.

Requirement 1: Systematic Observation

The WARF contains eight subscales, each having five items, making a total of 40 items. The subscales included are (a) Amount of Supervision Required, (b) Realism of Job Goals, (c) Teamwork, (d) Acceptance of Rules/Authority, (e) Work Tolerance, (f) Perseverance in Work, (g) Extent Client Seeks Assistance, and (h) Importance Attached to Job Training.

The WARF can be completed in 3 to 7 minutes depending on the rater. Scoring, using a key, takes approximately 5 minutes.

Each of these subscales is represented by items describing five different levels of performance from low to high. The following five items which represent the subscale "Amount of Supervision Required" are an example of this.

1. Client works with difficulty, even under constant supervision and after getting considerable training.

2. Client can work on his own after thorough training if his work is frequently observed and checked.

3. With training and direction, client can work independently under occasional supervision.

4. Once shown what he must do, client applies himself diligently without much supervision.

5. Client catches on easily and does his work with practically no supervision.

The items were selected a priori by the investigators on the basis of judgment. The

TABLE 2

INTERRATER RELIABILITY (PEARSON COEFFICIENTS) FOR WARF RATINGS AFTER 3 WEEKS (N SHOWN IN PARENTHESES)

	Rater		
Rater	Counselor B	Counselor C	Foreman
Counselor A	.78 (26)	.90 (26)	.98 (26)
Counselor B		.71 (39)	.67 (39)
Counselor C			.79 (39)

TABLE 3

MEAN WARF SCORES FOR VARIOUS OBSERVERS

Observer	Sample 1 ($N = 26$)	Sample 2 ($N = 39$)
Counselor A	23.85	—a
Counselor B	24.88	25.56
Counselor C	24.19	25.51
Foreman	17.19	16.54

a Not applicable.

items are rated by checking "yes" or "no" to each and they are scaled (Guttman, 1944) so that a positive response to an item at any level should also give a positive response to all items below that level. They are scrambled and the level and scale of items are not known by raters.

With these features, the WARF would seem to represent a systematic recording of observations.

Requirement 2: Relevance

The correlations between WARF scores and two criteria of job adjustment are given for four counselors and the workshop foreman in Table 1. The criteria for job adjustment were (*a*) pooled judgment of the same observers in ranking clients as to employability at the conclusion of a 36-week training program, and (*b*) actual record of employment obtained 2 years after the program. Success on the latter criterion was a minimum of 6 months of community employment. The pooled judgment of employability correlated .76 (phi) with the actual employment criteria.

These results show significant correlations (biserial) between WARF scores and both criteria of job adjustment for all observers. In fact, WARF observations made after just 3 weeks of the program were almost as predictive as those made after 16 weeks.

These results seem to support the basic contention that observable behaviors do occur before employment which are relevant to job adjustment after employment. They also seem to indicate that the WARF provides a basis for recording observations of such behaviors.

Requirement 3: Reliability of Observations

Two samples were available in which different observers rated the same clients on the WARF. The interrater correlations for various pairs of observers on these samples are given in Table 2. The pairs involve three counselors and the workshop foreman. The first sample of 26 clients is included in the 39-client sample.

Table 2 reflects fairly high interrater agreement ($r = .67$ to .98, product-moment coefficients) for all pairs of observers. Counselor B had the lowest correlations with other raters and tended to reduce the level of reliability achieved. These correlations appear high enough to suggest that the WARF has good interrater reliability.

As previously mentioned, interobserver correlations only reflect agreement in rank orders. They do not necessarily indicate agreement in absolute value or observer bias. The extent

of interobserver agreement in scale value is shown in Table 3. The mean WARF scores assigned by the three counselors and workshop foreman are for the same two sample groups used in Table 2.

In both samples, there were no significant differences in the means among counselors. However, there was a significant difference ($p < .01$; *t* test) in the mean score assigned by the workshop foreman and the nearest counselor in both samples, thus indicating that the foreman probably had a different point of reference.

These data indicate that observers generally agree well in observations recorded on the WARF, particularly in relation to rank order. There is enough difference among observers, however, to suggest that the WARF falls short in meeting the requirement for consistent agreement among observers in scale values. The subjective nature of WARF observations would make it exceedingly difficult to achieve ideal objectivity in scale values among different observers; however, its success in ranking would recommend its use.

Requirement 4: Identification of Behavior Patterns

Table 4 provides the pattern of correlations (phi coefficients) between the subscale observations on the WARF and the two criteria for Counselor A and the workshop foreman (these were the only two for whom sufficient data were available for this kind of comparison).

Both observers were able to make fairly consistent predictions from a differential analysis of client behaviors.

These patterns are difficult to interpret, and the data are not sufficient for conclusive analysis. However, they do suggest that the WARF shows potential as an instrument by which one can record observations of behavior in different areas which are meaningful in the development of the retardate toward job readiness.

One other analysis was made relative to behavior patterns. This concerned changes in job readiness behavior over a period of time. If the WARF were a good measure of job-readiness behaviors, then WARF observations made at different times during training should reflect progress. It should be possible to hypothesize that WARF scores would increase as clients develop and improve their behaviors. In this case, the WARF would act as the criterion measure of training achievement.

In this connection, Table 5 gives the means and standard deviations of WARF scores for four groups of clients for whom there were

TABLE 4

CORRELATIONS (PHI COEFFICIENTS) BETWEEN WARF SUBSCALE RATINGS AFTER 16 WEEKS AND
JOB ADJUSTMENT CRITERIA ($N = 19$)

| | Criterion | | | |
| | Job success | | Pooled judgment | |
Subscale	Counselor A	Foreman	Counselor A	Foreman
Amount of Supervision Required	.57	.51	.78	.58
Realism of Job Goals	.67	.52	.90	.63
Teamwork	.16	.50	.47	.53
Acceptance of Rules/Authority	.35	.10	.57	.15
Work Tolerance	.26	−.04	.48	−.04
Perseverance in Work	.60	.65	.81	.70
Extent Client Seeks Assistance	−.34	.46	−.34	.47
Importance Attached to Job Training	.69	.70	.47	.76

ratings after 3 and 16 weeks of training. The WARF scores changed significantly ($p < .05$; t test, one-sided) in the expected direction for three of the four observers, and insignificantly in the reverse direction for one observer. Also, the standard deviations tended to diminish with training in all samples. This is in the expected direction as training generally reduces variance by having a greater effect on those most deficient in the behaviors to be developed. This is especially true when the client group includes some who start at a level of achievement near the top of the criterion measure.

These results are not sufficiently comprehensive to provide the conclusive information needed for a sophisticated measure of job-readiness behaviors. They are presented here to illustrate the feasibility of identifying predictive behaviors in retardates through systematic objective observation.

To develop an instrument that meets all of the aforementioned requirements, it is necessary to exert greater effort in several directions.

1. More research needs to be done in defining the areas in which job-readiness behaviors occur. The WARF studies demonstrated that some areas of behavior are more fruitful than others in contributing to effective prediction of job adjustment. These help to give direction in identifying observable, predictive behaviors and patterns. Much more needs to be done in collecting data which will relate specific behaviors in these areas to job adjustment. Such efforts will give researchers a sound basis for constructing needed measures and applying the instruments to rehabilitation objectives.

2. Future efforts should be directed toward development of specific behavior descriptions which can be used for scaling of observations. The requirement for observer consistency in assigning scale values will always present problems so long as judgmental ratings form the basis for the instrument format. The WARF's "Guttman-type" scaling of yes or no questions probably gives better objectivity than graphic-type rating scales, but it still requires a subjective rating. Engineering of controlled situations in which behaviors can be repeatedly observed with standardized interpretation is also a possibility.

3. Once observer consistency is achieved, it is necessary that the measures of behavior be standardized. Also they should be subjected to studies of relationship to success in various job situations. Without observer con-

TABLE 5

MEANS AND STANDARD DEVIATIONS (SD) OF WARF RATINGS AFTER 3 WEEKS AND 16 WEEKS,
MEAN DIFFERENCES ($\overline{D}$), AND t VALUES

| Rater | N | After 3 weeks | | After 16 weeks | | $\overline{D}$ | t |
		Mean	SD	Mean	SD		
Counselor A	19	27.42	10.01	22.84	9.60	−4.58	−2.89
Counselor B	13	22.00	8.25	32.08	5.62	10.08	3.02**
Counselor D	8	29.00	6.94	31.63	5.95	2.63	2.42*
Foreman	39	16.54	10.63	20.82	6.60	4.28	3.81**

Note.—t computed for correlated means.
* $p < .05$.
** $p < .01$.

sistency neither standardization nor validity studies can have much practical application.

Summary and Conclusions

Measures of work-related behaviors which occur prior to employment and which are predictive of job adjustment after employment are needed. These are valuable as a basis for determining rehabilitation needs and for planning rehabilitation programs, including training, counseling, and job placement.

To be of maximum utility such measures must meet certain requirements. They must be easily used by observers to record behaviors in an objective and reliable manner. They must yield dependable relationships with accepted criteria of job adjustment, and they must provide information on behavior patterns which will help counselors to guide clients toward job adjustment.

There are indications from our analyses of the WARF and from the work of others (Gellman & Glaser, 1959; Jewish Vocational Service, 1964; Kolstoe, 1961; Peck & Stephens, 1964; Pinkard, Gilmore, Ricker, & Williams, 1963; Shafter, 1956; Warren, 1961) that behaviors in retardates which are predictive of job adjustment can be identified by counselors, workshop foremen, and perhaps teachers and others. These analyses also seem to indicate that these behaviors can be measured by means of client-rating devices. Good reliability and validity for these ratings can be demonstrated. They also yield helpful information on differential patterns of behavior as a basis for counseling and training.

However, most approaches in the development of job-readiness measures are deficient in several important respects: (a) They rely primarily on judgmental statements rather than verifiable behavior observations; (b) they are subject to interrater variations and, in turn, not subject to standardization or general interpretation; (c) they have not been sufficiently studied to provide a basis for relating patterns of measured behavior to rehabilitation needs.

The most important areas for needed research are in the identification of specific behaviors, attainment of observer consistency, and the development of normative information relative to predictive behaviors.

Assessment of the Physical Work Capacity of Institutionalized Mentally Retarded Males

A. Eugene Coleman
University of Texas at Austin

M. M. Ayoub
Texas Tech University

Dennis W. Friedrich
Texas Vocational Rehabilitation Department (San Angelo)

Educable and trainable mentally retarded males (*N* = 37) were examined for physical work capacity. Analysis of results indicated that the physical work capacity of the test population was 20 to 30 percent below that cited in the literature for nonretarded subjects of similar age and sex. Evidence also suggested that developmental and maintenance programs of physical fitness were required in order for mentally retarded persons to qualify for and maintain employment on most of the manual occupational tasks cited.

According to authorities in vocational rehabilitation and guidance (Cohen, 1960, 1963; Collman & Newlyn, 1956; Fraenkel, 1961; Wright, 1960; Greenblatt & Simon, Note 1), it is essential that the mentally retarded person be successful on his first employment position. Failure to match properly occupational capabilities to job requirements will precipitate failure which could lower the employee's feeling of worth and damage his outlook toward future employment and the attainment of occupational independence. While counselors (Michal-Smith, 1959; Warren, 1955) have devoted considerable attention to the task of matching the mental capabilities of mentally retarded persons to those required for the task, limited efforts have been made to match physical capabilities and requirements. Since the typical retarded employee most often is required to use motor rather than intellectual skills, his chances for success could be enhanced if the counselor were also able to match properly the physical requirements for the task to the physical capabilities of the employee (Nordgren, 1971; Nordgren & Blackstrom, 1971).

The purpose of this project was to serve as a pilot study to investigate the feasibility of generating a data bank on the physical work capacity of mentally retarded males. For purposes of this investigation, physical work capacity will be defined as the maximum level of metabolism (work) of which an individual is capable and will be expressed in terms of maximal oxygen uptake (l/minute and ml/kg/minute) and maximal work required to bring the heart rate to 170 beats per minute (kgm/170). It was anticipated that if the counselors could compare both the mental and physical capabilities of the retarded job applicant to those required for various physical tasks, they would be able to arrive at a better means of placement of mentally retarded persons on physical jobs.

On the basis of existing information related to the physical prowess of mentally retarded persons (Francis & Rarick, 1959; Howe, 1959; Stein, 1963), it is expected that the average physical work capacity of the mentally retarded population examined is less than that of nonretarded individuals of similar age and sex. If this expectation is verified, programs may need to be developed to improve physical work capacity of retarded persons and to help them delay the aging processes and enjoy occupational longevity.

Method

Subjects

The subjects were 37 mentally retarded males selected at random from the total

This investigation was funded by the Research and Training Center in Mental Retardation, Texas Tech University.

The authors would like to express gratitude to the residents and staff of the Lubbock State School for their assistance in this investigation.

"Assessment of the Physical Work Capacity of Institutionalized Mentally Retarded Males," A. Eugene Coleman, M.A. Ayoub, Dennis W. Friedrich, *American Journal of Mental Deficiency*, Vol. 80, No. 6, 1976, ©1976 American Journal of Mental Deficiency.

population of 16- to 25-year-old educable and trainable mentally retarded male residents of the Lubbock State School, Lubbock, Texas. All subjects were thoroughly screened, and only those free of physical and mental restrictions were selected. Each participant was engaged in a daily program that included dorm duties, vocational education, academic school, physical education, athletic training, dorm activities, and planned recreational activities. Due to the rural setting of the school, vocational education training for the majority of the students was horticulture-related.

Intelligence tests were administered to each resident prior to admission to the school and at 1-year intervals thereafter. For the purpose of this study, the most recent score on the Stanford-Binet Intelligence Scale was selected as the criterion IQ score for each participant (mean IQ = 48.56).

A narrative social history and scores on the Vineland Social Maturity Scale were obtained for each resident. These data, however, were not made available to the investigators. Principal anthropometric, physiological, and mental data for the test population are presented in Table 1.

Tests

All subjects were tested in a semirecumbent state, having had no strenuous exercise for 12 hours and no meals for 3 hours. Testing was performed in an air-conditioned clinic on the grounds of the school, with environmental conditions maintained at 70° farenheit and 50 percent relative humidity.

A modification of the Sjostrand (1947) technique was used for determining physical work capacity. After a 5-minute rest, each subject pedalled on a Monark bicycle ergometer for 4 minutes at a workload of 150 kgm per minute. Cadence provided by an electric metronome was used to ensure that the pedal frequency was maintained at 50 rpm. Upon completion of the 4-minute ride, the subject was exposed to an ergometer resistance increased to 300 kgm per minute. Following 4 minutes of pedalling at this resistance, the subject's ergometer resistance was increased 150 kgm (450 kgm) for an additional 4 minutes. At this point, the ergometer resistance was increased 150 rpm. The subject continued to pedal on the ergometer until his heart rate reached 150 beats per minute. The test was continuous, with no rest allowed between successive 4-minute rides.

Air volumes were monitored using a Max Planck respiration meter manufactured by Instrumentation Associates, Inc. Oxygen uptake was determined according to the metabolic techniques and procedure outlined by Consolazio, Johnson, and Pecora (1963). Heart rate was determined each minute from electrocardiogram (ECG) tracings. Heart rate and oxygen uptake measures recorded during the last minute of each 4-minute work interval were used as criterion scores. This procedure produced 3 to 6 pairs of heart rate and oxygen consumption points. Maximum oxygen uptake was determined by utilizing the essentially linear relationship between heart rate and oxygen consumption. Paired heart rate and oxygen consumption values recorded at each submaximal work level were plotted on the ordinate and abscissa, respectively. A linear extrapolation was then made to a heart rate of 170 beats per minute. The maximal oxygen uptake (VO_2 max) of the individual was predicted from the intersection of the heart rate 170 line and the line of least squares for the measured values.

Maximal work (kgm/170) was similarly extrapolated for each subject, utilizing the linear relationship between heart rate and work level (Sjostrand, 1947). This was determined for each subject by plotting the work load (kgm per minute) vs. the pulse rate (beats per minute). Heart rate and ergometer resistance values (kgm per minute) observed during the last minute of each 4-minute work interval served as criterion scores in the prediction process. The observed points were connected, and the work load where the line crossed the pulse-rate level of 170 was taken as the maximum working capacity (kgm/170). Although less accurate than direct measurement, these procedures yield high predictive accuracy while minimizing the discomfort and possible hazards attendant upon a maximum work load (Coleman, in press; Kasch, Phillips, Ross, Carter, & Boyer, 1966).

Results

The results of the data obtained in this investigation are presented in Tables 1 and 2 and Figure 1. In order to make comparisons between the results of this study and those reported by other investigators, the data have been expressed in terms of maximal oxygen uptake (1/minute and ml/kg/minute) and maximal work (kgm/170) and are presented in Table 1. In Table 2, these values are contrasted with those from previous studies in which subjects were nonretarded men 15 to 29 years of age. In Figure 1, the maximal physical work capacity for the test population is contrasted with the phys-

2. ASSESSMENT

TABLE 1

Means, Standard Deviations (SDs), and Ranges for the Anthropometric and Physiological Data of the Mentally Retarded Population ($N = 37$)

Characteristic	Mean	SD	Range
Age (in years)	18.60	± 2.70	16–24
Height (in cm)	164.70	± 14.32	153–171
Weight (in kg)	64.98	± 15.50	47–100
IQ[a]	48.56	± 8.86	33–70
$\dot{V}O_2$ (l/min)[b]	1.97	± .35	1.200–3.155
$\dot{V}O_2$ (ml/kg/min)[c]	31.68	± 7.51	22.89–45.83
Kgm/170 (kgm/min)[d]	754.05	± 46.48	200–1250

[a] Stanford-Binet Intelligence Scale.
[b] Maximal oxygen uptake.
[c] Maximal oxygen uptake in ml per kilogram of body weight per minute.
[d] Maximal work required to bring heart rate to 170 beats per minute.

TABLE 2

Physical Work Capacity Values of the Experimental Population vs. Nonretarded Populations

Reference	N	Age (in years)	Height (cm)	Wt (kg)	VO_2[a] (ml/kg/min)	Kgm/170[b] (kgm/min)	Test procedure
Present study	37	16–24	164.7	64.9	31.7	754.1	Bicycle
Adams, 1960	20	14–15	170.0	59.0		964.0	Bicycle
Alderman, 1969	19	15–16				948.0	Bicycle
Astrand, 1952	19	14–18	160.0	55.0	58.6		Bicycle
Astrand & Rhyming, 1954	44	20–29	176.7	70.4	58.6		Bicycle
Bailey, 1974	215	15–29	175.6	71.7	39.8		Bicycle
CAHPER, Note 2	171	16–17		64.7		865.2	Bicycle
Coleman & Jackson, Note 3	200	15–18	164.4	68.3	46.0		Field test
Cumming, 1963	15	16–30	175.5	72.0	53.2	968.0	Bicycle
Cumming, 1969	55	13–17	170.2	59.3	60.3		Bicycle
Dill et al., 1972	11	15–20	181.3	73.1	45.2		Treadmill
Ikia et al., 1971	77	15–20	165.5	65.6	45.1		Bicycle
Knuttgen, 1967	95	15–18	173.5	67.5	50.3		Bicycle
Matsui et al., 1972	194	14–18	166.1	55.7	49.2		Treadmill
Metz, 1970		14–15			53.3		Treadmill
Seliger & Zelenka, 1970	399	14–15	168.3	55.9	46.0	907.6	Bicycle
Shephard, 1966	190	16–29	170.0	59.2	47.9		Step test

[a] Maximal oxygen uptake in ml per kgm of body weight per minute.
[b] Maximal work required to bring heart rate to 170 beats per minute.

iological requirements of various manual tasks.

Physical work capacity scores of the test population were compared with those cited in the literature in order to determine whether or not the mentally retarded males examined in this study possessed work capacity scores equivalent to those of their nonretarded peers. Comparison of physical work capacity scores to job requirements should provide some insight into the ability of the test population to meet the physiological demands imposed by a variety of manual tasks. An attempt was made to select for comparison manual tasks which were representative of those for which mentally retarded males have been known to be employed.

Comparisons between different peer populations can be made only if it is noted that differences in testing procedures, samples, etc., may have influenced to some degree the discrepancies observed among the results obtained in the different investigations (Astrand & Rodahl, 1970). Subjects in the present investigation were institutionalized mentally retarded males tested on a submaximal bicycle ergometer test. Those cited for comparison were nonretarded males of similar age who were tested during maximal and/or submaximal performance on bicycle ergometer, treadmill, bench stepping, or distance running tests. In general, researchers with nonretarded persons as subjects have suggested that performance scores conducted on bicy-

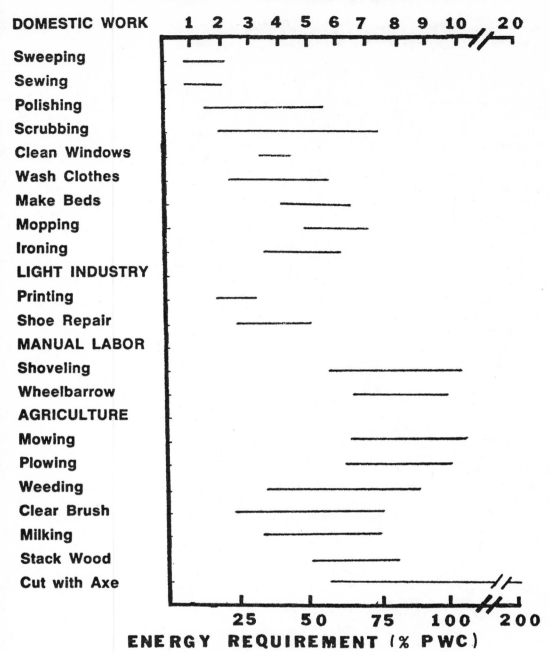

FIGURE 1. Energy requirements of various occupational tasks (data from Durin & Passmore, 1967). PWC = physical work capacity.

cle ergometers are slightly lower than those obtained on treadmills (Astrand & Rodahl, 1970). Likewise, submaximal tests tend to overestimate physical work capacity in poorly trained individuals and to underestimate physical work capacity in well-trained individuals (Astrand & Rodahl, 1970). Subjects in this investigation were considered active and had prior experience with bicycle riding.

Inspection of Table 2, in which physical work capacity values of the experimental population vs. the nonretarded population are presented, indicates that the physical work capacity of the mentally retarded male subjects was inferior to that of nonretarded subjects. Working capacities for the test subjects expressed in ml O_2/kg/minutes were 20 to 30 percent below those reported in comparable studies. Expressed in terms of kgm/minute, the average physical work capacity observed in the present study was 75 to 80 percent of that reported by other investigators.

2. ASSESSMENT

Figure 1 contrasts the average maximal physical work capacity value for the retarded subjects expressed in kilocalories (kcal) per minute with the requirements of various physical tasks. For purposes of this study, I assumed that one liter of oxygen corresponded to approximately 5 kcal per minute (Consolazio et al., 1963). Inspection of Figure 1 indicates that the typical retarded subject examined would have little difficulty performing tasks such as sewing, sweeping, and other forms of light domestic work. Prolonged effort on tasks such as scrubbing, shoveling, and agriculturally related tasks, however, would require that he utilize a greater percentage of his resources, i.e., work closer to his physiological maximum. Researchers in industrial situations (Durin & Passmore, 1967) have indicated that the average worker can perform a physical task for an 8-hour period with no undue fatigue or stress if he utilizes a work load equivalent to 50 percent of his aerobic capacity. The optimal 8-hour load for individuals with below average aerobic capacity values is less than 50 percent and directly related to the level of fitness (Astrand & Rodhal, 1970). Since the objective of most business enterprises is optimal productivity, the low-fitness individual must attempt to perform at a work level above that which is optimal for his capabilities in order to keep up or "do his share." Repeated performances at these levels could contribute to chronic physical and emotional fatigue which could eventually endanger his employment status. The retarded subjects in this study appeared to be in need of a vigorous physical conditioning program if they are to be successful in tasks similar to those identified in the literature.

According to information available for nonretarded subjects, a progressive decrease exists in man's physiological capabilities with the onset of advancing age and inactivity. While these decreases in physical prowess cannot be prevented or eliminated with regular activity, evidence does exist to indicate that the rate of decline can be delayed (Coleman & Burford, 1971). The experimental results of an investigation of two groups of nonretarded male adults, one active and one sedentary, indicated that active 40- and 50-year-old individuals possessed markedly higher physical work capacity values (ml/kg/minute) than their sedentary colleagues (Coleman, Burford, & Kreuzer, 1973). These individuals had a higher maximal energy expenditure level and could work at a similar load with less effort and have a greater reserve for later activity or could work at a higher load with

similar effort. The end result was that the conditioned individual was more productive.

Similar results have been observed for a population of retarded subjects (Nordgren, 1971), and several authorities have suggested that individuals with low physical work capacity levels would have difficulty performing most physical work tasks (Nordgren, 1971; Nordgren & Blackstrom, 1971; Rarick, Widdop, & Broadhead, 1970; Stein, 1966). These writers recommend regular participation in effective physical training programs as a means of helping ensure optimal work performance.

Historically, engineers have worked to match man and task so as to achieve optimal productivity (Passmore & Durin, 1955). This practice has been popular with both young and older employees and could involve moving an individual to a less demanding task or modifying the task so as to make it easier to perform. While these practices are commonplace in most "normal" work situations, their use for mentally retarded persons has been limited. Once the retarded worker finds a position for which he is suited, it is important that he retain it. Unlike the nonretarded worker, his tasks often cannot be modified nor is it easy to find another position for which he is ideally suited. If the retarded employee possesses a job for which he becomes physically unfit, he often becomes unemployed. We can neither economically nor socially afford to have segments of the population lose or jeopardize their occupational self-sufficiency, especially if it can be prevented or delayed.

The need does exist for organized physical development and maintenance programs for the retarded employee. Since these individuals often cannot afford to pay the membership fees required of private health or fitness clubs, they must find other sources. These services perhaps could be provided by concerned physical educators working with Human Development Centers, YMCAs, churches, schools, or interested civic groups.

Discussion

While the results of this investigation suggest that developmental fitness programs are needed in order for mentally retarded persons to qualify for most manual occupational tasks, they must be accepted in light of the following limitations. First, the sample population utilized was small ($N = 37$) and limited to the working males at one institution. There is a need to sample from other institutions and from populations of retarded individuals employed in jobs outside of institutional settings. Also, there should be a job analysis of specific work situations in which mentally retarded persons are employed. The energy costs utilized in this study were extracted from those cited in the literature and measured on nonretarded individuals. These tasks were selected because they could be performed by retarded workers. At present, no information exists as to the energy cost of specific tasks performed principally by retarded individuals.

While the procedure utilized in this study was successful, time and expense involved render it impractical for mass screening or office use by rehabilitation and placement officials. Attempts are being made to examine the feasibility of replacing the bicycle ergometer test with a step-test. This procedure is similar to that developed for the United States Forest Service (Note 4) and

involves the prediction of physical work capacity from recovery heart rate. While less accurate than direct methods, such a technique should be more feasible for office use and eliminate some of the problems attendant upon use of more sophisticated and expensive equipment (Kasch et al., 1966).

Reference Notes

1. Greenblatt, M., & Simon, B. *Rehabilitation of the mentally ill: Social and economic aspects* (Publication No. 58). Washington, DC: American Association for the Advancement of Science, 1959.
2. Canadian Association for Health, Physical Education, & Recreation. *The physical work capacity of Canadian children aged 7-17.* Edmonton, Alberta: Canadian Association for Health, Physical Education, & Recreation, 1966.
3. Coleman, A. E., & Jackson, A. S. *Texas Physical Fitness Motor Ability Test: Norms.* Austin: Governor's Commission on Physical Fitness, 1973.
4. U.S. Department of Agriculture/Forest Service. *Measuring physical fitness of forest service personnel.* Ft. Missoula, MT: U.S. Department of Agriculture/Forest Service, 1970.

A Vocational Assessment Battery For The Educable Mentally Retarded And Low Literate

Abstract: In developing a vocational assessment battery, attention was given to the special needs of the retarded: reading level, attention and interest span, following directions, time limitations and the need for format variety. Measures of intelligence, achievement, personality, aptitudes, and special abilities were included. Procedural steps are detailed for evaluating a group during a school day using cassette tapes, earphones and three trained evaluators. An immediate interpretation of the 16 Personality Factor Test is made through use of a programmable calculator. The final report, which includes an interview, places emphasis upon specific educational, vocational and behavioral recommendations useful to teachers and counselors.

CHARLES A. ALCORN *is Associate Professor of Education, North Carolina Central University, Durham.*

CHARLES L. NICHOLSON *is Professor of Education, North Carolina Central University, Durham.*

For the psychologist, vocational assessment of the mentally retarded and low literate individuals is particularly difficult because many general aptitude, personality, and other vocational assessment instruments are not applicable to these individuals. Low reading level, short attention and interest span, difficulty in following instruction and time limitations are some of the problems that plague the examiner who attempts to use assessment instruments not specifically designed for this group.

Limitations

Once aware of these limitations, it was the task of the authors to assemble a battery of assessment instruments which would yield data useful for making specific educational, vocational, and behavioral recommendations for the use of counselors and teachers. Indi-

viduals to be evaluated would qualify for the services of Vocational Rehabilitation because of some mental, physical, emotional, or other disability. An additional task was to assemble a battery, part of which could be used in a group testing situation. It was also necessary to organize the battery and necessary equipment so that it could be transported from place to place. In order to accomplish this, the authors had to take into account a number of factors related to validity of test results and administration procedures.

Validity and Test Administration

The principal difficulty is that most vocational assessment instruments have a reading level around the sixth grade, or higher, while the mentally retarded and low literate seldom read above the fourth grade level. As an example, a recent edition of the Kuder Vocational Interest Survey, Form E, reports a reading level of approximately fifth grade. The personal experience of one of the authors is that unless the individual has a reading level at the fifth grade, or higher, the results of the Kuder will be invalid, as indicated by the V Score, in about 50% of the cases. In another instance, instructions for the MMPI indicate that persons should have a reading level of at least the sixth grade. The authors examined the questions on the MMPI and, out of the total of 566 questions, found only 212 questions at the third grade level or lower. An additional 108 questions were at the fourth grade level. Even

"A Vocational Assessment Battery for the Educable Mentally Retarded and Low Literate," Charles L. Alcorn, Charles L. Nicholson, *Education and Training of the Mentally Retarded*, Vol. 10, No. 2, April 1975. ©Division on Mental Retardation of the Council for Exceptional Children.

when all 566 questions were presented orally to the client, many of the words were not comprehended.

Another problem involving many testing instruments is the time limitation. For example, the Differential Aptitude Tests have various timed sections. Again, the reading level is approximately the fifth or sixth grade. For the mentally retarded and low literate, the time limitation is just another obstacle that they must overcome in addition to the reading difficulty. Even when the retarded read at the fifth grade level, they frequently read at a slower pace than persons of average intelligence reading at that grade level; depressed scores are the result. The substitution of an oral presentation frequently does not benefit the low literate client, and in many cases the oral presentation is not practical. In addition, many instruments are standardized for timed presentation and with the subject reading his own material. Oral presentation thus violates the standardized procedure by setting a pace for item completion.

It has been the experience of the authors that short attention and interest span can invalidate test results of retarded individuals, as well as those of higher ability. Additionally, many retarded and low literate individuals approach the testing situation with a negative attitude because of past unpleasant experiences and frustrations with verbally-oriented tests. Length of testing session and number of different tests administered are factors to be carefully weighed. Through the use of a variety of tests, verbal and non-verbal, individually-administered and group-administered, paper-and-pencil tests and manipulative-type tests, attention and interest span can be somewhat controlled. Once these individuals learn that they are not required to read or do academic work on most of these instruments, they frequently develop a more positive and receptive attitude. Regardless of the task, it is essential that a trained evaluator work closely with those being evaluated, even in a group testing situation, to insure that directions are understood and consistently followed. Constant surveillance of the testing situation and periodic encouragement is often necessary.

Recommended Battery of Tests

The following battery of tests has been found useful and is presently being used by the authors in working with vocational rehabilitation counselors.

1. Wechsler Intelligence Scale for Children (or Wechsler Adult Intelligence Scale) — Verbal and Performance Scales of intelligence

2. Ravens Progressive Matrices (if time permits) — Nonverbal intelligence

3. Wide Range Achievement Test — Achievement in spelling, reading, and arithmetic

4. Bennett Mechanical Comprehension Test — Mechanical aptitude

5. Slosson Drawing Coordination Test — Visual Motor Perception

6. Differential Aptitude Tests:

   Clerical Speed and Accuracy — Routine clerical aptitude

7. Purdue Pegboard — Fine finger dexterity and assembly skills

8. Stromberg Test of Manual Dexterity — Gross arm dexterity

9. California Picture Interest Inventory — Vocational interest areas

10. 16 Personality Factor Test, Form E — Personality assessment with implications for educational, vocational, and personal adjustment

11. Bender Gestalt — Perceptual dysfunction and personality assessment

12. Minnesota Multiphasic Personality Inventory (to selected clients) — Personality assessment

2. ASSESSMENT

With the exception of the short oral reading test on the Wide Range Achievement Test (WRAT), the ability to read is not required. Directions, timing, and presentation of questions for a number of the tests have been recorded on cassette tapes. Other tests must be administered individually. Many of the instruments can be modified for administration without violation of the standardized procedure. For two tests, the 16 Personality Factor Test (16PF) and the Bennett Mechanical Comprehension Test (BMCT), commercial tapes are available from the test publishers. The spelling section of the WRAT, which is usually administered orally, can easily be taped, along with directions and control of time limits for the WRAT arithmetic section. This is also true for the Differential Aptitude Test: Clerical Speed and Accuracy (DAT: CS & A), which has standardized directions usually given orally, as well as a time limitation. It should be remembered that the tests described above may also be used with individuals of higher ability as well. In some instances, the person being evaluated will want to read the test question for himself without the use of the tape or he will want to follow along in the test booklet as he listens to questions presented on tape. The instruments for which directions and questions are taped do not require a high degree of training to administer and can be supervised by a competent individual with limited training in test administration.

Steps in Administration of Test Battery

In the administration of the tests, the authors have found from experience that eight to ten individuals is a feasible number to be evaluated in a school day. To accomplish this, three evaluators are required: two trained in individual testing (psychological examiner or practicing psychologist) and one trained for group administration of tests. The latter person can be easily trained in the administration of this battery since procedures are standardized.

The organization and administration of the battery of test in a school setting is accomplished through the following steps:

A. Initially, student clients are met as a group at which time the evaluators introduce themselves, and one of the evaluators explains the purpose of the evaluation and answers any questions students may have. A special effort is made to put students at ease with the following explanation:
"We are going to do a number of different things today: look at pictures, answer questions, work problems, and put pegs in holes. Except for a short reading word test, the ability to read is not required be-

cause we know that some people read well and some people do not read very well. We want to be fair with everyone, so most directions and questions have been recorded on cassette tapes. You can listen to them through earphones, if you like. Everyone has some things he can do better than other people. We want to find out what you can do best. This will help you and your counselor when you talk about getting along better in school and when you talk about what kind of job you can do best when you finish school. Some of the tests will be taken one at a time. Most of the time you will be working in a group. Do the very best you can."

At this time, polaroid pictures are taken; these will later be attached to reports which are sent to the vocational counselor. It is explained to students that this is to help us (the evaluators) remember names and faces. Each student is then furnished with a looseleaf notebook containing test booklets and answer sheets.

B. The group of eight or ten is arbitrarily divided into two subgroups. One group of four or five is seated around a table which is equipped with sets of earphones and a cassette tape recorder. Students listen to directions and mark answers as questions are presented. The 16PF, Form E, a personality test, which for most of the questions students pick statements that fit themselves best. This is followed by the BMCT, a mechanical aptitude test, also presented from a commercial tape. The WRAT spelling is presented next on a tape prepared by the authors. Level I is used because students of low ability typically have more success with this level. Next, the WRAT arithmetic is presented, with directions and timing included on tape. Again, most students of low ability prefer to work Level I, which begins with very simple problems that most can do. The last test on the tape is the DAT: CS & A, a short test of routine clerical speed and accuracy. As students begin each test, the group evaluator checks to make certain that all are following directions and are marking answer sheets properly. The group evaluator also spot checks and offers periodic encouragement.

At a nearby table, the other group of four or five will work with the group examiner on the Bender Gestalt, a test for identifying possible perceptual problems and also some personality characteristics, the WRAT oral reading test, and the PPB, all of which are administered individually. Students usually enjoy the Purdue Pegboard since manipulation of pegs and other parts is involved. Members of this group also take the California Picture Interest Inventory, a test of vocational interest areas, and the Slosson Drawing Coordination Test, a perceptual drawing test. If time permits, students do the Ravens Progressive Matrices, a nonverbal test of intelligence. These three tests are untimed. When necessary, the CPII is administered individually by the group examiner, especially if a client has a great deal of difficulty following directions or is very slow making responses.

C. From this group, students are taken one at a time for an interview and for individual administration of the **Wechsler Intelligence Scale**, which is a measure of general ability as well as a help in identifying possible perceptual problems. If administered before the Wechsler, the **Stromberg Test of Manual Dexterity** helps with the establishment of rapport between the examiner and the client. The Wechsler, of course, must be administered by a person especially trained in individual testing.

The tape runs about two hours, which is the time required for both groups to complete their respective tests. The groups are then switched so that by the end of the school day all students have taken both the individual and the group tests. A check sheet is used by the group examiner to make certain that all students have finished all tests. Brief rest periods are periodically given. Often the lunch break occurs near the mid point in the evaluation. The entire evaluation requires approximately four and one-half to five hours and can easily be accomplished within a school day.

Scoring Considerations

Scoring of most of the tests is accomplished through the use of hand scoring keys and manuals. The results of the 16PF are sent to the publisher for a printout interpretation. This is well worth the extra cost, as much information is provided in the area of personality, vocational predictions, behavioral characteristics, and treatment considerations. Form E should be used in conjunction with the tape presentation as the reading level of this form is approximately third grade. Utilizing the tape, the reading problem is further minimized. After one has used the printout of the 16PF over a period of time and has a library of statements from the 16PF, he can recognize values associated with statements and behavior characteristics. Many of the equation necessary for interpretation appear in the Handbook of the 16PF; others must be solved. A calculator which is programmable and which has a minimum of ten memories is needed for

these solutions. The authors use a portable Compucorp 142E calculator to furnish values for the 16PF interpretation. This immediate feedback is useful to counselors, as results may suggest that further behavioral evaluation is advisable. Depending on the client's reading level, the MMPI, or other instrument, may then be used.

Alternative Tests

From the battery which has been described, the psychologist has obtained a level of achievement, intelligence, dexterity, aptitude in two areas, vocational interests, as well as personality and adjustment information. Coupled with the interview and other available information from school records and the vocational counselor, this combined data can form the basis for meaningful recommendations. The above battery, however, is not without its limitations. Some of the instruments are poorly standardized, have somewhat complicated instructions and answer sheets, and other faults. Nor is the above battery complete. Other tests may be added or deleted, and other follow-up tests may be suggested by the results of this battery. In addition, work samples and work experience can be used. Two instruments not included in the present battery should be noted. The Wide Range Interest and Opinion Test, developed for the low literate and retarded consists of 150 pages, three pictures to a page. The client's task is to choose the picture of the work he would like to do and the work he would not like to do. This instrument contains pictures of both men and women, as well as both blacks and whites, in work situations. The scales and fields of interest are more complete than those for the CPII; however scoring this instrument by hand is not practical since a total of 22 keys is used. Machine scoring is available from the publisher. The authors have found that the retarded and low literate have some difficulty in taking this test and need to be very carefully supervised. If this is practical, the extra information is well worth the effort. The Jastak-King Work Sample is another instrument which provides valuable information concerning work aptitudes. The cost of this instrument is below the cost of many other work samples.

Reporting Test Results and Recommendations

Test data is then combined with information and impressions gained during the interview and is used as the basis for a written report. In addition to the basic identification of the client, the report consists of the following divisions: *Circumstances of Test, Objective Test Results, Summary of Test Results, and Recommendations.*

Under *Circumstances of Test*, the client's appearance, general attitude and manner (rapport, verbalization, assurance, mannerisms), ability to follow directions, and work habits as they apply to the Wechsler and other tests are noted. Information concerning home background, vocational aspirations, work experience, hobbies, school subjects liked and those disliked, as well as other pertinent information such as standardized test results and teacher or counselor comments is included.

On the page of *Objective Test Results* (mimeographed form), test data in the form of scaled scores, grade levels and percentiles is recorded. A *Summary of Test Results* follows. This includes the examiner's opinion of the client's mental ability, an interpretation of the Wechsler subtests, discussion of the possibility of a perceptual problem, as well as a narrative summary of test results. A printout of the 16PF (MMPI, when applicable) also appears in this section.

Recommendations are divided into three parts: Educational, Vocational, and Behavioral. Under Educational Recommendations, the client's achievement level in reading, spelling, and arithmetic is compared with the level expected of a person of his ability level. Depending on the nature and extent of his learning disability (low achievement, for example), remedial instruction, special education, or a basic occupational curriculum is recommended. The 16PF printout gives an indication whether this person can profit from further academic instruction, at his own level of abilities. Perceptual instruction may also be recommended. Vocational Recommendations are based upon the client's stated interests during the interview and upon results of the CPII, various dexterity tests, and aptitude tests. Predictions from the 16PF, which in-

clude such factors as accident-proneness, need for interpersonal isolation at work, likelihood of success in interpersonal areas, potential for leadership, dependability, and potential for growth to meet increasing job demands, are included. Behavioral Recommendations are based upon results of the 16PF, the Bender Gestalt, (MMPI or other test, in some cases), and upon school behavior reports furnished by the vocational counselor. Depending on anxiety level, acting out tendencies, behavior control, and self-concept, suggestions from the 16PF include such treatments as needed for a controlled environment, a graded series of success experiences to improve self-confidence, a structured active program to reduce anxiety, emotionally supporting situations, and emphasis upon plans and their execution.

Summary

In summary, the authors would like to emphasize the following points:

A. A carefully chosen battery of tests, administered within a school day, can provide useful data for making specific educational, vocational and behavioral recommendations.

B. Group administration of many of the tests is feasible with the use of cassette tapes and earphones.

C. Eight to ten clients is an ideal number for three evaluators (two trained in individually-administered tests and one trained in group-administered tests). The latter person can easily be trained in a short time since test procedures are standardized.

D. Immediate interpretation of the 16PF is possible through the use of a portable programmable calculator. Results may suggest the need for further behavioral evaluation.

VOCATIONAL BEHAVIORAL CHECKLISTS

Richard T. Walls

Thomas J. Werner

Authors: **RICHARD T. WALLS**, Ph.D., professor of educational psychology and research associate of the Rehabilitation Research and Training Center, West Virginia University, Morgantown, WV 26506; **THOMAS J. WERNER,** M.A., instructor of psychology, and doctoral candidate, West Virginia University.

ABSTRACT. Thirty-nine behavior checklists containing items (behavior descriptions) related to pre-vocational, vocational, occupational, and work behaviors were reviewed, categorized, and evaluated. The items were counted and categorized into eight subclasses of vocational behavior: prevocational skills, job-seeking skills, interview skills, job-related skills, union-financial-security skills, work performance skills, on-the-job social skills, and specific-job skills. Checklists were classified áccording to objectivity (degree of behavioral specificity), scope (number of items per subclass), observation setting, and prescriptive-descriptive nature. Strategies for selecting and utilizing vocational behavior checklists to facilitate training and assessment are discussed.

In many types of training programs there is a need for frequent assessment of client, student, or trainee skills in vocational or occupational areas.

Apart from casual or anecdotal observation, there have been two major types of formal observation tools: rating scales and behavior checklists. The primary emphasis of this report is direct observation of behaviors as represented by behavior checklists.

In an attempt to determine the number of behavior checklists available and in use, an advertisement was placed in several periodicals requesting, ". . . behavior checklists used in tabulating behaviors or skills" of various populations. The same request was sent to 883 state schools and rehabilitation facilities.

More than 200 checklists were received; they varied greatly in the extent to which they represented carefully specified and observable behaviors and in item formats and scoring requirements. Classes such as the following were represented: eating, toileting, dressing, health, grooming, communication, mobility, dexterity, vocational, recreational, socialization, orientation, motor skills, self-help, daily living, independence, alcohol and drug use, household responsibility, and work habits. Each of these classes included behaviors representative of that class. Details of 157 of them are reviewed in an annotated bibliography (Walls, Werner, Bacon, Zane, 1977).

As part of the continuing analysis of independent living skills and vocational behaviors, the authors reviewed and evaluated all items related to the assessment of vocational behavior. The goal was a comprehensive reference guide to the selection of vocational behavior checklists. While the same class was sometimes labeled "prevocational," "occupational," "job," or "work" behaviors, any items representing behaviors associated with employment are considered herein as "vocational."

Vocational items from each of 39 checklists were counted and sorted into eight subclasses. Descriptions of these subclasses and representative items follow.

Prevocational Skills include verbal behaviors related to job definitions, the client's job interests and job skills, as well as various prework skills. Item examples are (a) names jobs he could hold related to his own skills; (b) matches items by size; (c) names necessary tools required for specific jobs.

Job-Seeking Skills include searching skills leading to a job interview. Item examples are (a) reads newspaper to locate jobs or training; (b) fills out job applications; (c) determines job opportunities in the community.

Interview Skills include behaviors required during initial contacts with a potential employer. Item examples are (a) wears clothing suitable for the occasion; (b) gets to the appointment on time; (c) answers all questions.

Job-Related Skills include essential job behaviors that are not related to production, but rather to transportation to and from the job, work clothes, meals on the job, and orientation to work area. Item examples are (a) travels to and from work; (b) pays for lunches and transportation, making correct change, if required; (c) goes to each area in center when requested without getting lost or retracing his steps or entering 'off limits' areas.

2. ASSESSMENT

Union-Financial-Security Skills include all behaviors related to job and financial security. Item examples are (a) calculates wages for hours worked minus approximate deductions; (b) works out a simple budget and budgets paycheck; (c) knows the function of union picketing.

Work Performance Skills include the primary production and performance characteristics such as punctuality, tool and work station maintenance, work rate, evaluation of own performance, persistence, work quality, and safety. Item examples are (a) follows instructions when job involves three or more specific tasks; (b) assembles materials needed on which to work; (c) begins work and continues for thirty minutes.

On-the-Job Social Skills include appropriate interpersonal skills with both peers, customers, and supervisors. Item examples are (a) interacts with others during breaks or lunch; (b) offers assistance when someone he is working with needs help; (c) works to improve from criticism.

Specific-Job Skills include information and behaviors related to particular occupations. Item examples based on "sales" behaviors are (a) stocks shelves; (b) cleans stock; (c) wraps packages.

As noted, 39 of the behavior checklists contain vocational items. They vary widely with respect to scope, objectivity, setting, and prescriptive-descriptive nature.

Scope connotes two dimensions, (a) total number of vocational items and (b) number of different subclasses represented. Scope, as represented by number of items in each subclass, may be noted in Table 1. For example, the *Behavioral Characteristics Progression* and the *Eastmont Training Center Checklist* differ greatly with respect to scope. Although they both contain approximately the same total number of items (50 and 56 respectively), the distribution of those items among the eight subclasses is dissimilar. The *Behavioral Characteristics Progression* contains 3 items in Prevocational, 7 items in Job-Seeking, 2 items in Interview, 10 items in Job-Related, 10 items in Union-Financial-Security, 16 items in Work Performance, and 2 items in On-the-Job Social. In contrast, the *Eastmont Training Center Checklist* contains 53 items in Prevocational and 3 items in Work Performance. To illustrate the other connotation of scope, the total number of vocational items for the *Group Home Candidate Checklist* is 254, but for the *Track Profile* only 9 items.

Objectivity is another important variable in the consideration of vocational checklists. The objectivity of these checklists is also represented in Table 1. "Objectivity" refers to how observable (i.e., behavioral) the checklist items are. The checklists were evaluated independently by two trained reviewers. They assigned a value from 1 to 5 based on the following criteria: Rating 5 clearly specifies (a) observable behaviors, (b) standards of performance (rate or accuracy of response), and (c) conditions of performance (situation prior to response). Rating 4 indicates one of the above (a, b, or c) is poorly specified or omitted. Rating 3 indicates two of the above are poorly specified or omitted. Rating 2 indicates behaviors not observable (poorly defined but potentially specifiable), and the standards and con-

ditions are poorly specified or omitted. Rating 1 indicates the items are so vague and general that specification would be difficult or impossible, and the standards and conditions are poorly specified or omitted. When a rating difference of not more than one point on the five point scale was considered agreement, the agreement/agreement + disagreement index of interrater reliability was 0.974.

Objectivity also varies greatly among the vocational checklists. Items from the *Colorado Master Planning Guide for Instructional Objectives* specify (a) observable behaviors and (b) standards of performance. For example one item states, "Begins work at the beginning of the day and continues to work throughout the day, except for scheduled breaks." *North Central Regional Center Skill Evaluation and Assessment* items are behaviorally stated but do not include standards or conditions of performance; such an item is, "reads newspaper". Items that would not be readily specified objectively appear in the other scales. An example reads, "Enthusiasm towards work."

Specification of setting or place of observation is not usually included in a checklist or manual. Since items geared toward on-the-job settings may not be useful in prevocational or classroom training, (and *vice versa*), we have attempted to categorize items according to one of three settings (On-the-Job, Training Class, or Both). Some items illustrate an on-the-job or non-classroom setting. For example, the *Nebraska Client Progress System* contains the following item: "States prescribed policy for receiving paychecks, calling in sick, leaving work station at nonroutine times, etc." An item from the *Mid-Nebraska Competitive Employment Screening Test and Teaching Manual* illustrates a training class setting. It states, "Sees advantages to outside employment." Some items might be observed either on-the-job or in a training class. As an illustration, the *Adaptive Functioning Index #2* lists, "Works through small disruptions, e.g., phone rings, someone walks by." In Table 1, on-the-job settings are coded as OJ; training class settings are denoted by TC. B indicates that behaviors in the subclass may be observed in either setting or that both OJ and TC items are included in that subclass.

The only other descriptor included in Table 1 is an indication of whether the checklist is prescriptive (P), descriptive (D), or marginally prescriptive-descriptive (M). In a descriptive checklist, definition of an individual's current skill repertoire is the central concern. If a client "assembles two-part objects that fit together in a simple but secure way" (as indicated on the *Minnesota Developmental Programming System*), that action is known to exist in the client's vocational repertoire. If the client cannot perform the task, remedial training may be implied, but the training procedures are not specified. A prescriptive checklist goes further by describing the means for training the skill deficit. To illustrate, the *COMPET (Commonwealth Plan for Education and Training of Mentally Retarded Children)* not only describes whether the individual, "names necessary tools required for specific jobs," but then prescribes procedures for training the skill. It suggests that the trainer should "bring tools into classroom and discuss domestic and vocational use of each; provide

TABLE 1
VOCATIONAL BEHAVIOR CHECKLISTS[a] CLASSIFIED BY EIGHT SUBCLASSES, NUMBER OF ITEMS PER SUBCLASS, OBJECTIVITY,[a] SETTING,[c] AND PRESCRIPTIVE-DESCRIPTIVE NATURE[d]

Title	Prescr/Descr/Mar	Pre-vocational Skills #	S	Job-Seeking Skills #	S	Interview Skills #	S	Job-Related Skills #	S	Union, Financial & Sec. Skills #	S	Work Performance Skills #	S	On-The-Job Social Skills #	S	Specific-Job Skills #	S
Objectivity Range 4.0 – 5.0																	
Behavioral Char. Pgrsn.	M	3	TC	7	B	2	B	10	OJ	10	OJ	16	OJ	2	OJ	0	
Colorado Mast. Guide	M	0		4	OJ	5	OJ	4	OJ	6	OJ	45	OJ	8	OJ	6	OJ
COMPET	P	61	TC	2	TC	2	TC	8	TC	8	TC	0		0		98	TC
Higginsville Beh Scale	D	0		1	OJ	0		5	OJ	5	B	18	OJ	1	OJ	0	
Job Seeking Skills Ref. Manual	P	0		2	TC	13	TC	0		0		0		0		0	
Minnesota Dev. Pgm Sys.	D	13	TC	0		0		2	B	0		4	B	0		0	
Nebraska Client Pgs.	M	0		0		1	OJ	2	OJ	3	OJ	17	OJ	1	OJ	0	
Washington Assessment & Tr. Scale	D	7	TC	0		0		0		0		17	B	1	TC	0	
Objectivity Range 3.0 – 3.9																	
Adult Sv. Eval. Form	D	14	TC	0		0		0		0		1	OJ	0		0	
Beh. Profile Eval. Booklet	D	11	TC	1	OJ	1	OJ	2	B	15	B	9	B	0		0	
Camelot Beh. Check.	M	15	TC	1	OJ	1	OJ	2	OJ	4	OJ	10	OJ	4	OJ	0	
Eastmont Tr. Ctr. Checklist	D	53	B	0		0		0		0		3	B	0		0	
Household Act. Eval.	D	113	B	0		0		0		0		0		0		0	
W. A. Howe Ctr. Check.	D	16	TC	0		1	B	5	B	1	B	6	B	4	B	0	
Mat. Development Ctr. Beh. Identification	D	4	B	0		0		2	TC	0		26	B	12	B	0	
Mid-Nebraska Compet. Emp.	P	45	TC	3	TC	9	B	4	TC	5	TC	50	TC	10	TC	0	
NYU Voc. Status Indicators (Draft)	D	0		17	OJ	15	OJ	0		24	OJ	45	OJ	18	OJ	0	
North Central Skill Eval.	D	5	TC	7	OJ	7	OJ	7	B	0		5	B	4	B	0	
Roadmap to Eff. Teach.	D	89	TC	0		0		0		0		0		0		0	
Track Profile	D	8	TC	0		0		0		0		1	OJ	0		0	
Vineland Soc. Maturity	D	14	TC	0		0		0		0		2	OJ	0		0	

TABLE 1 (continued)

Title	Prescr/Descr/Mar	Pre-vocational Skills		Job-Seeking Skills		Interview Skills		Job-Related Skills		Union, Financial & Sec. Skills		Work Performance Skills		On-The-Job Social Skills		Specific-Job Skills	
		#	S	#	S	#	S	#	S	#	S	#	S	#	S	#	S
Objectivity Range 2.0–2.9																	
Adaptive Funct. Index#	D	10	TC	0		0		4	B	0		45	B	22	B	0	
Adult Perform. Scale	D	64	TC	0		0		0	OJ	1	OJ	16	B	3	B	0	
Class. Code for House Act.	D	0		2	B	1	B	5	B	3	B	8	B	0		7	B
Craig Ctr. Prog. Rpt.	D	14	TC	0		0		2	TC	1	OJ	6	B	0		0	
Fairview Social	D	13	TC	0		0		4	TC	0		13	B	0		0	
Group Home Candidate Check.	D	96	TC	37	B	14	B	19	B	49	B	21	B	18	B	0	
Life Skills for DD	M	37	TC	0		0		0		0		8	TC	0		0	
Obs. & Client Eval. Guide	D	6	TC	0		0		4	B	0		56	B	56	B	0	
Scale of Employability	D	15	B	5	OJ	7	OJ	7	OJ	1	OJ	45	OJ	18	OJ	0	
Selinsgrove (mild)	D	0		0		0		1	OJ	0		14	OJ	3	OJ	0	
T.M.R. Perform. Profile	D	2	TC	0		0		2	B	1	TC	3	B	2	B	0	
Voc. Behaviors Scale	D	3	TC	1	TC	4	B	2	B	3	B	8	B	5	B	0	
Work Beh. Rating Scale	D	0		0		0		0		0		10	B	3	B	0	
Objectivity Range 1.0–1.9																	
AAMD Adapt. Beh. Scale	D	3	TC	0		0		0		0		9	B	0		0	
Comprehensive Eval. Form	D	32	TC	0		0		6	B	0		36	B	17	B	0	
Porterville Eval. Form	D	0		0		0		3	OJ	0		12	OJ	9	OJ	0	
Tech Counselor's Evaluation	D	82	TC	0		0		4	TC	0		20	TC	14	TC	0	
Vocational Training Evaluation	D	5	TC	0		0		1	OJ	0		8	B	6	OJ	0	

[a] Checklists are listed alphabetically within objectivity ranges. Full names and sources are listed under Reference Notes.

[b] 1.0 Least Objective; 5.0 Most Objective, as described earlier in the present article.

[c] OJ =On-the-Job (non-classroom setting).   [d] P =Prescriptive.
TC=Training Class.   D =Descriptive.
B =Either setting *or* both OJ and TC items.   M=Marginally Prescriptive-Descriptive.

practice in actual use." Marginally prescriptive-descriptive refers to checklists that are extensively sequenced and suggest training, but do not specify explicit prescription. Only three were determined to be prescriptive, five were marginally prescriptive-descriptive and the remainder were descriptive (see Table 1).

The vocational checklist characteristics presented (scope, objectivity, setting, and prescriptive-descriptive nature) must be considered in relation to the needs of the checklist user. Different populations, facilities, training programs, and staffing patterns dictate different weightings among the characteristics. By any analysis, objectivity and scope are prime considerations. Ideally, both high objectivity and wide scope would be present in a given checklist. Unfortunately, no vocational behavior checklists reviewed fully meet these requirements.

One strategy might be to select subclasses from the higher objectivity checklists. If a sufficient number of items are not available in those subclasses of that checklist, then the user might broaden scope by selecting items from less objective checklists. For example, if clients in a training program need Job-Seeking Skills, trainers could begin by examining the seven items from the *Behavioral Characteristics Progression* (see Table 1). If a greater variety of Job-seeking behaviors is required, the trainers could then refer to the 37 items of the *Group Home Candidate Checklist*. Although these latter items are less objective, they provide increased scope.

The current state of vocational checklisting demands consideration of a trade-off between scope and objectivity. This trade-off is one of relative merits. Objectivity is crucial if reliable observation of behaviors is to occur. But a subclass with only two items, however objective, may be of little value in a comprehensive training effort.

Vocational behavior checklists are not training programs. The prime reason for use of checklists is careful assessment of individual competencies. They provide direction and may serve as either foundations for new training programs or adjuncts to revision of existing ones. First and foremost, they are behavior description and curriculum planning tools. Their potential usefulness will depend on an interaction of several factors (type of training program, clients' initial vocational behavior repertoire, training setting, scope and objectivity of the checklist used, and the capability of the checklist to provide prescription).

In the final analysis, the best measure of training program effectiveness is client progress in the acquisition of vocationally relevant skills. Careful specification and reliable observation of those relevant skills is central to effective training. Vocational behavior checklists are intended to be tools in that process.

Checklist References

All behavior checklists cited herein are listed in alphabetical order by checklist title to facilitate location. The authors are listed in parentheses following the title. The source from which we obtained the checklist is then noted.

AAMD Adaptive Behavior Scale (1974 revision). American Association on Mental Deficiency, 5201 Connecticut Avenue, N.W., Washington, DC 20015.

Adaptive Functioning Index #2. (Marlett). The Vocational and Rehabilitation Research Institute, 3304 33rd St., N.W., Calgary 44, Alberta, Canada.

Adult Performance Scale. Michael R. Dillon, Superintendent, Connecticut State Dept. of Health, Central Connecticut Regional Center, Box 853, Meriden, CT 06450.

Adult Service Treatment Team Resident Evaluation Form. John Campfield, Syracuse State School, P.O. Box 1035, Syracuse, NY 13201.

Behavior Profile Evaluation Booklet. Anna State Hospital, Developmental Disabilities Division, Anna, IL 62606.

Behavioral Characteristics Progression. VORT Corporation, P.O. Box 11132, Palo Alto, CA 94306.

Camelot Behavioral Checklist. (Foster). Camelot Behavioral Systems, P.O. Box 607, Parsons, KS 67357.

Classification Code for Household Activities. (Chapin). In *Human Activity Patterns in the City* by F. Stuart Chapin, Jr. Wiley-Interscience, John Wiley & Sons, 605 Third Avenue, New York, NY 10016.

Colorado Master Planning Guide for Instructional Objectives. (DD Master Planning Committee). Division of Developmental Disabilities, 4150 South Lowell, Denver, CO 80236

COMPET: Commonwealth Plan for Education and Training of Mentally Retarded Children. (PA Departments of Education and Public Welfare). Department of Education, Box 911, Harrisburg, PA. 17120

Comprehensive Evaluation Form. William R. Phelps, West Virginia Rehabilitation Center, Institute, WV 25112.

Craig Developmental Center Educational Progress Report. Craig Developmental Center, Sonyea, NY 14556.

Eastmont Training Center Checklists. Eastmont Training Center, Little Street, Glendive, MT 59330.

Fairview Social Skills Scale. (Giampiccolo). Research Department, Fairview State Hospital, 2501 Harbor Blvd., Costa Mesa, CA 92626.

Group Home Candidate Checklist. (Turnbull). Ann P. Turnbull, Dept. of Special Education, University of North Carolina, Chapel Hill, NC 27514.

Higginsville State School and Hospital Behavioral Scale. Higginsville State School and Hospital, P.O. Box 522, Higginsville, MO 64037.

Household Activities Performance Evaluation. (Phelps). William R. Phelps, Disabled Homemaker Program, Division of Vocational Rehabilitation, Charleston, WV 25305.

W. A. Howe Development Center Behavioral Checklist. R. J. Van Dyke, W. A. Howe Developmental Center, 7600 W. 183rd Street, Tinley Park, IL 60477.

Job Seeking Skills Reference Manual. (Prazak, Walter). Multi Resource Centers, Inc., 1900 Chicago Avenue, Minneapolis, MN 55404.

Life Skills for the Developmentally Disabled (Vol. III: Manual for Training Clients). Geneva Folsom, The George Washington University, Div. of Rehab. Medicine, 2300 Eye Street, N.W., Washington, DC 20037.

Materials Development Center Behavior Identification Form: MDC. Materials Development Center, Department of Rehabilitation and Manpower Services, University of Wisconsin-Stout, Menomonie, WI 54751.

Mid-Nebraska Competitive Employment Screening Test and Teaching Manual. (Schalock). Robert L. Schalock, Mid-Nebraska Mental Retardation Services, 518 East Side Blvd., Hastings, NE 68901.

Minnesota Developmental Programming System. (Bock, Hawkins, Jeyachandran, Tapper, Weatherman). Warren H. Bock, Outreach Training Program, 301 Health Service Bldg., St. Paul, MN 55108.

Nebraska Client Progress System. Special Education Section, Department of Education, Lincoln, NE 68508.

NYU Vocational Status Indicators (Experimental Draft). Margret Brown, Rehabilitation Indicators Project, N.Y.U. Medical Center, Institute of Rehabilitation Medicine, 400 East 34th Street, New York, NY 10016.

North Central Regional Center Skill Evaluation and Assessment. North Central Regional Center, 73 Rockwell Avenue, Bloomfield, CT 06002.

Observation and Client Evaluation Guide. Research

2. ASSESSMENT

Utilization Laboratory, Jewish Vocational Service, 1 South Franklin St., Chicago, IL 60606.

Porterville State Hospital Work Evaluation Form. Porterville State Hospital, P.O. Box 2000, Porterville, CA 93257.

Roadmap to Effective Teaching. Monterey County Office of Education, Special Education Department, P.O. Box 851, Salinas, CA 93901.

Scale of Employability. (Original version). Research Utilization Laboratory, Jewish Vocational Service, 1 South Franklin St., Chicago, IL 60606.

Selinsgrove State School and Hospital Resident Rating Scale for Mildly Retarded. Selinsgrove State School and Hospital, Selinsgrove, PA 17870.

T.M.R. Performance Profile for the Severely and Moderately Retarded. (DiNola, Kaminsky, Sternfeld). Educational Performance Associates, 563 Westview Avenue, Ridgefield, NJ 07657.

Technical Counselor's Evaluation Form. William R. Phelps, West Virginia Rehabilitation Center, Institute, WV 25112.

Track Profile. State of Oregon, Mental Health Division, Salem, OR 97310.

Vineland Social Maturity Scale. (Doll). American Guidance Service, Inc., Publishers' Building, Circle Pines, MN 55014.

Vocational Behaviors Scale. (Krantz). Gordon Krantz, Ph.D. Dept. of Educational Administration, 225 Health Services Bldg., University of Minnesota, St. Paul, MN 55108.

Vocational Training Evaluation. Central Connecticut Regional Center, Undercliff Road, Box 853, Meriden, CT 06450.

Washington Assessment and Training Scales: WATS. Dr. Sandra Belcher, Fircrest School, 15230-15th Ave., N.E., Seattle, WA 93155.

Work Behavior Rating Scale. Exceptional Children's Foundation, 2225 West Adams Blvd., Los Angeles, CA 90018.

References

Walls, R. T., Werner, T. J., Bacon, A., & Zane, T. Behavior checklists. In R. P. Hawkins & J. D. Cone (Eds.), *Behavioral assessment: New directions in clinical psychology.* New York: Brunner-Mazel, 1977.

VOCATIONAL CHOICES: AN INVENTORY APPROACH

Abstract: A representative sample of educable mentally retarded males and females in public secondary day schools and state residential institutions participated in standardizing the Reading-Free Vocational Interest Inventory, *a recently devised nonreading method to measure vocational likes and dislikes. Separate norms tables were prepared for males and females to convert raw scores on each interest scale to standard scores and equivalent percentile ranks. Test-retest reliability on subsamples were highly satisfactory. Validity coefficients obtained with concurrent testing were encouraging with many values significant at high levels of confidence. Predictive validity is yet to be established as well as needed research with populations other than the mentally retarded.*

RALPH L. BECKER

RALPH L. BECKER *is Research Psychologist, Ohio Department of Mental Health and Mental Retardation, Division of Mental Retardation and Developmental Disabilities, Columbus, Ohio.* The research reported herein was performed pursuant to a grant from the US office of Education, Department of Health, Education, and Welfare, Project No. 452227, Grant No. OEG-0-8-080188-4421 (607). (Because of the recent submission of the Reading–Free Vocational Interest Inventory to test publishers, the author is unable, at this point in time, to give interested educators a date for marketing of the Inventory. Other inquiries may be directed in care of the author at the Columbus State Institute, 1601 West Broad Street, Columbus, Ohio 43223.)

Interests have been the object of much attention from vocational and counseling personnel during the past generation. At least two scholarly books (Strong, 1943; Darley & Hagenah, 1955), a collection of eight significant monographs (Super, 1940; Darley, 1941; Carter, 1944; Barnett, 1952; Brogden, 1952; Guilford, 1954; Strong, 1955; Layton, 1960), and a number of published reviews in the journals (Berdie, 1944; Super, 1945, 1954; Roe, 1957), all dealing with the nature and role of interest are the result.

Implicit in these and other vocational studies by research personnel is the definite positive relation between inventoried interests and job satisfaction. The results indicate that the person who enters an occupation consistent with his interests is more likely to be a satisfied worker than the person who does not. Moreover, in assessing a person's interest the accumulated evidence shows that expressed interests have somewhat less permanence than inventoried interests—inventoried interests, on the other hand, are more stable and provide useful data for prediction (DiMichael & Dabelstein, 1947; Nunnally, 1959; Cronbach, 1960; Craven, 1961).

The review of relevant literature in the field of vocational measurement over the past 30 years clearly indicates: (a) the interest dimension may be critical to job satisfaction and adjustment; and (b) inventoried assessment of a person's vocational likes and dislikes are more permanent and stable than expressed interest. These findings by researchers were obtained from studies dealing with high school, post high school, and college students of normal intelligence aiming at the middle through the upper range of the occupational hierarchy. Attempts to measure vocational preference in the educable mentally retarded using the inventory method has generally not proven fruitful. This has been largely a matter of the inappropriateness of inventories requiring a level of reading comprehension beyond that achieved by a large proportion of mentally retarded persons; or unrealistic occupations for which the mentally retarded could not genuinely aspire.

In view of the value of the interest dimension as a positive component of job satisfaction and adjustment, the present project was undertaken to prepare an inventory that would: (a) assess the vocational choice of educable mentally retarded subjects in occupations in which they are proficient and productive; (b) have acceptable reliability for retarded persons in different types of training facilities; and (c) have acceptable correlates of validity.

Method

Based on the results of a pilot study (Becker, 1967; Becker & Ferguson, 1969), an extensive review of vocational literature dealing with the mentally retarded was made. Jobs demonstrating productive and proficient performance were analyzed for possible sorting of similar job tasks (i.e., sweeping, mopping, and dusting; serving, waiting tables, and preparing salads) into clusters that would be independent and mutually exclusive categories of known task activities performed by mentally retarded workers. The success of the sorting process and confirmed by extensive item analyses (Becker, 1971), resulted in 11 male clusters and 8 female clusters and they were as follows:

Males. Automotive, Building Trades, Clerical, Animal Care, Food Service, Patient Care, Horticulture, Janitorial, Personal Service, Laundry Service, and Materials Handling.

Females. Laundry Service, Light Industrial, Clerical, Personal Service, Food Service, Patient Care, Horticulture, and Housekeeping.

Clusters consisted of 15 pictorial items each with all illustrations depicting different occupational activities as reported in the literature. For males, 165 activities were illustrated and for females an additional 120 illustrations were prepared. All illustrations consisted of clean, bold, line drawings, and free of fine detail and figure—ground problems of perception. In addition,

pertinent occupational hardware and environment were included in the illustrations (see Figure 1).

For purposes of administering the inventory, pictorial items were grouped by

FIGURE 1. Sample of pictorial items presented in triad form by sex.

threes (triad) for a total of 55 triads in the male inventory and 40 triads in the female inventory. For each of the male and female forms, pages were bound into 8½" by 11" test booklets including a cover page of instructions and the purpose of the inventory. Examinees were administered the inventory for self estimates using a forced-choice technique, that is, given three alternative choices, subjects are instructed to select one item on a "like best" basis though all three may seem equally attractive or unattractive to them. Selections may be made directly in the test booklet by making a circle on the desired drawing, or scoring an answer sheet form that identifies each item in each triad. Items are keyed to arrive at raw score totals in each interest cluster. Depending on the agency type, public day school, or residential institution examinees' raw scores were converted to normalized standard scores (T score) and percentile ranks using the appropriate agency norm.

To record a subject's performance on the interest scales, an individual profile sheet was prepared for permanent keeping in the subject's school folder. A feature of the profile sheet is a percentile graph whereby a subject's rank in each of the interest scales is plotted for a visual chart of high and low interests.

To meet the demands of representative sampling in preparing the norms, a sample of 6,400 educable mentally retarded subjects from all geographical regions of the United States and from urban, rural, and inner city divisions were included. The strategy was contingent upon obtaining similar proportions of the regional distribution of the standardization sample with regional distribution of actual enrollment in public secondary day schools for the school year 1969-70. A discussion of the comparison study and efforts to obtain regional and institutional proportions were reported in a previous investigation (Becker, 1971).

Findings

Inventory Reliability

The reliability of the inventory was reported for four educable mentally retarded groups: public day school and institutionalized males, and public day school and institutionalized females. Subsamples from the standardization study were administered the inventory and retested after a 2 week interval. The Pearson product-moment method was used to compute the correlations.

Table 1 presents reliability coefficients for each interest scale (cluster) by agency type for subsamples of males. Table 2 presents reliability coefficients on subsamples of females.

TABLE 1

Test-Retest Correlations of the Interest Scales for a Subsample of Males: Public Day Schools Grades 9-12, and Ungraded Institutions

| | Test-retest reliability* | |
| | Public day schools (N=143) | Institutions (N=50) |
Interest scales		
Automotive	.91	.94
Building trades	.86	.89
Clerical	.79	.80
Animal care	.89	.94
Food service	.83	.88
Patient care	.87	.89
Horticulture	.84	.89
Janitorial	.86	.85
Personal service	.88	.83
Laundry service	.75	.74
Materials handling	.73	.82

*Interval of 2 weeks.

TABLE 2

Test-Retest Correlations of the Interest Scales for a Subsample of Females: Public Day Schools Grades 9-12, and Ungraded Institutions

| | Test-retest reliability* | |
| | Public day schools (N=90) | Institutions (N=45) |
Interest scales		
Laundry service	.72	.89
Light industrial	.73	.87
Clerical	.68	.85
Personal service	.80	.78
Food service	.78	.65
Patient care	.85	.88
Horticulture	.87	.89
Housekeeping	.86	.85

*Interval of 2 weeks.

Correlations were mainly in the 70's and 80's for subsamples of males and at high levels of statistical significance. Coefficients ranged from .73 to .91 in public day schools, and .74 to .94 in residential institutions. Correlations of institutionalized males were generally higher than their counterparts in public schools, indicating greater reliability of the scores. Since the institution sample averaged 2 years, 5 months older (mean CA, 19-10), the higher reliabilities could be explained, as experience has shown, by the more mature group being the more stable and thus illustrating the expected higher correlations. Group mean IQ's were not significantly different with the larger value observed in the public school sample (public school IQ, 69; institution IQ, 62).

Correlations in Table 2 for subsamples of females were mainly in the 70's and 80's and at high levels of statistical significance. Coefficients range from .68 to .87 in public day schools, and .65 to .89 in residential facilities. Institutionalized females obtained generally higher test-retest coefficients indicating greater reliability of the scores for the more mature group of girls (mean institution CA, 20-0; mean public school CA, 17-4). Group mean IQ's were not significantly different with the larger value observed in the public school sample (public school IQ, 68; institution IQ, 62).

Inventory Validity

Validity of the inventory was obtained with concurrent testing using the research instrument and a standardized vocational preference inventory. The *Geist Picture Interest Inventory* (GPII) was selected since it contains male and female forms (Geist, 1964) and may be administered as a group test. A random sample of subjects who were involved in the collection of test-retest data on reliability, were also administered the GPII at the initial testing for correlates on concurrent validity. Correlations were computed between the raw scores of the research instrument, the *Reading-Free Vocational Interest Inventory* (R-FVII), and raw scores of the GPII. Coefficients of correlation were computed when the interest scales, by inspection, appeared to be positively related. To interpret the relationship between the two instruments, a brief description of each of the selected inventory scales is worthwhile.

R-FVII

Automotive. Enjoys servicing and repairing all types of vehicles.

2. ASSESSMENT

Building Trades. Enjoys using small and large hand tools or heavy equipment in construction work.

Clerical. Enjoys general office work; delivers mail or messages.

Animal Care. Enjoys tending domestic animals and pets.

Food Service. Enjoys preparing or serving food to guests and patrons.

Patient Care. Enjoys assisting patients in hospitals or clinics.

Horticulture. Enjoys greenhouse, gardening, and dirt farming activities.

Janitorial (Housekeeping-Females). Enjoys performing light maintenance and house-keeping services.

Personal Service. Enjoys providing a wide variety of services to guests or patrons.

Materials Handling. Enjoys general warehouse and delivery work.

Light Industrial. Enjoys using small hand tools in assembly or factory-type work.

GPII

Persuasive. Enjoys dealing with people, selling and promotion work.

Clerical. Enjoys keeping records, accounts, correspondence, and office work.

Mechanical. Enjoys exercise of manual skills; working with tools or machines.

Scientific. Enjoys field and laboratory sciences dealing with things and people.

Outdoor. Enjoys a variety of outdoor or open-air activities.

Literary. Enjoys reading; may enjoy writing.

Computational. Enjoys numerical activities; computing, counting, figuring, or keeping numerical records.

Social Service. Enjoys helping others; assists the sick, destitute, or unfortunate.

Personal Service. Enjoys providing services to people.

Table 3 presents correlations between selected scales of the GPII and R-FVII for samples of educable mentally retarded males in public day schools (mean CA, 17-7; mean IQ, 68) and state institutions (mean CA, 19-6; mean IQ 61). Inspection of the 30 coefficients shows the Materials Handling versus Computational scales to be the only relationship that is not statistically significant in either agency sample. All other correlations show at least one agency in each relationship at the .05 or .01 levels of confidence and beyond.

Differences in the magnitude of the coefficients between agencies on the same paired scales may suggest group differences in the educational and vocational training, work experience, and background of the sampled subjects, as well as differences in the way pictorial items are perceived on the two inventories. In general, correlations are very satisfying with many significant at the .01 level and beyond and with few low positive values. Most coefficients are in the 30's and 40's and although modest, reach levels of statistical confidence.

Table 4 presents correlations between selected scales of the GPII and R-FVII for public day school (mean CA, 17-6; mean IQ, 67) and institutionalized (mean CA, 19-8; mean IQ, 62) educable mentally retarded females. Inspection of the 30 coefficients shows three pairs of relationships not statistically significant in either agency sample. These are the Clerical versus Clerical, Horticulture versus Outdoor, and Personal Service versus Personal Service scales. All other correlations show at least one agency in each relationship at the .05 or .01 levels of confidence and beyond.

Differences in the magnitude of the coefficients between agencies on the same paired scales suggests there may be real group differences between the two samples for such characteristics as educational and vocational background, training, and work experience, and in the perception of a wide range of pictorial items having occupational significance. Correlations are generally satisfying with many significant at the .01 level and beyond. Most coefficients are in the 30's and 40's and reach levels of statistical confidence. In most cases, a low positive value in one agency sample is balanced by a high positive value in the second agency for the same relationship.

Job Trainee Profiles

In the process of collecting standardization data in local public day schools and state institutions in Ohio, work-study coordinators suggested that the project staff examiner obtain verbal data on subjects' vocational likes and a comparison be made

TABLE 3

Product-Moment Correlations Between Scales of the GPII
and Reading-Free Vocational Interest Inventory
(R-FVII) for Samples of Males

| R-FVII scales | GPII scales | Correlations | |
		Public day schools (N=38)	Institutions (N=38)
Automotive	Mechanical	.36*	.29
Building trades	Mechanical	.71**	.53**.
Clerical	Clerical	.35*	.35*
Clerical	Literary	.21	.50**
Clerical	Computational	.40*	.39*
Clerical	Persuasive	.22	.35*
Animal care	Outdoor	.28	.46**
Food service	Persuasive	.49**	.17
Patient care	Social service	.55**	.37*
Patient care	Scientific	.47**	.35*
Horticulture	Mechanical	.35*	.28
Horticulture	Outdoor	.50**	.47**
Janitorial	Mechanical	.17	.37*
Personal service	Social service	.26	.46**
Materials handling	Computational	.16	.16

*Significant at the .05 level.
**Significant at the .01 level.

TABLE 4

Product-Moment Correlations Between Scales of the GPII
and Reading-Free Vocational Interest Inventory
(R-FVII) for Samples of Females

| R-FVII scales | GPII scales | Correlations | |
		Public day schools (N=38)	Institutions (N=40)
Light industrial	Mechanical	.39*	.32*
Clerical	Clerical	.29	.25
Clerical	Literary	.48**	.09
Clerical	Computational	.42**	.12
Clerical	Persuasive	.40*	.26
Personal service	Personal service	.14	.19
Personal service	Social service	.26	.46**
Food service	Personal service	.42**	.38*
Food service	Persuasive	.06	.37*
Food service	Clerical	.41**	.46**
Patient care	Scientific	.78**	.59**
Patient care	Social service	.67**	.75**
Horticulture	Outdoor	.12	.18
Horticulture	Mechanical	.39*	.10
Housekeeping	Mechanical	.48**	.29

*Significant at the .05 level.
**Significant at the .01 level.

99

between expressed and inventoried results.

Within the limits of a working schedule, a total of 10 subjects were interviewed by the same project examiner for their vocational likes. Each subject was asked to name three kinds of jobs or types-of-work that he liked to do. They were cautioned to name as first, the work or job they liked best; to name as second, the work or job they liked next best; and to name as third, the job they liked to do but not as much as their first and second choices.

Of the 10 subjects for whom both interviews and inventory scores were obtained, data on four cases is presented as generally typical of the findings for the two kinds of information. Figures 2 and 3 present profiles of 2 males and 2 females, respectively, with a male and female, each, from work-study and vocational training programs in public secondary day schools and residential state institutions.

Subject 1. John is a 23 year old resident at a state institution for the mentally retarded. His IQ is 58 and he has attended the academic, prevocational and vocational training programs at the institution. For the last 3 years he has been the full time mail boy at this facility. John expressed his preference for a variety of job tasks including:

First: "Hospital work, mostly."
Second: "Mail boy."
Third: "Work in a theatre and shine a flashlight to show people where to sit; and help people in a motel and carry packages."

John was insistent in adding that he wants "no kitchen work and no maintenance work like fixing lights." (Note John's performance on the BTr and FS scales in Figure 2.)

Figure 2 presents John's inventoried profile on the 11 vocational interest scales. Inspection of his profile reveals a cluster of three interest areas with percentile ranks (PRs) of 95 and 98. The Personal Service (PSv) area ranks as his first choice (PR 98), with Patient Care (PCr, PR 95) and Clerical (Cl, PR 95) tied for second, for three areas of highest measured interest. The Laundry Service scale (Ly, PR 70) might be an alternative position for job entry if highest interest areas were closed out in the institution.

There is substantial agreement between John's stated interests and his measured interests. Though he expresses preference to work in a hospital, his measured interest shows a first choice in the Personal Service category with Patient Care in a very strong

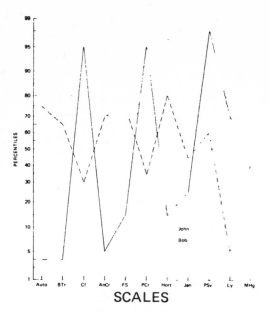

FIGURE 2. Job trainee profiles of male institutional and public day school workers.

second position. As a working mail boy, the Clerical scale in a second position tends to confirm John's positive feelings about his job when confronted with many other vocational activities. John's interest in working in a theatre or motel to assist patrons and guests as his third verbal choice, was his first measured choice in the Personal Service category.

Subject 2. Bob is an 18 year old special education student enrolled in the 11th grade at a public high school. His IQ is 75 and he has attended special classes for the educable retarded since the fourth grade. He is presently participating in the work-study curriculum for juniors. Bob indicated the following are the work activities he would like most to do:

First: "Remove trees and tree stumps."
Second: "Probably work on cars and repair them."
Third: "Get a job doing carpentry work—I like to work outside."

Figure 2 presents Bob's inventoried profile on the 11 vocational interest scales. Inspection of Bob's performance indicates that most scales are moderately above and below the median (PR 50). The Horticulture scale (Hort, PR 80) and Bob's verbal first choice along with the Automotive (Auto, PR 75) and Food Service (FS, PR 75) scales, are three areas of highest measured interest. Bob's verbal desire to "work on cars" appears to be borne out by his preference for automotive activities when faced with many alternative choices. The expressed interest in carpentry was only moderately borne out by measurement as indicated by the Building Trades scale (BTr, PR 65). Although the expected relationship did not occur, the fact that the Food Service scale did emerge as an interest area does identify a potential work field for exploration leading to job entry.

Subject 3. Judith is a 21 year old resident at a state institution for the mentally retarded. She was admitted at the age of 14 and has since attended programs in education and vocational training within the facility. On a recent intelligence test she earned an IQ of 64. Judith is presently working in the employee's cafeteria and is being considered for transfer to the commissary. She expressed vocational preference for the following types of work:

First: "I like to be a waitress."
Second: "Factory work; do rubber work like making rubber gloves or balloons."
Third: "Do laundry work."

Figure 3 presents Judith's inventoried

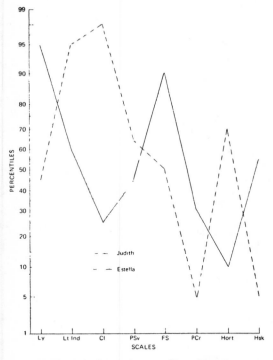

FIGURE 3. Job trainee profiles of female institutional and public day school workers.

profile on the eight vocational interest scales. Inspection of her profile indicates two scales with high measured interest: Laundry Service (Ly, PR 95) in the first position and Judith's third verbal choice, and Food Service (FS, PR 90) in a second position and her first expressed choice. Her verbal preference for "factory work" was only modestly borne out by measurement

on the Light Industrial scale (Lt-Ind, PR 60). Judith's measured interest was also her expressed interest although a difference in the rank order of job preferences did result.

Subject 4. Estella is a 19 year old student enrolled in special classes for the mentally retarded at a public high school. Her recent IQ was 62. She is completing her senior year in the educable mentally retarded program while working full-time in the school office as a clerical trainee. Estella gave as her vocational preferences the following activities:

First: "Be a secretary and work in a office."
Second: "Make things—do reupholstery work, sew, things like that."
Third: "Be a waitress in a cafeteria."

Figure 3 presents Estella's inventoried profile on the eight interest scales. Inspection of this profile demonstrates a wide scattering of values of extremely high and low interests coupled with average to near-average interests. The Clerical scale (Cl, PR 98) as her first measured interest, was also her first expressed interest. Of the 16 pictorial items keyed to the Clerical scale, Estella chose 15 clerical activities in discriminating the wide range of different job tasks. The Light Industrial scale (Lt–Ind, PR 95) as her second measured interest, was also her second verbal interest. Estella's expressed preference to "be a waitress in a cafeteria" was not borne out by measurement. The Food Service scale (FS) obtained a PR of 50, below the third position Horticulture (Hort, PR 70) and fourth position Personal Service scale (PSv, PR 65). Though the expected relationship did not occur, work sampling opportunities in both food service and horticulture would tend to confirm the preference of one job type over the other.

Summary

The present project was undertaken to develop a nonreading method of assessing vocational preference in educable mentally retarded youth enrolled in public secondary day schools and state residential facilities. Areas of commerce and industry in which retarded workers demonstrated proficiency and productivity were analyzed by job tasks and resulted in 11 male and 8 female interest categories. Extensive item analyses and subsequent reliability and validity studies established test-retest reliability of the scores and concurrent validity of the interest scales. Individual inventoried profiles of educable retarded job trainees were analyzed against present job status and expressed interest.

2. ASSESSMENT

The results showed high agreement among the three variables while identifying emerging inventoried interests for potential job entry.

Future use of the scales will require long term studies on predictive validity to establish some confidence in the predictive quality of the tool in making guidance recommendations to clients. Studies dealing with populations other than the educable mentally retarded, such as the trainable mentally retarded, the disadvantaged, the illiterate, and those with reading problems would determine the feasibility of this type of design in counseling and guidance of verbally handicapped persons.

References

Barnett, G.J., Handelsman, I., Stewart, L.H., & Super, D.E. The occupational level scale as a measure of drive. *Psychological Monographs*, 1952, 342.

Becker, R.L. *Vocational Picture Interest Inventory.* Columbus, Ohio: Columbus State Institute, 1967.

Becker, R.L. *Reading-free Vocational Interst Inventory.* Final Report. US Office of Education, Research Project No. 452227, Grant No. OEG-0-8-080188-4421, 1971. (Mimeo)

Becker, R.L. *Reading-free Vocational Interest Inventory:* Measurement of job preference in the EMR. *Mental Retardation*, 1973, **11**, 11-15.

Becker, R.L., & Ferguson, R.E. A *Vocational Picture Interest Inventory* for educable retarded youth. *Exceptional Children*, 1969, **35**, 562-63.

Becker, R.L., & Ferguson, R.E. Assessing educable retardates' vocational interest through a non-reading technique. *Mental Retardation*, 1969, **7**, 20-25.

Berdie, R.F. Factors related to vocational interests. *Psychological Bulletin*, 1944, **41**, 137-157.

Brogden, H.E. The primary values measured by the *Allport-Vernon Tests*, a study of values. *Psychological Monographs*, 1952, 348.

Carter, H.D. Vocational interest and job orientation. *Applied Psychological Monographs*, 1944, 2.

Craven, E.C. *The use of interest inventories in counseling.* Chicago: Science Research Associates, 1961.

Cronbach, L.J. *Essentials of psychological testing.* New York: Harper and Brothers, 1960.

Darley, J.G. Relationships among the *Primary Mental Abilities Tests*, selected achievement measures, personality tests, and tests of vocational interests. *University of Minnesota Studies in Higher Education*, 1941, 192-200.

Darley, J.G., & Hagenah, T. *Vocational interest measurement.* Minneapolis: University of Minnesota Press, 1955.

DiMichael, S.G., and Dabelstein, D.H. Work satisfaction and work efficiency of vocational rehabilitation counselors as related to measured interests. American Psychologist, 1947, **2**, 342-343. (Abstract)

Geist, H. *Geist Picture Interest Inventory.* Beverly Hills: Western Psychological Services, 1964.

Guilford, J.P., Christensen, P.R., Bond, N.A., Jr., & Sutton, M.A. A factor analysis of human interests. *Psychological Monographs*, 1954, 375.

Layton, W.L. (Ed.) *The Strong vocational interest blank: Research and uses.* Minneapolis: University of Minnesota Press, 1960

Nunnally, J.C., Jr. *Tests and measurements.* New York: McGraw-Hill, 1959.

Roe, A. Early determinants of vocational choice. *Journal of Counseling Psychology*, 1957, **4**, 212-217.

Strong, E.K., Jr. *Vocational interests of men and women.* Stanford: Stanford University Press, 1943.

Strong, E.K., Jr. *Vocational interests 18 years after college.* Minneapolis: University of Minnesota Press, 1955.

Super, D.E. *Avocational interest patterns: A study in the psychology of avocations.* Stanford: Stanford University Press, 1940.

Super, D.E. Strong's vocational interests of men and women: A special review. *Psychological Bulletin*, 1945, **42**, 359-370.

Super, D.E. The measurement of interests. *Journal of Counseling Psychology*, 1954, **1**, 168-173.

SEX ROLE STEREOTYPING IN SPECIAL EDUCATION: A LOOK AT SECONDARY WORK STUDY PROGRAMS

PATRICIA THOMAS CEGELKA

PATRICIA THOMAS CEGELKA *is Assistant Professor, University of Kentucky, Lexington, Kentucky*

Abstract: An examination of special education practices relative to secondary work study programs for the mentally retarded reveals sex biases in favor of the male enrollees. These biases are apparent in program admission, program offerings, and program evaluation. Both ethical and legal considerations dictate that those practices which serve to doubly handicap individuals labeled both retarded and female be eradicated. Suggestions are made for assessing and restructuring secondary work study programs in order to provide equal quality of participation for all.

Commenting on the high placement ratio of boys to girls in classrooms for the educable mentally retarded (EMR), Mercer (1973) observed that girls must be slower than boys in order to be labeled and placed in special classes. She suggested that society is more tolerant of lower levels of intellectual ability in females. An analysis of special education curriculum reveals that sex role stereotyping is prevalent in all aspects of special education programing (Gillespie and Fink, 1974). The purpose of this article is to extend Gillespie and Fink's analysis by examining the literature on secondary work study programs and the subsequent adult adjustment patterns of those served. The focus is on the extent to which these programs may have provided differential training opportunities for the sexes, resulting in differentiated patterns of adult adjustment.

Effectiveness of Work Study Programs for EMR

Over the past century considerable progress has been made in the area of secondary vocational preparation programs for the retarded. Early efforts were, of course, centered exclusively in institutional settings. An institution in Kentucky took the lead by developing what was considered a mature vocational training program, with academic learning being confined to the mornings, the afternoons devoted to trade training (Doll, 1967). Stewart's report in 1882 of this program stated that:

> Those unable to master whole trades were trained in specific operations. Many were able to live without outside aid and the best girls were discharged to work for wages in families. (p. 237)

During the first few decades of the century, institutional colonies developed specifically for the rehabilitation of the mentally retarded; trade extension classes were begun and vocational education/special education liaisons budded. During the 1950's, monies from the Office of Vocational Rehabilitation (OVR) stimulated the development of model demonstration projects, resulting in the proliferation of secondary level work study programs for the mentally retarded.

An impetus to the expansion of vocational training programs for the mentally retarded, as well as a consequence of that expansion, has been the plethora of studies on adult adjustment patterns of the mentally handicapped. Some of the early studies (Baller, 1936; Muensch, 1944; Fairbanks, 1933; Hegge, 1944) suggested that even without special education programs, retarded individuals tended to make adequate adult adjustments. With employment ranging anywhere from 33% during the Depression to 89% during the war years, the retarded were found to be employed in all categories listed by the Dictionary of Occupational Titles. Boys were most frequently employed in labor occupations and girls in domestic service occupations. The marriage rates tended to be somewhat lower than for the average population, with divorce rates somewhat higher, particularly for girls. Run-ins with the law were somewhat greater for males, while there was a higher incidence of promiscuity among the girls than found in the general population.

Environmental intervention such as that reported by Skeels and Skodak, 1966 and specific training programs (Abel, 1940) indicated that the adult adjustment patterns of mentally retarded could be enhanced. More recent studies have attempted to determine the extent to which special class training and specific vocational training were affecting adult adjustment of EMRs. Acceptably high success rates have been reported for former special class students. Porter and Milazzo (1958) found that 75% of those in special classes were employed, compared with 17% of the nonspecial class group. Phelps (1956) found that 68% of his sample were employed, with an additional 11% listed in the categories of housewife, armed services, and unemployed. Dinger's (1961) followup reported an 83% success rate for his retarded sample.

A 1971 report of students who participated in the Kansas Work Study Project addressed the question of the efficacy of the OVR sponsored secondary programs (Chaffin, Spellman, Ragen & Davison, 1971). It concluded that cooperative work study programs of this nature were achieving at least limited success insofar as the project students were earning significantly more than a comparison group of nonproject students ($90 per week compared with $63 per week). However, while 83% of the experimental students were employed, 75% of the nonproject students were also employed, which corresponds to the rates reported in prework study followups. This lead to the conclusion that the goal of work study programs should not be to make students employable (which, apparently, they already are) but to enhance this employability.

Sex Role Stereotyping in the Curriculum

A careful analysis of followup studies of former special education pupils has led the author to conclude that although secondary programs may have enhanced the employability of their male clients, these programs have made no discernible impact on the employability of females. This is true in terms of percentage of employment, type of employment, and comparative female-male earnings. It does not appear that either the philosophy or the curriculum for training mentally handicapped females has altered much in the last hundred years.

The focus of vocational preparation training efforts for the mentally retarded continues to be on the male portion of the population. A sampling of the literature turned up reports of 10 model projects designed exclusively for boys and one such project for girls. Those projects serving both males and females reported sex ratios of from 2:1 to 4:1, boys to girls. The curricula of these programs are reflective of differential expectations for the sexes. For instance, the Illinois Curriculum Guide developed by Goldstein and Seigle (1958) suggested in the unit on Occupational Adequacy that girls engage in sewing and boys in woodworking. Dinger (1961) recommended units of instruction for boys which included home repairs—carpentry, plumbing, electrical and masonry. The girls' units in home economics involved grooming, child care, sewing, and cooking. Syden (1963), in recommending guidelines for cooperative work study programs, stated that:

> Each student should be given an opportunity to work in a school shop or home economics room. Boys should be assigned to one semester of general shop and one semester to specific shop class, such as metal, printing, and possibly, machine shop. Girls should be given the opportunity to participate in cooking, sewing, ceramics and typing classes. (p. 91)

It would appear that both the classroom training and the work placement components of the secondary programs have provided boys with sets of skills which are potentially transferable to higher levels of occupational attainment than the skill areas in which girls are trained. Kokaska (1964), in discussing a work study program in Phoenix, admitted that sex was a handicapping variable in finding job training samples for girls. Faced with this same problem, the Kansas Work Study Project developed a Domestic Work-Sample (Spellman, Chaffin, & Nelson, 1970) for girls, in which female students were placed in private homes to learn housecleaning skills in preparation for possible permanent job placements as cleaning ladies.

The extent to which these school experiences have resulted in differential adult occupational patterns for the sexes is impossible to assess precisely. Frequently, the reports list jobs held by the retarded (and possibly a comparison group of normals) but do not specify which jobs were held by boys and which by girls. Further, because wages are usually reported as a general mean or median for the total retarded sample, the wages of males and females cannot be compared. Thirdly, the reporting of gross percentage data of successful and unsuccessful subjects does not allow comparisons by sex. A final complicating factor, and a telling index of differential expectations, is the variance in criteria of success applied to males and females. A much more stringent criterion of success is applied to boys—they must be employed and economically self supporting. For a girl, being categorized as "successful" may mean any one of a variety of things:

1. She is fully employed and self-supporting;
2. She is a housewife and supported by her husband;
3. She may be married and also working outside the home; or
4. She is a *homemaker* or a *housekeeper*, neither label implying marriage. In other words, a woman meets success criteria if she helps around the house—her own, her parents', or others'.

Those reports where sufficient data are presented to determine the level or type of employment support the contention that there has been little alteration in the adult adjustment patterns of females, at least over the past 40 years. Fairbanks (1933) reported that 40% of her adult female sample were employed in domestic services (including marriage). Charles (1953) categorized 50% of his females as housekeepers (marriage not implied). Bobroff (1960) reported that 59% were employed as homemakers (again, marriage not implied). Chaffin's (1971) study found 50% of the females from the experimental work study population either in domestic service or married. Interestingly, 50% of the nonwork study females were similarly "employed."

Not only is the literature fairly consistent in reporting the category of jobs held by retarded women, it is also fairly consistent in reporting the relative earnings of retarded males and females. Phelps (1956) found the pay earned by retarded females to be 58% that of the retarded males. Although the avowed purpose of this study was to analyze the individual characteristics of those earning more and less than the median wage, females were excluded from the analysis because of their low salaries. Bobroff (1960) reported that earnings for the retarded females in his sample were 66% those of the retarded males. Peterson and Smith's (1960) study particularly dramatized the differential earnings picture. Figure 1 presents a comparison of the weekly earnings of the retarded and normal sample.

The retarded males and the normal females earned approximately 62% of what the normal males did. This suggests that being a female of average intelligence is an economic disability equal to being a male who is mentally handicapped. The retarded female earnings were approximately 35% of those of the former two groups, highlighting the double disability of being both retarded and female.

Conclusions

There are basically four conclusions that can be reached from this survey of the relationship of special education work study programs to mentally handicapped females. These are:

	Male	Female	Comparative earnings—male/female
Nonretarded	89.30	55.00	62%
Retarded	54.85	19.25	35%
Comparative earnings—nonretarded/retarded	62%	35%	

FIGURE 1. Comparative median weekly wages of retarded and nonretarded subjects.

1. Fewer girls than boys are found in special vocational preparation programs. Mercer's observations that girls, particularly Anglo girls, are less apt to be labeled as retarded and placed in special classes than boys with similar intelligence quotients, suggests that sex per se may be a determining variable in placement.

2. Once in, girls are not provided with equal vocational training opportunities. They are trained for jobs of low or no financial remuneration. The jobs for which they are trained frequently are not covered by minimum wage laws and often promise less stability than the occupations for which

males are trained.

3. The field expects lower levels of adjustment from females. Girls are expected to be more dependent, as reflected by the differential criteria for success. In order to be counted as successful, a male generally must be fully employed and economically self sufficient while a female need not be employed, economically self sufficient or married. The emphasis on training girls primarily for marriage has serious implications. Given national divorce rate estimations of from 25 to 40%, it appears that girls should be trained for more stable employment futures. Further, it is probable that a large number of married females will have to contribute to the family income through employment outside the home. Special education programs have been negligent in preparing girls for such employment other than in low paying jobs.

4. By using nonspecific success criteria (housewife, homemaker, etc.) for girls, the field has been able to report higher success rates than would otherwise be possible. For instance, Dinger (1961) optimistically reported an overall success rate of 83% for his group of former special class pupils. The revised percentage of 60% employed for pay, with the remainder being either housewives or still in school, is comparable to that of studies reporting the adult adjustment of nonspecial education mentally retarded.

It is more difficult for girls than boys to get into special education classes for the mentally handicapped. Once in, lesser training is provided for them and lower levels of adult adjustment are expected of them. Their ability to meet these lower success criteria is then interpreted as justification for the special education programs.

Recommendations

The history of education reveals that in primitive cultures girls were taught to cook, to make clothes, to care for children and to perform similar domestic tasks (Atkinson & Maleska, 1962). In 1882, the first mature vocational training program for the mentally handicapped sent "the best girls to work for wages in families" (Stewart, 1882). In the 1960's, Domestic Work Samples (Spellman, Chaffin, & Nelson, 1970) were developed for training girls enrolled in a model work study program. The fact that special education curricula continue to emphasize domestic skills for girls suggests that little has been done in the last century to enhance their employability. Both ethical and legal considerations dictate that those practices which serve to dou-

bly handicap individuals labeled both retarded and female must be eradicated. Various components of program admission, curriculum, and evaluation should be examined for evidence of discriminatory practices. The following considerations might serve as a framework for assessing and restructuring secondary work study programs for the EMR:

• Admission to special education programs. Assuming that secondary work study programs are educationally defensible in that they render a unique and positive training function, educationally relevant criteria for admission to these programs must be developed and applied equally to the sexes. Retarded females should be afforded the same opportunities for participation as retarded boys.

Biases of curriculum and training opportunities. Responsible special education personnel should examine the curricula (instructional units and materials, course offerings, and general program emphases) of individual secondary programs for sex biases, particularly where such biases predict differential patterns of adult adjustment. Equality of opportunities, in terms of the salary potential, job stability, training and placement aspects of work study programs. While federal equal rights legislation and the women's liberation movement have made obtaining quality job placements for females a somewhat less difficult task than it once was, nonetheless, it will continue to require an extra measure of diligence and ardor on the part of the work study coordinators to ensure equality of training opportunities.

• Program evaluation. Efforts at evaluating the successfulness of secondary school programs must focus on the vocational and adult adjustment patterns of all participants, using a single set of criteria for both sexes. Adult independence or success status must be defined, with particular emphasis on the parameters, quantitative and qualitative, of the nonsalaried occupation of homemaking. If such evaluation efforts should demonstrate differential adjustment patterns for the sexes, these data must be analyzed to determine the responsible components and remedial steps that should be initiated in the training programs.

Not only must both females and males be provided with equal opportunity for participation in work study programs, but they must be afforded an equal quality of participation as well. Only then can special education begin to obtain its goal of maximizing the potential of all eligible participants.

The Use of the PROGRAM ANALYSIS OF SERVICE SYSTEMS (PASS) Technique in the Evaluation of Vocational Services for Mentally Retarded People

Ron Goodridge

Abstract. A brief introduction to the background of and rationales for the Program Analysis of Service Systems (PASS) and its use as a means of program evaluation and planning is given. Recurring service issues in assessments of vocational rehabilitation programs done to date by means of PASS are discussed. A PASS assessment includes major issues identified by the assessment team, program strengths and weaknesses, and recommendations and priorities for change. PASS evaluations separate and specify service weaknesses in vocational rehabilitation and provide means for planning and monitoring service improvements.

Program Analysis of Service Systems (PASS) was first developed in Nebraska in 1969 by Wolfensberger and Glenn and used only in that state as a means of more objectively allocating funds to newly developed community mental retardation services. A second edition (PASS 2), revised to make it applicable to the broad range of human services, was published in 1973 and received wider exposure through its use in training events across North America. From extensive experience gained through training exercises and actual team assessments, a considerably revised third edition (PASS 3) (Wolfensberger & Glenn, 1975) was published in 1975 and is currently in use.

Prior to the first PASS training workshop in June, 1973, only a few people outside Nebraska were familiar with the PASS technique. Since then, several thousand people in North America, and now others in various nations, have heard presentations or read about PASS. Approximately 3000 individuals have learned how to use it through participating in intensive, 5-day introductory training workshops throughout Canada and in several states of the United States. About 200 people have attended "advanced" PASS training; and about 20 have gained enough training and experience to teach others in the use of PASS.

PASS is fundamentally a technique for external program evaluation. It is based on the principle of normalization as well as other principles of sound human service planning and effective administration. As a means of quantitatively assessing the quality of any human service agency, program, or entire service system, PASS has been used to evaluate many different kinds of services in educational, residential, vocational, recreational, correctional, or counselling services. These services have been addressed to an equally wide range of human problem areas and disabilities: physical disability, sensory impairment, emotional disorder, mental retardation, aging, social disadvantage, delinquency, alcohol, drug addiction, etc.

Because PASS focuses on universal aspects of service quality which are applicable to any type of human service or helping program, it is possible to compare dissimilar services. Also, PASS can document the increase or decrease in quality of a single service over time.

In the assessment of a particular human service program or agency, a team of qualified "raters" familiarizes itself thoroughly with all aspects of the service, drawing upon a combination of written descriptions of the project, site visits, and interviews with clients and key administrative and direct-service staff. Applying well-defined guidelines and criteria, the raters then evaluate the project on 50 "ratings," which are statements about various universal aspects of service, the physical comfort of the service setting, the intensity and relevance of programming, individualization, etc. Each rating is scored by means of a rating scale which has three to six "levels," with the lowest level of each implying poor or even unacceptable service performance, and the highest one implying near-ideal but attainable performance. Each level earns a different number of points, according to the degree of adherence of a particular service characteristic or practice to certain desirable standards and rationales, which are explained in the *Field Manual*. The significance of the ratings is not indicated by the order in which they occur on the score

2. ASSESSMENT

sheet, but rather by the scoring weights assigned to them. Those ratings which carry the highest positive and lowest negative scores are the most important. For instance, the largest weight assigned to any rating is 40 points (which can mean +40 on the high side, or −40 on the low side) for the rating "Model coherency." This is followed closely by "Socially integrative social activities," and "Intensity of relevant programming," each with a range of +39 to −39 points.

The highest attainable score for all ratings combined is +1000; the lowest is −947. A score of 0 (either overall, or for a specific rating) reflects a "minimally adequate" level of performance, while anything below 0 is considered to fall into the "unacceptable" category. Thus, when a rating is reported as being at a "minimally adequate" level, it means that the score for that rating was 0. A total score of +711 is the "expected" level of performance for any human service. Sometimes, high scores in one element may be balanced out by low scores in another, and a system with some outstanding features may still receive a low or even negative score because of major shortcomings in other areas.

When the demanding criteria of PASS have been applied, most human services have been closer to a minimally acceptable (0 points) than to expected level (+711 points) of performance for two major reasons: (a) PASS judges services according to optimum standards: standards which are near-ideal, but which are by no means impossible to attain. Thus an agency which simply does what most other agencies are doing, without going beyond current mainstream practices, and without incorporating the knowledge already available at the frontier of the field, will not rate very high on PASS. Also, services which have been highly competent and/or innovative will only continue to score high if their initial vitality and momentum are maintained over time in many of the higher-weighted rating areas. (b) PASS also rates a service according to its quality, rather than according to the quantity of service which it delivers. On this basis, PASS is different from many other evaluative instruments. PASS is not concerned with how many people an agency or service system manages to accommodate. Rather, since it is based largely on the principle of normalization, PASS credits services for the degree to which they create normalizing environments for, and positive social interpretations of, their clientele. Many human services attempt to serve large numbers of people, often in a central facility and are not, or are only partially, oriented to social integration of the clients, as required by the normalization principle. Thus, although most human services do perform some service to their clientele, the quality of that service is often only a fraction of what it conceivably might be.

Where shortcomings do exist, PASS makes no allowance for the cause of, or reason for, these shortcomings. Thus, it asks "what," and not "why," and weaknesses lose credit points no matter how reasonable the cause (e.g., bad laws, unfavorable location, lack of funds). The "why" must be considered in understanding the history of an agency, and in charting a course of action, but not in describing or evaluating the current reality. This approach is taken in order to objectify assessment, be able to compare different types of services with each other, and prevent compromises from being reinterpreted as ideals — as is often the case soon after a compromise is made.

PASS was intended and has proven to be much more than an · evaluation technique. In addition to evaluative criteria, PASS also provides concrete guidelines and serves as a useful "check-list" for planning new services or for improving existing services. Additionally, PASS can be used in many instances to evaluate programs which are in the planning or proposal stage.

Initially, PASS was designed to serve simultaneously and equally as a tool for service assessment and for training

personnel in the principle of normalization. Here, perhaps, lies PASS' greatest current utility. Many human service planners, administrators, and workers have come to comprehend the complexity and subtlety of normalization for the first time after an intensive exposure to PASS. It is mainly a consequence of PASS' intent to "teach" normalization thoroughly and consistently that efforts are made to ensure that those who apply it in any "official" way have received extensive training in its meaning, rationales and use. So far, PASS is not self-teaching, because potential raters have to work through and internalize the intent of the normalization principle before they can learn to apply PASS reliably and consistently. However, a thorough reading of PASS, especially the *Field Manual*, could provide a person with sufficient background to use it in service planning or for informal, "internal" service appraisal.

In the context of any discussion of PASS, a brief exposition of the normalization principle itself is appropriate and often necessary. A full 734 of the theoretical maximum of +1000 points a service might conceivably attain on PASS are related to how well the service meets the criteria and ideals of normalization. This principle is thoroughly explained in the textbook on that topic. PASS "breaks down" or "operationalizes" the principle into its practical human service implications; but while it provides more details in some respects, it does not cover the principle as globally as does the textbook.

To summarize briefly: the principle of normalization is a relatively recent ideology and derives from Scandinavian human service practices of the 1950's and 1960's. Its initial application in North America was to the field of mental retardation. However, it is now being increasingly applied to other fields of human service involving handicapped or disadvantaged persons who have been traditionally perceived as different and devalued (seen as "deviant") by society. The approach of normalization is to assist and/or allow persons to achieve a normal pattern of life, to achieve fuller participation in conventional community services, to secure the opportunities, rights, benefits, recognition, acceptance and valued status of citizens of dignity and worth. This is the goal of normalization. However, normalization also implies that the means to that goal be typical of our culture and as appropriate as possible so as not to attract attention to persons with special needs, thereby further reinforcing their perceived differentness.

Normalization is a conscious, explicit, systematized, operational and optimistic ideology. It is concerned with and seeks to promote devalued persons' social integration and social acceptance. It is concerned with the ways people are interpreted to other citizens, e.g., how they are labelled and talked about. Normalization seeks to accentuate similarities and commonalities with fellow citizens and peers, rather than differences and stigmata. Normalization focuses on potential, rather than past lack of performance, and implies that human service managers should have a positive orientation to and high expectations for the devalued person's development and capacity to learn and grow.

Normalization, therefore, provides a positive and implementable set of ideals for a service and specifies the service goal. PASS furnishes practical guidelines for means and methods of reaching that goal.

PASS is not "traditional program evaluation" or a design for "evaluative research." Carol Weiss (1974) makes a distinction between "alternative models of program evaluation." One such model, according to Weiss, is a "social experiment," which is true experimental research and is governed by control conditions and before-and-after measurement. Examples may include experiments in guaranteed annual income, negative income tax, health insurance, etc.

"Traditional program evaluation," Weiss' second model, is a catchall term to describe methods used to study ongoing programs. These essentially involve before-and-after assessment of the extent to which programs are achieving stated objectives, without any form of control group or conditions. PASS seems to fit best in Weiss' third category of "accountability systems." PASS was designed to contribute to greater accountability in human services in a number of ways by providing a means for objectively and quantitatively assessing programs according to universal standards of service quality; by comparing services over time and by comparing dissimilar services.

PASS is not a method for evaluating an individual's performance or potential, whether that individual be staff or client. Stated more simply, PASS is not a measure of traditional service "outcomes." PASS is primarily concerned with assessing "processes" which human service agencies apply to their clients as opposed to traditional outcomes (or what might be called "processes emitted by clients"). It is possible to debate both (a) the merits of "process" versus "outcome" evaluation, and (b) what in fact actually constitutes an "outcome." This paper is not the appropriate place to debate either of these points. For now it is sufficient to say that one of the basic assumptions underlying PASS is that the processes which a service applies to its clientele are as important as what results from the service. Therefore, PASS looks at service policies, structures, practices, interpretations, etc. and assesses both (a) how these directly affect the client's experience and (b) how these indirectly interpret the client to other people (the larger public and society). Many of the universal human service *desiderata* with which PASS identifies and which are embodied in ratings are simultaneously "processes" and "outcomes." For example, one service characteristic assessed in PASS is "Socially integrative social activities." As one of the most important and heavily-weighted ratings in PASS 3, this rating assesses the extent to which a handicapped person is meaningfully integrated with and accepted by his non-handicapped peers. The activities, supports and structures which the service undertakes or provides to facilitate the person's integration really constitute a "process of social integration;" and this process is also evaluated via this rating.

PASS is not, nor have its authors or proponents ever claimed it to be, a perfect or all-inclusive evaluation method for all aspects of a single service or system. PASS is primarily a method for external program evaluation. PASS itself rewards (or penalizes) a service for its utilization (or failure to utilize) other means of both internal and external assessment at all levels (client, staff and program). A specific PASS rating, "Program evaluation and renewal mechanisms" takes this into account.

Some Recurring Issues in Vocational Programs

A very conservative estimate would place the total number of team assessments done to date (1973-1976) with PASS 2 and PASS 3 at somewhere between 500 and 600. (This does not include assessments done in Nebraska with the first version of PASS.) Many if not most of these assessments were training or practicum evaluations conducted in connection with training workshops. Based on this author's fairly considerable experience with and knowledge of PASS utilization across North America, another conservative and very reasonable estimate would be that approximately 20% of these assessments were conducted on vocational programs.

The one major piece of research done to date on PASS tends to substantiate this latter estimate. Flynn's monograph *Assessing Human Service Quality With PASS 2: An Empirical Analysis of 102 Service Program Evaluations* (1974) included a sub-sample of 22 vocational services. Flynn's further research (unpublished) on an expanded sample of 151 services includes a sub-sample of 31 vocational programs.

Based on experience and knowledge to date, it is possible to point to definite recurring issues in the PASS assessments of different types of services and services to different disability groups. This is indeed possible with respect to vocational programs for mentally retarded people; and the remainder of this paper will identify and discuss briefly several of these issues.

What emerges from a typical PASS assessment is a lengthy, detailed written report which usually presents findings in terms of the following outline:

1. The overriding or major issues, or major concerns about service quality as identified by the assessment team;
2. Program strengths according to the criteria contained in PASS (ratings);
3. Program weaknesses according to PASS criteria;
4. Recommendations and priorities for change.

The overriding issues may be identified in terms of one or more single, important (and usually heavily-weighted) ratings; or in terms of a "cluster" or group of related ratings.

In PASS assessments of vocational services for mentally retarded people, four issues which tend to recur are these:

1. A lack of program intensity and relevancy; i.e., vocational programs tend to be non-challenging and non-(real) work-like;
2. A lack of specialization and of a coherent model; i.e., vocational programs generally tend to confusingly, inappropriately and ineffectively mix training, sheltered employment, "educational" functions, and counselling together in one program;
3. A general age-inappropriateness; i.e., program structures, practices, activities, routines, etc. tend to interpret clients as younger and less capable than they are;
4. A lack of comprehensiveness in the area of vocational services generally; i.e., vocational programs tend to operate in an isolated, uncoordinated, non-systematic fashion so as to produce discontinuity for clients who may need or want to move on in terms of training or employment potential.

Intensity of Relevant Programming

This heavily-weighted rating (point range from -39 to $+39$) is the most important "clinical" rating in PASS. It assesses both the level and the temporal massing of challenge in terms of (a) whether and to what extent the program meets the service needs of the client, and (b) whether and to what extent the program "graduates" the client along to greater independence or at least more advanced challenges. Secondly, this rating asks "Is the service relevant to the client (regardless of intensity)?"

Many vocational rehabilitation programs have found to be lacking in both respects. After one looks beyond what is often a superficial "busy-ness" in sheltered workshops and other vocational programs, one is frequently struck by the inactivity, lethargy and apparent boredom of clients. Sometimes, one encounters clients who are performing the same or similar tasks day after day, month after month, year after year. Some complicated and challenging machinery (one determinant of intensity) may be present, but it is operated only by a select few clients or only by staff. In short, growth-producing challenge is lacking in many programs on the vocational service scene.

Much of the "work" engaged in by vocational programs is at best marginal in terms of (a) training potential, (b) remuneration for the client, or (c) (additional) revenue-production for the program. Sometimes it is simply irrelevant activity. Much of the simplistic and repetitive "subcontract" work (stuffing envelopes, packaging seeds, etc.) or

2. ASSESSMENT

the arts-and-crafts activities (ceramics, etc.) engaged in by clients is rationalized on the basis of being "easy to get," "the only thing available" or "what the clients like to do." Much if not most of this "work" bears no resemblance to what would be expected in competitive job situations. It does little to equip clients with the competencies to move on to advanced tasks or eventual dependent or semi-independent employment.

Model Coherency

This rating is the most important, heavily-weighted (point range: −40 to +40), complex and difficult one in PASS. It used to be called "Specialization" in PASS 2 and is concerned with the degree of specialization among a number of variables within a program and with whether these combine harmoniously so as to meet the specific needs of clients. These variables are: (a) client grouping, or whether clients are grouped appropriately in terms of similar age categories and disability levels; (b) the human management model, or whether there is a clearly defined service model (e.g., vocational, residential, etc.); (c) manpower identity, or whether the training and/or experience of staff "fit" the type of job they are doing; (d) program content or what is being done in the program; (e) program process, or how it is being done. Another way to draw the issue is to ask: Are the right people working with the right clients, doing the right things, using the right methods, and consistently so?

Recurring problems which affect the coherency of vocational programs for retarded people can be identified in relation to all of these variables. (a) Vocational as well as other types of programs for mentally retarded individuals frequently attempt to serve a broad group of clients of widely varying ages and levels of ability. This variance is often so broad that a program cannot specialize; it becomes "all things to all people," and thus fails to serve any single group of the clients effectively. (b) Many vocational programs attempt to provide both training and sheltered employment but do so without clearcut objectives and priorities. Often service personnel find it difficult to identify which clients require sheltered employment and which need training (to move on to independent job opportunities). Thus, a confused mixture of "models" is often present in vocational programs. This is compounded by the inclusion in the program of "academic upgrading" or "social/life skill development." These latter services are no doubt required by many mentally retarded individuals. What is being questioned here is the appropriateness of providing these services within a vocational (work) context. (c) Many of the staff, dedicated and hardworking, to be sure, employed in vocational programs possess training and skills of questionable relevance to the functions of the programs. One would have to question whether a person trained in social work and counselling is the best person to teach an industrial skill (e.g., operating a printing press) to a retarded worker.

These various incongruities directly affect (d) "program content" and (e) "program process." Programs without a clearly defined model and with inappropriately trained or skilled personnel are bound to have and do employ a confused mixture of techniques, methods, approaches, etc. The end result, observed repeatedly by PASS teams assessing vocational services, are programs which simply fail to meet the vocational needs of retarded people: the need to be trained in specific job competencies or the need to have meaningful and rewarding (personally and monetarily) employment opportunities.

Age-Appropriate Interpretations and Structures

A third recurring issue in vocational programming has to do with the group of "cluster" of seven ratings under the general PASS heading of "Age-appropriate interpretations and structures." In North American culture, at least, it is generally more demoralizing to be reduced in age than advanced. This is so in spite of (a) the youth-orientation of our culture, and (b) our increasing tendency to devalue elderly citizens and cast them into a deviancy role.

Numerous examples from assessments of adult vocational programs can be çited to illustrate general age-inappropriateness:

1. Shorter (school-like) days;
2. Child-like furniture and appointments in vocational settings (school desks, blackboards, etc.);
3. Presence of child-like artwork and decorations in vocational settings;
4. Use of "school buses" to transport retarded people to sheltered workshops;
5. Prolonged periods of recreation or non-work activity during the work day (e.g., exercise periods);
6. Repeated references to adult workers as "boys" and "girls" by vocational service personnel.

All of these things can contribute to retarded adults being perceived by the general public as younger and less capable than they are. Thus, these interpretations pose barriers to retarded clients being socially accepted and viewed as productive workers.

Comprehensiveness

This rating is based on a human service planning principle which in turn derives from ideological considerations other than normalization. A full discussion of this concept is beyond the scope of this paper. All that can and need be done here is to list the four components of a comprehensive system:

1. A clearly defined, geographically cohesive, manageable service region;
2. An appropriate regionag population (200,000-600,000);
3. A range of service, wide and complete enough within the region, so a client/consumer need not go outside the geopolitical service area;
4. Effective ("empowered") coordination of services so clients/consumers experience continuity in receiving services.

Within an envisioned comprehensive system of services for mentally retarded people, several major sub-systems can be identified: residential services, developmental (educational) services, vocational services, family resource or support services, and central or administrative services. The vocational system, for example, would need to include a range or continuum of individual services to meet the range of needs among retarded people in a particular region for vocational training, employment or job support.

There are few examples of comprehensive systems of services. Not surprising then is the lack of comprehensive vocational services across North America. Typically, vocational services exist in isolation or in a fragmented service delivery pattern. As a result, retarded people might remain in a job assessment program, or in a sheltered workshop, or in a training-on-the-job (TOJ) placement much longer than necessary because there is nowhere (no service as a "next stop") to go, or because the system is so fragmented that coordination and referral is virtually impossible.

This paper has been intended to highlight several recurring service issues in vocational programs for retarded people. These are by no means the only service weaknesses identified via PASS assessments of vocational services. Nor is it the intent of this paper to imply that all vocational programs have these weaknesses or that there are no positive programs in existence. Indeed there are innovative, challenging, coherent and dignifying programs in operation. Sadly, experience tends to show these are few and far between.

The above service weaknesses have recurred often enough to be identified as common and major, even overriding, issues facing the field of vocational rehabilitation for retarded people. PASS has served to provide a means to separate and specify these issues. In doing so, PASS might also provide the means for planning and monitoring service improvement in the future in this area.

References

Flynn, R. *Assessing human service quality with PASS 2: NIMR monograph 5*. Toronto: National Institute on Mental Retardation, 1975.

Weiss, C. Alternative models of program evaluation. *Social Work*, 1974, *19*(6) 675-681.

Wolfensberger, W. *The principle of normalization in human services*. Toronto: National Institute on Mental Retardation, 1972.

RON GOODRIDGE was born and educated in the United States. He obtained a B.A. degree in 1969 from Kalamazoo College in Michigan and did graduate work in education and special education at Northeastern Illinois State College in Chicago, where he also worked for two years as a special education teacher with the Chicago Board of Education (1969-1970). In early 1971 he moved to Winnipeg, Manitoba, where he served as a program coordinator with the Winnipeg Branch of the Canadian Association for the Mentally Retarded (1972), and Executive Director of Citizen Advocacy Manitoba (1973-1975). In March 1975, he joined the staff of the (Canadian) National Institute on Mental Retardation where he specializes in the areas of service system planning and evaluation, and manpower development and training.

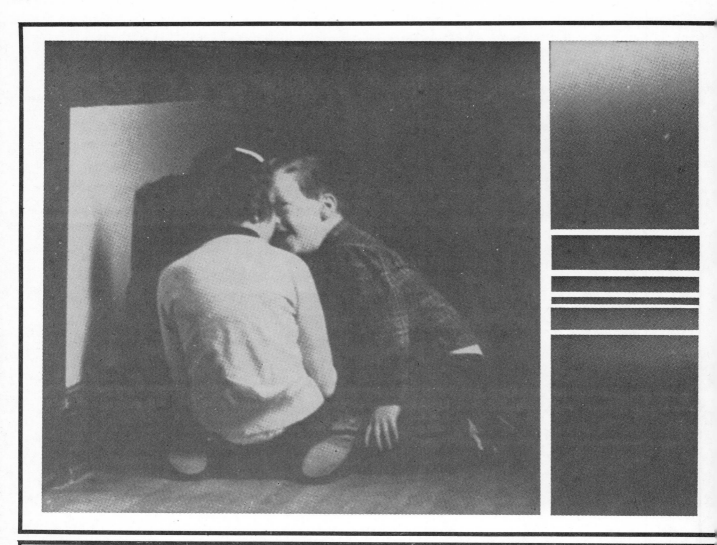

"Photos courtesy of the President's Committee on Mental Retardation"

SPECIAL
EDUCATION'S
RESPONSIBILITY

Education is just beginning to view employment as a goal for the mentally retarded. Vocational evaluation and training needs to be an integral part of the school curriculum. Teachers must be skilled in evaluation, work adjustment and placement. There is no set time to begin preparing for competitive employment. Positive work attitudes fostered on the elementary level are the foundation for later success.

Articles included in this section illustrate the success of job experience simulation and work study programs in junior high and high school. The effect made on both vocational skills learned and the changes in self concept are encouraging. The mentally retarded student is given the chance to be successful before entering the job market.

There is much work to be done. In many schools there is poor communication between teachers and vocational rehabilitation workers. There is only a limited time for development and supervision of work experience. Teachers often lack vocational education skills. Communication between teachers and the rest of the student's community is sporadic or not at all. All services need to cooperate for successful placement. The student must be allowed to learn to perform a job under normal circumstances with the same time limits they need to master for competition in the job market. They need to develop specific occupational skills for advancement to their potential ability levels.

There is a major problem facing the family and community after graduation. Most sheltered workshops have waiting lists. The future holds isolation from peers, segregation from community and dependence on the home environment for any growth and stimulation. Schools spend at least twelve years developing potential. The commitment must be extended to include placement and continued services.

VOCATIONAL EVALUATION: SPECIAL EDUCATION's RESPONSIBILITY

Abstract: Many educable mentally retarded persons continue to lead a marginal life after school despite higher potentials. Schools can and should provide more relevant vocationally oriented programs to help eliminate the barriers formerly encountered by the mentally retarded after they leave school. Initiating vocational evaluation programs in the school is recommended and the components of the process are described. A model for operating a vocational evaluation and placement program is suggested.

DONN BROLIN *is Associate Professor, Department of Counseling and Personnel Services, University of Missouri—Columbia. He was formerly Director, Special Education Project, University of Wisconsin—Stout, Menomonie.* This article is based on a speech given at the Special Study Institute on Vocational Evaluation and Curriculum Modification, Department of Public Instruction, Des Moines, Iowa, February 1, 1972.

The majority of persons who are labeled as educable mentally retarded could achieve higher levels of personal, social, and vocational functioning if they had better educational and vocational opportunities. Too many retarded persons are not learning to live and work successfully in our society.

One reason is a lack of public understanding about the ability of the educable mentally retarded. Most of these students are not significantly brain damaged or otherwise medically disabled and have many positive abilities that can be converted to vocational assets. However, there is still a tendency to place the mentally retarded in routine, repetitive, simple, and low paying jobs even though many could perform successfully in more highly skilled and highly paid occupations (Kokaska, 1971; Oswald, 1968).

Another reason is the lack of appropriate educational and vocational programs in the secondary schools. Many professionals believe that too much emphasis is placed on academic instruction and too little on the development of socio-occupational competence (Goldstein, 1969). This criticism is being leveled against special education in secondary schools even though there has been a greater emphasis on vocational pro-

graming in the secondary schools in the last decade. Work experience has been incorporated into the high school curriculum, often with the cooperation of the state rehabilitation agency, employment service, and sheltered workshops. These work study programs have had the benefit of getting the agencies involved in the vocational problems of the educable retarded students before graduation, but yet they have not worked as efficiently as was hoped.

Communication problems, in many cases, have existed between the secondary school and the rehabilitation agency, resulting in sporadic services and inadequate continuity of service (Hammerlynck & Espeseth, 1969). The same has been true of the relationship between the school and the employment service. In a recent study, Colorado State Employment Service counselors indicated that they did not feel it was their responsibility to find employment for the mentally retarded and were not knowledgeable about mental retardation; moreover, 38 percent of the counselors surveyed said that they often did not have any working relationship with special classroom programs for these students (Smith, 1970).

Sheltered workshops have provided vocational evaluation, training, and placement services for many of these students, thereby relieving participating schools of vocational responsibilities. But again the help provided by the workshops often has not met the needs of the students. Often workshop personnel are not well trained in mental retardation and are neither aware of the student's background nor are able to observe his functioning over a long period of time. Consequently, the students have not been able to receive the individual and specialized assistance they need. In addition, the performance of many educable retarded students has been lower than their actual potential because they have not yet reached a certain level of vocational maturity, motivation, and experience.

Giving the responsibility for vocational evaluation and training of these students to rehabilitation agencies, employment services, and sheltered workshops will not totally solve the problems. These agencies have many types of vocationally handicapped clients to serve and cannot be expected to train their already overloaded staff to deal effectively with all the vocational problems of the educable retarded student. Some secondary schools have provided vocational evaluation for their students, but this usually has not been done in any systematic way.

Up to this point the extent and quality of vocational programing for these students has depended primarily upon the individual teacher's inclination, ingenuity, training, vocational experience, and the like. Some teachers have developed good vocational programs; others have not, placing students in jobs with the hope that some vocational skills and interests will develop. Schools can and should be providing better programs to help eliminate the educational and vocational barriers that the retarded student encounters.

The secondary school program must assume a larger responsibility for the vocational development of its educable retarded students by initiating a vocational evaluation program as an integral part of its curriculum. This is consistent with the recent statement by US Commissioner of Education, Sidney P. Marland (1972) who listed career education for the handicapped as one of the nation's primary educational needs.

The Vocational Evaluation Procedure

Vocational evaluation, according to Gellman (1968), is concerned with the prognosis of whether a person can work, what kind, and what types of training are needed. Although there are varying opinions on how to do this, it is my opinion that vocational evaluation should consist of the following components: clinical assessment, work evaluation, work adjustment, and on-the-job tryout.

Clincial Assessment

There are four types of clinical assessment: medical, social, educational, and psychological.

Medical Assessment. This assessment involves evaluating the individual's physical capacity, general health, brain damage, vision, hearing, speech, perceptual motor functioning, coordination, dexterity, and any suspected or evident anomalies pre-cluding optimal health and physical functioning. In addition to pointing out limitations to vocational functioning, a medical assessment should indicate whether treatment can modify or remedy some or all of the limitations and this information should be used for vocational planning.

Social Assessment. This assessment involves evaluating the educable retarded student's family relationship, social skills, interpersonal relationships, care of his personal needs, and ability to use leisure time. For example, it has been found that the parents have a significant influence on the student's eventual vocational outcome (Brolin, 1969). Moreover, lack of appropriate social skills, rather than inability to do the job, is the major reason for loss of employment.

Educational Assessment. This assessment involves evaluating the student's academic ability for job placement. Many jobs do not require a high academic level but a certain academic level is needed for care for one's everyday affairs. Proper educational assessment could assist in preventing a mildly retarded student from being placed in an unchallenging position and in becoming underemployed.

Psychological Assessment. This assessment at its best involves evaluating the educable retarded student's verbal skills, performance skills, special interests and knowledge, and the like. In the past, psychological assessment has focused on IQ scores despite their insignificance in determining the individual's vocational potential. The psychologist can be of real help in assessing the individual's skills and in pinpointing intellectual and personality strengths and weaknesses for eventual vocational programing.

Work Evaluation. The second component, work evaluation, in the vocational evaluation procedure consists of: intake and other counseling interviews; interest, dexterity, and other standardized vocational tests; work and job samples; and situational assessment. *Interviews.* These are extremely important in the work evaluation process, for they can provide essential information on the interests, needs, knowledge, and personality of the student.

Standardized Testing. This testing should be used with caution. The tests are often inappropriate for educable mentally retarded students because of the verbal ability required and/or the norm groups used. While there have been attempts to develop less verbal measures, such as *Standardization of*

3. RESPONSIBILITY

the Vocational Interest Sophistication Assessment (VISA), (Parnicky, Kahn, & Burdett, 1968), *The Geist Picture Interest Inventory*, (Geist, 1959), and the new *Reading-Free Vocational Interest Inventory*, the validity of all these measures is questionable and any interest test should be used with care. The *Purdue Pegboard* (Tobias & Gorelick, 1960), is perhaps the best fine finger dexterity test to use. The *General Aptitude Test Battery* (GATB), (US Department of Labor, 1966), should be used with caution despite a recent study in Minnesota (Lofquist, Dawis, & Weiss, 1970) concluding that it si appropriate.

Work and Job Samples. These are becoming increasingly important components of the work evaluation process and range from simple to complex operations. Work samples are simulated tasks or activities but do not actually replicate a specific job whereas a job sample is a model or replication of an actual job or part of a job that exists in industry. Both are set up like a testing procedure where there are definite instructions, standards, time and/or units performed requirements, and hopefully norms on which to compare the individual's performance with other groups. They do not consist merely of giving individuals work and seeing how they do on it.

Unlike standardized tests, however, work and job samples have these advantages: (a) they are more like jobs than tests are; (b) they are more motivating, less anxiety producing, and more appropriate than tests for persons with cultural and language difficulties; (c) they may sample actual operations of a job, and (d) they provide better evidence for the prospective employer of the types of abilities the client has.

The disadvantages most frequently cited of work and job samples are: (a) many clients may not take work samples related to jobs that they do not like; (b) it is difficult to develop enough representative job samples to cover all the major occupations; (c) they are expensive and time consuming to develop; and (d) there is still much subjective evaluation in the use of work and job samples. *The Dictionary of Occupational Titles* (DOT), (US Department of Labor, 1965), is valuable in conducting job analyses which is a first step in developing work and job samples.

Situational Assessment. This assessment is the typical technique used by sheltered workshops and is oriented toward simulating actual working conditions. Instead of focusing on specific work skills, as in the

work or job sample, the situational assessment forcuses on general work habits and behaviors. The client usually works on subcontracted, production assembly work that is fairly simple. Clients are systematically observed and rated on their work personality and their behaviors are compared to behaviors deemed necessary to secure employment.

Work Adjustment

The third component work adjustment, of the vocational evaluation procedure is particularly helpful for the educable retarded student who is inexperienced and unmotivated. The work adjustment program is planned individually for each student and concentrates on his particular deficiencies that have been delineated in the work evaluation period. The work adjustment program helps the student develop adequate physical tolerances, change work behaviors, and acquire new vocational related information and experiences.

There are several different kinds of work adjustment techniques. One is a simulated work experience setting that provides work activities and that emphasizes productivity. Another is individual and group counseling. A third, and perhaps the most effective with many retarded individuals, is behavior modification in which operant conditioning focuses on reinforcement to control and shape behavior. The goal in the behavior modification approach is to alter the client's work environment so that appropriate behaviors are learned and maintained and inappropriate behaviors extinguished. After a period of work adjustment, a more realistic assessment of the educable retarded student's vocational strengths, weaknesses, and potentials can be made.

On-the-Job Tryouts

The final component of the vocational evaluation process, on-the-job tryouts, provides perhaps the only realistic assessment of the client's abilities. On-the-job tryouts should be separate from work evaluation because the former gives the student the opportunity to perform an actual job under the supervision of industrial and business personnel. Prerequisite to a relevant decision about the job tryout is the conducting of a job analysis, focusing on a description of the work to be performed and on the required characteristics of the worker.

Job analysis takes into consideration what the worker does, how he does it, why he does it, and the skill involved in doing it. When the student is engaged in the on-the-job tryout, the job analyst can observe him at the place of work and give whatever training and instruction is needed before making a final judgement as to the student's potential for that type of work. Neff (1970) has stated that perhaps "the site of the vocational evaluator ought to be in the work place itself [p. 29]." If the vocational evaluator has done his job, the student should be ready for the on-the-job experience and should do well. The on-the-job tryout should reflect the actual vocational capacities of the student, provided that the evaluation and adjustment that preceded it was adequate.

The above comprises the vocational evaluation process. It appears that special education teachers must have the competencies of a social worker, psychologist, counselor, evaluator, and placement specialist if vocational evaluation is their responsibility. This may well be true, but someone has to conduct and coordinate the vocational evaluation and it is going to have to be the teacher if the students are to be served adequately. Other resources should be utilized if they are available and appropriate.

A Vocational Evaluation Model

To make sense out of the mass of vocational evaluation data collected on students, there must be some systematic framework or model from which the teacher can operate so appropriate evaluation, adjustment, and placement techniques can be employed. One

that could be useful is the *Minnesota Theory of Work Adjustment* (Dawis, 1967). This theory is concerned with placing the individual on an appropriate job and is based on the assumption that work adjustment depends on the correspondence between the individual's work personality and the work environment.

The individual's work personality is made up of his abilities and needs, and the work environment consists of the abilities required for satisfactory work performance and the needs that can be satisfied by the job reinforcer system. This can be depicted as seen in Figure 1.

When the individual's abilities correspond to the abilities required to do the job, there is *satisfactoriness*. When the individual's needs correspond to the job reinforcer system, there is satisfaction, that is, the individual is happy with what he is doing. There are well designed followup questionnaires to assess these two areas. If there is both satisfactoriness (the individual can do the job) and satisfaction (the individual is happy about his job), there is work adjustment and job stability (Dawis, 1967).

To measure the various components in the model, the following can be used:

• *Abilities* These can be measured by work samples, situational assessment, on-the-job tryouts, GATB, *Purdue Pegboard*, and other vocational aptitude tests and clinical assessments.

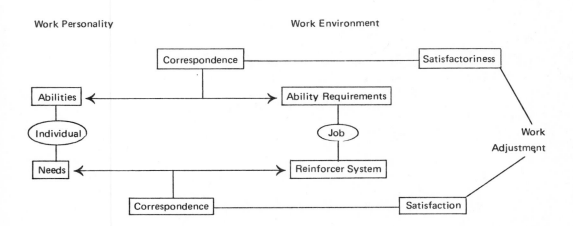

FIGURE 1. Minnesota Theory of
Work Adjustment

3. RESPONSIBILITY

- *Ability Requirements.* These can be measured by the DOT, job analysis, *Guide to Jobs for the Mentally Retarded*, (Peterson & Jones, 1964) and *Occupational Adjustment Patterns*. (US Department of Labor, 1962).
- *Needs.* These can be measured by the *Minnesota Importance Questionnaire* (MIQ) (Lofquist, Dawis & Weiss, 1970), interest inventories, personality measures, expressed needs, and past history.
- *Reinforcer System.* These can be measured by the DOT, job analysis, and *Occupational Reinforcer Patterns* (ORPs), (Borgen, Weiss, Tinsley, Dawis, & Lofquist, 1968).

The *Minnesota Theory of Work Adjustment* provides a systematic framework for operating a vocational evaluation and placement program. It is a way to obtain information about work personalities, abilities, needs, and work environments to find the correspondence between all these factors that will lead to successful work adjustment.

A successful and effective vocational evaluation program can be designed within the school structure and be complemented by an appropriate community job site experience. By using the techniques described above, the secondary special education teacher will be able to enhance the opportunities for our mentally retarded citizens and truly provide a career education.

References

Borgen, F., Weiss, D., Tinsley, H. Dawis, R., & Lofquist, L. The measurement of Occupational Reinforcer Patterns. *Minnesota Studies in Vocational Rehabilitation.* 1968.

Brolin, D. E. The implementation of recommendations from an evaluation center for the mentally retarded and an analysis of variables related to client outcome. Unpublished doctoral dissertation, University of Wisconsin, 1969.

Dawis, R. The Minnesota studies in vocational rehabilitation. *Rehabilitation Counseling Bulletin,* 1967, **11**, 1-10.

Geist, H. *Geist Picture Interest Inventory.* Berkeley: Southern Universities Press, 1959.

Gellman, W. The principles of vational evaluation. *Rehabilitation Literature,* 1968, **29**, 98-102.

Goldstein, H. Construction of a social learning curriculum. *Focus on Exceptional Children,* 1969, **1**, 1-10.

Hammerlynck, L. A., & Espeseth, V. K. Dual specialist: Vocational rehabilitation counselor and teacher of the mentally retarded. *Mental Retardation,* 1969, **7**, 49-50.

Kokaska, C. The need for economic security for the mentally retarded. In Brolin, D., & Thomas, B. (Eds.), *Preparing teachers of secondary level educable mentally retarded: Proposal for a new model.* Menomonie, Wisconsin: Stout State University, 1971. Pp. 18-21.

Lofquist, L., Dawis, R., & Weiss, D. *Assessing the work personalities of mentally retarded adults.* Minnespolis: University of Minnesota, 1970.

Marland, S. Career education 300 days later. *American Vocational Journal,* 1972, **47**, (2), 14-17.

Neff, W. Vocational Assessment - theory and models. *Journal of Rehabilitation,* 1970 **36**(1), 27-29.

Oswald, H. *A national follow-up study of mental retardates employed by the federal government.* Grant RD-2425-6, Washington, D.C.: Department of Vocational Rehabilitation, 1968.

Parnicky, J., Kahn, H. & Burdett, A. *Standardization of the Vocational Interest and Sophistication Assessment (VISA): A reading free test for retardates.* Bordentown, N.J.: Johnstone Training and Research Center, 1968.

Peterson, R., & Jones, E. *Guide to jobs for the mentally retarded.* Pittsburgh: American Institute for Research, 1964.

Smith, G. The mentally retarded: Is the public employment service prepared to serve them? *Mental Retardation,* 1970, **8**, 26-29.

Tobias, J. & Gorelick, J. The effectiveness of the *Purdue Pegboard* in evaluating the work potential of retarded adults. *Training School Bulletin,* 1960, **57**, 94-104.

US Department of Labor. *Dictionary of occupational titles.* (3rd ed.) 1965.

US Department of Labor, United States Employment Service. *General Aptitude Test Battery.* Washington: USGPO, 1966.

US Department of Labor, *Guide to the use of the General Aptitude Test Battery.* Section II: Norms; Occupational Aptitude Pattern Structure, 1962.

Special Students and the World of Work

TEACHING WORK ATTITUDES AT THE ELEMENTARY LEVEL

Joseph E. Justen III
Terry G. Cronis

Joseph E. Justen is Assistant Professor, Special Education, University of Missouri, Columbia.

Terry G. Cronis is Assistant Professor, Special Education, University of South Alabama, Mobile.

■ Studies of job failure in mentally retarded populations have consistently indicated that most retarded individuals lose their jobs, not because of inability to do the work but rather because of a failure to adjust to the social demands of the world of work (Gold, 1973; Kolstoe, 1961; Kolstoe & Frey, 1965). In addition, there is some evidence that retarded individuals are unrealistic in the establishment of their vocational goals (Knight, 1972). Introducing vocational and career education to the retarded child at the secondary level may well be too late. Job attitudes and work habits are formed early. By exposing young retarded children to the world of work and by fostering proper work attitudes and habits at an early age, a sound foundation can be established for later success on the job. Thus, curricula for the primary and intermediate level special class should contain experiences for each of these two areas.

THE WORLD OF WORK

While even preprimary level retarded children are generally aware that people work, retarded children are often unaware of the various occupations that exist in modern society. They are even less aware of the requirements needed to fulfill those jobs. If one were to ask a retarded child what he wished to be when he finished school, likely responses would be "an airplane pilot," "a race car driver," "a nurse," and so on. If the child were then asked what a person needs to know or do to become qualified for such work, the retarded child would probably not be able to answer. Thus, the purpose of career education for the young retarded child should be (a) to introduce them to typical occupations performed by average citizens as opposed to the highly idealized and publicized jobs to which they are typically exposed, (b) to acquaint them with the qualifications required and the duties and responsibilities expected in these occupations, and (c) to aid students in establishing effective vocational choices by comparing their interests and abilities with the requirements of the various jobs surveyed. The following activities were designed as an aid in accomplishing these goals.

Job of the Week

Before the mentally retarded can develop an interest in jobs within their capabilities, they must be introduced to these jobs. A simple means of providing exposure to a wide variety of occupations is to select a new job for discussion each week. A special section of the bulletin board can be set aside for pictures and other information illustrating this job. Each day a specific period of time, preferably 15 to 20 minutes, should be set aside for discussion of the "job of the week." On the first day of the school week the new job should be introduced to the class, the appropriate section of the bulletin board pointed out, and a discussion conducted on basic aspects of the particular job. On each of the following days a brief discussion should be devoted to a different aspect of the job of the week. Topics for discussion and presentation might include skills and abilities required on the job, tools and equipment required on the job, the role the job plays in the community, and the need for persons interested in performing the job.

Job Work sheets

Studies of memory in the mentally retarded have generally indicated that a retarded person's short term memory is defective (Robinson & Robinson, 1965). This leads to problems in the acquisition of new information. Once a retarded individual has thoroughly learned something, however, he is likely to remember it. Thus, if a retarded child is provided with but one brief exposure to a new occupation he will probably forget much of the important information concerning this job. However, if the child is given multiple exposures to the important aspects of the job, his recall will be greatly improved. An effective means of following up discussions of jobs available in the community is the job work sheet. These work sheets are essentially drill sheets prepared on standard ditto masters and duplicated for the class. At the lowest level these sheets might involve matching a picture of a worker with a job (fireman with crew putting out fire) or a tool with a worker or job. At a more complex

3. RESPONSIBILITY

level they might involve reading a brief question and selecting the correct answer.

Meet the Worker

A motivating way to introduce students to the world of work is through a modification of the television show *Meet the Press*. By periodically having representatives of various occupations discuss their jobs for the class (or for several classes together), students are afforded an opportunity to ask the experts. It is surprisingly easy to obtain workers from various fields for student interviews. Most companies are more than willing to release or supply persons to serve in this capacity. Whenever possible, a "meet the worker session" is an invaluable means of reinforcing the job of the week.

Job Analysis

If mentally retarded individuals are to develop realistic vocational choices, they must be made aware of the requirements of various jobs as well as their own strengths and weaknesses. One means of increasing pupil awareness in these areas is to have students perform job analyses on different occupations. In this activity the student is read a story, shown a film, or otherwise exposed to a specific job. After this presentation the teacher conducts a class lesson aimed at analyzing the attributes needed to fulfill the requirements of this job. Generally, this lesson would consist of a class discussion in which students explore questions such as: Does a person who works at this type of job need to be able to stand on his feet for long periods of time, lift heavy weights, distinguish between fine shades of colors? These discussions should be followed up with discussions of individual strengths and weaknesses as they relate to the job presented (e.g., Could Betty load cement bags on a truck?).

What's My Job

Assuming teachers have introduced a program to expose children to the world of work and the requirements of various occupations, a way to increase motivation and reinforce information previously learned is through the game "What's My Job?" This game is basically a modification of the television panel show *What's My Line?* To start the game the teacher thinks of a job and the students must ask questions which can be answered by a *yes* or *no* in order to gain clues about the job. When a student thinks he knows the job, he may raise his hand and guess. If he is correct he wins the game and may pick the next job. If incorrect he may not guess again, though he may continue to ask a *yes* or *no* type question and confer with others who are preparing to guess.

A Class Business

In addition to exposure to the various types of occupations available, it would also be advantageous for retarded individuals to be exposed to business operations. This exposure should not be aimed at producing future entrepreneurs; rather it should be cursory, designed primarily to enhance the retarded child's understanding of the factors involved in even the smallest business. A class business can be an excellent way to accomplish this end.

Such an operation should be constructed along lines similar to that of Junior Achievement. While the teacher or school will supply ample capital to initiate the business, students must return a portion of their income toward paying off the loan granted them for initial wares and toward the purchase of new materials. Class art projects, foodstuffs from the class kitchen, and car washes can be excellent starting places for a class business.

WORK HABITS AND ATTITUDES

Vocational education for the elementary age level mentally retarded child should emphasize the development of adequate work habits and good job attitudes rather than specific job skills or on-the-job training. This is not meant to suggest that these latter skills have no place in a curriculum for the elementary age retarded child. Early work experiences such as those in the school cafeteria or with the school janitor can provide the child with invaluable initial on-the-job training. Likewise, many of the skills subsumed under the heading of practical arts are actually skills which will be useful to the vocational training of the mentally retarded.

Sign In Sheets

By requiring students to sign in and out of the classroom, the teacher can reinforce one of the primary prerequisites to success on the job, that of being on time. The sign in sheet may be varied in complexity to suit the level of the class. At the lowest level it could consist of laminated cards bearing a photograph and the name of the child with a space for the child to write in his time of arrival (in grease pencil) copied from a digital clock. The higher level students could be expected to fill out a work sheet providing their name, the time, and so on. Whatever format is used, the activity should resemble punching a time clock on a job. To provide transfer, much discussion could be centered on who was earliest, who was latest, and who arrived at the same time. One novel method consisted of a teacher-made tape recording of the time, each minute repeated every 15 seconds before the new time was given. This tape was started 5 minutes before class and played for 10 minutes. Students had to write the time they heard on the tape, then put their paper in a time clock for validation.

Work Wheels

The ability to assume responsibility is essential for success on even the simplest jobs. Assigning students a certain job to perform each day is one method of developing responsibility not only in performing an assigned task but also in being aware of a responsibility that changes daily or weekly. A work chart or wheel may be constructed by the teacher and class. It may be a simple slot chart or a large

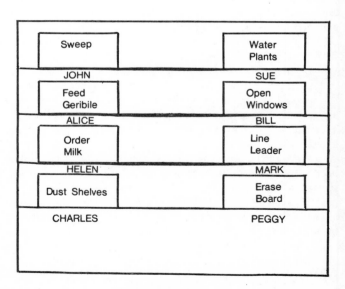

FIGURE 1
A SLOT CHART

wheel which matches a student to a job (see Figures 1 and 2). Nothing more than the name of a job is necessary because a reference book may contain an illustrated description of each job.

Tool License

The tool license is a simple means of providing status (reinforcement) for gaining skill with various equipment and tools. This procedure gives students a realistic view of job qualifications.

Such licenses may be limited in design only by the teacher's imagination and creativity. A wallet size card which depicts the tool, the bearer's name, and perhaps his picture can be obtained by each student who successfully demonstrates his skill by a series of training periods and competency checks. Such licenses may be given for scissors, ruler, paper cutter, claw hammer, stapler, staple gun, etc. No large classroom chart need be kept because part of the status of achieving the license is showing it on request when the teacher needs someone to use the particular tool or to help train another individual. A plain white card may indicate apprentice status and a colored card with picture and place for the bearer's signature may indicate journeyman status. A scissors license, for example, may require competency checks on safely carrying, passing, and holding scissors, as well as cutting along lines of varying difficulty marked on duplicated work sheets.

Task Sheets

One of the most important concepts for retarded individuals to internalize is the notion that a certain amount of work must be accomplished in a day's time. Various assignments may be listed, such as work sheets for math, spelling, and reading. Classroom tasks such as sweeping or opening the windows may also be put on the task sheet. Another item might be a particular "special" activity that will be included in the day's curriculum such as music, physical education, or art. A space may be provided for the student to check

or have the teacher check off each completed task. These sheets may be taped to the desk or hung at a work area, locker, or mailbox so that both student and teacher will have ready reference to the progress being made.

Job Evaluation

Quality is an important aspect of work and should be introduced early. Students are not always aware of the vast number of gradations between not doing a job and doing it well. Establishing a quality evaluation rather than a simple *done/not done* standard can be essential in developing pride and extending skill attainment. At first, such quality checks can be simple levels such as *not done, not OK, needs improvement, OK,* and *good*. Using general descriptors allows for variations of ability and for working up to one's ability level. Care should be taken to use an absolute standard at both ends of the scale, however. This provides needed reality which enables a mentally retarded child to assess his own ability level when called upon to do so.

Worker of the Week Award

A weekly award for a selected good worker (not necessarily the best) can be established as a means of reinforcing good work habits or production. Varying criteria such as most improvement or consistent high quality may be used. A plaque, certificate, or picture on the bulletin board may be used with whatever ceremony the teacher may wish to include. Using the principal to present the award can elevate the worker of the week award to a very high level of status.

Hopefully, the above ideas will provide special educators with at least a meager start towards providing for the vocational and career education needs of the young retarded child. With a little extra effort, classroom teachers can lay a solid foundation for the future vocational success of their pupils.

FIGURE 2
A WHEEL CHART

REFERENCES

Gold, M. W. Research on the vocational habilitation of the retarded: The present, the future. In N. R. Ellis (Ed.), *International Review of Research in Mental Retardation* (Vol. 6). New York: Academic Press, 1973.

Knight, O. B. Occupational aspirations of the educable mentally retarded. *Training School Bulletin*, 1972, 69, 54-57.

Kolstoe, O. P. An examination of some characteristics which discriminate between employed and not-employed mentally retarded males. *American Journal of Mental Deficiency*, 1961, 66, 472-482.

Kolstoe, O. P., & Frey, R. M. *A high school work-study program for mentally subnormal students*. Carbondale: Southern Illinois Press, 1965.

Robinson, H., & Robinson, N. *The mentally retarded child: A psychological approach*. New York: McGraw-Hill, 1965.

An Experiment in the Pre-Occupational Education of Mentally Retarded Students on the Junior High School Level

CAROL N. FLERES

CAROL N. FLERES *is a doctoral candidate, University of South Carolina, Columbia and Assistant Professor of Special Education, Baptist College, Charleston, South Carolina. The author expresses appreciation to Dr. Harold Robbins of Queens College, City University of New York and to Mr. Phillip Allopenna, Principal of Harry B. Thompson Junior High School, Syosset, New York for their assistance with this program.*

It has been common practice for many districts to provide career exploration opportunities for mentally retarded adolescents within the school. The purpose of this exploration is to familiarize youngsters with behavioral expectations of daily employment. While this type of program serves a useful purpose, it does, nevertheless, fall short of providing the necessary awareness of occupational alternatives available to the mentally handicapped. It was, therefore, our belief that simulating realistic occupational experiences would permit these youngsters to develop skills necessary to make a better match between their own capabilities and an occupational choice.

Central School District Number Two, Syosset, New York and the Nassau County Board of Cooperative Educational Services (BOCES) combined resources to provide a multi-occupational program designed to meet the needs of the mentally retarded. Five broad areas were selected for the program: Health Services (Nurse's Aide), Offset Printing (Printer's Helper), Auto Mechanics (Gas Station Attendant), Cosmetology (Manicurist), Electronics (Assembly Line Worker). Staff representing both the public school and the vocational center cooperated in developing behavioral objectives.

To modify behavior and, at the same time, to introduce concepts of banking, students were paid "school dollars" according to their individual work performance. (Attitudes were stressed, not skills.) Token payments were deposited in the student's personal checking account. Checks drawn could then be used for the purchase of items in the class store. To promote delayed gratification, articles of differing value were offered and students encouraged to save in order to purchase quality items.

For illustrative purposes two specific areas of the program will be outlined.

Health Services [Nurse's Aide]

The first three weeks of the program were spent in Health Services, an area in which persons of retarded intellectual ability may find a variety of occupational opportunities such as nurse's aides, laundry room workers, cafeteria workers, laboratory attendants (washing test tubes and cleaning slides or other equipment), or as hos-

"An Experiment in the Pre-Occupational Education of Mentally Retarded Students on the Junior High School Level," Carol N. Fleres, *Education and Training of the Mentally Retarded*, Vol. 10, No. 1, 1975. ©Division on Mental Retardation of the Council of Exceptional Children.

pital supply room attendants.

Following are the objectives developed to introduce some of the skills required of a nurse's aide:

1. To demonstrate the correct technique for washing hands
2. To identify equipment used in a hospital unit (bedside table) and be able to equip such a unit
3. To clean an empty unit using the aseptic technique
4. To make a closed (unoccupied) bed
5. To read an oral thermometer
6. To count a pulse at the radial artery (wrist)
7. To comprehend the essentials of food service and demonstrate:
   a. setting a basic tray
   b. serving patients and making them comfortable
   c. feeding a blind person

The behavioral checklist by which students received token payment included using good manners, following the nurse's orders, displaying a kind and cheerful disposition, working well and helping others, and appearing well-groomed. Students could earn a maximum of five dollars in each category.

An effort was made to point out numerous areas of related employment opportunities. Two field trips were taken to nursing homes and one to a retirement home for the blind. Although a trip to the local hospital would have been desirable, arrangements were not possible.

While the girls enjoyed the total experience, the boys expressed concern that a nurse's aide was essentially "woman's work." No amount of convincing satisfied them to the contrary.

Auto Mechanics [Gas Station Attendant]

Retarded students wishing to enter the automotive trades might find employment as gas station attendants or, in some cases, mechanic's helpers. While both men and women are employed by the industry, the girls' interests lie more in other areas. Therefore, they spent only one week in the gas station business while the boys remained for four weeks.

Objectives for boys and girls were:

1. To be able to read the air pressure gauge for tires
2. To clean a windshield thoroughly using a squeegee
3. To demonstrate the procedure for checking:
   a. oil level
   b. water level in the radiator
   c. anti-freeze
   d. water in the battery
4. To fill the windshield washer bag

Additionally, the boys were to demonstrate ability to:

5. Change a tire
6. Change spark plugs on American made automobiles
   a. remove and replace spark plugs
   b. file the plugs
   c. gap a spark plug
7. Fill the radiator with anti-freeze
8. Fill the battery with water
9. Inspect:
   a. transmission oil
   b. brake fluid

The behavioral checklist sought the following goals: clean work habits, following directions, working safely, working hard, and cooperating with fellow workers. Each category was weighted five points equally.

The vocational teacher felt that the students' achievements were comparable to those of a first month regular high school class with one exception, the retarded youngsters lacked the physical strength needed for changing a tire. One might speculate as to causes. Perhaps the relatively small stature of most of the boys was a factor. It is also quite possible, however, that lack of physical training and normal social outlets resulted in their underdeveloped muscular proficiency.

Throughout the automotive program a high school senior assisted the teacher in insuring safety. This was a difficult task for any one person, as the shop was large and, at any given moment, a variety of activities was in progress.

Supplementary Instruction

Activities in the junior high school special class supplemented the mini-vocational experiences by means of discussion, "coffee" breaks, and the study of available part-time jobs for teenagers. Also, by delivering the New York Times, students learned to deal with subscribers, make change, categorize coins and bills, compute totals with an adding machine and fill out a bank deposit slip. Before receiving permission to write out a check negotiable for cash, the delivery boy or girl reviewed the meaning of terms used on his pay stub (gross pay, social security, other deductions, and net pay). In-school work experiences were announced as Classified Advertisements on the blackboard with application and interview prerequisite to employment.

Grooming was stressed and a special area set up to encourage good grooming practices within the classroom. A certificate was awarded each student who demonstrated ability to mend tears in clothing, sew buttons, shine shoes, shampoo hair, care for face and hands, press a dress or slacks, and pass an oral test on general aspects of grooming. Notable improvements were apparent.

3. RESPONSIBILITY

Student Aides

Through a program of independent study, two senior high school students interested in pursuing careers in special education helped to plan and execute projects and make purchases for the class store. Because of their enthusiasm, the project had been successful in achieving its goals. Nine out of ten parents responding to a questionnaire favored continuation of the program while many volunteered positive comments throughout the project as well. Of course, meaningful evaluation will come later when the students acquire and, hopefully, maintain positions in the working community. innovative suggestions, and sense of professionalism beyond their years, the contributions of both the girls were indispensable to the program.

Results

On initiation of the program absenteeism dropped by approximately one-third. Students became excited about working and began, for the first time, to refer to themselves as workers. They made numerous inquiries regarding employment and also said that they preferred working to either seeing a filmstrip about a job or merely talking about employment. Nine of the ten said that they were happy to have participated and six thought they had found an occupational area to possibly pursue in the future.

Incentives were of obvious value. Individual student behaviors improved in direct relation to the number of school dollars earned and, in areas where grooming was reinforced, improvement was dramatic. Eight out of ten students responding to an oral questionnaire said that they felt earning school money had been worth the effort regardless of their feelings about working at a particular job. In addition, students showed increased eagerness to perform paper and pencil tasks such as filling in banking or employment forms. By the end of the school year, oral testing revealed that each student understood, at least fundamentally, the concept of checking as well as the terms deposit, balance forward and total.

Through encounter with many different teacher-employers, students lost their initial timidity, thus moving easily from one mini-experience to another. They learned to approach less familiar adults and to make their needs and desires known when necessary. Four of the five vocational teachers maintained that the retarded students could be integrated into regular classes provided that placement was restricted to one or two retarded youngsters in any one regular class.

All areas of the curriculum were illuminated by the simulated work experiences. Students showed increased desire and ability to engage in meaningful discussions regarding employment. Occupational living had become an integral part of their experience.

The John F. Kennedy High School Work-Study Program

Classroom Techniques

SANDY ALPER
RAY DeNEVE
PAUL M. RETISH

SANDY ALPER *is a work-study teacher at the John F. Kennedy High School, Cedar Rapids, Iowa.*

RAY DeNEVE *is a Curriculum Coordinator of Special Education Classes, Dubuque, Iowa.*

PAUL M. RETISH *is an Associate Professor, Division of Special Education, College of Education, The University of Iowa, Iowa City.*

Abstract: Sandy Alper, Ray DeNeve, and Paul M. Retish discuss a work-study program which was initiated to provide a real-life experience for educable mentally retarded students attending The John F. Kennedy High School in Cedar Rapids, Iowa. The lab offers a school without walls and its purpose is to ease the transition from school to job.

John T. Wilson and John J. Koran identify a variety of behaviors and material modifications employed by a teacher relative to the adaption of elementary science curriculum materials (SAPA) for use with special education children. Tentatively, it appeared that both teacher behaviors and material modifications tended to increase lesson structure as a means to guide acquisition and facilitate mental integration of content. WAYNE D. LANCE, Department Editor

The difficulties the educable mentally retarded encounter on the job due to social and emotional factors has been documented by several authors (Kolstoe, 1961; Michael-Smith, 1950; Howe, 1967). The evidence suggests that the retarded persons rarely remain established in their first or second positions. In the first few years of employment, they show a history of movement among jobs with little or no locomotion to positions requiring higher level skills. The reasons for this movement seem to be directly related to their frequent inability to get along with others.

The Work-Study Program

The work-study program at John F. Kennedy High School in Cedar Rapids, Iowa, was established 5 years ago to provide academic and work experiences for educable mentally retarded sophomores, juniors, and seniors.

Academic classes in language arts, social studies, math, and science are held in the mornings. These classes meet the Iowa Department of Public Instruction's requirements for a high school diploma. Juniors and seniors work at various jobs within the community during the afternoon. Many students have, however, experienced the types of difficulties mentioned above on the job situation.

In an attempt to prevent such failures and frustrations before students are placed on jobs in their junior and senior year, an Actual Life Experience (ALE) was initiated during the 1969-70 school year. This program was an attempt to prepare sophomores

"Classroom Techniques, The John F. Kennedy High School Work Study Program," Sandy Alper, Ray DeNeve, Paul M. Retish, *Education and Training of the Mentally Retarded*, Vol. 8, No. 2, 1973.

125

3. RESPONSIBILITY

for the actual work experiences they will encounter in their junior and senior years.

The heart of the ALE program is a work laboratory which was set up in a former nightclub in the downtown business district of Cedar Rapids. Since the building is in an area designated for urban renewal, it was available to the school district rent free.

The ALE lab offers simulated work experiences in several areas: crafts, production, a kitchen-restaurant, nursing, and clerical duties. In each area the student has the opportunity to perform a number of tasks. For example, in the kitchen students learn to prepare and serve meals to the public. A restaurant atmosphere is established and the students perform the duties of a short-order cook, waitress or waiter, and dishwasher. Students in the craft areas make items such as lamps, candles, wreaths (and other seasonal items), in addition to learning sewing skills, and shopping for supplies.

The production area makes and repairs puzzles, cardboard puppets, games, and other educational materials for use in local elementary schools. Students are able to follow the progress of their work and see the final result as they help to deliver these items to the elementary schools. The students also learn to work with basic tools. The nursing area centers around duties expected of a nurse's aide (as well as home care for the sick) and includes instruction by Red Cross nurses. The clerical area emphasizes message-taking, telephone procedures, alphabetizing, filing, etc.

Sophomores attend the lab in the afternoons on a 3 week rotating basis. They are transported downtown to the lab for a 3 week period and assigned to a particular area of the lab. The next 3 week period is spent at school in mini-mod courses. These mini-mod courses are designed to reinforce tasks at the lab and include areas such as time, measurement and money, crafts, first-aid, driving laws, and other relevant areas.

Results of the Lab

The intent of the ALE lab is not to teach a specific job skill, but rather to introduce each student to a number of work tasks which should prove valuable to him in any job situation. As Smith (1968) points out, it is probably unreasonable to assume that the retarded student will remain in the original job in which he is placed. The instructional component of the work-study program, therefore, should prepare the student to perform satisfactorily in a variety of settings and not in a circumscribed, narrowly defined occupation.

The emphasis at the ALE lab is on dependability, cooperation, punctuality, and related qualities demanded by any employer. The problem of social adjustment encountered by these students is also taken into consideration by allowing them to work with a variety of people and to meet the public.

The success of the ALE lab is at this point difficult to measure in terms of job success for these students. A followup study which will include both occupational and personal adjustment is, however, being planned. It is felt that the ALE lab does offer the student an environment in which he is allowed and encouraged to seek experiences often outside the scope of the traditional classroom setting. A result of the lab that has been felt by those who participate there as well as those in the home-school setting has been one of changing self concept. In interviews with students, teachers, and paraprofessional persons, the unanimous feeling is that the lab offers an environment more relevant to the needs of these students and affords them an opportunity to be successful.

Two Followup Studies of Former Educable Mentally Retarded Students from the Kansas Work-Study Project

JERRY D. CHAFFIN
CHARLES R. SPELLMAN
C. EDWARD REGAN
ROXANA DAVISON

JERRY D. CHAFFIN *is Associate Professor of Education and Coordinator of Special Education Administration Programs;* CHARLES R. SPELLMAN *is Operations Coordinator, Special Education Instructional Materials Center;* ROXANA DAVISON *is Research Assistant, School of Education, Department of Special Education, University of Kansas, Lawrence; and* C. EDWARD REGAN *is Coordinator of Programs for the Mentally Retarded, Shawnee Mission School District #512, Shawnee Mission, Kansas. The original Kansas Project was supported in part by a grant from Social Rehabilitation Services RD1548.*

Abstract: Two followup studies were conducted to investigate the postschool adjustment of educable mentally retarded subjects from the Kansas Work-Study Program and a comparison sample from neighboring school districts. The results indicated that most of these educable mentally retarded students would be employed in the competitive labor market without the benefits of a work study program. Students who had participated in the work study program, however, were graduated more often, held their jobs longer, and earned more money than did the students from the comparison group.

PROVIDING educable mentally retarded students with both educational and vocational experiences is generally accepted as the means to insure later social and economic adjustment. The responsibility for work study programs is being assumed by public schools in cooperation with state vocational rehabilitation, employment service, and vocational education agencies. Nearly 10 years ago, these cooperative efforts were seen as a significant development in rehabilitation of the retarded (HEW, 1961). Even so, the efficacy of cooperative work study programs for the retarded has not been demonstrated as yet.

A number of writers have reviewed followup studies of the postschool adjustment of mentally retarded individuals from public schools and residential centers (Carriker, 1957; Goldstein, 1964; Shafter, 1957; Tizard, 1959; Voelker, 1962; Windle,

1962). These reviews provide the reader with a summary of studies involving retarded adults of various ages, intelligence quotients, socioeconomic groups, and educational backgrounds who were contacted during different economic periods. These reviews of followup studies, however, do not focus on former students of *work study* programs.

In a recent publication, Stachlecker (1967) assembled 79 selected articles pertinent to the education and training of the mentally retarded, including descriptions of 7 work study programs and reports on 8 followup studies. Other work study programs (Carson & Arveson, 1963; Muller & Lewis, 1966) have been published, but like Stachlecker's text, they are primarily descriptive, and they do not report the results of their program.

Spellman (1968) attempted to compare

the results of 10 work study programs which had emphasized the cooperative efforts of vocational rehabilitation and public schools in the preparation of the mentally retarded for later adjustment. Spellman noted that the employability of the graduates of these programs ranged from 46 percent to 86 percent. He was cautious in drawing conclusions regarding the results of these projects since they had been conducted in different localities and many important variables, such as IQ, socioeconomic status, specific training procedures, and status of dropouts were often not clearly explained in the documents he reviewed. All of these projects emphasized administrative or descriptive aspects rather than the merits of the program in regard to student outcomes. Spellman concluded that this emphasis on demonstration "may account for the fact that these reports did not provide impressive evidence to support the work study arrangement [p. 36]." Without supportive evidence, the efficacy of work study programs must remain speculative.

Purpose

The purpose of this article is to report the comparative vocational status of the students who participated in the Kansas Work-Study Project during the years 1964-67 and of a comparison group who participated in the summer of 1964. A followup study of these two groups was conducted in 1967 and 1969 in an attempt to evaluate the efficacy of the high school work-study program. A detailed description of the 1967 followup study and a comprehensive account of the work study program have been reported previously (Chaffin, Smith, & Haring, 1967; Spellman, 1968). The initial followup study and the Kansas Work-Study Project will be reviewed briefly to provide background for the 1969 followup study.

A Review of the Kansas Project

The Kansas Work-Study Program was a 3 year selected demonstration project which had as its major purpose the development of procedures for vocational evaluation and training of educable mentally retarded adolescents in two Kansas school districts. Specifically, the Kansas Project sought to provide: (a) comprehensive rehabilitation, diagnosis, and evaluation of employment potential; (b) actual job tryout and job training; (c) job placement supervision; (d) practical curricula activities; (e) social work services to enlist pa-

rental support and cooperation; and (f) evaluation of project procedures. The project sought to achieve these objectives through the concerted efforts of rehabilitation counselors, school administrators, regular class teachers, and special education personnel.

Eligibility. Selection criteria specified intellectual retardation (about 45-80 IQ), retarded achievement (3 or more years), and the probability, after training, for social and occupational competencies. These criteria were consistent with the eligibility requirements for educable mentally retarded students in special education classes in Kansas public schools. In practice, therefore, students who were eligible for special education classes in their respective school districts were also eligible for the Kansas project.

Work samples. All students in the Kansas Work-Study Program participated in a series of work samples in the community; these served, in part, as an evaluation of their working abilities. A work sample consisted of a short term placement (2-4 weeks) in the community for approximately 2 hours each day. Generally, the students were required to participate in at least three different work samples. The primary function of these work samples was to familiarize the student with a variety of different vocational environments and to provide the teacher and counselor with a comprehensive vocational evaluation.

On the job training. From these evaluations a vocational-educational plan for on the job training and classroom instruction was developed. Job training differed from the work sample both in duration and emphasis. While in training, students worked approximately 4 hours and attended special education classes for 3 hours per day. The emphasis therefore changed from evaluating vocational abilities to the eliminating of behaviors inconsistent with work, teaching specific skills important for a given job, and initiating instructional programs designed to develop generally desirable work habits and attitudes. Classroom instruction concurrent with the evaluation and training phases was designed to enhance the work experience program by providing a curriculum which centered around functional application of the academic subjects and activities for daily living.

Placement phase. During the last semester of the senior year, students entered the placement phase in which they were required to work fulltime in the competitive labor market. Continued training and evaluation of the working seniors was conducted through weekly meetings and by regular contact with their employers.

Selection of Sample

During the summer of 1964, the first year of the Kansas Project, two groups of educable mentally retarded students were identified for later comparison, as one method of evaluating the program. The experimental sample consisted of the first 30 students from the two school districts participating in the work study project. These 30 subjects were matched with a comparison group consisting of students who were referred by their high school counselors from neighboring school districts. Each student referred by these counselors was evaluated on IQ, achievement, and socioeconomic status. From these data a comparison population was selected. No attempt was made to exclude subjects from either group on variables other than age, sex, intelligence, achievement, and socioeconomic status. A few students from the comparison group were enrolled in secondary special education programs; however, none participated in an organized work study plan involving both vocational rehabilitation and special education. A comparison of the two groups on the selection variables is provided in Table 1.

The IQ scores were obtained from individually administered intelligence tests, either the *Stanford Binet* or the *Wechsler Adult Intelligence Scale*. Academic achievement in the basic skill subjects was assessed by the *Wide Range Achievement Test*. Both achievement and intelligence tests were individually administered by certified school psychologists.

TABLE 1
Group Comparison of Age, IQ, Sex, Occupational Rating, and Wide Range Achievement Scores

Variables	Comparison (N = 30)	Experimental (N = 30)
Mean age (9–1–64)	16.36	16.65
Mean IQ	63.40	63.77
Mean occupational rating of parents	59.77	59.10
Mean reading grade level	4.30	4.20
Mean arithmetic grade level	4.65	4.32
Mean spelling grade level	4.05	3.72
Sex: Boys	21	21
Girls	9	9

Socioeconomic status was based on an occupational rating scale developed by the National Opinion Research Center (Bendix & Lipsett, 1953). The scale assigns an occupational rating to the parents based on the social prestige associated with their occupation.

Results of the 1967 Followup Study

The immediate results of the project were determined by individual interviews with 59 of the 60 subjects during July and August, 1967. Only one of the 59 subjects located refused to discuss his vocational status, except for stating that he was employed fulltime. In the remaining cases the employment status was verified with each subject's employer. Table 2 provides a summary of the school and employment status of the subjects at the time of the 1967 followup.

The experimental group had more subjects who were graduated and fewer who dropped from school, although the comparison group had more students who were still in school. A comparison of all students who were out of school, including those who were graduated or dropped, revealed that 92 percent of the experimental group and 68 percent of the comparison group were considered employed. Students were considered employed if they were working full or parttime, were in advanced vocational training programs, or were housewives. A comparison of graduates revealed even greater differences. Of the experimental graduates, 16 of 17 (94 percent) were employed, in training, or housewives, compared with 4 of 7 (57 percent) of the comparison graduates.

Even though 94 percent of the experimental graduates of the Kansas Project had achieved satisfactory vocational adjustment, the reader is reminded that about 68 percent of all comparison subjects had achieved similar adjustment status. Thus, the project claimed intervention effects for only about 30 percent of the graduates served, assuming that at least 70 percent of the experimental group would have been employed without project intervention. Interpretation of the results of this followup was confounded since three subjects from the experimental group and nine subjects from the comparison group were still in school. Two other experimental subjects and one comparison subject had transferred to another school. Other students from the comparison population had been out of school only a short time. As a result it was posited that a number of students who were placed by the project might not maintain their employment status and a

TABLE 2

School and Employment Status: 1967 Followup Study

	Experimental (N = 30)			Comparison (N = 29) [a]		
	Employed [b]	Unemployed	Total	Employed [b]	Unemployed	Total
Graduated	16	1	17 (68%)	4	3	7 (37%)
Dropped out	7	1	8 (32%)	9	3	12 (63%)
Total out of school	23 (92%)	2 (8%)	25 (100%)	13 (68%)	6 (32%)	19 (100%)
In school			3			9
Transferred; in school			2			1

[a] One subject dropped out of school, employment status unknown.
[b] Full or parttime, vocational training, or housewife.

number from the comparison group, recently out of school, might not have been successful in finding a job during the competitive summer market. The 1969 followup negates the above limitations since all subjects had been out of school at least one year.

Results of the 1969 Followup Study

During August and September, 1969, interviews with the subjects were conducted either by the authors, students in a special education teacher training program, or former staff of the Kansas Project. All 30 experimental and 28 of the comparison students or their families were located and interviewed. One subject from the comparison group was deceased and one could not be located; therefore, the present data are available for 58 of the original 60 subjects. Fifteen subjects (9 experimental and 6 comparison) had moved from the Kansas City metropolitan area. In 4 cases, the subject was interviewed by phone and in 11 instances the data was obtained from interviews with the subject's immediate family. It should be emphasized, however, that with one exception, employment status was verified with each employer.

The results of the 1969 followup with regard to school and employment status are presented in Table 3. An analysis of these results shows that more experimental subjects graduated from high school than did

subjects from the comparison group, and the vocational adjustment of the two groups was essentially the same.

Additional findings from the 1969 followup include the following:

1. A comparison of the salaries of the two groups reflected a substantial difference. Actual wages which could be verified by the subject's employer were available for 42 subjects (23 experimental and 19 comparison). The mean gross weekly wage was $90.45 and $62.84 for the experimental and comparison groups, respectively. The data were analyzed by means of the Mann-Whitney U Test, resulting in a significant ($p < .05$) difference favoring the experimental group.

2. The length of time each subject had been employed in his present job was also investigated. The experimental subjects had been in their present positions an average of 18.7 months whereas the comparison subjects had been in their present jobs an average of 10.6 months. These differences were also significant ($p < .05$). Chart 1 provides a more detailed description of the types of jobs held by the experimental and comparison subjects.

3. Data on the marital status of subjects in this study indicated that 4 of the experimental subjects were married compared with 8 of the comparison subjects. Two of the married subjects from the comparison group were living with their parents. All of the married subjects from the experimental group were

School and Employment Status: 1969 Followup Study

TABLE 3

Subjects	Experimental (N = 30)			Comparison (N = 28) [a]		
	Employed [b]	Unemployed	Total	Employed [b]	Unemployed	Total
Graduated	19	3	22 (73%)	13	2	15 (54%)
Dropped out	6	2	8 (27%)	8	5	13 (46%)
Total out of school	25 (83%)	5 (17%)	30 (100%)	21 (75%)	7 (25%)	28 (100%)

[a] One unknown and one deceased.
[b] Full or parttime, vocational training, or housewife.

living independently.

4. An analysis of the living arrangements showed that a total of 32 subjects were living with their parents or immediate family. Thirteen experimental students were living alone, with spouse, friends, or in military housing compared to 10 from the comparison group. One student from the experimental group and 2 from the comparison were living in residential state institutions at the time of the followup.

5. Other available data from the 1969 followup indicated there was no significant relationship beetween IQ and employability, IQ and wages earned, occupational status of parent and employability, occupational status of parent and wages earned, or length of employment and wages earned.

CHART 1
Employment by Job Title: Data from the 1969 Followup Study

Experimental	Comparison
2 Military service	4 Military service
1 Housewife	2 Housewife
6 Labor[a]	6 Labor
2 Assembly line	2 Assembly line
1 Salesclerk	1 Salesclerk
4 Hospital worker	1 Car washer
1 Garment cutter apprent.	1 Dishwasher
1 Ambulance attendant	1 Machinist apprent.
1 Spot-welder	1 Pressman apprent.
1 Motel maid	1 Baby sitter
1 Beautician's helper	1 Door to door sales[b]
1 Baker's helper	
1 Carpenter apprent.	
2 Vocational training	
25 Employed	21 Employed
5 Unemployed	7 Unemployed
	1 Deceased
	1 Unknown
30 Total	30 Total

[a] One parttime.
[b] Parttime.

Discussion

The initial results of employment status favored the experimental group of whom 92 percent were employed, compared with 68 percent of the comparison subjects. However, during the 2 year period between the 1967 and 1969 followup, the employment of the experimental group *decreased* from 92 percent to 83 percent and the employment of the comparison group *increased* from 68 percent to 75 percent, virtually eliminating any differences between the two groups. These results suggest that at least three-fourths of the edu-

cable mentally retarded are capable of some kind of employment without the intensive vocational preparation purportedly inherent in cooperative work study arrangements. It would appear that the goal of the work study program *is not to make students employable*; rather the goal is to *enhance the employability which already exists* for most of the students in the program. This can be carried out by developing deliberate work training programs in the skilled and semiskilled occupations with a goal of increasing substantially the earning potential of the more capable educable mentally retarded students. In this respect the Kansas Project was moderately successful. Subjects from the experimental group had an average earning of more than $90.00 weekly, more than $25.00 greater than the weekly earnings of the comparison group. Six of the experimental subjects earned $100.00 or more per week and one subject earned $200.00 per week; four of these subjects had annual incomes exceeding $6,450.00, which was the average starting salary for teachers in the Kansas City, Kansas school district during the 1969-70 school year. This is consistent with Dinger's (1961) findings. He reported that 42 percent of the employed group in his study had an annual income greater than the 1958 Pennsylvania salary ($3,600) paid the beginning teacher.

Despite the efforts of the project staff, a number of the students dropped out of school, some were unemployed, and a few underemployed. Kolstoe (1961) and Warren (1961) suggest that employers can accurately predict an employee's later potential for successful employment. By placing all mentally retarded students on work samples, and having the employers predict the clients' later employment, school programs could develop a dual approach to the work experience program. Students who were judged successful could immediately receive extensive training to upgrade their employment potential. Unsuccessful clients could continue to receive training in in-school training stations, or in highly supervised or semisheltered settings in the community.

In conclusion it would appear from the results of these followup studies that cooperative work study programs which operate similarly to the Kansas Work-Study Project may be achieving limited success. Continued efforts directed toward adding precision to present procedures should result in achievement of maximum vocational potential for every educable mentally retarded individual.

Costs and Benefits of Training Educable Students: The Kansas Work-Study Project Reconsidered

John W. Muth/Larry D. Singell

John W. Muth is a graduate student and *Larry D. Singell* is Professor of Economics, Department of Economics, University of Colorado, Boulder.

The purpose of this article is to suggest that projects which have the employability or earnings potential of students as their major objective should consider the economic costs and benefits involved in such projects. In a previous article in this journal, Chaffin, Spellman, Regan, and Davison (1971) analyzed two followup studies of projects designed to provide educable mentally retarded students with both educational and vocational experiences. The postschool adjustment of the students who had participated in the Kansas Work-Study Project were compared with a sample from neighboring school districts, and the results clearly suggested that participants graduated from high school more often, held their jobs longer, and earned more money than did students from the comparison group. The authors thus drew the conclusion that this, or similar programs, "may be achieving limited success" (p. 738).

Using cost data provided to us by Chaffin and the data reported in the 1971 article, we made an economic evaluation of the Kansas Work-Study Project. Our findings suggest that, when the costs of this project are compared with the gains in earning potential of the students involved, the project was very successful rather than achieving the "limited success" described in the followup evaluation.

The conceptual framework for economically evaluating such a project is quite simple. The project represents an investment of funds at or over some specified time period and then hopefully a flow of benefits over the remaining life of the students involved. These costs and benefits can then be compared and the "profitability" of such a project to society evaluated. Hence, the relevant questions at the outset are: What were the costs of the Kansas Work-Study Project? And

TABLE 1

Present Discounted Value of Benefits over Costs and the Rate of Return for Alternative Number of Years

| Number of years elapsed since project | Net present discounted value of the investment | | | Internal rate of return |
	3%	6%	9%	
3	- $16,024	- $27,124	- $36,555	- .6%
4	15,229	- 816	- 14,305	5.8%
5	43,701	22,472	4,851	9.9%
10	165,534	114,130	74,468	17.9%
15	270,628	182,622	119,713	20.0%
20	361,283	233,804	149,120	20.6%

what benefits did the students participating receive which they would not have received in the absence of the project?

Chaffin's followup study focused on a selected group of only 30 of the students involved in the project. In our study the marginal or extra costs were adjusted to determine the relevant costs for this group only. These project costs were $72,400; $46,432; and $38,245 for each of the three years of the program, respectively. Thus, over the three years the total project costs were $157,077 in excess of the costs of educating these students in regular classrooms.

For the purpose of our evaluation, we used the most conservative estimate of benefits, that is, the wage differential between those in the experimental group of 30, matched closely in terms of IQ, age, occupational rating of parents, sex, and grade level equivalent. The followup study for the Kansas Work-Study Project in 1969 found the average weekly wages of those in the experimental group to be $27.61 greater than average weekly wages of those in the comparison group without special training. Thus, the annual total income differential, adjusted for the difference of the unemployment rates between the two groups, amounted to $60,724 in the first year after the program and declined to an estimated $32,718 in the sixth and successive years.

This flow of benefits should be converted into their value at the present time. If the benefits described above were all available for use now, they could be invested in some other capital project, and thus, it would be possible to earn interest or direct benefits in some other form. However, since waiting is required, the benefits must be "discounted" to allow for this potential loss in earnings.

Table 1 summarizes the results of the economic evaluation of the Kansas Work-Study Project. The first column shows the number of years elapsed since the end of the project. The three middle columns show the net present discounted value of the investment, that is, the discounted benefits net of costs, at various discount rates. These benefits are based on the assumption that the wage differential between the experimental and comparison groups continues for the number of years described. Thus, 5 years after the program ended and adjusted by a 6% discount rate, the value of wages received by program participants was $22,472 higher than it would have been in the absence of the program even after the costs of the program were deducted. The last column shows the internal rate of return for each year listed. Thus, if wage differentials continue for 10 years, the state could pay any cost for capital, in terms of the interest rates up to 17.9%, and still show a net gain in benefits over costs.

The results as presented in Table 1 suggest that the project was a success if income differentials between experimental and comparison groups continue for a period of only 3 to 5 years. These returns are considered respectable in both the private and public sector.

Reference

Chaffin, J. D., Spellman, C. R., Regan, C. E., & Davison, R. Two followup studies of former educable mentally retarded students from the Kansas Work-Study Project. *Exceptional Children*, 1971, *37*, 733-738.

CAREER EDUCATION NEEDS OF SECONDARY EDUCABLE STUDENTS

DONN BROLIN

Abstract: The major purpose of this study was to identify the needs of secondary level educable mentally retarded students and the competencies teachers must have to meet these needs. From the data received at a conference for state and national authorities, a field questionnaire was developed and sent to 30 randomly selected administrators and 251 secondary level teachers of the educable retarded in Wisconsin. The results showed that a greater emphasis is needed to prepare secondary teachers of the educable retarded with knowledge and skills in vocational rehabilitation and vocational education. The teachers indicated that increased involvement of other school and out-of-school personnel was needed to meet some of their students' primary needs, and that a prevocational coordinator position was especially needed. The study reflected needed changes in both regular and special education teacher preparation.

Donn Brolin is Associate Professor of Education, Department of Counseling and Personnel Services, University of Missouri—Columbia. He was formerly the Initiator and Director of the Special Education Project at the University of Wisconsin—Stout, Menomonie, Wisconsin. The research reported herein was performed pursuant to a grant from the US Office of Education, Department of Health, Education, and Welfare. However, the opinions expressed herein do not necessarily reflect the position or policy of the US Office of Education, and no official endorsement by the US Office of Education should be inferred.

Work-study programs, in which students spend part of the day or week acquiring work experience and skills in specific jobs in the community, have developed rapidly in many high school programs during the past decade. Nevertheless, special education teachers are still trained to teach primarily academic skills, and their classrooms place much emphasis on purely academic instruction and little emphasis on vocational evaluation, adjustment, training, placement techniques, and other important career education areas. Hammerlynck and Espeseth (1969) indicated that another problem is inadequate communication between the teacher and vocational rehabilitation workers. This results in a sporadic and inadequate continuity of services as students progress through work-study programs. Other problems are the limited time to develop and supervise work experiences, the lack of vocational education skills by the special education teacher, limited teacher communication with and use of other school disciplines, and insufficient knowledge of mental retardation by supporting personnel (e.g., sheltered workshop, employment service, social service, and rehabilitation workers).

Martin (1972) pointed out that the educational system is just beginning to view employment as an important subgoal, and he presented these disturbing statistics:

> Only 21 percent of handicapped children leaving school in the next 4 years will be fully employed or go on to college. Another 40 percent will be underemployed, and 26 percent will be unemployed. An additional 10 percent will require at least a partially sheltered setting and family, and 3 percent will probably be almost totally dependent [pp. 523-524].

Martin recommended redefining our basic instructional program and developing career edu-

"Career Education Needs of Secondary Educable Students", Donn Brolin, *Exceptional Children*, Vol. 39, No. 8, May 1973 © by The Council for Exceptional Children, 1973.

cation programs where work habits and skills related to future employment could be learned.

The primary purpose of this study was to identify the instructional needs of secondary level educable retarded students and the competencies teachers must have to meet these needs so that relevant teacher education changes can be initiated. A second purpose was to determine the extent to which other types of personnel should be involved in meeting student needs.

Method

A 2 day conference was held at the University of Wisconsin—Stout on November 12-13, 1970. The purpose of the conference was for national and state authorities and special education practitioners to provide their input on the needs of secondary educable students and the teacher competencies necessary to meet these needs. Before the conference the participants were asked to send to the project staff a list of what they believed to be the needs and competencies. During the conference the participants were asked to develop the lists further and rate all identified needs and competencies according to degree of importance. At the end of the conference all the participants were shown the group consensus on each item and then each individual participant was asked either to revise his opinion (if it differed from the consensus) or to specify his reason for remaining outside the consensus.

The conference participants identified and rated the importance of over 200 needs and competencies by using the above method (the Delphi technique). They were classified into one of four curriculum areas, i.e., academic, activities of daily living, psychosocial, or occupational. The project staff then used the statements and the ratings to refine and compile a revised and more condensed list of the 31 most highly rated competencies for the secondary level teachers of the educable. These competencies were included in a field questionnaire developed by the project staff. Conference participants were asked to react to the instrument prior to its use, and based on their suggestions, a number of modifications were made before the questionnaire was finalized.

The questionnaire was sent to all secondary (grades 10-12) special education teachers in Wisconsin ($N = 251$) and to 30 randomly selected administrators. Two followup mailings at 3 week intervals were conducted; total response was 73 percent ($N = 205$). The teachers varied considerably in age, education, teaching experience with educable students, and nonteaching work experience. There were 115 men teachers, 83 women, and 7 unidentified (respondents were not required to identify themselves). All but 4 percent were either certified or working toward certification in special education; 20 percent had a master's degree and 24 percent a bachelor's degree in special education.

The questionnaire consisted of two parts. Part I included a list of the four curriculum areas—psychosocial, activities of daily living (ADL), academic, and occupational. The re-

TABLE 1
Percent of Time Needed for the Four Curriculum Areas as Rated by Three Groups of Respondents

| Curriculum area | Respondents' classroom teaching responsibility | | | |
	Major (N=149)	Minor (N=24)	None (N=25)	Total[1] (N=198)
Occupational	28	32	34*	30
ADL	25	26	22*	24
Psychosocial	24	24	19*	23
Academic	23	18	25**	23
TOTAL	100	100	100	100

[1] Of the 205 respondents 7 failed to indicate the percentage of time they spent teaching educable students.
*$p < .05$
**$p < .01$

TABLE 2

Ranked Mean Priority of 31 Competencies

Rank	Mean	Curriculum area	Teacher competency
1	4.72	Occupational	Using appropriate work adjustment techniques
2	4.57	Occupational	Teaching job seeking skills
3	4.56	ADL	Preparing students to care for personal needs
4	4.54	Psychosocial	Teaching social behavior expression
6	4.52	Occupational	Finding appropriate job tryout sites
6	4.52	Occupational	Finding the student suitable employment
6	4.52	Occupational	Conducting a vocational evaluation program
8	4.49	Psychosocial	Developing the students' self confidence
9	4.42	Occupational	Providing vocational guidance
10	4.41	ADL	Teaching responsibilities to self and others
11	4.40	ADL	Developing the students' communication skills
12	4.38	ADL	Instructing in home management
13	4.36	Academic	Teaching adequate academic skills
14	4.29	Occupational	Using community agencies that assist in vocational adjustment
15	4.22	Occupational	Writing reports to agencies
16	4.19	Psychosocial	Providing opportunity for interaction with normal students
17	4.17	Psychosocial	Providing professional guidance in developing personal responsibility
18	4.05	Occupational	Coordinating postschool activities
19	4.03	Occupational	Developing the students' manual abilities
20	4.02	ADL	Instructing in uses of leisure time
21	4.01	ADL	Teaching home mechanics
22.5	4.00	ADL	Teaching civic responsibilities
22.5	4.00	ADL	Using transportation methods
24	3.98	Academic	Organizing academic instruction appropriately
25	3.95	Occupational	Providing specific job training
26	3.94	Psychosocial	Developing social, emotional, & intellectual functioning related to students' environment
27	3.93	ADL	Using community resources
28	3.92	Psychosocial	Helping parents meet student needs
29	3.87	Psychosocial	Providing for independent thinking
30	3.84	Academic	Providing ongoing evaluation of academic abilities
31	3.46	Psychosocial	Teaching aesthetic values

spondents were asked to indicate the percentage of curriculum emphasis that they believed should be given to instructing secondary educable students in each of the four areas.

Part II included the same four curriculum areas accompanied by a list of the teacher competencies needed to meet the student needs listed in Part I. The number of competency statements were 11 occupational, 9 ADL, 8 psychosocial, and 3 academic. The respondents were asked to rate (on a 5 point scale) how important they judged each of the 31 competencies to be for a secondary teacher of the educable to adequately meet students' needs and to indicate what personnel they thought ideally should be responsible for each competency and which ones in practice were doing it. Choices of personnel included a special education teacher, prevocational coordinator, other school personnel (counselor, psychologist, regular class teacher, social worker), or others outside of school (welfare, vocational rehabilita-

tion agency, sheltered workshop). More than one person could be checked.

Results

Part I

Table 1 presents the percentage of emphasis that the respondents indicated should be devoted to each of the four curriculum areas of secondary educable programs. The respondents were categorized as those who spent the majority of their time in classroom teaching (> 50 percent), those who spent a minority of time (< 50 percent), and those who did no teaching (administrators). The ratings support the position that a high school curriculum for the educable retarded should contain as much or more emphasis in occupational skills and activities of daily living as in psychosocial and academic instruction. The ratings of the administrators indicated somewhat different expectations about curriculum emphasis than did the teachers' ratings.

TABLE 3

Frequency of Competencies Categorized by Their
Ranked Importance and Curriculum Area

	Curriculum area	
Ranking of importance	Occupational	All other
Most important (1-10)	6	4
Intermediate (11-20)	4	6
Least important (21-31)	1	10

NOTE: Overall chi square = 6.12; df = 2; $p < .05$

Part II

Teacher competencies ratings. The 31 teacher competencies resulting from the Stout conference were rated on a 5 point scale of importance. These ratings were 1 for not important, 2 for slightly important, 3 for moderately important, 4 for important, and 5 for very important. Table 2 presents, in rank order, the mean rating and curriculum area of each teacher competency.

Table 2 reveals that a large proportion of the occupational competencies were rated highly. To determine whether occupational competencies were rated significantly different from the other competencies, a chi square analysis was conducted (Table 3). The analysis was statistically significant at the .05 level of confidence indicating that significantly more occupational competencies were rated as most important than the other three types of competencies combined.

Ideal versus in practice ratings. Analysis of the respondents' indications of what personnel are and should be responsible for the 31 competencies is summarized in Table 4. For the 11 occupational competencies, the percent of respondents who indicated that in practice special education teachers are primarily responsible ranged from a low of 32 percent for coordinating postschool activities to 96 percent for teaching job seeking skills. The median percentage was 60 percent. This degree of competency responsibility did not differ significantly from their ratings of how they ideally should be responsible for these occupational competencies (56 percent). Significantly greater responsibility was endorsed for a prevocational coordinator for the occupational area competencies, i.e., ideally, 60 percent, and in practice, 30 percent. Similarly, the ideal and in practice percentages for out-of-school personnel were significantly different, 28 and 17 percent.

Further inspection of Table 4 reveals that, in contrast to the ratings of the occupational competencies, the respondents (special education teachers and administrators) rated the special education teacher as the one who should assume primary responsibility for the students' instruction in the ADL, psychosocial, and academic areas with some assistance from the other disciplines, particularly other school personnel. Although a prevocational coordinator

TABLE 4

Median Percent of Respondents' In Practice and Ideal Endorsement of Specific Competencies
in Each Curriculum Area for Four Types of Personnel

Personnel type	Endorsement	Curriculum areas			
		Occupational	ADL	Psychosocial	Academic[1]
Special education	Ideally	56	81	81	87
teacher	In practice	60	88	90	86
Prevocational	Ideally	60*	17*	26*	33
coordinator	In practice	30	7	12	15
Other school	Ideally	39	54	55*	43
personnel	In practice	25	42	33	27
Out-of-school	Ideally	28*	33*	38*	14
personnel	In practice	17	17	19	17

NOTE: Median test computed on the arrays of percent endorsement of the specific competencies in a given curriculum area for the ideal and in practice categories.

[1] The 3 academic competencies were too few to be statistically analyzed by this procedure.
*$p < .05$

and out-of-school personnel were not frequently checked as providing these competencies, significantly more involvement was indicated. Other school personnel were also checked as needing significantly more involvement in the psychosocial area. The three academic competencies were too few to be statistically analyzed by this procedure

Discussion and Implications

The results indicate that secondary teachers of educable students should be prepared to provide considerable instruction in the occupational, ADL, and psychosocial areas as well as in strictly academic material. The study found that the importance of occupational curriculum competencies was rated significantly higher than the other three curriculum areas. Also, administrators rated the curriculum emphasis differently than the classroom teacher in the occupational area. However, the respondents (primarily teachers) believed that many of these competencies should not be the primary responsibility of the traditional special education teacher. Instead, they expressed the need for a prevocational coordinator for secondary programs, i.e., a special educator who is concerned both with educative and habilitative functions but gives greater attention to the latter (Younie & Clark, 1969; Clark, 1971). However, only 4 of the 205 respondents indicated that they could be considered prevocational coordinators.

It seems that administrators employing more than one special education teacher should consider a prevocational specialist. Otherwise, because of the discrepancies between ideal and in practice ratings for the prevocational coordinator, special education teachers have to assume much more responsibility for meeting the students' occupational development needs. However, many do not believe some of the occupational competencies are their main responsibility, particularly providing skill training, job tryouts, job placement, and postschool activities, and writing reports to agencies. Thus, despite its high rating of importance, the occupational area appears the most neglected of the four areas studied (Table 4).

The findings indicate that other school personnel should become more involved in meeting some of the primary needs of the educable student. Other school personnel are involved somewhat in helping with personal care instruction, home management, interaction with "normal" students, development of manual abilities, home mechanics, mobility training, vocational skills training, parental assistance, and evaluation of academic abilities. However, many respondents felt that more involvement is needed, particularly in the psychosocial development area (Table 4). Perhaps the new thrust

toward career education will force this involvement.

Many respondents indicated that out-of-school personnel should be accepting more responsibility in a number of areas, e.g., postschool activities, leisure time training, and parental assistance. They indicated that presently there is too little involvement in the occupational, ADL, and psychosocial areas (Table 4). Thus, there is evidence of a need for community agencies to provide more direct services to special education programs.

This study has significant implications for both regular and special education teacher preparation. Probably few special education teacher preparation programs provide the opportunity for students to develop the majority of competencies found to be most important in this study. However, a clearly expressed need for a prevocational coordinator or a more vocationally oriented and prepared special educator was indicated. Therefore, future special education teachers must receive training in vocational rehabilitation and vocational education for the handicapped if they are adequately to perform vocational evaluation, work adjustment, and job placement and to prepare their students in the independent living skills areas. A few years ago Hammerlynck and Espeseth developed a master's degree training program for a dual specialist—a vocational rehabilitation counselor and teacher of the retarded. The Stout project has resulted in the promotion of a new undergraduate preparation model for secondary special education teachers of the educable retarded at that university combining these components and those of vocational education (Brolin & Thomas, 1972).

With the current emphasis on career education, this study supports those who strongly recommend redirecting curricula and teacher education so they really begin meeting students' needs. Coursework for regular class teachers focusing on the unique characteristics and needs of special education students and techniques of teaching them is highly recommended. More understanding and cooperation with community agencies is also an area needing improvement.

This study should be considered exploratory because of its limited generalizability, i.e., on Wisconsin teachers only. The absence of test-retest reliability and the small number of academic competencies may also be considered limitations (many of the ADL competencies were academic in nature). In several states there are undoubtedly many prevocational coordinators employed in the schools. It is hoped that many of them have the competencies found necessary in this study. However, the general positive reaction and interest throughout the country in the Stout project (Brolin & Thomas,

1972) reflects the nationwide concern in improving our educational services to handicapped children and several related projects have been generated from this study. Further research of this nature is highly recommended.

Conclusion

Teachers of the secondary educable retarded are currently responsible for meeting most of the many needs of their students, and these students require and deserve a quality education which can be provided only by specially prepared teachers. Since educable students do not generally go on to other education, it is even more essential they they receive the career education they need at the secondary level. If the educators of special education personnel do not redirect their curricula more toward career education, there may be no market for their graduates in secondary programs. Today, there are many who advocate that other types of teachers can better meet these student needs. Thus, teacher education programs must prepare

their student teachers more appropriately so that educable students may be better equipped to meet the stringent demands of today's society.

References

Brolin, D., & Thomas, B. *Preparing teachers of secondary level educable mentally retarded: A new model.* Final Report. University of Wisconsin—Stout, Menomonie, Wisconsin, August 1972.

Clark, G. M. Secondary pupil needs and teacher competencies. In D. Brolin & B. Thomas (Eds.), *Preparing teachers of secondary level educable mentally retarded: Proposal for a new model.* Project Report No. 1, University of Wisconsin—Stout, Menomonie, Wisconsin, April 1971, Pp. 41-50.

Hammerlynck, L. A., & Espeseth, V. K. Dual specialist: Vocational rehabilitation counselor and teacher of the mentally retarded. *Mental Retardation,* 1969, 7, 49-50.

Martin, E. W. Individualism and behaviorism as future trends in educating handicapped children. *Exceptional Children,* 1972, 38, 517-525.

Younie, W. J., & Clark, G. M. Personnel training needs for cooperative secondary school programs for mentally retarded youth. *Education and Training of the Mentally Retarded,* 1969, 4, 186-194.

Using a Pictorial Job Training Manual in an Occupational Training Program for High School EMR Students

GREG R. WEISENSTEIN

GREG R. WEISENSTEIN *is currently a doctoral student in Special Education and evaluation coordinator to the Habilitation Personnel Training Project at the University of Kansas, Lawrence, Kansas.*

It has been well documented that a number of factors are working together in limiting the employment success of the educable mentally retarded. The majority of studies tends to reveal individual characteristics which have served to act as performance inhibitors once the retarded person is already employed. The obvious question asks if those factors which cause failure after the retarded person is employed are the same set of factors which serve to limit him from gaining employment in the first place. My experience would suggest that indeed some of the same factors which are detrimental to the employed are also deterrents to those looking for employment, although the rank order of their importance varies in the two different situations. Even though personal attributes rank high in determining whether retarded persons will remain on the job once hired, the most critical factor in finding employment is their actual ability to learn to perform the job under normal circumstances and within normal time limits so that they can compete with more capable job seekers who require no training at the lower levels of employment.

Considering these factors that influence employability, the truly effective vocational program for the EMR at the secondary level should be a composite of two distinct experiences. The first experience is common to most special students enrolled in high school work-experience programs and includes general development in work related skills resulting from various working experiences. The second and much less common experience is specific occupational training. Since many special education programs have not incorporated specific occupational training into their curricula, most EMR students are leaving the public schools unprepared to compete with more capable job seekers and are being allotted positions in competitive employment that are not commensurate with their potential ability levels.

Port Angeles Project

In response to this marginal economic adjustment experienced by most retarded adults, the following specific occupational training program was developed to act as an adjunct to the regular high school work-experience program currently operating in Port Angeles, Washington. The purpose of the project was to demonstrate the feasibility and effectiveness of short term community-based training and a locally developed pictorial job training manual.

The project was designed to teach EMR girls, within the period of six weeks, the skills which would enable them to gain employment in motels and hotels as maids. The occupation of nonhousehold maid was chosen as the area of specific training for the following reasons: its utility as an occupation, the apparent number of job openings which could occur in the Port Angeles area, and the generalization from occupational training in this area to general skills that are essential to homemaking.

It was predicted that a concentrated six week training program, utilizing both supervised on-the-job training within the community and the pictorial job training manual, could prepare mentally handicapped girls for work as household maids and therefore facilitate the job seeking process. It was also predicted that the training received in such a program could have generalizing effects upon the homemaking behavior of the student participants and, further, that the program could be feasibly supported by local school district funds.

Preliminary Surveys

Two preliminary surveys were taken prior to the beginning of the program. The first was conducted within the community and served to measure the employment potential for EMR girls with no experience or training, seeking jobs as motel or hotel maids, and to assess the employers' criteria for personnel selection when considering EMR girls in competition with more capable job seekers.

The results of the employer survey revealed that motel and hotel managers in the Port Angeles area would more readily hire the slow learner if she had had prior training or experience. Although only ten of the fourteen employers who were contacted responded, a majority indicated that though hiring preference would be given to normal students if neither normal nor slow students had experience, slow students had a distinct employability advantage when pre-trained. In addition a response of 70 percent or greater on any one question was established as significant in giving direction to project development.

The second survey was conducted to determine the homemaking behavior of student participants before their entrance into the program and upon completion of the program. The purpose of this assessment was to reveal any changes that might have occurred in homemaking behavior as a result of occupational training.

Program Development

The first step in program construction was to determine aspects of the job involved. To do this a job analysis was conducted at the motel where the on-the-job training portion of the project would take place. The analysis revealed job skills and vocabulary that are definite prerequisites of maid work. It was also determined that the work performed by motel maids could be broken down into units of similar skills such as dusting or bed making. These groups of skills were referred to as phases and represented several small jobs or skill areas.

A curriculum guide was next developed from the job analysis to coordinate these four major components of the program: (1) six weeks of in-class training, taking place at the high school special education Home Living Center; (2) four weeks of on-the-job training, carried on concurrently with the last four weeks of in-class study; (3) a slide presentation of job skills; and (4) a pictorial job training manual. Daily activity in the Home Living Center and on the job were outlined with the participating teacher encouraged to supplement in areas of student weaknesses. Total training hours were established at 45 for in-class work and 30 for on-the-job training.

The final step in program construction was to develop the pictorial job training manual. The manual was developed from over 250 slides of experienced maids performing routine tasks. Of the slides taken, 149 were selected to be illustrated. For each illustration, low readability captions were written that would serve to clarify the specific job skill that was being illustrated. The job vocabulary was included in the job training manual to provide students with the necessary vocabulary to communicate with other motel staff members both during and after training, and to familiarize students with those words that are found in the manual. In addition, the personal qualifications of a maid were listed under the section entitled "A Code for Maids," and the number of guests per room had been established, in relation to the number and size of beds, under the section entitled "Mathematics." The manual was previewed and a copy given at the beginning of training to each of the participating students to be used as an integral part of the in-class and on-the-job portions of the program.

Evaluation Techniques

Throughout training performance rate served as both a diagnostic device and an evaluation tool. Prior to the initiation of the program, three experienced motel maids were timed during each phase of the job over a three week period. Resulting times were established as minimum, average, and maximum times both for each job phase and for the cleaning of an entire motel room. The average minimum room cleaning time computed for the three maids was 35 minutes and 7 seconds while the average maximum time was 52 minutes and 22 seconds.

3. RESPONSIBILITY

Dust the closet shelf. Also dust the coat bar.

Check the hangers. There should be four per guest.

Check the rack on top of the table. It should have have schedules, writing paper and postcards. You may need to refill the rack.

There should be writing paper in a drawer. There should also be envelopes. Make sure there are two of each per guest.

FIGURE 1.

Maximum times represented target times for the program participants and served as indicators of skill efficiency or deficiency in a particular phase of the job.

During on-the-job training, student performance was continually monitored and charted through each job phase, with quality held consistent so that inferior work would be repeated until the quality that had been established by the motel manager was attained. Increases of time thus reflected inferior work during the affected job phases. As students became more competent in the varied job phases, their reduced times reflected fewer mistakes and an increase in the quality of work. When the student's measured room cleaning times were less than or approximated the average maximum times recorded by the experienced maids, she was considered adequately trained to enter competitive employment.

Project Participants

For involvement in the program eight girls of varying intellectual ability levels were chosen from a special education class for the mentally retarded at Port Angeles High School. For the purposes of the project, no criteria was placed on having had prior experience at any one level of work-experience training for entry into the program. Intelligence test scores were recorded for each student, and the Wide Range Achievement Test was administered so that the level of intellectual functioning and prior academic achievement could be considered when reviewing the program results. No attempt was made to rank the subject population on mental, physical or achievement levels.

The participating school and motel personnel were as follows: (1) the work experience coordinator, (2) the special education home and family life instructor (in-class and on-the-job instructor), (3) two motel maids and the motel manager (consultants, guest speakers and instructor aides), and (4) two high school volunteers (timers and quality supervisors).

Training Schedule

The project was designed so that the on-the-job training portion of the six week program took place during the early spring, making optimum use of the participating motel with little disturbance, if any, to their seasonal trade. Early spring seemed best since maids are in greatest demand during summer months. Thus, training and the move into competitive employment was kept as close together as possible.

Results

Results of this project should be interpreted with consideration given to three distinct limiting factors which were at work in affecting the program data: internal inconsistencies resulting from slightly different room cleaning schedules used by the experienced maids, unchecked variables which may have affected learning, and lack of a longitudinal follow-up study.

Comparative data was received from three sources: pre and post tests, the initial parent survey and follow-up, and periodic monitoring of phase times throughout the four weeks of on-the-job training. Arithmetic graphs designed for the project were used to record times from both the pre and post tests and monitoring, with each job phase being represented on a different graph for every student. Target times were also provided on each of the corresponding graphs.

Student performances during the first period of monitored times substantiated the pretest findings and were indicative of significant skill deficiencies in both household skills and skills required of a motel or hotel maid. It was obvious at this point that none of the students were prepared to enter competitive employment and could not compete with more capable job seekers. Even if employment had been attained without job preparation, the increases in cleaning times recorded for most students during the first week of on-the-job training would have rendered them susceptible to employer criticism and possibly job termination.

Following six weeks of program involvement, all participants experienced a 50 to 75 percent reduction in time on many job phases, with several students bettering the average total room cleaning time recorded by the experienced maids. Six out of eight participating

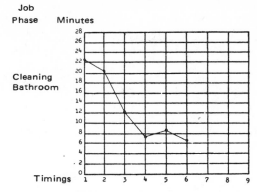

FIGURE 2. Charting Procedure Used in Data Collection

students were able to approximate or better the original target time of 52 minutes and 22 seconds for cleaning an entire motel room. These six students were considered to be work ready, capable of assuming positions in competitive employment as motel or hotel maids.

Not only was project success measured in terms of decreased cleaning times, increased employability, and number of trainees hired, but also in terms of the amount of learning transfer that occurred between the training program and home environment. Here there was a correlation between successful program participation and the amount of learning transfer, with all students reported to have experienced some improvement in homemaking skills. The second parent survey indicated that the most meaningful improvements in homemaking behaviors seemed to result from the student's realization of the importance and need for cleanliness and routine housekeeping. However, the degree of improvement that had been predicted in this area did not materialize. Many students were still reflecting a need for homemaking guidance.

Discussion

A subjective analysis of the instructional materials by the project and motel staff indicated that the training manual was the most valuable media used. It facilitated the learning process by providing a stimulus for recall, establishing a cleaning sequence to be followed and reportedly shortening the transition from in-class studies to on-the-job training.

As training sites the motel and the Home Living Center proved to be satisfactory. The Home Living Center was equipped with furnishings generally found in a motel room and served as an excellent location for the pre and

3. RESPONSIBILITY

post tests as well as initial training. The motel used for on-the-job training inclined to be more strict and demanding than other motels in the Port Angeles area and therefore provided an excellent test of the training program. It was felt that the students who had reached target time and were prepared for competitive employment would be capable of meeting the standards established by all other motels in the immediate area, if they had first met the standards imposed by the training motel.

Performance rate proved to be an excellent unit for evaluating student performance. Since timings were used for both the pre and post tests and for monitoring on-the-job behavior, the two evaluative devices could be compared on the basis of equal time units. Although time did not reflect the direction of change, whether toward quantity or quality, it was sensitive to sufficiently small increments of positive or negative change.

Program

A breakdown of the program expenses, excepting clerical and labor, follows:

```
250 colored slides
    (purchase and processing) ............65.00
Job training manual illustrations ........75.00
1st printing of the manual ..............35.00
Replacement of cleaning supplies .......10.00
Transportation at 10 cents a mile ........16.00
Certificates of completion .............. 2.00
                                        $203.00
```

This expense figure represents a per student cost of approximately $25.00 for the six weeks of training. However, the larger cost items such as slides and the illustrations for the job manual are not consumable materials and can be used in subsequent years. Therefore, subtracting the larger nonconsumable expenses would reduce the per student cost to slightly under $8.00 per student.

Short Term Follow-up

A short term follow-up of program participants, one year after training, revealed the following positions currently held: two participants are working in a local sheltered workshop (the same two that did not achieve target times), two are attending vocational schools, two are still in the special education program, one is working at another job for a higher rate of pay, and the last is employed as a motel maid. Although most trainees are not now employed in the motel industry, it is important to note that many could be and that the single employee in the industry recently acquired her job as a result of her training. Initially three trainees had been hired as part-time summer employees following the conclusion of the program.

Conclusion

Instructional devices such as the pictorial job training manual, on site experiences, and slide presentations have proven extremely successful in teaching vocational skills to project students. The duplication of these devices for training the mentally handicapped in other occupational areas or home living skills may prove equally effective. It is hoped that future investigators will see fit to apply tighter controls in studies to determine more fully the value of the instructional techniques originated in this project.

Graduation: What Happens to the Retarded Child When He Grows Up?

JAMES STEPHEN STANFIELD

Abstract: Interviews were held with parents or guardians of 120 graduates of classes for the moderately (trainable) retarded in a large southern California metropolitan school district in the years 1968, 1969, and 1970. Information was gathered to assess the quality of community life experienced by these moderately retarded adults after graduation from school. Recommendation is made for (a) new criteria for evaluation of community adjustment of the moderately retarded which emphasizes comprehensive postschool programing to meet the recreational and social needs of the retarded as well as to provide occupational and vocational training and (b) community based residential facilities to provide such programing as an alternative to the parent care model and the permanent parent-child relationship it reinforces.

James Stephen Stanfield is Assistant Professor, Department of Special Education, California State University, Los Angeles.

With strong support from parent organizations, professionals in the field of mental retardation are beginning to see their recommendations realized for infant stimulation programs and full day public school classes through age 18 years (in some cases, 21) for the moderately or "trainable" retarded child. Their concern has and should continue to draw returns for the retarded young—but what of the retarded adult?

Charney in 1963 alluded to the need for increased professional attention to the retarded adult when he commented, "The question of postschool services for the trainable is one which is becoming increasingly intense as more and more such children complete their schooling [p. 109]."

Yet in 1969 Cobb, in an exhaustive bibliography (168 entries) of descriptive studies of community adjustment of the retarded adult, reported only three such studies relating to the postschool adjustment of the moderately retarded. The most recent of these had been completed 10 years before Cobb's publication. In an intensive interest in bringing services to the retarded young, educators seem to have neglected the question of what happens to the retarded child when he grows up.

Past Studies

Delp and Lorenz (1953) reported the "outcome of public school training programs for so-called noneducable children" in St. Paul, Minnesota. Eighty-four former pupils (median IQ 36) who had been enrolled in classes for the moderately retarded at some time during 1934 to 1951 were studied. Of the 41 who were found living outside an institutional setting all were living at home. Five had found gainful employment on a regular basis (two full time). Eighty percent were reported to have adequate self help skills and contribute to home maintenance. Few were mobile beyond their immediate neighborhood. Eighty-eight percent (36) were involved in no structured postschool work or habilitative program.

Saenger (1957) studied the community adjustment and life styles of a sample of 520 moderately retarded adults drawn from a census of 2,640 students formerly in classes for the trainable retarded (40-50 IQ) in New York from 1929 to 1956. There were 343 living in the community, with the majority being able to dress and feed themselves and to help in home upkeep. Twenty-three percent were gainfully employed outside a sheltered setting (most part time). One-third traveled in the community at large and were able to use public transportation. Seventy-three percent (250) were active in no postschool habilitative program.

Tisdall in 1958 studied 126 children originally enrolled in 1953 in classes for the trainable retarded (mean IQ 33) in Illinois. Of the 48 individuals in this study who had reached maximum school age and "graduated," 38 were living at home. The majority of parents reported that their children were able to care for their personal needs and to be responsible for specific duties of home maintenance. Seven were in sheltered workshops, 1 was gainfully employed, 16 were in activity centers, with 40 percent in no postschool program. The degree of community mobility was not reported.

Purpose of Present Study

The purpose of the present study was to gather information which might reflect on the quality of community life experienced by the moderately retarded adult after graduation. Interviews were held with the parents or guardians of those who had graduated from classes for the moderately retarded in a large southern California metropolitan school district in the years 1968, 1969, and 1970.

Method

Subjects

Of an original census of 161 graduates, 120 formed the study population: 15 had moved, 25 failed to respond to requests for participation, and 1 parent refused to participate. Two of the 120 graduates included in the study were residing in state institutions, and information for those two was available only in the areas of vital statistics and school history.

Section 6901 of the California *Education Code* (California State Department of Education, 1966) defines mentally retarded minors as follows: " . . . all minors who because of the retarded intellectual development as determined by individual psychological examination are incapable of being educated efficiently and profitably through ordinary classroom instruction [p. 467]." It is the practice of the school district from which the present study sample was drawn to place a child in a class for the trainable retarded if his IQ falls between 30 and 50 and his social and developmental functioning levels are such that he could not profit from regular classroom instruction.

Procedure

Letters explaining the study and requesting participation were sent to the parents or guardians of all graduates of classes for the moderately retarded in the district during the years 1968, 1969, and 1970. The portion of the population which did not respond to either the initial letter or a second registered letter or which could not be reached by telephone was visited personally. The total number eventually reached and included in the sample was 120, or 75 percent of the actual census of 161.

A modified version of Saenger's (1957) Depth Interview Schedule was administered to the parents or guardians. Data were gathered and reported in five areas: (a) vital statistics, (b) school history, (c) work and postschool habilitation programs, (d) life at home, and (c) life in the community.

Results
Vital Statistics

The population of 65 boys and 55 girls ranged in age from 19 to 21 years. The majority of the graduates (113 or 94 percent) were living with their families. Four were living at board and care homes, 2 were institutionalized, and 1 was living by himself.

Forty-two percent of the graduates came from families whose average yearly income was under $5,000 per year. The majority of these families (which composed 52 percent of the total sample studied) were minority families. Twenty-eight percent of the parents had an income from $5,000 to $10,000, with 30 percent reporting an annual income in excess of $10,000 per year.

School History

The graduates had an average of 10 years of school experience. Mean age of starting school was 7 years.

Work and Postschool Habilitation Programs

Forty percent (48) of the graduates were in a sheltered workshop program. Eighty percent of those 48 graduates in the workshops were earning under $10.00 per week for full time labor, and nearly half were earning less than $5.00 per week. The majority of the workers (75 percent) had been working for longer than one year.

No graduate was self supporting; however, 3 percent (three) of the graduates were working in unsheltered settings. One was earning $15.00 per week from a newspaper route, another $20.00 per week as a classroom attendant, and a third averaging $55.00 per week as a laundry worker. All three were working part time.

Two percent (two) of the graduates were working for the family business. One was earning $10.00 per week helping his father in a window display business; the other, the most financially successful of all those studied, was earning $300.00 per month for his services to his father who was a distribution agent for a local newspaper.

Eleven percent (13) of the graduates found a place in one of five activity centers in the Los Angeles area offering a program for the moderately retarded adult. Nine of these graduates had been in the program for more than one year.

Forty-four percent (52) of the graduates were involved in no postschool work or habilitation program. When parents were asked to give reasons why their son or daughter was not in a postschool program or presently working, 55 percent of them responded that it was due to the severity of the graduate's handicap, 30 percent reported transportation difficulties, and 20 percent reported lack of proper referral to job or postschool habilitative programs.

Life Style Within the Home

Ninety-four percent of the parents reported the graduate capable of caring for his personal needs and able to protect himself against injury. When asked if they could leave their child alone, however, only 23 percent reported they felt confident to do so for extended periods. Fifty-six percent had reservations concerning the well being of their children if left alone for more than short periods. Although the parents felt that their children could provide for themselves, i.e., make simple meals, entertain themselves, and protect themselves against injury around the home, they were fearful that the children would not know how to handle an emergency if one arose. Twenty-one percent of the parents questioned felt their children should never be left alone. Of the 25 graduates in this group, 16 were girls and the major fear of the parents was that they would "open the door to strangers."

Nearly 90 percent of the graduates studied had specific responsibilities for household chores. These included such activities as making one's bed, picking up trash, etc. Parents felt that such contributions were very helpful.

When asked how the graduate occupied his time while at home, the parents mentioned most often solitary activities, such as watching television, listening to records and the radio, and looking at books and magazines. For the 52 graduates who were not in a workshop or activity center, watching television was their major daily activity.

The majority of parents reported that family interaction among graduates, parents, and siblings was generally favorable. When asked if there was anything they would like their retarded child to do that he does not do now, the majority of replies involved acquiring greater self reliance. Learning to read, write, and compute were also heavily desired. Many parents felt that if their child could learn to read and compute that employment and independence would follow.

Life in the Community

Sixty percent of the graduates were mobile within their immediate neighborhood, but only 10 percent ever left their neighborhood to travel about the community at large. This was true in spite of the availability of public transportation. Forty-eight graduates (40 percent) never went unescorted beyond the front yard of their homes.

When asked where their children (young adults) traveled alone outside their homes, the activity most frequently mentioned (37 percent) was going to the neighborhood shopping center, either on an errand for the parent or to " . . . get a coke or some laundry or simply to look around." Idly walking about the neighborhood was reported as the second most frequent activity. Only 23 of the graduates had friends to visit. Again, 40 percent never left their homes to go anywhere unchaperoned.

The majority of the graduates (84) were reported to have friends. Friends, with few exceptions, were acquired while attending a workshop, activity center, or social-recreational program specifically designed for the retarded. Only a few of the graduates reported to have friends in the immediate neighborhood and only 2 in the community at large. Although girl friends and boy friends were mentioned, these relationships were, with two exceptions, not of a courting nature. Two of the graduates were reported to go on unchaperoned dates; both were girls who had had sexual relationships, one being pregnant at the time of the study.

Forty-six (38 percent) of the graduates were found to be participating in one or more postschool social-recreational programs for the retarded. Participation in bowling leagues and dances were the most often mentioned activities. Time involved in such social-recreational

3. RESPONSIBILITY

programs averaged less than 6 hours a week with 37 percent spending no more than 2 hours a week.

Considering the limited association of the retarded graduate with peers outside of a sheltered workshop or activity center and the lack of involvement of 62 percent of the population in any social or recreational program for the retarded, it may be concluded that for the majority of the graduates studied there was virtually no social or recreational life apart from that with the immediate family.

Although the majority of parents reported only limited involvement of their offspring in neighborhood and community life, most felt that the general population living within the same neighborhood had positive attitudes toward the retarded. However, they felt that the community at large held more negative attitudes. This latter perception may be due to the lack of support many parents felt was given by public service agencies. When asked if such agencies were helpful, 76 of the parents responded negatively. When asked what problems the parents felt they needed help with now from community agencies or elsewhere, parents most frequently stated the need for family counseling, planning for the future, and family adjustment problems and the need for more social-recreational programs and vocational guidance for their children.

Regarding current status of their retarded offspring, 63 percent of the parents reported that the condition of their child (his general life style) had improved since graduation, 33 percent felt that no improvement had occurred, and 4 percent felt that things had worsened.

Recommendations and Implications

New Criteria for Evaluating Community Adjustment

The 1953, 1957 and 1958 followup studies indicated that most moderately retarded adults graduating from public schools possess adequate self help skills, can make a worthwhile contribution to home maintenance, and interact reasonably well with parents and siblings. Data from the present study give further proof of the ability of graduates to meet these criteria and support the conclusion that the moderately retarded can function outside the state institution.

However, the current study, like those before it, also reveals a significant part of the moderately retarded population not being involved in any postschool habilitative program, not participating in social or recreational activities other than those provided by the immediate family, never traveling beyond the confines of the immediate neighborhood, and spending the majority of the day in solitary

activities. When evaluated on the basis of the degree of participation in activities which lead to self growth, increased independence, and social maturity, community adjustment of most moderately retarded individuals after graduating from school can be considered deficient.

New criteria for evaluating success in community adjustment must be adopted if educators are to be sensitive to more than the subsistence needs of the retarded. Guaranteed comprehensive postschool programs, including residential facilities, must be made available.

Guaranteed Comprehensive Postschool Programing

Fifty-two (44 percent) of the graduates were found not to participate in any postschool habilitative programs. For these young adults graduation from school marked the beginning of a life of relative isolation from peers and segregation from the community at large. Although they had gained a degree of independence in caring for their personal needs, they were totally dependent upon their parents and the immediate environment of their homes to provide any self actualizing or growth producing experiences. What was once the responsibility of the schools became, upon graduation, an obligation of the home. Few parents could be expected to meet successfully such an obligation:

> At first it wasn't too bad (after graduation). He enjoyed his vacation as he called it—and then he began to ask when school would start again. I don't have the time it takes—and I don't always know what to do for him.

These graduates spend the majority of their day engaged in passive, solitary activities. The TV addict was often found in this group as well as one individual who sat all day "watching cars."

If the school district is willing to commit up to 12 years of programing and specialized personnel to develop within students the potential for functioning in a postschool sheltered setting, then it should be equally committed to assuring graduates placement in such a setting or providing services until such facilities become available. Either the objectives of public education of the moderately retarded must be changed from their present terminal nature or a system of publicly supported postschool facilities must be established to assume responsibility for such graduates.

There are at least 25 sheltered workshops for the handicapped which accept the mentally retarded in the area surrounding the school district in the study. Only nine were known to serve any of the moderately retarded graduates studied. The majority of these workshops restricted participation to those with mild and borderline intelligence.

An area of 4,069 square miles is served by nine workshops and five activity centers. It is apparent why those parents reporting their child not involved in any postschool program listed transportation problems as one of the major obstacles to placement. The typical graduate in a postschool sheltered workshop or activity program spent an average of 2 hours per day in transit. More postschool programs must be established if the needs of the moderately retarded in the area are to be met.

Needed facilities would ideally be within easy traveling distance to avoid the currently excessive time spent on buses. In addition to occupational training, social and recreational and leisure time activities would be part of the daily program. The current study found that the majority of the graduates had no involvement in any organized social or recreational program.

Community Based Residential Facilities

The current model of provision of services to the retarded assumes a permanent parent-child relationship. As a result, successful community functioning for the retarded individual is considered synonomous with being able to live with at least a minimum degree of harmony within the sheltered environment provided by a parent.

When asked if there was anything they would like their retarded child to do that he does not do now, the majority of the parents wanted him to become more independent: they wanted their children to grow up. When asked what their retarded offspring would like to do that he is unable to do, activities to achieve adult status were most often mentioned: the graduate also wanted to grow up.

Community based communal residential facilities that would provide a total day program of occupational, social, recreational, and leisure time activites—using community work and recreational resources—would be an alternative to life long family bound care. The majority of the moderately retarded will always be dependent on someone to help them meet their human needs. Parents, being human, cannot carry the responsibility of providing life long care for their children. The community has made great strides in sharing with the parent the responsibility for the retarded child; it must do so for the retarded adult.

References

Cobb, H. The predictive assessment of the adult retarded for social and vocational adjustment. In *A Review of Research. Part I, Annotated bibiliography*. Vermillion: University of South Dakota, Department of Psychology, 1969.

Delp, H. A., & Lorenz, M. Follow-up of 84 public school special class pupils with I.Q.'s below 50. *American Journal of Mental Deficiency*, 1953, 58, 175-182.

California State Department of Education. *Education code*. Sacramento: California State Department of Education, 1966.

Charney, L. The trainable mentally retarded. In S. A. Kirk & B. B. Weiner (Eds.), *Behavioral research on exceptional children*. Washington, D.C.: The Council for Exceptional Children, 1963. Pp. 90-113.

Saenger, G. *The adjustment of severely retarded adults in the community*. Albany: New York State Interdepartmental Health Resources Board, 1957.

Tisdall, W. J. A follow-up study of trainable mentally handicapped children in Illinois. Unpublished master's thesis, University of Illinois, 1958.

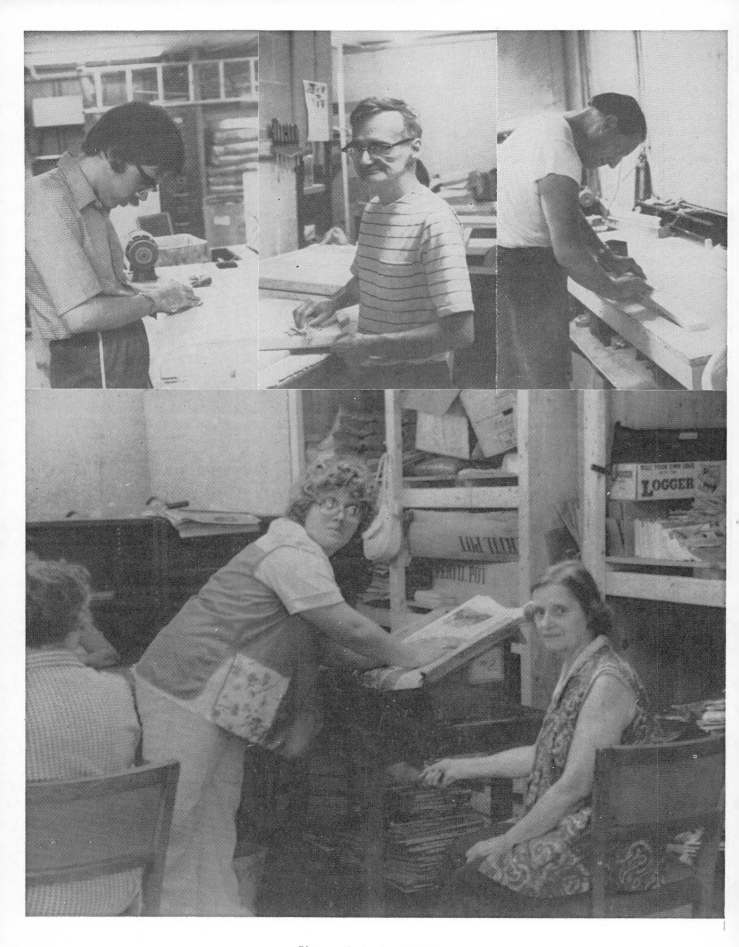

Photographs by Ann Rivellini

MANPOWER DEVELOPMENT AND UTILIZATION

The federal government has hired over 7, 500 mentally retarded workers for a variety of positions since 1964. Two thirds have never worked before, and at least one half had not completed the third grade. Reports show that 93 percent have mastered their jobs successfully. Only 7 percent have been terminated because of unsatisfactory performance.

The National Association for Retarded Citizen's (NARC) "On the Job Training Project" (OJT) has been successful in promoting meaningful employment by business and industry. Firms are assisted in identifying job areas where the mentally retarded can best utilize their skills. Employers are refunded a portion of the training cost, one half of the entry wage for the first four weeks, and one quarter of the wage for the second four weeks. Funding is provided by the U.S. Department of Labor and State agencies through the Comprehensive Employment and Training Act.

In the fall of 1976, the 15,000th person entered the program. Over a ten year period at least 85 percent of those hired have been able to keep their positions or advance. OJT provides an effective method of alleviating manpower shortages and promote training and employment of the mentally retarded.

Section four is devoted to the "normalization principle." Programs are discussed that are involved in the identification of new areas of employment and the most efficient (and successful) methods of training. The mentally retarded are being given the chance to compete, to fail and to care for their own needs.

THE STORY
OF
SARAH

Unlike most workshops where programs are limited to benchwork, the vocational program at SARAH has been adapted to the suburban/semirural area in which they reside.

H. Douglas Neumann

The Shoreline Association for the Retarded and Handicapped (SARAH), is a private non-profit organization founded in 1957 for the purpose of enriching the lives of the mentally retarded and handicapped inidividuals living in the five town area of Branford, Clinton, Guilford, Madison and North Branford, Connecticut. SARAH provides social services; vocational training and placement in the fields of horticulture, food services, industry and landscaping; internal evaluations; advocacy and adult education. Such services as recreation, transportation, leisure time, medical and legal services are coordinated with local community agencies. SARAH operates a Day School and Day Care Program for pre-school mentally retarded and "normal" children living in the area as well as the "Apple Doll House Tea Room" in Guilford, and a thrift shop known as "SARAH'S Cupboard" in Branford. SARAH also has launched a major effort to provide residential services including community-based residential (long term) and respite (short term) services for mentally retarded adults in the area. These homes give the mentally retarded individuals a chance to live in a group as a family unit away from their parents. The acquisition of homes is essential to the well-being of mentally retarded and handicapped citizens. It is the insurance that the individual will not be institutionalized but will continue a productive life. SARAH has three homes in existence and looks forward to acquiring two more.

A major effort is under way in the state of Connecticut to de-institutionalize mentally retarded people. They are being placed in large numbers into nursing homes and group homes of 10-25. In most instances, they are placed in these homes with no meaningful program available to them for their daytime hours. SARAH has made the commitment that there will be a vocational program for each mentally retarded or handicapped individual living in the five towns. Unlike most workshops where programs are limited to benchwork, the program has been adapted to

the suburban/semi-rural area in which they reside. SARAH'S vocational program is defined to be in harmony with its communities.

The Vocational Training Program provides work adjustment, sheltered employment and skill training in three major areas. The program includes two food service programs; one of which serves luncheons to the public from 11 a.m. -2 p.m. Monday through Friday, and the other which serves hot lunch to staff and clients--and also delivers hot lunches to the Day School. The landscaping and greenhouse training program comprise the Horticultural component. The landscaping crew maintains lawns, plants, shrubberies, and all other related jobs. They also run a firewood business, cutting, splitting and delivering wood during the fall and winter. The greenhouse crew grows herbs and house plants that are sold to the public between 9 a.m. - 3 p.m. Monday through Friday and also at plant parties. The third major area is light industry, where the clients either do work which is also done by employees at local manufacturing companies, or work on two prime products: paper logs and birdfeeders.

The Vocational Training Program services, in conjunction with the Guilford School System, provides speech therapy, adult education and tutoring in reading. The clients are primarily from the five communities, but referrals from any community are accepted if appropriate services can be offered. Transportation is provided. Some of the Vocational Program's population are students, who spend one-half of each day and their transportation is provided by the school system. Recreational programs are provided for the clients in the community, and transportation is made available for these events.

In today's technically oriented society, a basic knowledge of industry working, principles, and processes are essential for clients to function at any relative degree of independence. The industry program offers this training on all levels of social, intellectual and manual functioning.

Ann Rivellini

(the training) also encourages the development of individual thinking and mutual respect within the larger group context in regard to quality, personal accomplishment, and foresight.

From simple assembly, bagging and packing to piecework, the training involves skills needed to succeed in a work situation. The industry program affords the opportunity for all levels of clients to participate in a group process in which each step is vital to the next. It also encourages the development of individual thinking and mutual respect within the larger group context in regard to quality, personal accomplishment, and foresight.

Through the various processes and skills learned; through adequate individual programming, they (the clients) will be readied for placements in more highly competitive and demanding environments than presently existing within the sheltered workshop.

Skills learned in the workshop setting can elevate the severely handicapped worker from that of unskilled, expendable labor to the status of a productive component in today's society, whose talents are respected and valued--a contribution not only to the individual, but in the market place and community as well. Two skilled staff members were hired through a CETA (Comprehensive Employment and Training Act) Grant to develop and operate the log making and woodworking projects, just started this spring. The log making involves tightly rolling paper into logs which will be marketed this fall. Clients doing woodworking are making bird feeders which will be sold by mail order.

The Horticulture Program at the vocational training center not only teaches the basic principles of horticulture, but also teaches in an interesting way fundamental work concepts applicable to many other fields. Areas covered include greenhouse maintenance, plant propagation, physiology, plant pathology and identification, different types of gardening (annual, perennial, herb, etc.). The study of soils is also included, and all are presented on a level understandable to the clients.

The objectives of the program are to train individuals with mental and physical handicaps as horticultural workers, to identify and modify objectionable behaviors which interfere with work performance and inter-personal relationships, and to place the individuals trained in this program in competitive employment in the community on jobs for which they are trained.

Working in conjunction with the Horticultural Program, a commercial landscaping service offering professional ground maintenance to area businesses and industries is operated at competitive prices.

The North Branford School System has contracted them to do their lawn maintenance.

Sarah operates and maintains a selection of grounds care machinery of the highest caliber, producing professional results enabling them to handle most any grounds maintenance, parking area maintenance, watering, weeding and fall leaf removal.

Recently the town of Guilford has agreed to rent their golf course to SARAH for the sum of one dollar per year. Beginning in the spring, they will provide grounds care and upkeep for this community facility.

The landscaping division also operates a firewood business during the fall and winter months; cutting, stacking and splitting. Cords of wood are cut, split, and delivered in the shoreline area.

The primary goal of the food service program is to teach clients complete independence in all areas of food preparation and service. Cooking is only a small part of what vocational clients learn. They are involved in menu planning, with consideration to nutrition, and then take part in shopping for necessary items. Tasks are assigned in the kitchen and each client is responsible for following his or her program. Duties learned include dishwashing, recipe following, cooking, using equipment safely and properly, and serving food efficiently and on time. Personal and kitchen hygiene are part of every phase of food service work. The clients are assigned work areas to clean daily as part of their program. This includes equipment, floors, counters, and dishes. At present, the food service daily cooks for 67 clients and the vocational training program staff. This food service also is used as a training situation for those who will eventually work in the Apple Doll House Tea Room as waitresses, waiters, dishwashers and food handlers.

Working in conjunction with other food service is the Tea Room program. Clients are first trained in the food service program to prepare them for the Tea Room. The Tea Room offers a unique blend of work experience and working directly with the public who patronize the restau--

Photographs by Ann Rivellini

rant. In the Apple Doll House Tea Room, training is taken one step further to include not only preparation of food and housekeeping but social amenities and good grooming as well.

The main objectives in the Tea Room experience for the client are to be able to set a table properly, correctly take a complete luncheon order, mix and serve beverages with help, serve meals correctly, pass the hostesses cleaning inspection and be able to demonstrate appropriate behavior in a work environment. Clients are further taught to handle money.

Clients dress in early American garb and a luncheon at the Apple Doll House Tea Room will take you on a journey through the Guilford of yesteryear. Sitting atop an apple knoll, the Tea Room affords the visitor a panoramic view of the rolling Connecticut countryside.

The ability to communicate one's thoughts, needs and desires to others is one of man's greatest assets. For most of us this ability develops easily, for others it is something to be obtained only through years of concentrated effort,

...one's educational opportunities need not be terminated solely because a chronological age limit has been reached.

where each step forward is a major accomplishment. It is the goal of the speech and language program to aid each individual in acquiring the skills necessary to enable them to participate in the daily communication process and thus grow from this interaction of ideas and feelings.

The program contains a total communication system (sign-language plus oral speech). For some of the trainees, the establishment of an annual hearing program and the concurrent follow-up of hearing problems, the speech program also coordinates a continuing process of speech-language education with area school systems.

Through the combined efforts of the Guilford Board of Education and the vocational training progam services, an adult education program was established in 1975. It was felt that one's educational opportunities need not be terminated solely because a chronological age limit has been reached. The idea of continuing education for handicapped people was a relatively new concept then. It now seems to be gaining support at a rapid rate and more towns are starting similar programs---SARAH'S program was the first.

Most of the clients at the workshop participate in some aspect of the program. Instruction is individualized according to the needs of the particualr student involved. Curriculum emphasis is placed on fundamental living skills and academic achievement in the areas of reading, writing, number concepts and language development.

In order to meet the ever increasing need for the vocational training program, SARAH recently purchased the Country Squire Inn, Killingworth, Connecticut, situated on 6 acres of land.

The main building was built in 1780. The restaurant seats 200. There is also a corn crib that has been converted to a small home and the original barn has been converted to shops and offices. It is proposed to initially open the Country Squire Inn for a luncheon business. A minimum of 10 clients could be employed as either food handlers, dishwashers, or waiters and waitresses. Future programs might include a weaving shop, a tin making shop, a thrift shop, a furniture refinishing shop, an apron and what-not shop. Each shop could employ up to five clients who would work under the direct supervision of an instructor. All the skills needed for these shops the clients are capable of developing, all of these skills are needed in today's society, all of these skills conform to our community, and all of the products are in demand.

The Country Squire Inn opens up the room to expand in the two areas SARAH has been most successful--food service and retailing. The shops will be a chance for clients to develop other marketable abilities. One of the most exciting prospects will be stables and use of the grounds for the care of horses.

Many of the larger stables in this country employ mentally retarded people in their stables. It seems that the retarded individual, when properly trained, is more proficient with horse care than the average stable hand. All too often a "normal" groom will overlook certain details that are truly necessary for the well-being of the horse, whereas the retarded groom would find it essential in the care of "his" horse. Horses have a keen sense of "feeling out" those that handle them. Retarded peopole reach out with love and understanding to an animal. The animal senses no fear or danger when approached by the retarded. Through observing many retarded stable hands at work one can realize that the pride and accomplishment put into their grooming shows in the gentle behavior and health of the horse.

Naturally, of course, for the individuals and the animals involved, there will be a "breaking in" period as with any unfamiliar relationship in all of life. The horses must become accustomed to the noisy excited clients and the clients must be properly trained step by step in safe enjoyable stable work. It is necessary, of course, to always have a knowledgeable supervisor present to teach, assist, and manage the stable. In the beginning of training, the client would be taught the proper way to approach a horse-- how to stroke him, how to give him a carrot or hold him. Also in the first stage is daily upkeep of the stable and grounds. It's a nice feeling to know you've taken a messy stall and made it nice and clean with the scent of fresh bedding for the horse to sleep in. At the same time, fresh hay is put in the racks and water pails are filled. The second stage begins the actual handling and becoming a groom. Each is taught the correct way to lead a horse and tie him in cross-ties (a set of ropes across an aisleway which

Photographs by Ann Rivellini

keep the horse in one position). At first they will learn to curry (round and round) and brush the horse's body.

Eventually the client will be taught to pick up each hoof and clean it out--checking for stones, etc. For many clients this stable care and grooming will be a great accomplishment and something that broadens the horizons in their lives.

This first section on horse care could be mastered by most any person. For those that really enjoy it and are enthusiastic, further training will come in the areas of feeding, turning out, cleaning tack and exercising. Once a client feels confident around the animals, he can learn to handle the horses well enough to move them about-- walking them, putting them in and out of the stall, etc. The barn will provide boarding of 20 horses, a feed room and tack room, and two stalls for client horses. Their own horses will be of a gentle disposition and used for initial client training--in grooming and handling; plus--for advanced trainers--as school horses for exercising and riding

In actual operation, the trainees would work with customers' horses--feeding, grooming, and cleaning the stall. In the shoreline area the horse business is booming-- with people moving to large indoor facilities at a great pace. Active horsemen desire an attractive, convenient stabling facility where their horse will get individual personalized care. People like to show off their horse and his home, and the Country Squire's stable will provide a large indoor facility that can be an asset to the entire area. People of all types will enjoy visiting the horse farm just as much as a lunch at the restaurant. The facility would be dual-purpose--for the training of clients and the public's usage. The horse has been man's companion for hundreds of years--a point well-worth pondering. People, whether retarded or normal, are at peace with animals.

The Country Squire Inn

Photographs by Ann Rivellini

Teaching the Unteachables

JOHN FLEISCHMAN

A group of caring people in Oregon are proving that the profoundly retarded can learn to lead happy and useful lives. Yet the mind of the retardate is full of the human mystery. How does one survive and another fail?

John Fleischman is an assistant editor of HUMAN BEHAVIOR.

In Oregon's Willamette Valley, rain is what falls with very little interruption from November to May. If this is October, the drizzle frosting the windshield can't be rain. Some locals put on hats for the autumn storm clouds scudding east into the Cascades, but the army surplus ponchos, the rubberized trousers, the L.L. Bean's moosehunting shoes are held in reserve. In the fall, moss gathers strength on the northern exposures.

Picking up the McKenzie River highway heading northeast out of Eugene, Dan Close is trying to reconstruct a dry July Sunday last summer when a year's work almost died on a highway bridge 48 miles up into the Cascades. Close was then the director of a new group home in Eugene for 10 severely and profoundly retarded adults. He had been off that Sunday climbing Three Sisters Mountain while three of his weekend staff had taken the "folks" for a carefully planned hike along the McKenzie River. The folks were becoming accomplished walkers. Graduating from walks around town, the group-home residents were taken hiking at least every other weekend, usually along logging roads or major trails. The week

before, a staff member had driven up to the tiny town of McKenzie Bridge to alert the rangers and to scout the trail.

It was a flawless summer day—so clear that when Close reached Three Sisters' summit he could see the snowy top of Mount Rainier to the north and, faintly but unmistakably, Mount Shasta over 200 miles south. He took color slides to prove it.

Tired from the day's climb, yet still exhilarated by the view, Close drove home along the river road—unaware that two of his folks had walked away from the hike. In the long July daylight, it was still bright when Close crossed the river above the little village of McKenzie Bridge and continued down the twisting valley towards home. He didn't know that less than two hours before, one of the missing residents had been struck and killed on the bridge itself by a woman motorist who told police that the man had lunged out into the roadway in front of her. When Close reached home, the phone was ringing. John Collier was dead, and Jim Clay had disappeared into the rugged woods.

Jim Clay was a strong, healthy 30-year-old with a measurable IQ below 20. He had almost no language and was wearing no coat. At about the same time that John Collier was run down on the highway bridge, Jim was spotted not very far away on the other side of the river. Crossing the McKenzie on a ramshackle log bridge, Jim encountered a local boy. The boy spoke to him, and Jim became frightened and bolted up a power-line break. The boy's father called the ranger station to report that his son had seen a strange man who looked to be on drugs.

By morning, Close was on his way back up the river road for the first of a dozen runs that July to join a search force of rangers, deputy sheriffs, group-

home staffers, state police and volunteers backed by helicopters and light planes. A nearly equal force of television camerapersons and reporters—as well as the curious—turned up to watch the operation. The news media were very helpful, Close says, by emphasizing that Jim was not dangerous but only hungry and frightened. In their zeal to be of assistance, the people of McKenzie Bridge phoned in every report of an overturned garbage can or mysterious thump in the night. These false reports turned the search away from the rough hills and back towards the village.

Seven days after Jim disappeared, a man hiking up to his remote cabin spotted Jim standing in the cabin's doorway holding a jug of water. The man ran for help, and when the group-home staff came back with him, they found Jim sitting up in bed with his clothes neatly folded at the foot. He was 30 pounds lighter, spotlessly clean and very hungry.

In October, the mountains are black walls of thick fir and pine; the rainclouds, white dragons snuffling eastward up the narrow valley. The tires hiss on the asphalt. "I used to think these were the ugliest hills in the world," Close says, staring off into the wet wilderness, "because I thought Jim was up there." Close remembers the police conducting the hunt with thoroughness, gallons of coffee and the idea that Jim was "escaping." It was the only way they could conceptualize Jim's elusive behavior. As misconceptions go, it was very minor. But while the search continued, there was an unspoken fear in the minds of Close and the others connected with the group home—the fear of much larger misconceptions.

"People think the greatest risk in group homes is the risk of death," says Close. They had had a death. But while the search for Jim continued, the reality of John's loss didn't have time to sink in. But what if Jim was never found or was found dead? If the police saw Jim as an escapee, would the public see the group-home staff as delinquent custodians? What were two such helpless men doing hiking around in a wilderness area? Surely the severely and profoundly retarded had to be protected from themselves and the outside world.

A death seemed a disastrous way to introduce the public to a novel treatment for the severely and profoundly retarded. The very label makes professionals wince. The severely and profoundly retarded are those with IQs below 35, the bottom limit of the trainable mentally retarded (TMR) category. That sounds splendid except that it is very difficult to accurately measure an IQ below 50. The subjects have little or no language, and often cannot hold a pencil in a way that could possibly be construed as functional. Behavioral-inventory tests are the only way to measure their IQ. You find out if the subjects can eat with a fork. Do they wash behind their ears? Can the men close their own flies? Are they toilet trained?

The severely and profoundly retarded don't do very well on these kinds of tests, either. Which may explain why most of the severely retarded, especially the adults, are stored in institutions where attendants close their flies, cut their food, wash behind their ears and clean them up when they forget their toilet training. These custodial institutions are filled with severely retarded adults because their natural parents wear out or die or are told to do the "best thing" or throw up their hands in despair once the impact of their child's condition sinks in. Also children, even retarded children, are cute. Children are symbols of hope, but a 20-year-old man with three days of stubble and an IQ estimated below 20 looks neither cute nor hopeful.

"The adult severely and profoundly retarded population is not in the forefront of the public consciousness. The attitude is 'Let's get the children and prevent them from ending up like this,'" says Close. "They've lived in institutions all their lives. They're those retarded people you've heard about. Maybe you've seen one on the street with his mother, but you've never thought about them." In institutions and nursing homes, the severely and profoundly retarded exist out of sight and out of mind. "This group has been kissed off," says Close.

The group Close talks about is larger than we like to think. A 1972 HEW

"They've lived in institutions all their lives. They are those retarded people you've heard about. This group of people has been kissed off."

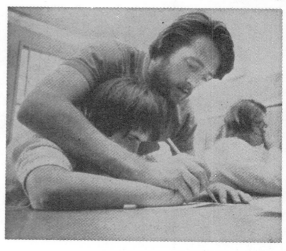

study shows that there were 200,000 mentally retarded Americans of all ages and levels in institutions. Dr. Richard Eyman, a demographic researcher at Pacific State Hospital in Pomona, California, has looked at it more closely. His studies have shown that in a hypothetical community of 100,000, there are 25 profoundly retarded adults (measurable IQ below 20) and 100 severely retarded adults (measurable IQ below 35). He points out that these figures can be extrapolated for the nation as a whole, giving a figure of 275,000 severely and profoundly retarded Americans.

A 1970 study conducted by Eyman in Riverside, California, showed that the severely and profoundly retarded have a "well over 80 percent" probability of being committed to an institution at some point in their lives. In particular, the profoundly retarded are likely to be institutionalized—a probability of 95 percent. "The place you are going to find the profoundly retarded is in an institution," says Eyman. "There are not many homes that can stand up to that kind of thing."

The Eugene home wanted to try. The idea of group homes for the handicapped and the retarded has been around for years. But as far as Close or any of the others involved in the Eugene home could discover, it had never actually been attempted with this class of retarded adults. The low level of the subjects' intelligence, combined with their adult strength and size, had discouraged this kind of treatment.

The problem with a group home is what to do with the residents during the day. Retarded children can be sent off to special schools. Moderately retarded adults can work in sheltered workshops. But here was a group seemingly too old to educate or too slow to work. Still, the last 10 years have seen

a revolution in the behavioral sciences that seemed to promise both a solution to the daytime problem and the means to operate a group home for so difficult a population.

Tom Bellamy, a young doctoral candidate in special education at the University of Oregon, started a workshop for severely and profoundly retarded adults in Eugene. He adapted some of the techniques pioneered by Marc Gold, whose work at the University of Illinois had opened up the whole field of vocational training for the severely retarded. Through a method called task analysis and sequential training technique, Gold divided the assembly of a 15-piece bicycle brake into its smallest discriminations and successfully taught the steps to a group of 64 moderately and severely retarded individuals in sheltered workshops. Gold had opened the door to useful and commercially valuable work for the retarded.

Bellamy set up a shop to subcontract the assembly of electronic subunits. Bellamy's severely and profoundly retarded workers were able to put together a 52-piece cam switch actuator at a rate close to industry standard and with quality equal to or higher than that of industry. Bellamy's first workers lived at home, but there simply weren't enough uninstitutionalized potential subjects living in Eugene to give his program a meaningful sample. The population Bellamy wanted was living outside town at the state hospital, Fairview.

Meanwhile, Dan Close was working with Gold in Chicago. Initially, Close worked with severely and profoundly retarded adults at Camarillo (California) State Hospital as a psychology undergraduate at California Lutheran College. Pursuing a master's degree at Idaho State University in Pocatello, he became involved with a sheltered workshop for TMR adolescents and adults. Marc Gold was consultant to the project; and the first time Close heard him speak, he knew this man was onto something. Gold invited him to Chicago to run the research on a vocational-skill training experiment. Close says flatly of Gold, "He taught me everything I know."

Close had become interested in the community-living approach; and when he heard about the proposed Eugene group home, he came out to Oregon to join Bellamy.

Bellamy found a sponsor through the Alvord-Taylor Homes, a nonprofit organization operating a group home for the mildly retarded and another as a respite care center in Eugene. Through the state Mental Health Division, he found money and access to the patients at Fairview.

In the fall of 1974, Close drove out to Fairview for an initial look at his future residents. He knew what institutions were like, but he was momentarily overwhelmed by the scene. Fairview is an excellent institution of its kind with a cooperative director backed up by a progressive state mental health establishment. Still, the first encounter unnerved Close. "They looked bizarre," he recalls. "You go out to a state hospital, and you'll find people sitting around in white shirts and pants and bowl haircuts. Some with shoes, some barefoot, some with snot running down their faces. I thought there was no way we were going to be able to work with these people."

Institutions teach institutional behavior. Stereotypical institutional behavior for the mentally retarded is head banging, floor searching, hand rubbing and throwing tantrums. After 20 years in institutions, the patients often curl into a permanently stooped posture, the shoulder blades half-folded around the chest. Sitting aimlessly in wards, the retarded become addicted to self-stimulation, or "self-stim" as it is called—crotch rubbing, earhole grinding and endless rocking back and forth. The line between the symptoms of the retardation itself and the institutional stereotype is blurred.

The journey from the institution to the normal world is a cultural ocean as frightening and as wide as the one many Europeans crossed seeking a New World. Close likes the metaphor: "Our people are like that—immigrants from another land. They don't understand our language, and their culture is the culture of the institution."

In a ward of endless rockers and

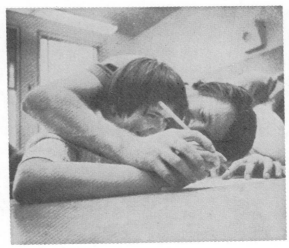

"Our people are like new immigrants from another land. They just don't understand our language, and their culture is that of the institution."

shriveled men, Dan Close found 27-year-old John Collier sitting immobile in front of a TV set. John hated to move, and he had discovered that if he parked himself in front of a TV, no one would disturb him. But Dan Close had plans to disturb him. "The thing about John was that he acted as if he knew nothing, but then he would come out with things like counting to 10," he explained.

For his generation, John's case was unusual. The cause of his retardation was unknown, and it was only after he started school that he was given the dread label of mentally retarded. He lived with his parents until he was 19, when the strain of caring for and supervising him every minute became too great. But even after he was committed to a state institution for the retarded, his family stayed in contact—coming to visit, sending presents and asking about his living conditions. Most of the severely and profoundly retarded John's age were committed early, and their families lost touch with them. "It becomes pretty unrewarding to visit a child who is unresponsive," says Close.

Because of his parents' attention and his relatively short period of institutionalization, John had the most going for himself of the eight chosen in the fall of 1974 for the new group home. John was selected by the toss of a coin from a group of 17 retarded adults at Fairview Hospital and Training Center outside Eugene. The "target" population was made up of those patients who were over 18, able to walk and use a spoon and who tested out as "severely or profoundly retarded." Because of the funding through the Oregon Mental Health Division, the target group had to have been committed from Eugene or the surrounding Lane County. Eight were arbitrarily picked for the group home, and nine people remained at Fairview as a control group. Subse-

quently, two more residents were added to the home, but they remained outside the "experiment."

Less than a year before his death John Collier emigrated to a new world. He was in the first group brought to the electric-blue house at 670-16th Street, the group home that would much later be called the John Collier House.

* * *

A few minutes before nine, they straggle up 16th Street on their way to work. There is no mistaking the six women and four men. Some walk fast intent on their goal. Others shuffle looking lost to the world. Louie, the "Big L," lopes along in great strides, then stops to survey the scene, then bounces forward again. Jim, clad in a bright yellow windbreaker, brings up the rear. His hand is clenched just in front of his eyes, his fingers working up and down like a trumpet player's. When the front of the group reaches Alder Street, Jim screws his eyes tight and waits, his fingers marking time.

At every corner, Jay Buckley, who has taken over after Close went back to school to get his doctorate, puts the folks through the street-crossing program one at a time. Buckley takes Alice's hand and points down the street "Car's close," says Jay. "Car's close," says Alice. She tracks the car with her outstretched finger as it speeds past "Car's far away," Jay says. "Car's far away," she repeats. Under his direction she tracks both directions and then steps off on her own. In ones and twos the group repeats the corner drill.

Alder Street borders the University of Oregon campus. On the far side, the folks turn right and follow a sidewalk past the tennis courts and up a small rise to the new special-education building where the workshop is located. The university is a hotbed of behaviorism where the first tenet is "Show me the data." The special-ed building was designed for data collection. A darkened gallery runs above the classrooms. Beveled one-way windows look down into the workshop. Directional microphones are positioned in the ceiling. Perched on hard metal stools, "coders" sit in the shadows watching the scene below. Disembodied voices from the wall speakers echo in the gallery. A beeper sounds every 10 seconds, and the coders dutifully mark down on special sheets what their subject is doing at that moment—looking around, "self-stim," attending to directions, working and so on.

Graphed and computerized, the results are empirical, tangible and comparable. Can "self-stim" be decreased in X? Code the behavior and find out its exact rate of occurrence. Design a program to change the behavior. Code the subject's behavior during the correction program and afterward. Then compare the numbers. Has there been a change? Is the program effective? Behavioral science marches on to the beep of a 10-second timer.

The workshop is an ordinary-looking classroom furnished with evenly spaced trapezoidal tables. Each table has a row of shallow bins and the necessary forms and tools for the task. The folks manufacture cable trusses, plugs and switches for oscilloscopes. The key to the workshop is task analysis. A job is broken down into its tiniest steps, and the necessary discriminations are plotted. Then the job is taught tidbit by tidbit, and the worker is reinforced every step of the way.

Assembling a switch becomes a series of small discriminations and simple operations. Take one piece out of a bin. Fit it in a wooden form. Place the second piece on top. Screw the two together. Lay the unit on a marked card. Repeat the process until the card is filled. Call for a supervisor to count the units and check the quality. Start another card.

Louie has been institutionalized for 34 of his 38 years. His hair is long and lank, and he has grown a full beard that, at first glance, gives him a vaguely sinister air. It is a false impression. Louie fits the first piece into the form. He studies the result with melancholic concentration; then he snatches the second piece and slaps it carelessly into place. The workshop supervisor squats at his elbow. She puts the second piece back in the bin. "Fix it, Louie," she says.

His frustration boils over, his arms jerking back at his head, the forearms locked at the wrists. "Fix it, Louie," she says. His locked arms slowly uncoil. He snaps up the returned piece and slaps it back. She puts it back. "Fix it, Louie." His arms fly up again, his head twisting backward. Suddenly he pulls his arms down again and quickly fits the piece correctly. "All right, Louie," she congratulates, "all right, Louie. Very nice." He races through the card, assembling the units with spasmodic intensity. He jerks his head away and throws one arm up in triumph.

"Hey, Louie, you've got your one hand up." She comes over to inspect the card, poking the pieces to make sure they are screwed tightly. Satisfied, she offers Louie a penny, an immediate reward for the job. "Let's trade," she suggests. Louie studies the coin. "What did you get, Louie?" she asks. "What did you get?" "Penny," says the bearded man in the softest of voices. "Way to go, Louie, way to go." He slips his reward into a plastic cup taped to his workbench and starts another card.

The pennies are the basis of a token economy to reinforce correct behavior. Besides pennies, everyone earns a flat piece rate. Some exceed minimum wage because of high productivity. But for many, paychecks and even tokens are too remote. They work for the constant verbal and social reinforcements the supervisors lavish on them.

Barry is on the token economy. All day he works at his station screwing plugs together, shaking them at his ear and tapping them against his face to insure they are tight. The pennies mount up. At 4 p.m., he grasps his money tightly in his fist and goes to the "store," a table spread with small plastic boxes of raisins and cookies. The boxes are arranged by price, and he walks up and down the row, deciding. He settles on a box of animal crackers, which he takes to a table and opens with great care. Satisfied, Barry munches his day's earnings.

The house on 16th Street comes alive when the folks come home. Sam, the house mongrel, barks like crazy. Mark heads straight for the stereo, stuffs "The Who" into the machine, and Friday night is off and running. Soon there are dancers in the living room and vegetable choppers in the kitchen, where Jeanne Bell is patching together a dinner without a stove, since the old one gave up the ghost that morning. Jay Buckley is out in the driveway wrestling a donated replacement off a pickup truck.

Jeanne started out as an elementary school teacher and then became interested in "exceptional" children. Together with Dan Close, she helped to set up the group home. When Close left, she stayed on to work with Jay. They are supposed to work a roughly normal Monday-through-Friday week. When stoves burn out, or other problems mount, the week becomes longer.

Two other staff members come in first thing in the morning, and two more after dinner. There is also a different weekend staff. The night manager is the only staff member who lives in, in a room in the basement. The group home also has a stream of volunteers and practicing students from the university.

"At first, we hired a man to stay up all night. We didn't have any idea what would happen," Jeanne remembers. "But it turned out that they sleep like anybody else."

The folks do most of the work—the cooking, the laundry, the housecleaning, the dishwashing, the yard work, the table setting and emptying the garbage cans. They feed the pets and make the beds—just like in a real home.

Barry is methodically slicing up apples for a salad while a staff member half-watches him and half-watches two sandwichmakers. One of the sandwichmakers has changed her clothes twice since she came home from work. Changing your clothes when you want is an example of the distance between the institution and 670-16th Street. Jeanne says, "In an institution, they slept in a large room. There was another room where their clothes were kept locked up. But when they came here, suddenly they had bedrooms, dressers and drawers with clothes in them."

The house on 16th Street is not just a bunch of nice people being nice to retarded people. The ideology of the group home is behaviorist, and the methodology is thumbtacked to the pantry wall. The wall is covered with programs for problems great and small —to get Bonnie to say certain sounds, to teach shoe tying, to toilet train Alice. For example:

Name: Barry. (Desired) Behavior: Keeping his clothes to himself. Objective: Barry will tell Louie to take off any article of clothing that is rightfully Barry's.
If Louie has Barry's clothing—
(1) Get Barry, point at Louie and at the article of clothing, say, "Barry, Louie has your ——— on."
(2) Nudge Barry and get him involved.

4. MANPOWER

(3) Tell Barry to tell Louie, "Hey take my pants, etc., off."
(4) Wait for Barry's verbalization.
(5) Then tell Louie to take off Barry's article of clothing.
Note: This is especially important for you morning folks.

Another part of the group home's behaviorist approach is the use of systematic coding observations to generate data for the experiment and also to analyze specific behavior problems.

When Louie first came from Fairview, he spent hours on his hands and knees searching the floor. The behavior showed up on the community-living observations as a form of "self-stim" because of the way Louie rubbed the carpet with his fingers. A program was written up to "overcorrect" the searching. Anytime a staff member found Louie searching, Louie was made to wash his hands and was then given paper to scribble on. Now Louie collects pencils like a magnet. He scribbles intently and then stops to study the circles. Then he returns to scribbling.

The Friday night excitement is heightened by the news that Alice is going out to dinner with Bob Johnson. Bob is a severely retarded young man from a foster-care home. Alice, who is 10 years older chronologically but his equal mentally, is beside herself with anticipation. "You're going out to dinner with Bob Johnson?" asks Jeanne. "Bob Johnson," blushes Alice, tucking her chin under.

Just as the group sits down to dinner, Bob arrives. Bob is delighted to be there, delighted to be going out to dinner, delighted to be going out with Alice and delighted to see Jeanne. He shakes everybody's hand. Along with two staffers, they are off to Mama's Truckstop. Bob is slipped a few bucks to pay for the outing and with much hand-

shaking and at least two complete sets of farewells, the couple sets out.

Jeanne seems almost as delighted as Bob. Sex has never been a problem, she says. Quite the contrary, many of the residents have little idea how to show even elementary affection. "It's hard to believe, but some of them don't know how to hug and kiss." Hugging and kissing are an unofficial priority. There is no program on the pantry wall, but the staff teaches it, anyway.

Eating is a big part of the official program. Institutions don't spend a great deal of time on table manners; they don't even teach chewing. Since institutional food is soft and bland, the patients only have to master the spoon. The severely and profoundly retarded often choke on foods such as apples that require chewing. Louie is a chronic choker. He eats with the same wild abandon with which he walks. Once he was surprised stealing a potato from the kitchen. He jammed the whole thing down his throat and was nearly asphyxiated.

Eight residents sit at the main table while two others work on eating programs with Jay at the small "training table." Jeanne presides at the main table. "Isn't everyone sitting up straight? Isn't Sally sitting up straight? Good, Sally, really good." Sally beams from her seat. In institutions, the patients slump at the table, their noses in their plates, shoveling the food into their mouths. In the group home, everyone sits up straight to eat. After a few meals spent reinforcing the residents, staffers find themselves eating with the carriage of ballet dancers.

Louie eyes an extra sandwich. "Would you like another sandwich, Louie?" Jeanne asks, offering him the plate. He picks up a half and takes one small bite. "Good chewing," says Jeanne. "Isn't everyone sitting up straight?" Every-

one, staff included, is sitting bolt upright.

Saturday morning, staff member Tama Levine sets out for the local Y with five of the folks. Underlying the group home's philosophy is the principle of normalization; retarded people should lead as normal a life as possible in the least restrictive setting. The folks go bowling. They go to movies and to concerts. Three nights a week, the folks study rudimentary arithmetic, handwriting and reading at a local school. Normal people go to baseball games, so the folks go see Eugene's minor league Emeralds. Whether they understand the rules is not important; they cheer from beginning to end.

Normal people like to work out, and so do the folks. They play a unique brand of basketball. Jan, who is 24 and suffers from Down's syndrome, can barely manage the ball. She seems frozen; yet slowly she coils her body for a two-handed cradle shot straight from the knees. Jim has a different approach: shouldering the ball one-handedly, he advances on the basket with one eye screwed shut, his free hand working its continual trumpet-playing routine. At 15 feet, he pops the ball through the hoop with the assurance of Wilt Chamberlain. He squeezes both eyes shut in delight.

Tama puts the group through calisthenics. Down's people are incredibly limber. Jan drops easily into a full leg split, then tucks both legs behind her head. Then they all jog around the gym. Barry, who is the state champion in the Special Olympics 50-yard dash, leads the way, squealing in a high voice, his left hand raised over his head.

It is too late for a swim, but Tama takes them down to the weight-lifting room. As the group enters, the lifters look up in amazement. Tama soon gets everyone lifting something, and the body builders go back to the serious business at hand. Fifteen minutes later, the folks have blended into the strange rituals of weight lifting. Jim kneels before an iron bar connected through a pulley to a stack of iron discs. As he pulls, his face continues its perpetual grimacing. Next to him, a weight lifter staggers under an immense barbell resting on a foam-rubber backpad. The lifter's face is contorted with strain as his buddy shouts encouragement:

"Work it, work the weight." Tama urges Jim on: "Pull, Jim, pull. All right, Jim. All right." Jim lets the pulley down with a clang. He shakes his wrists wildly. "All right, Jim. Way to go," says Tama.

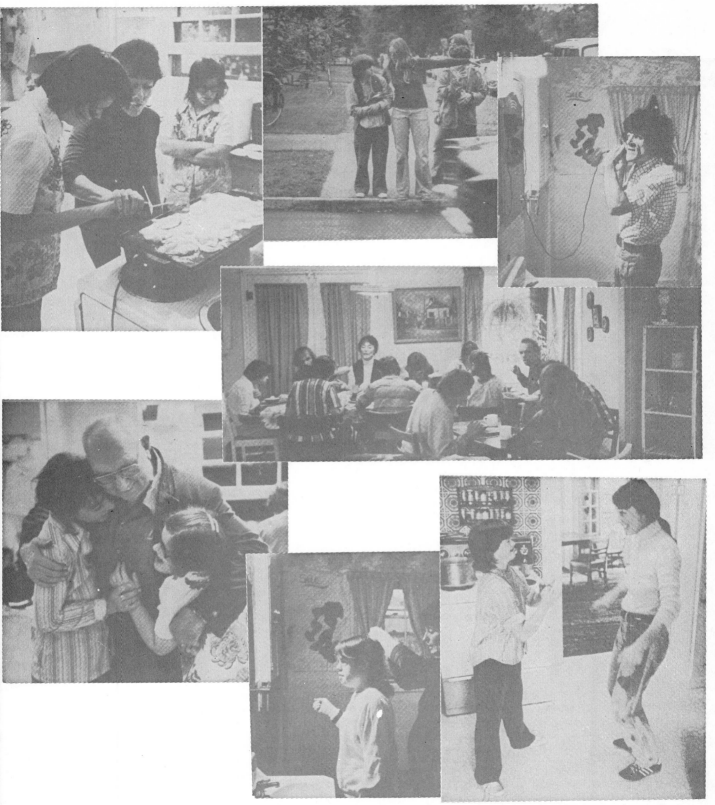

Having spent most of their lives stored in various state hospitals, 10 severely and profoundly retarded adults now have their own home. It's a place (clockwise from lower left) where one can stand at the front window watching for the paperboy, and where codirector Jeanne Bell can share a hug with a visiting father and his stepdaughter. Bell and the staff teach such basic how-tos of living as frying an egg, crossing a street, shaving, tripping the light fantastic in the kitchen, amateur hairstyling and minding one's table manners at dinner.

Prevocational Training of the Severely Retarded Using Task Analysis[1]

William P. Friedenberg
Andrew S. Martin

Authors: WILLIAM P. FRIEDENBERG, M.S. (Syracuse University), currently completing work for his Ph.D. in clinical psychology at Texas Tech University, Lubbock and is also a research assistant at the Research and Training Center in Mental Retardation, Texas Tech University; ANDREW S. MARTIN, Ph.D. (University of Connecticut), a research scientist at the Research and Training Center in Mental Retardation, P.O. Box 4510, Texas Tech University, Lubbock, Texas 79409.

ABSTRACT. Two severely retarded students were trained on a task requiring multiple, multidimensional discrimination. Two procedures for accomplishing the task were subjected to task analysis and training procedures for each devised. Each student was trained on both a hand and machine procedure for stapling labels on plastic bags. Subsequent production tests suggested that tangible reinforcement may be a necessary ingredient in maintaining low-error performance with an inherently non-reinforcing task. Recommendations are made for in-depth analysis of tasks prior to setting up training programs.

Prevocational programs for the mentally retarded are designed to evaluate and train potential workers in basic skills. Gold (1973b) shows that intelligence tests, manual dexterity tests, and work sample tasks are of limited usefulness in predicting work performance. An actual work assignment is preferred because it can develop valuable skills in the client while it is being used for evaluation.

Crosson (1969) set the standard for extending behavioral techniques to sheltered workshop settings through his use of task analysis and intensification of cues by the trainer. In this training procedure, "the trainer demonstrates each of the component behaviors in the proper sequence and prompts the trainee to immediately model the behavior. This can be accomplished by verbal or gestured command although it is occasionally necessary to mold the response by physically guiding the trainee through an appropriate topography" (p. 815). Other researchers have since added evidence that laboratory techniques can be used with success in the real life setting of the workshop (Zimmerman, Stuckey, Garlick, & Miller, 1969; Gold, 1972; Gold, 1973a; Brown, Bellamy, & Sontag, 1971).

The current study applied task analysis procedures to train students in the prevocational area of a sheltered workshop. Gold's thesis (1973a) that pay or praise in some form are not the only reinforcers available for work was tested using a task with different reinforcing properties from that used by Gold. The assumption that retarded students would require more training time and have lower subsequent production rates using a "complicated" piece of equipment than they would with standard techniques was also investigated.

Participants. Patrick, a 21-year-old severely retarded male (IQ = 30) and Tommy, a 30-year-old male with a measured IQ of 36 were assigned to the prevocational area of the workshop since neither was judged to be ready for work in the sheltered workshop.

Setting. The state school where the study took place is a residential facility for the mentally retarded. The school has a sheltered workshop of the extended care type and a newly instituted pre-vocational training area.

Training Task. The workshop presently has several contracts involving production of goods for local businesses. One such contract consists of the bagging, labeling, and displaying of spices for sale in grocery stores. Stapling labels onto plastic bags filled with garlic bulbs was chosen as a training task since the skills involved were applicable to other workshop jobs.

Task Analysis. The task of putting a label on a plastic bag filled with two garlic bulbs was analyzed for economy and ease of physical movement using task analysis procedures adapted from Gold (1975). The task was first method-analyzed to establish the method or methods which would be easiest to learn or teach. Two alternatives were designated—stapling by hand and stapling using a foot-operated machine (See Figure 1). This machine required coordinated use of eyes, hands, and feet in a sequence unfamiliar to the trainees. Based on the fact that the machine required more effort from the student and more input from the instructor, it would not appear at first glance to be the method of choice. Content analysis was used to break the two tasks into teachable units. The steps for hand and machine stapling are presented in Table 1. Finally, process analysis determined the format and type of feedback used in training. Following a procedure developed for use with housekeeping tasks (Brown, Bellamy & Sontag, 1971), four levels of instruction were used: nonpunitive indication of error, verbal direction, modeling, and priming.

FIGURE 1

Foot-operated stapling machine

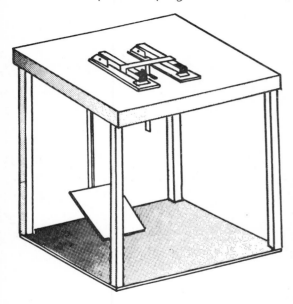

General Procedure. Each student was trained to staple labels onto bags using one of the two methods, machine or hand, for approximately 20 minutes each day. This period was lengthened to allow a block of 10 trials in progress to be completed. After the student met the criterion of 20 consecutive trials without error, he was tested for production in three 20-minute sessions. During these test sessions, the student was told to work as fast as he could and staple as many labels as possible for 20 minutes. When the production test was completed, each student was trained using the alternate production method. Three production test sessions followed to test speed and accuracy using the second stapling method. A production test session using the hand method was given between the 1st and 2nd machine production sessions for Patrick, and a machine session was given between the 2nd and 3rd sessions for Tommy. These interpolated trials were used to test for practice effects.

Training. The trainer began by physically modeling the steps necessary to obtain a completed product while stating verbally the operations he was performing according to the task analysis. He then told the student to try the task. An inability to complete a step correctly was dealt with first

TABLE 1

Steps in Machine and Hand Stapling from Task Analysis

LABEL STAPLING — MACHINE

1. Pick up one label with one hand.
2. Place the label in front of you (face down with the open end of the flap facing you).
3. Retrieve a bag of garlic from the tray, with both hands, holding only the corners of the open end.
4. Insert the mouth of the garlic bag into the "v" shaped space made by the raised flap of the label.
5. Hold the bag in place with the thumbs.
6. Now press the flap down (over the mouth of the bag) with the forefingers.
7. Carefully put your thumb on the flap also and press down.
8. Now remove your forefingers and carefully pick up the bag without moving your thumb.
9. Insert under the stapler and staple by depressing the pedal.
10. Place the labeled bag in a tray.

LABEL STAPLING — HAND

1. Pick up one label with one hand.
2. Place the label in front of you (face down with the open end of the flap facing you).
3. Retrieve a bag of garlic from the tray, with both hands, holding only the corners of the open end.
4. Insert the mouth of the garlic bag into the "v" shaped space made by the elevated bag.
5. Hold the bag in place with the thumbs.
6. Now press the flap down (over the mouth of the bag) with the forefingers.
7. Carefully put your thumb on the flap also and press down.
8. Now remove your forefingers and carefully pick up the bag without moving your thumb.
9. Insert under the stapler, carefully letting go of assembly on side of label to be stapled first.
10. Using free hand, hit or push down on stapler.
11. Push label over, keeping assembly under stapler.
12. Grasp with free hand, letting go with other hand.
13. Position and staple other side of label.
14. Place labeled bag in a tray.

by a non-punitive indication of error ("Try it another way"). If this had no effect, a verbal direction was given such as "hold the bag tightly." If the verbal instruction did not result in the performer correcting his error, a physical cue was given in the form of the step being modeled by the trainer with accompanying verbal instructions. The fourth level of correction (priming) consisted of manipulating the boy's hands to help him complete the step correctly. No tangible reinforcement was given. The experimentor tried as much as possible not to make eye contact or provide other social reinforcement since the student's constant checking with the trainer to see if he is correct can easily disrupt learning (Gold, 1973c).

4. MANPOWER

Production Test. When criterion was reached, three production test sessions of 20 minutes each were given. In these sessions. the student was encouraged to complete as many units as he could with no corrections made by the trainer. Earlier experience had indicated that production rates were not easily maintained without any reinforcement so non-contingent verbal reward was included in this stage. This consisted of dramatic exhortations to try hard and work quickly, and praise of current performance. The verbal reinforcement was not tied to specific performance of the student at that moment.

Results

Figures 2 and 3 show the number of errors and the number of completely correct products made for each block of 10 trials during training for both procedures. Patrick took only two sessions or approximately 40 minutes to meet the criterion of 20 consecutively correct responses using the hand stapling procedure. He quickly went from 10 step

FIGURE 2

Number of substep errors and completely correct products produced per block of ten trials during training.

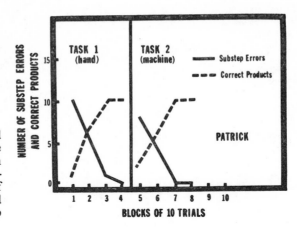

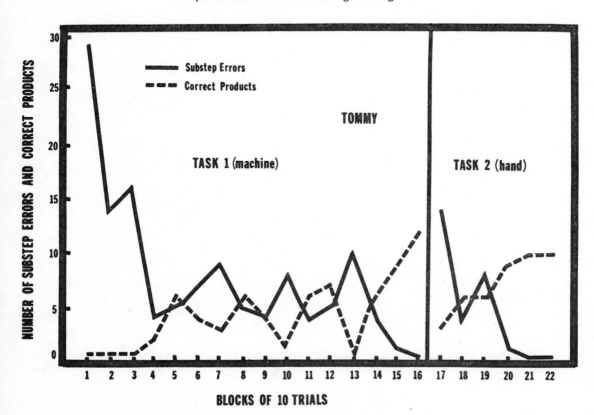

FIGURE 3

Number of substep errors and completely correct products produced per block of ten trials during training.

errors per 10 products to zero errors. The transfer of training to the second method can be seen in lower initial step errors, higher initial number of completely correct products, and shorter training time (approximately 20 minutes for the machine training). Tommy took longer to learn the machine procedure than Patrick took to learn the hand procedure. His total training time over 6 days was, however, less than 2 hours (107 minutes). He started with lower overall performance characteristics than did Patrick, reached a plateau for several sessions, then quickly reached criterion within one day's session. This fast rise to criterion after a period of plateau performance has been described by Zeaman and House (1963) for visual discrimination learning in retardates. Transfer was accomplished (lower step errors and more correct products), with complete training taking place in 2 days (60 trials) on hand stapling.

Table 2 shows the relative numbers of completely correct products and unacceptable products for each test session, and the mean performance on these two measures for both students.

Patrick produced an average of 21 correct products by hand with an average of 9.5 unacceptable. This represents an average unacceptable rate of 31%. When tested after being trained on machine stapling, he produced an average 20 correct with an average 7.34 unacceptable. This yields an unacceptable product rate of 27% —an improvement of 4% for machine over hand stapling. Tommy produced 31.75 correct and 6.5 unacceptable by machine with an unacceptable product rate of 17%. His performance after being trained to staple by hand shows 29 correct and an average 6.0 unacceptable for an error rate of 17%—the same as for machine stapling. No apparent differences are seen between interpolated and original test session production rates, thus indicating that the second stapling technique results were not enhanced by practice effects.

In test sessions the average number correct produced by both students was 26.7 by machine and 24.4 by hand. For both the average number of unacceptable products was 6.85 by machine and 8.0 by hand, representing an unacceptable product rate of 20% and 25% respectively.

TABLE 2

Mean Production in Test Sessions on
Machine and Hand Stapling

	MACHINE						HAND				
	Sessions							*Sessions*			
	1	2	3	4	$\overline{X}$		1	2	3	4	$\overline{X}$
TOMMY											
Number Correct	31	30	33	33*	31.74		30	20	37		29.0
Unacceptable	6	7	8	5	6.5		6	8	4		6.0
PATRICK											
Number Correct	23	10	27		20.0		22	28	8	26*	21.0
Unacceptable	10	10	2		7.34		6	6	13	13	9.5
Machine Correct	$\overline{X}$ = 26.7					Hand Correct	$\overline{X}$ = 24.4				
Machine Unacceptable	$\overline{X}$ = 6.85					Hand Unacceptable	$\overline{X}$ = 8.0				

*Interpolated trials — using alternate method

4. MANPOWER

Discussion

In addition to showing that training was successfully completed for both students within a very short period of time, the results tend to favor machine stapling slightly over hand stapling in number produced, unacceptable products, and error rate. One of the aims of this study was to see if possible increased training time on machine stapling would be offset by improved performance. Although no conclusions can be drawn from such a small sample, the results at least indicate that one should consider possible gains in the long run production obtainable by investing in a longer initial training period, and the fact that quality may deteriorate less over time due to the standardization provided by the machine. In addition, the trainer should not be overly apprehensive about the use of work aids that seem complicated but which are contributory to increased production. A careful study of potential work aids and training methods to teach use of these aids should be made before assuming a simpler method is preferable.

Concerning the high unacceptable rate seen in production after errorless performance had previously been reached in training, the possibility that the criterion was too low for assurance of complete learning or that over-learning should have been instituted to insure retention is discounted. The criterion for acquisition used in the present study (20 consecutive correct trials) is considerably higher than that used in other studies. In addition, Gold (1972) found no positive effect of over-learning on retention rates. A more likely explanation is that the inherent interest in the task (Gold, 1972; Gold, 1973a) and social reinforcement was not strong enough in the present study to maintain performance at a high level. The present task is a fairly difficult one, and unlike the bicycle brake used by Gold, the discriminations necessary for successful completion of this task are multiple and multidimensional rather than simple 2-choice discriminations. The fine motor coordination necessary for holding a thin plastic bag and stapling a label is substantial. There are many possible errors in such fine work and any lack of precision would result in an unacceptable product. Once the task had been learned, the inherent reinforcement value of the task may have been low compared to that of longer-cycle assembly tasks with an impressive "mechanical" look. Lack of interest may have caused attention lapses, resulting in small errors. Thus, either tangible rewards (Logan, Kinsinger, Shelton, & Brown, 1971), tokens (Zimmerman, Stuckey, Garlick, & Miller, 1969), competition (Huddle, 1967), or more explicit social reinforcement (Logan, Kinsinger, Shelton, & Brown, 1971) are probably necessary to maintain performance. Both students were aware that workers in the sheltered workshop were paid for their work. One finished his first performance trial by asking the trainer for payment. Although Gold's (1973a) students received no response-contingent reinforcement, they still received their regular workshop pay.

References

Brown, L., Bellamy, T., & Sontag, L. (Eds.) The development and implementation of a public school prevocational training program for trainable retarded and severely emotionally disturbed children: Progress report part I. Unpublished manuscript, Madison Public Schools, Madison, Wisconsin, 1971.

Crosson, J. E. A technique for programming sheltered workshop environments for training severely retarded workers. *American Journal of Mental Deficiency*, 1969, 73(5), 814-818.

Gold, M. W. Factors affecting production by the retarded: Base rate. *Mental Retardation*, 1973, 11(6), 41-45(a).

Gold, M. W. Research on the vocational habilitation of the retarded: The present, the future. In N. R. Ellis (Ed.), *International review of research in mental retardation*, (Vol. 6). New York: Academic Press, 1973 (b).

Gold, M. W. Stimulus factors in skill training of retarded adolescents on a complex assembly task: Acquisition, transfer and retention. *American Journal of Mental Deficiency*, 1972, 76(4), 517-526.

Gold, M. W. Utilization of task analysis and task complexity in training. Paper presented at Training Techniques and Approaches for the Mentally Retarded, Research and Training Center in Mental Retardation, Texas Tech University, Lubbock, Texas, May, 1975.

Huddle, D. D. Work performance of trainable adults as influenced by competition, cooperation, and monetary reward. *American Journal of Mental Deficiency*, 1967, 72(2), 198-211.

Logan, D. L., Kinsinger, J., Shelton, G., & Brown, J. The use of multiple reinforcers in a rehabilitation setting. *Mental Retardation*, 1971, 9(3), 3-6.

Zeaman, D. & House, B. J. The role of attention in retardate discrimination learning. In N. R. Ellis (Ed.), *Handbook of mental deficiency*. New York: McGraw-Hill, 1963.

Zimmerman, J., Stuckey, T., Garlick, R., & Miller, M. Effects of token reinforcement on productivity in multiply handicapped clients in a sheltered workshop. *Rehabilitation Literature*, 1969, 30, 34-41.

Acknowledgments

The authors wish to express their appreciation to Mr. Jerry L. Morris for his assistance in designing and building the stapling apparatus, Dr. Carol K. Sigelman and Dr. Robert W. Flexer for their editorial assistance, and Ms. Jan Chapman for her help in preparing the manuscript.

The Use of Operant Techniques in Teaching Severely Retarded Clients Work Habits

SHLOMO KATZ
JOEL GOLDBERG
ESTHER SHURKA

Abstract: Four severely retarded clients who had never adapted to the work requirements of a sheltered workshop underwent a special training program based on operant conditioning techniques. Because of the low intellectual level of the subjects, and the general complexity of the work tasks available in the workshop, it was decided to first teach them the general principle of a job, using a simpler work task. The model task was broken down into four stages and taught in isolation from the other clients in the workshop. Each stage was taught in gradual steps with concrete reinforcements for successful responses. Once the model task was mastered, a work task from the workshop was introduced. After the subjects mastered this task, they were returned to the workshop where they continued to receive reinforcements. Three of the four subjects successfully completed the training and are currently achieving an acceptable productivity level in the workshop.

The use of operant techniques has opened up many new possibilities of treatment for the severely retarded who previously were assumed to be beyond help. Watson (1967), in a review of the use of operant techniques, has shown that operant techniques have been successfully used in institutions to develop self help and social skills in severely and profoundly retarded children. The skills developed were self feeding, self dressing and grooming, toilet training, social interaction and play. Smolov (1971) provides an extensive review of the effective use of operant techniques for the modification of self injurious behavior. The use of the technique in teaching severely retarded work skills has been reviewed by Gold (1973).

As in developing self help skills, the emphasis in workshops is on the acquisition of new behaviors, rather than on the modification of existing rates of behavior. While a number of studies has been carried out, Crossen, Youngberg and White (1970); Gold (1973), Gold and Barclay (1973) in the area of teaching the severely retarded work skills, generally the literature on methods of improving acquisition of new behaviors in workshops is fairly sparse.

Purpose

The purpose of this study was to investigate the use of a successive approximation technique in teaching severely retarded clients vocational tasks in a sheltered workshop. The study was aimed at those clients generally below the intellectual level of the general client population and who have never adjusted to the work requirements of the workshop. These are clients who, because of lack of institutional space or parental refusal to institutionalize, are placed in the workshop but spend most of their time sitting around doing nothing and generally making a nuisance of themselves. These kind of clients are found in most sheltered workshops in

4. MANPOWER

TABLE 1

Description of Each Subject

Subject	C.A.	M.A.	Sex	Behavior Profile
A	27 years	3 years	Male	Has been in workshop for a year. Non-verbal, but understands when spoken to. When angry makes loud noises. Eats continuously and often wets his pants. Spends his day sitting, passively watching the other clients at work. No contact with others.
B	20 years	2 years	Female	New immigrant. Has been in workshop for a year. Completely non-verbal and does not understand Hebrew, but does understand Persian. She is partially blind, has no contact with others and has no behavior problems. Passes the time sitting around and gazing into space.
C	19 years	2? years	Female	Although says a few words, her verbal understanding is low. She is able to relate to others and has one friend, an older female client. She has been in the workshop for over two years, but has never been productive.
D	25 years	—	Male	Although he has been in the workshop for five years, they have never succeeded in getting him to work or break his social isolation. He spends his day wandering around, picking up papers which he then places in his mouth and eats. There is no contact with anyone in the workshop. Completely non-verbal.

Israel and help with these problems would be of value to the personnel and the workshop. All previous attempts to teach vocational skills to these subjects had failed and they were considered to be nonproductive workers and non-trainable.

Method

Subjects

Four subjects, two males and two females, were selected on the basis of their limited productivity in the workshop. A description of each subject is given in Table 1.

Description of the Workshop

Generally, the workshop caters to moderately and mildly retarded clients with an IQ range between 35 and 60, on the WISC and Stanford Binet Scales. However, due to the reasons given in the purpose, there are a number of severely retarded who have been placed in the workshop. The workshop provides sheltered employment and social and educational experiences. Most of the work is subcontracting jobs, assembling of manufactured goods, mainly in the electrical field. The clients work for most of the day, with a number of hours devoted to academic skills. In addition, a social club functions after work and all are free to attend.

Procedure

A successive approximation procedure was set up with different types of candy, chocolate and popcorn as the reinforcements. These were varied so as to provide a maximum range of type of reinforcer and to prevent satiation of a specific reinforcer.

The work task selected was the screwing of three small screws into three holes with a screwdriver into an electric plug. This task is one of the regular subcontracting items supplied to the workshop. As the task was fairly complicated for their level, it was decided to first teach them the general principles of the task, i.e., parts discrimination, correct hand use and screwing, using a simpler model. The model chosen was a large bolt with a nut, and the task required was similar to the target behavior, i.e., picking up a nut and screwing it onto the bolt. It was anticipated that once they had mastered this task, the skills learned would then be generalized to the actual work task, and it would then be easier to teach them the prescribed work task.

The subjects were separated from the rest of the clients and underwent the training individually in a secluded room with a minimum of interference.

First Stage—Learning with Model Task

The model task was broken down into four component steps: (1) pick up nut from box of nuts with left hand; (2) pick up screw with thumb and forefinger of right hand; (2) simultaneously pick up nut and screw with respective hand, and (4) simultaneously pick up nut and bolt and screw nut on bolt.

In the first step the subject was trained to pick out and raise a nut with his left hand. The task was demonstrated by the investigator, and the subject urged to attempt the task. Every correct attempt was reinforced by giving the subject one of the candy reinforcers. This was carried on until 10 consecutively correct responses were achieved.

The second step procedure was the same, learning to pick up the screw with the thumb and forefinger and then to replace it in the box. Every correct response was reinforced until 10 consecutively correct responses were achieved.

In the third step the subject was taught to lift the nut and bolt simultaneously from the respective boxes and to replace them. A reinforcement was immediately presented. This was carried on until 10 consecutively correct responses were achieved.

In the final step the subject was required to lift the nut and bolt simultaneously and to screw the nut onto the bolt. Every correct response was reinforced and the activity was terminated after 10 consecutively correct responses.

Generally it took two to three days, with 15 to 20 minute sessions to achieve the required performance for each component step. Thus, 10 to 12 days were required to master the training task for all the subjects. The training was carried out by a research assistant and not by the regular staff.

Once the subjects had mastered the model task, they were now exposed to the actual work task.

Second Stage—Work Task Electric Plug Assembly

The second stage was also initially carried out individually. A pile of plugs and a box of screws were placed before each subject. The experimenter then demonstrated how to lift up one screw with the left hand and a plug with the right hand, then placing the screw into position and then, with a screwdriver, screwing the screw into position. After this demonstration the subjects were prompted to attempt and were reinforced with candy for every screw correctly placed and screwed in. Each subject received a daily hour long session for six days to master the task. The criterion for having mastered the task was an average of four completed plugs.

Once having mastered the task in isolation, they were returned to the general workshop where they began to work a full day. In the workshop they were reinforced with candy for every plug completed during the entire day, for a period of six days, i.e., one work week.

At the beginning of the following work week, that is, 22 days after initiation of the training, the concrete reinforcers were gradually removed and replaced by verbal reinforcers. The verbal reinforcers consisted of phrases like "very good," "good show," "nice," etc. The reinforcement schedule for this period was as follows: For one week, every one correct plug received a verbal reinforcement and for every three plugs, a concrete reinforcer. During the following week, they received a verbal reinforcement

4. MANPOWER

for every three correct plugs and a concrete reinforcer for every five correct plugs. This schedule was carried on for two weeks, after which it was changed to verbal for every 10 correct and concrete for every 15 correct. A week later reinforcement was limited to only verbal reinforcement, dispersed at random during the course of a work day. During this stage the regular staff of the workshop also began to dispense verbal reinforcers. Up to now the reinforcement had been given by the research assistant only.

At this stage the subjects went on a ten day vacation. On their return the reinforcers were reactivated and they received a verbal reinforcement for every correct plug and a concrete reinforcer for every three correct plugs, for a period of three days, after which the reinforcers were terminated.

Third Stage—Follow-Up

The subjects carried on working in the workshop without the presence of the investigator under normal workshop conditions for another 50 days. There were no reinforcements other than the usual verbal reinforcers dispensed to all clients. Measurement of performance was carried out for three successive days at the beginning of the period and then one day a week over the next four weeks.

Results

Results of Model Task

Although four subjects were initially selected, one of the four refused to cooperate and insisted on continuing with his old behavior pattern of picking up and eating papers. Thus, the results relate to the three subjects who cooperated.

The results of this period are presented in Figure 1. As can be seen from the figure, all three subjects learned the model task in a total of 10 days.

Generally there were very few problems with the model task. Subject A, because of his insistence on putting the bolts in his mouth, which made them slippery and thus difficult to handle, had some problems initially but once this problem was eliminated by negative reinforcement, it went smoothly. Subject B had problems because of her poor eyesight, but once she was taught to use touch instead of sight, she mastered the task. Having to use touch only affected her speed of performance which is reflected in the results. The third subject, C, displayed initial problems of concentration, but using a time out technique (removing her from the room) this behavior was soon eliminated.

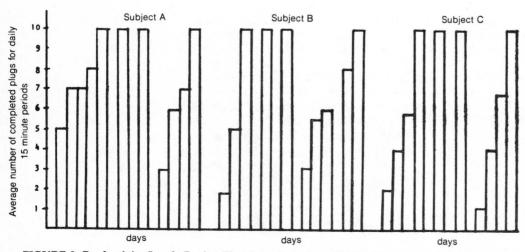

FIGURE 1. Productivity Levels During First Stage Learning with Model Task for All 3 Subjects

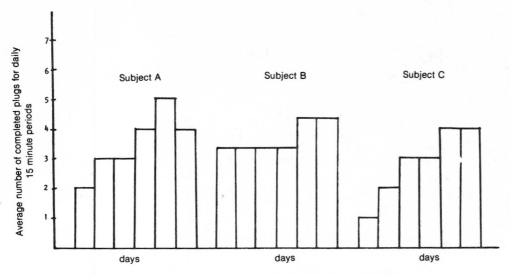

FIGURE 2. Productivity Levels for 6 Days of Training in Isolation on
Assembly of Electrical Plug for All 3 Subjects

Results of Work Task

In this stage the procedure was divided into two substages. The first stage consisted of individual training sessions alone with the experimenter for a period of six days. The results are presented in Figure 2.

All three subjects were able to achieve an average of four or five completed plugs for 15 minute periods during the first six days.

The subjects were then returned to the workshop with the other clients. Their individual performance is presented in Figures 3, 4 and 5. The results cover 30 days of production and are presented in average productivity over a 15 minute period.

The return to the workshop did not affect subject A, and his productivity remained stable, gradually increasing over the 30 day period, with minor fluctuations. The reduction of reinforcements, and the change from concrete to verbal reinforcements did not have any effect on his performance. Towards the end of the period he was averaging 10 completed plugs for

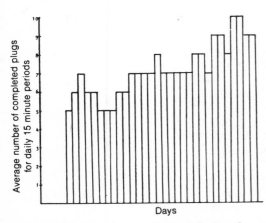

FIGURE 3. Subject A's Productivity Levels
Over 30 Days on Assembly of Electrical
Plugs in Workshop

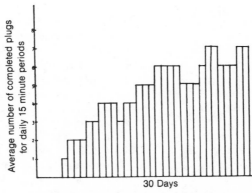

FIGURE 4. Subject B's Productivity Levels
Over 30 Days on Assembly of Electrical
Plugs in Workshop

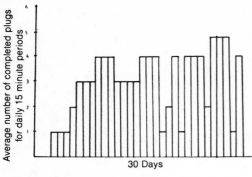

FIGURE 5. Subject C's Productivity Levels Over 30 Days on Assembly of Electrical Plugs in Workshop

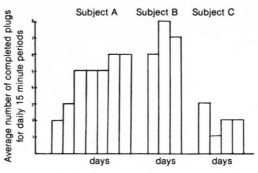

FIGURE 6. Productivity Levels During Follow Up Period for All 3 Subjects

15 periods, which was very comparable to the norms of the workshop.

The results for Subject B are presented in Figure 4.

The return to the workshop had an effect on Subject B and her productivity fell off. With time, however, it increased and at the end of the period she was averaging between six and eight completed plugs for 15 minute periods. For this subject the concrete reinforcers were of little significance, even at the beginning, and so no reduction in productivity was anticipated once concrete reinforcers were removed.

The results for subject C are presented in Figure 5.

Subject C also had problems on her return to the workshop and her productivity fell off. With time, however, her productivity increased, but was inconsistent. She was in constant need of supervision, especially to prevent undesirable behavior, such as talking to others, etc.

Results of Follow-Up Period

The subjects were followed-up and their performance measured. During this period there were no verbal or concrete reinforcers.

The results are presented in Figure 6.

Subject A's performance was measured for seven days; three days at the beginning of the follow-up and one day a week for an additional four weeks. His productivity fell off initially but over the period of time it improved. However, it never reached the same level as during the reinforcement period. The complete reduction of reinforcement seems to have affected his production. Subject B's productivity was measured for three days only, as she became ill and was removed from the workshop. During the three days there was no decline in productivity. For this subject, concrete reinforcement did not appear to be effective and she seemed to be motivated more by intrinsic motivation, working and being busy, than by extrinsic reinforcement.

Subject C's performance was measured over four days. Her performance dropped and continued to decline. It appears that for this subject the reinforcement, especially the verbal reinforcement, was important as it also provided close supervision in the workshop and the verbal reinforcement appeared to facilitate work performance.

Discussion

Three out of four subjects were taught to work during the study and continued to work during the subsequent follow-up. The fourth subject refused to cooperate, and insisted on continuing his old behavior pattern of picking up and eating papers. Perhaps with this client a reinforcement schedule procedure might have been set up to eliminate the negative behavior prior to the work procedure. However, it was assumed that the negative behavior was far too deeply ingrained and the training schedule could not compete with it.

As the experimenters were interested in the learning of new behavior, the typical

ABAB design, Sidman (1960) was not applicable, and therefore it is difficult to draw conclusions as to which of the environmental consequences were of importance in modifying the behavior. This weakens the conclusions that can be drawn from the study, but does, however, indicate the usefulness of the method in at least teaching the clients to work. It should be stressed that all prior attempts to get them to work have failed. It would appear that the method of individual supervision and the use of the successive approximation technique has the best results. It is doubtful that we would have succeeded had the subjects remained in the workshop during the initial training period. Removal from the workshop was an important environmental consequence, and the subsequent personal attention and praise appears to have been more important than the concrete reinforcers. Further support for this hypothesis was found when the subjects returned to the general workshop. Their productivity dropped off in spite of the fact that they continued to receive concrete reinforcement. The subsequent gradual removal of the reinforcers did not have any marked effect on the production.

The fact that they were working in the company of the other clients appears to be reinforcement for production. While prior to the study they were socially isolated, both from the rest of the clients and the workshop staff, they now were part of the work cycle and used the fact of their working as a means to social interaction. Their productive behavior tended now to increase social interaction and personal status. They now received a work card, salary and were regarded as members of the work group.

The study has demonstrated that it is possible to teach severely retarded (IQ less than 30) work skills and enable them to achieve an acceptable level of production and find their place in the workshop. However, more research is needed to study improved training techniques and in more clearly estimating the effects of environmental control. This study suggests the value of developing reinforcement programs to achieve higher standards of performance, both social and work, in the mentally retarded.

References

Bandura, A. *Principles of behavior modification*. New York: Holt, Rinehart & Winston, 1969.

Crosson, J. E., Youngberg, C. D. & White, O. R. Transenvironmental programming: An experimental approach to the rehabilitation of the retarded. In: H. J. Prehn (Ed.) *Rehabilitation research in mental retardation*. Rehabilitation Research and Training Center in Mental Retardation, University of Oregon, Eugene, 1970, Monograph 2, 19–34.

Gold, M. W. Research on the vocational habilitation of the retarded, the present, the future. In: Ellis (Ed.) *International review of research in mental retardation*. Vol. 6, New York: Academic Press.

Gold, M. W. & Barclay, C. R. The effects of verbal labels on the acquisition and retention of a complex assembly task. *The Training School Bulletin*, 1973, **70**, 38–42.

Sidman, M. *Tactics of scientific research*. New York: Basic Books, 1960.

Smolov, S. R. Use of operant techniques for the modification of self-injurious behavior. *American Journal of Mental Deficiency*, 1971, **76**, *3*, 295–305.

Watson, L. S. Application of operant conditioning techniques to institutionalized severely and profoundly retarded children. *Mental Retardation Abstracts*, **4**, 1967.

This investigation was supported by the Bar-Ilan University Research Fund.

Although several demonstrations are available that severely retarded persons can learn difficult vocational tasks, little effort has been made to determine whether this learning occurs as a result of the reported training procedures. Therefore, a severely retarded woman learned to assemble a saw chain when teaching procedures involving differential reinforcement, modeling and physical priming were used. The use of a multiple baseline design across task segments allowed for the interpretation that the procedures were functionally related to the trainee's gains.

Evaluation of a Procedure for Teaching Saw Chain Assembly to a Severely Retarded Woman

Candace T. O'Neill
G. Thomas Bellamy

Acquisition and performance of vocational tasks by severely and profoundly retarded persons have been reported with increasing frequency during the last two decades. It now seems clear that to label a person "retarded," even "severely retarded," implies no necessary restriction on the individual's potential to learn a variety of work behaviors (Bellamy, Peterson, & Close, 1975; Clarke & Hermelin, 1955; Crosson, 1966; Gold, 1976; Hunter & Bellamy, 1976; Karan, Eisner, & Endres, 1974; Martin & Flexer, Note 1).

The demonstrational emphasis of much of this literature motivated the present research. Acquisition of vocational skills by severely retarded adults has been reported often, but little effort has been made to determine whether those gains are actually the result of reported teaching procedures. For example, none of the studies cited utilized experimental designs which rule out the possibility that learning resulted simply from extended exposure to the task or trainer. Therefore, the purpose of this research was to ask if the learning of a difficult vocational task was functionally related to the defined training procedures.

Specifically, a case study in vocational training will be presented to illustrate the ability of a severely retarded woman to learn to assemble saw chain, a task potentially available to sheltered workshops. In the study the relationship between

training procedures and task acquisition was assessed in a multiple baseline design across task segments.

Method
Trainee

The trainee was a 30-year old woman labeled either severely or profoundly retarded on the basis of several standardized intelligence tests administered over the last 10 years. At the time of the research she had been a participant in a community vocational training program for fourteen months. Prior to that, the trainee had resided in a state institution for nine years with neither vocational nor educational programming. She had no functional expressive language, but followed some simple verbal directions and imitated some movements.

The Work Task

The task involved assembly of 11 small parts to form a repeating segment of saw chain, the cutting portion of chain saw blades. Each of the components measured approximately 1.5 × .5 cm. Assembly involved stacking the components in three levels, with each piece requiring correct rotation on both horizontal and vertical axes. Stacking was done on a masonite strip with grooves which held the bottom set of components in a straight line. Assembly of the product involved performing in sequence a chain of behaviors which was defined in 47 steps, or discriminated operants. At the com-

This research was supported in part by the Developmental Disabilities Office, Region X and the Bureau of Education for the Handicapped.

"Evaluation of a Procedure for Teaching Saw Chain Assembly to a Severely Retarded Woman," Candance T. O'Neill, G. Thomas Bellamy, *Mental Retardation*, Vol. 16, No. 1, 1978.

pletion of training the subject was expected to complete the task without assistance. This involved moving a place marker in front of each parts bin in turn, picking up a component from the bin and placing it correctly on the chain assembly.

FIGURE 1. SAW CHAIN MATERIAL USED FOR ASSEMBLY.

Training Materials

In addition to the task itself, training involved the use of a parts bin apparatus, in which parts were stored separately in the order of assembly. The apparatus consisted of a row of 11 3-inch (7.6cm.) square compartments. In front of each compartment was a small platform on which the trainee moved a wooden block to mark her place in the assembly. Small edibles and later pennies which could be exchanged for edibles were delivered contingent upon task-related behaviors during training.

Data Collection

Correct responses for each discriminated operant in the task were recorded during probes which occurred after every 20 minutes of training. During probes the trainee responded to the discriminative stimulus defined for each step in the task. This was accomplished by letting her continue without interruption when a step was completed correctly and by having the trainer complete the step after incorrect responses (thereby creating the discriminative stimulus for the next step). During probe trials the trainer made comments like, "You are really trying hard," *etc.*, while the trainee was manipulating task components, regardless of whether responses were correct.

A response was scored as correct if the trainee responded to the discriminative stimulus without prompts or cues of any kind, performed the movement correctly, and made all necessary rotational discriminations. Any other response or failure to respond within 10 seconds was scored as incorrect. Observer agreement was checked during

the first five probes and every eighth probe thereafter. During these 16 probes performance was scored simultaneously by the trainer and a second individual with vocational training experience.

Training Procedures

Training was conducted on one task segment at a time to allow measurement of progress within a multiple baseline design. Training continued on each segment until the trainee performed all steps in the segment correctly on three consecutive probes.

The trainee was seated in front of the task with the trainer either sitting beside or standing behind her. Early training sessions began when the trainee attended to the task for a few seconds. The trainer then modeled the first step, asked the trainee to perform the step, and provided differential consequences for correct and incorrect imitative responses. Correct responses were followed by compliments, physical contact, and small edibles. Incorrect responses were terminated by the trainer as soon as they occurred. The trainer returned the task to the last correctly completed step and, using more complete modeling or physical priming, assisted the trainee through a correct performance of the step. The trainer then returned the task once more to the last correctly completed step and repeated the procedure, providing much less physical or modeling assistance.

Each step was introduced in sequence via this modeling and priming procedure. After a step was performed correctly, the trainer no longer provided the modeling cue prior to the trainee's response. The trainee was expected to perform the step without prompts of any kind from the trainer, the relevant discriminative stimuli being provided by the task itself. Differential consequences for correct and incorrect responses were then provided as described above.

These procedures were modified during the training periods between probe trials 30 to 70 when the data indicated lack of progress. These modifications were based on the trainer's hypothesis that correction procedures might be functioning as reinforcers for error responses. First, an attempt was made to maximize the difference between consequences for correct and incorrect responses. Incorrect responses were followed by a firm "No" before the correction procedure. When this had little effect, it was hypothesized that the physical contact involved in priming correct responses might be a strong reinforcer. These were deleted, but with little effect. Finally, an attempt was made to eliminate corrections altogether. This involved attempting to anticipate incorrect responses and provide necessary verbal or physical assistance before an error was made. When the trainee began to emit the correct response, the assistance was gradually removed by providing it earlier in the behavior chain (Bellamy, Inman, & Schwarz,

4. MANPOWER

1976) or making it less and less specific. This procedure continued throughout the remainder of training.

Results

Observer Agreement

Agreement between observers was computed by dividing the total number of agreements by the agreements plus disagreements on the 47 discriminated operants in the task. Agreement ranged from 98–100 percent. It is possible that this represents an overestimate, in that complete independence of observers was not achieved. Progression through the task during probes required the trainer (first observer) to complete a step performed incorrectly by the subject in order to assess responding to the subsequent step. Therefore, the second observer was aware when the trainer considered a step incorrect. After the two initial probes, however, the second observer reported no instances when she felt the trainer had intervened inappropriately.

Task Acquisition

Acquisition data are presented in Figure 2. During the three probes before instruction, the subject made one correct response on Segment 1 (attending to the task) and no correct responses on either Segments 2 or 3.

Training on Segment 1 was conducted during 28 hours and 40 minutes over a two month period. A total of 82 probes were taken during this time, with performance on Segment 1 increasing from 4 correct responses on probe 4 to a criterion of 3 consecutive correct responses on probes 83 to 85. Correct responding on the remainder of the task ranged from 0-5 on Segment 2 and 0-6 on Segment 3. Inspection of Figure 3 reveals that little apparent progress was made during probes 30-70, the period in which several procedural modifications were made.

Training on Segment 2 required a total of 7 hours and 40 minutes during eight days of training. During the 23 probes taken during this time, the subject's correct responses to Segment 1 remained perfect; those to Segment 2 increased from 6 and 5 on probe trials 86 and 87 to a criterion of 3 consecutive correct trials on probes 107–109; correct responses on Segment 3 ranged from 0–9.

Training on Segment 3 was completed during 8 hours of instruction over nine days. During the 24 probes taken during this period, the subject main-

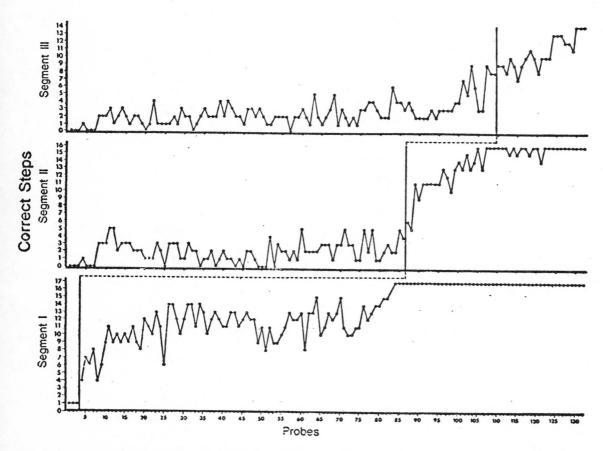

FIGURE 2. NUMBER OF STEPS COMPLETED CORRECTLY DURING UNASSISTED PROBES CONDUCTED BEFORE AND AFTER TRAINING (VERTICAL INTERVENTION LINE) ON EACH TASK SEGMENT.

tained correct responding to all steps on Segment 1 and ranged from 14–16 correct on Segment 2. Correct responding on Segment 3 increased from 9 on probe 110 to the criterion level on probe 131 to 133.

Discussion

The subject learned to perform all three segments of the task independently after the training procedures were implemented. This result provides evidence for the existence of a functional relationship between the vocational training procedures and the trainee's skill acquisition. Because a multiple baseline design was used, attribution of skill acquisition to simple repeated exposure to a task or trainer, which has not been ruled out in most previous literature, could be seriously doubted in the present study. The trainee appears to have acquired each segment of the task as a function of beginning systematic instruction.

The results also provide a clear demonstration that a severely retarded person can learn the skills required to perform a complex vocational task. This is consistent with several other reports of the potential vocational competence of severely retarded persons (Bellamy, Peterson, & Close, 1975; Clarke & Hermelin, 1955; Crosson, 1966; Gold, 1976; Martin, & Flexer, 1975). Spanning two decades, these reports have illustrated that, with systematic training, severely handicapped adults could participate in remunerative work activity. However, their impact on vocational service programs seems to have been considerably less significant than the positive results might suggest. In spite of their apparent vocational potential, severely retarded adults frequently receive no work opportunities (Rowitz, O'Connor, & Boroskin, 1975), or else participate only in programs designed for adults whose "productive capacity is inconsequential" (Federal Register, 1974; Commission on Accreditation of Rehabilitation Facilities, 1976).

Therefore, the question arises as to what researchers should now do to decrease this apparent gap between research and service programs. One approach is to continue reporting practical procedures for teaching vocational tasks which may be available to sheltered vocational programs. By illustrating the abilities of severely retarded adults to perform these tasks, an increased willingness to include these individuals in vocational programs may be fostered.

A second task for applied researchers appears to be the development of training procedures which are increasingly efficient, thereby reducing the cost of including severely retarded persons in sheltered vocational programs. Related to this issue is the apparent increase in efficiency of training on successive task segments in the present study. Acquisition of segment 1 required 28 hours, 40 minutes, while segments 2 and 3 required only 7 hours, 40 minutes and 8 hours respectively. A possible explanation for this dramatic reduction in training time is that the subject acquired behaviors which facilitated performance in the training setting, including sustained attention to the task and consistent responding to verbal, physical and gestural cues used by the trainer. Another potential explanation is the possibility of an increase in the trainer's skills in obtaining and reinforcing correct responses. A third possible explanation for the reduction in training time during Segments 2 and 3 seems particularly important. Training may have become more efficient because the trainee developed generalized skills or "operations" (Becker, Englemann, & Thomas, 1975), which resulted in the correct performance of some untaught steps which were similar to those taught previously. For example, steps 7, 11, 15, 19, 23, 27, and 31 all involved obtaining one part from the bin behind the marker immediately after the marker had been moved. After training on a few of these steps in the first two segments, the trainee also began responding correctly to the steps which had not been taught. That is, the trainee had developed an operation of following a particular stimulus characteristic (the marker in front of a parts bin) with the response of reaching into that bin to obtain one part. This would suggest that generalization had occurred across the irrelevant dimensions of location of the bin and particular type of part.

This generalization poses a set of particularly interesting questions for future research on vocational training. Can a set of generalized skills, or operations, be identified which are applicable across several tasks typically found in sheltered workshops? Will pre-training on these skills increase a severely retarded individual's overall success in community vocational programs? And finally, can these operations be used as a basis for task selection and assignment decisions within workshops?

Redundant Cue Removal in Skill Training for the Retarded

MARC W. GOLD

MARC W. GOLD *is Research Assistant Professor, Children's Research Center and Institute for Research on Exceptional Children, and Assistant Professor of Education, University of Illinois at Urbana—Champaign.*

Abstract: 36 mildly and moderately retarded sheltered workshop clients learned to assemble a 12 piece unit for which the parts were color coded. Subjects received one of three different procedures designed to efficiently remove the color cue. All three procedures worked equally well. Implications are given for the application of the procedures used.

The use of a cue redundancy—color—to facilitate the acquisition of a complex assembly task was clearly demonstrated in an earlier study (Gold, 1972), in which subjects with color coding available learned to assemble a 15 piece bicycle brake in half the trials needed by the subjects without color coded parts.

The theoretical support for this procedure is from the "Attention Theory" of Zeaman and House (1963). According to this theory, the more relevant and redundant the cues, the more efficient the learning. This means, for instance, that if a problem can be solved using cues from both the color and the form dimensions, it will be solved more efficiently than if the only cues available are on the form dimension (Gold & Scott, 1971).

With the efficiency and effectiveness of cue redundancy in aiding task completion previously demonstrated, the purpose of this study was to investigate means of fading it out in such a way as to make color coding an efficient learning procedure on tasks where the coding must be removed following acquisition and prior to production. This is often necessary since in many tasks color coding cannot be used in production because of the cost and impracticality of painting every part.

Method

Subjects

The subjects were 36 adolescent and adult sheltered workshop clients. Descriptive data for the sample are presented in Table 1. The sample was drawn randomly from the workshop populations, the only restriction being that subjects had to be able to see and hold the parts. Twelve subjects were randomly assigned to each of the three groups: (a) complete removal group, (b) incremental removal group, and (c) forced choice group.

Materials

The apparatus was a tray containing 15 compartments. A divider runs parallel to and 3 inches back from the front of the tray.

TABLE 1

Descriptive Characteristics of Subjects

| | IQ | | | |
| | Mildly retarded | | Moderately retarded | |
Group	Mean	SD	Mean	SD
Complete removal	62.50	10.80	29	11.83
Incremental removal	57.90	7.53	31	9.66
Forced choice	59.80	8.53	34	11.12

The purpose of this divider is to separate the parts that are being used for a particular trial from the parts to be used in subsequent trials (Gold, 1972). The parts of the assembly are sequenced in the tray, rather than having the subjects learn the sequence. This is consonant with industrial procedure, where parts are stored in a sequence most conducive to assembly rather than randomly or in a pile.

The task was a Bendix RB-2 coaster brake. In the earlier study (Gold, 1972) the complete 15 piece assembly was used. For this experiment the assembly consisted of 12 pieces. The three parts left out were a lock nut and two shoes.

The cue redundancy consisted of painting (red) the surface of each part that is facing the subject when it is placed in the proper position for assembly. Ten of the 12 parts can be put on two ways, one of which is correct. The addition of a color cue to one of the two alternatives to this two choice problem means that attention to the cue can provide solution.

Procedure

The general procedure consisted of one demonstration of the task by the experimenter, showing correction of errors and reinforcement procedures (Gold, 1972). The experimenter assembled the unit once, then the subject assembled the unit until a criterion of six correct assemblies out of eight consecutive trials was reached using the noncoded parts. A correct trial was one complete assembly of the brake without error or assistance. The subject did four trials per day until the criterion was reached.

Three procedures for fading the color coding were used. Subjects in the complete removal group were brought to six correct out of eight consecutive trials on the cue redundant brake (color coded parts) and then brought to criterion on the noncoded brake. Subjects in the incremental removal group started out on the cue redundant brake. Color coded parts were replaced with noncoded parts following three consecutive correct discriminations, and were reinstated following three incorrect discriminations, not necessarily consecutive, on that part. Trials were considered correct when no errors were made and only noncoded parts were used. Subjects in the forced choice group were first brought to six correct out of eight consecutive trials on the cue redundant brake. They were then transferred to the form only brake (no cue redundancy).

When a discrimination error was made, the assembly was taken from the subject and placed on the table; then the following procedure was used with the part on which the error was made:

1. A color coded part was placed in front of the subject, noncolor side up.
2. Three form only parts were given to the subject with instructions to place them on the table in the same position as the color form part (a match to sample discrimination task), forcing the subject to solve the problem using the form dimension.
3. The procedure was repeated with the coded side of the part up.
4. The subject then continued on the partially completed assembly until criterion was reached.

Subjects in any group who failed to reach criterion by 55 trials were given a score of 55 and terminated. Their data were included in the analyses.

Results

An independent groups design was used. The reliability of the effects were assessed via one way analyses of variance using trials, manipulation errors, and discrimination errors to criterion as dependent measures. No effects approached significance. The data are presented in Table 2.

Discussion

The principle value of this study is to demonstrate three techniques for eliminating color coding on a task where it has been added for training purposes. The different procedures might provide sufficient variety so that various tasks and various children

TABLE 2

Group Means and Standard Deviations

| | Groups | | | | | |
| Measures to criterion | Complete removal | | Incremental removal | | Forced choice | |
	Mean	SD	Mean	SD	Mean	SD
Trials	32.33	16.36	20.83	10.37	26.08	11.16
Manipulation errors	10.08	10.07	5.66	4.37	7.33	10.94
Discrimination errors	35.16	34.75	27.92	20.87	28.83	34.54

could be efficiently taught. With color coding a common phenomenon in educational settings these techniques would appear to be of use.

be replaced. Second, they should be run clinically. That is, procedures from other groups in the experiment or completely different procedures should be used until the subjects reach criterion on the task. The procedures for these subjects should be reported separately from the group data but included in the same publication. This would provide both experimental and clinical data resulting in increased applicability for the practitioner.

Subsequent experiments will include the above methodological changes and will investigate the use of other color coding and fading procedures on the acquisition of bench assembly tasks with the intent of contributing to a much needed expanded technology of instruction for the retarded. Data from the research program described give strong support for the benefits of such a technology. The data also point up the disparity between what the retarded are capable of doing vocationally and the low level to which the retarded have been relegated by our society and our profession.

For this particular task and sample population, inspection of the data shows considerable within group variance, suggesting the possibility of large individual differences related to the relative effect of

each procedure. The present design did not allow administering more than one procedure to a given subject. In the absence of a clear-cut hierarchy of training procedures, however, the data do suggest a strategy for training on tasks where a cue redundancy can be added temporarily for training. One could begin with the incremental removal procedure. If the subject requires the reinstatement of color more than three or four times, suggesting that the cue redundancy is not facilitating the use of the form cue, switch to one of the two alternate procedures, both of which require that the subject first reach the criterion of six correct out of eight consecutive trials on the entire task before the cue redundancy is removed. Some individuals might acquire the task more efficiently this way.

In the present study, three of the 36 subjects completed 55 trials without reaching criterion, two in the complete removal group and one in the forced choice group. The methodology of the present study precluded giving them additional trials or different training. Procedural flexibility should be kept to a minimum in the experimental setting (and where group designs are used). But in the applied setting flexibility is a necessity. Several changes should be made in our procedures related to subjects who fail to reach criterion. First, their data should not be included in the parametric analyses. These subjects should

WORKSHOP SUPERVISION:EVALUATION OF A PROCEDURE FOR PRODUCTION MANAGEMENT WITH THE SEVERELY RETARDED

G. Thomas Bellamy
Dean P. Inman
John Yeates

The ability of severely and profoundly retarded adults to learn remunerative vocational skills has been demonstrated periodically for two decades (Bellamy, Peterson, & Close, 1975; Clarke & Hermelin, 1955; Gold, 1976; Karan, Wehman, Renzaglia, & Schutz, Note 1). After such skills have been learned, however, an individual's vocational success depends largely on the maintenance of acceptable production rates for extended time periods.

Research on increasing the productivity of severely retarded individuals has been sparse, no doubt reflecting their relative absence in vocational programs. Reviews of the available research are consistent in concluding that different supervision methods can have quite different effects on worker productivity (Bellamy, Inman, & Schwarz, in press). Yet the relevance of these findings to vocational programming is limited by both the brief time frame of many studies and the unusual staff or equipment resources used in conducting others (Screven, Straka, & LaFond, 1971). The purpose of this study is to evaluate the effectiveness of a practical supervision method during employment periods of up to eighteen months.

Method

Subjects. Production data are presented for three women employees of the Specialized Training Program, a community workshop for severely and profoundly retarded adults at the University of Oregon. They ranged in chronological age from 19 to 26 years, in MA (Stanford-Binet) from 2.6 to 3.2 years and at the time the experiment began, had been community residents for approximately 10 months after having been institutionalized for most of their lives.

This research was supported by the DHEW Developmental Disabilities Office, Region X, and the Bureau of Education for the Handicapped, Research Branch.

The Work Task and Setting

Each subject was assigned the job of assembling a cable harness which contained eleven color-coded wires. Assembling involved threading the wires in sequence in a plywood board, which was marked with a channel where wires were placed according to cues for beginning and termination points for each wire. A continuous elastic cord was then used to tie the cable with approximately 75 self-tightening knots.

In the production room two supervisors were responsible for 14 workers, each of whom worked independently on an assigned task. Data on production rates of all workers were recorded continuously by the supervisors. That is, as soon as a worker completed a task, the supervisor recorded the time in which the assembly was completed, the time the next assembly was begun, and the amount paid to the worker. Reliability of production records was assessed during 90-minute work periods at intervals of approximately six weeks for one year. Reliability, computed by dividing the number of agreements (in work start times, work stop times, and units completed in a period) by the number of agreements plus disagreements in each work period, ranged from 85 to 100 percent and averaged 95 percent.

Procedure

A multiple baseline design across three subjects was used to measure the effects of a timer contingency which differentially reinforced higher production rates. During baseline the following conditions were in effect: When a subject finished a task, she raised a hand to signal a supervisor. The supervisor then conducted a brief quality check of the completed cable and, if it was constructed correctly, delivered one penny to the subject. For Subject 2, an immediate-store contingency was added to the original baseline conditions approximately four weeks after baseline had begun.

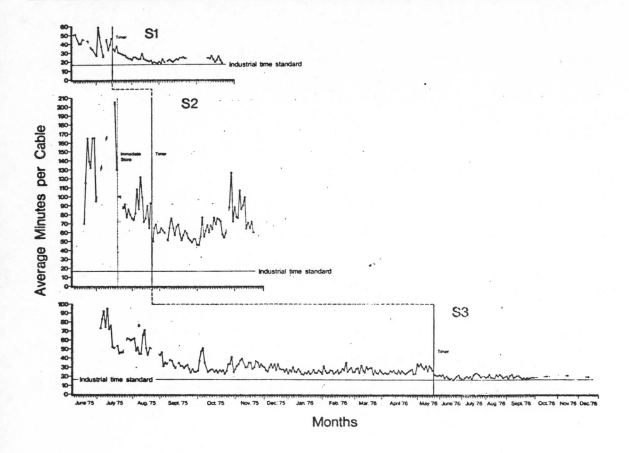

FIGURE I. AVERAGE NUMBER OF MINUTES REQUIRED EACH DAY BY THE THREE SUBJECTS TO CONSTRUCT AN ELEVEN-WIRE CABLE HARNESS UNDER BASELINE, IMMEDIATE STORE, AND TIMER CONTINGENCIES.

Under this condition, she was allowed to spend her partial payment immediately after earning it. This was done in an attempt to decrease the delay between reinforcement and token exchange thereby increasing the effectiveness of the token reinforcer.

When the timer contingency was first imposed for each subject, a supervisor informed her that if she completed her cable before the timer bell sounded, she would receive two pennies for the completed unit instead of the usual one. The timer was then set for the average time required by that subject to complete a cable over the previous five days. If a subject finished an assembly before the timer bell sounded, she raised her hand as a signal to the supervisor who then performed a quality check, praised the subject for completing the work before the bell sounded, gave her two pennies and allowed her to turn off the timer. If a subject failed to beat the timer, the procedure was the same except that only one penny was delivered upon task completion. For Subject 2, the immediate-

store contingency remained in effect for the first eleven weeks of the intervention.

Results and Discussion

Figure 1 reflects mean cable assembly time per day for three subjects. Visual inspection reveals a significant effect for subjects one and three in that there is a definite and sustained reduction in task completion time and in day-to-day variation as a function of imposing the timer contingency. That these results are also *ecologically significant* (Brooks & Baumeister, 1977), is supported by the fact that (a) the degree of reduction was significant, *i.e.*, production time closely approximated the industrial time standard of 17 minutes, and (b) the time periods over which the contingencies had an effect were sufficiently long to be of vocational importance. (See Table 1.)

For Subject 2 the advent of the timer contingency did not produce meaningful changes. Although average production time decreased by ap-

TABLE 1

SUMMARY DATA FOR THREE SUBJECTS REFLECTING MEAN CABLE-ASSEMBLY TIME, STANDARD DEVIATION AND RANGE DURING THE LAST THREE WEEKS OF BASELINE AND THE FIRST THREE WEEKS OF THE TIMER CONTINGENCY.

	Baseline			Timer Intervention		
	Mean (Minutes)	Standard Deviation	Range (Minutes)	Mean (Minutes)	Standard Deviation	Range (Minutes)
Subject 1	39.8	11.76	50	26.3	4.70	24
Subject 2	75.0	19.45	87	65.3	16.9	93
Subject 3	27.9	6.65	40	19.9	3.06	16

proximately ten minutes immediately after the intervention, the resulting rate was still far removed from the industrial standard on which wages and shop earnings are based. Further, the duration of the behavioral change (approximately 6 weeks) was probably too short to meet normal job requirements for dependability in this and other work settings.

To accommodate individual differences and at the same time establish competent work performance at normal rates, a supervisor can manipulate any of a constellation of variables relating to the organization of the work setting, consequences for task attending, consequences for task completion, and the contingencies which determine delivery of these consequences. The present research suggests that the task at hand is to identify *combinations* of supervision variables which result in competent work behavior in severely retarded adults. Moreover, the gains made through programming efforts should be evaluated in terms of the duration of their effect as well as degree since vocational competence should maintain for extended periods of time.

FACTOR STRUCTURE AND CORRELATES OF ADAPTIVE BEHAVIOR IN NONINSTITUTIONALIZED RETARDED ADULTS

Vincent J. Guarnaccia
Hofstra University

Forty mentally retarded adults working at a vocational training center were rated by their counselors on the 10 behavior domains of the Adaptive Behavior Scale. A factor analysis yielded the following factors: 1, personal independence; 2, personal responsibility; 3, productivity; and 4, social responsibility. A regression analysis of the four factors on the variables of age, sex, verbal IQ, performance IQ, and maternal trust showed that the predictors together accounted for 75 percent of the variance in Factor 1 and very little of the variance in the other factors. Theoretical and practical implications of the results were discussed.

The practical limitations of standard intelligence tests as predictors of the success with which mentally retarded individuals cope with the physical and social demands of the environment are widely acknowledged. Increasing attention is now being given to the concept of adaptive behavior and to the assessment of deficits in such areas as personal independence, personal responsibility, and social responsibility (Leland, 1973).

A recently devised instrument which holds considerable promise for measuring level of adaptive functioning is the Adaptive Behavior Scale (Nihira, Foster, Shellhaas, & Leland, 1969). In the present study, the applicability of the Adaptive Behavior Scale to noninstitutionalized mentally retarded adults was explored, and the factor structure of the scale for this population was delineated. In previous factor analytic studies with institutionalized children and adults, Nihira (1969a, 1969b) found the Adaptive Behavior Scale to be measuring three major dimensions: personal independence, personal maladaptation, and social maladaptation. It is possible that the emphasis on pathology in the latter two factors reflects the institutional condition rather than the nature of the scale itself and that use of the scale with other populations might yield different factors.

The relative contribution of organismic and environmental variables to adaptive functioning, as measured by the Adaptive Behavior Scale, was also explored. Age, IQ, and sex were included because they are reported most often in the literature, particularly in multiple correlation studies designed to predict performance on various tasks (Cobb, 1972). The environmental variable of interest was parental trust, which was thought to act as an "exposure" variable in the sense that it increases, decreases, prevents, or delays effective interaction of the individual with the environment. Leland (1973) has suggested several ways in which parental trust may be particularly important in the lives of mentally retarded persons.

Method

Subjects

Forty mentally retarded adults (20 male, 20 female) were selected from a total population of 350 trainees at the Vocational Training Center of the Nassau County, New York Chapter of the Association for the Help of Retarded Children. All trainees were ambulatory and without major physical defects or emotional problems, able to understand and follow simple directions, and socially adjusted to the degree that they presented no hazard to themselves or others. Moreover, all trainees had been at the Center for more than 1 year but not more than 10 years; the average was 6.5 years. None had spent time in an institution, and all were living at home or in hostels. The age range of the subjects was 17 to 45 years, with a mean of 31. Verbal

"Factor Structure and Correlates of Adaptive Behavior in Non-institutionalized Retarded Adults," Vincent J. Guarnaccia, *American Journal of Mental Deficiency*, Vol. 80, No. 5, 1976. ©1976 American Journal of Mental Deficiency.

and performance IQs, based upon the Wechsler Adult Intelligence Scale administered within a year of this study, ranged from 48 to 75, with a mean of 61. Both the age and IQ distributions were approximately the same for males and females. There were 6 subjects with Down's syndrome.

Maternal Trust

Maternal trust was measured with the Interpersonal Trust Scale (Rotter, 1972). This scale is a 40-item Likert-type scale on which a respondent is asked to judge whether he agrees or disagrees with statements concerning a wide variety of social "objects" such as friends, physicians, politicians, salesmen. The total score is considered to reflect the level of expectancy held by an individual that the word, promise, verbal or written statement of another individual or group can be relied upon. Rotter contends that it represents a disposition to consider the environment relatively safe, reliable, and trustworthy. Test–retest reliability coefficients are reported to range from .56 to .68 under varying administration procedures.

Adaptive Behavior

The Adaptive Behavior Scale (Nihira et al., 1969), the dependent variable in this study, has two main sections. In the first an individual's skills and habits are assessed in the following areas: Independent Functioning, Physical Development, Economic Activity, Language Development, Number and Time Concepts, Occupation-Domestic, Occupation-General, Self-Direction, Responsibility, Socialization. There are 69 items in the first section, and each area yields a separate score. The second part of the scale, related to personality and behavior disorders, was not included in the analysis because it yielded an extremely irregular distribution of scores. Reliabilities reported for the area scores ranged from .43 to .86, with a mean of .74.

Procedure

Mothers of the trainees in the sample were called on the telephone and asked to come to the training center where they were individually administered the Interpersonal Trust Scale by the author. The mothers were told that the data would be used as part of a research project, but the details of the study were not explained.

Concurrent with Interpersonal Trust Scale data collection, the trainees were rated by their rehabilitation counselors on the Adaptive Behavior Scale. The counselors were aware of the purpose and basic design of the study. Six counselors were involved, although not all counselors had the same number of trainees to rate. The counselors rated only the trainees who were part of their own caseload. In all instances, the counselors had long-standing contact with their trainees and had excellent knowledge of them. When there was some doubt about how to rate a trainee on a given item, counselors conferred with the director of rehabilitation and other personnel who were familiar with the trainee.

Data Analysis

In computing the factor analysis of the Adaptive Behavior Scale, I used the 10 area scores rather than the more specific, but less meaningful, item scores. In addition, an independent measure of productivity was included in the analysis which was the average weekly earnings of each subject over the preceding 6-month period. The data were subjected to a principal-component analysis, and the number of factors was determined by plotting eigenvalues and cutting off at the first significant drop. The derived factors were then rotated orthogonally to a varimax solution with the Fortran BMDX 72 program. Interpretation of the rotated factors was based upon variables with loadings of .40 or more.

The next step was to compute step-wise multiple regression equations with age, sex, verbal IQ, performance IQ, and maternal trust as predictor variables of the derived Adaptive Behavior Scale factors. The program was the Statistical Package for the Social Sciences.[1]

Results

The analysis yielded four fairly independent and psychologically meaningful factors which are presented in Table 1. These factors were the first four extracted and together accounted for 61 percent of the total variance in the correlation matrix.

Factor 1 was labeled Personal Independence and is represented by five Adaptive Behavior Scale areas. All of them seem to relate to cognitive (knowledge and skills) and motivational elements which are requisites for autonomous functioning. This factor seems to contain the basic tools for independent living and some inclination on the part

[1] All computations were done at the Hofstra University Computing Facility.

TABLE 1
PRIMARY FACTOR LOADINGS OF THE ADAPTIVE BEHAVIOR SCALE (ABS)

Factor[a]/ABS area	Loading
Factor 1	
1 Independent functioning	.89
3 Economic activity	.85
5 Number and time concepts	.82
4 Language development[b]	.70
8 Self-direction[b]	.59
Factor 2	
9 Responsibility	.72
Factor 3	
2 Physical development	.57
11 Earnings[bc]	.51
6 Occupation-domestic	.40
Factor 4	
10 Socialization	.78
7 Occupation-general	.58

[a] Factor 1: personal independence, Factor 2: personal responsibility, Factor 3: productivity, Factor 4: social responsibility.

[b] Areas with significant loadings on more than one factor.

[c] Not part of Adaptive Behavior Scale.

of the individual to use them. The other factors have slightly lower loadings but, in general, are defined by areas which relate to interaction with the environment.

Factor 2, labeled Personal Responsibility, is defined solely by that Adaptive Behavior Scale area. The ability and willingness to meet specific obligations and expectations seems to be important in this factor. Also, it is interesting that physical development is found here instead of in Factor 1. No doubt this reflects the fact that jobs found in the workshop setting are predominantly repetitive, assembly-line operations which depend much more upon dexterity, coordination, and sometimes speed than upon cognitive skill. In fact, many jobs are structured in such a way that initiative and individual decision-making are discouraged or prevented.

Factor 4, Social Responsibility, is defined by two areas which relate to such things

as work habits, consideration for others, cooperativeness, and participation in group activities. Perhaps the term "other-directedness," at work and elsewhere, best sums up the quality of this factor.

Examination of the regression of Personal Independence (Factor 1) on the five predictor variables, summarized in Table 2, indicates that this criterion can be predicted most effectively by Verbal IQ ($F = 19.11$, $1/38\ df, p < .001$), Sex ($F = 9.51$, $2/37\ df, p < .001$), and Maternal Trust ($F = 18.42$, $3/36\ df, p < .001$). Verbal IQ was selected first and entered into the equation with a very substantial positive Beta-coefficient. By far, this was the most effective single predictor of personal independence, accounting for almost 40 percent of the variance. Next to be entered successively into the equation were sex and trust, both resulting in increments in R^2 (.56 and .74, respectively). The addition of age at the fourth step and performance IQ at the fifth step contributed very little ($R^2 = .75$). The negative Beta-coefficients of sex and age suggest that the most independently functioning retarded adults are likely to be young and male.

The five variables included in the regression equation for Personal Independence resulted in an R of .867 and explained about 75 percent of the variance in this criterion. This R yielded a highly significant F ratio of 14.54 ($5/34\ df, p < .001$). Thus, the relationship between Personal Independence and the five predictor variables was not only highly significant but also rather substantial.

In interpreting the relative contribution of each predictor variable to the variance in Factor 1, it should be noted that estimation of the factor scores was done by weighting each variable (Adaptive Behavior Scale area) with a factor score coefficient. Table 2 shows a substantial decrease in the Beta-coefficient for Verbal IQ after Step 2 of the regression procedure. It appears that while a certain basic level of verbal competence is required for independent functioning, being a male and having a relatively trusting

TABLE 2
REGRESSION FOR PERSONAL INDEPENDENCE (FACTOR 1)

Variable	Beta-coefficient at each step					R	R^2
	1	2	3	4	5		
1. Verbal IQ	.637	.570	.286	.253	.267	.637	.405
2. Sex		−.399	−.512	−.475	−.473	.748	.560
3. Trust			.515	.491	.493	.861	.742
4. Age				−.113	−.111	.866	.751
5. Performance IQ					.021	.867[a]	.752

[a] An F ratio of 14.54 ($5/34\ df, p < .001$) was computed for the R of .867 obtained at the final step of the regression procedure. This statistic should not be confused with the F ratios for sequential increments R^2 which are reported in the body of the table.

mother are advantages. The zero-order correlation matrix indicates, however, that verbal IQ is correlated quite highly with all of the other predictors and for this reason needs to be taken into account at all steps.[2]

A summary of the regression results on the other factors—Personal Responsibility, Productivity, and Social Responsibility—was not tabulated because the F ratios for increments in R^2 were not significant. With respect to Personal Responsibility (Factor 2) and Productivity (Factor 3), the five predictors together accounted for no more than 20 percent of the variance in each factor. Social Responsibility (Factor 4) had such low R^2 values that there is virtually no value in using the predictors individually or in any combination for this factor.

Discussion

From the standpoint of applicability, the Adaptive Behavior Scale appears to be well-suited for use with noninstitutionalized retarded populations, although, as might have been expected, Part II, in which maladaptive behavior related to personality and behavior disorders is measured, is of more limited usefulness since those persons with severe problems in this area are usually institutionalized.

The results of the factor analysis corresponded very closely to the theoretical proposals of Leland (1973) concerning the basic structure of adaptive functioning. Personal Independence (Factor 1), Personal Responsibility (Factor 2), and Social Responsibility (Factor 3) seem to embody precisely the same elements as Leland discussed. Nevertheless, these results must be interpreted with caution. Although some authors allow that the minimum subject-to-variable ratio can be as low as 4:1 (Clyde, 1972), most agree that much higher ratios are desirable. Given the greater variability typically found in mentally retarded samples, it is uncertain whether the factors found in this study would be reproduced with a larger sample. Consequently, these findings should be considered tentative and in need of corroboration.

The emergence of productivity as an independent factor (Factor 3) seems to make sense in terms of the sample studied. For retarded adults employed in a workshop setting, productivity is considered a prime indication of maturity and adaptability. Moreover, workshop jobs tend to involve sustained and repetitive visual-motor activities that require some physical endurance. Not surprisingly, measures of manual dexterity have been found to be the most stable predictors of work competence (Cobb, 1972).

The results of the regression analysis are interesting from both theoretical and practical standpoints. Clearly, age, sex, IQ, and maternal trust—individually or in combination—did not emerge as powerful predictors of overall adaptive functioning. Nevertheless, they did account for 75 percent of the variance in independent functioning. It is instructive to note also that in terms of relative weight, verbal IQ is by far the most influential of the predictors, accounting for 40 percent of the variance in independent functioning. One may speculate that sex and maternal trust operate as qualifying variables in the sense that they become important only after a minimal level of verbal competence has been reached.

The failure of the five predictors to account for a significant proportion of the variance in personal responsibility, productivity, or social responsibility is not surprising since the predictors reflected a rather limited range of variables. Better coverage might have occurred had measures of personality, motivation, and manual dexterity been included. But from a practical standpoint, the results highlight the fact that we should be careful not to oversimplify the criteria on which successful adaptation is judged. This is particularly important in the selection of clients as feasible for rehabilitation services.

Finally, some words of caution are in order. The statistically significant relationship between the predictors and the criterion of independent functioning should be considered quite stable as a probability in the noninstitutionalized retarded adult population, but this finding in itself contributes very little to predictability of outcomes in the individual case. In fact, the best judgments of the caseworker may involve many considerations not touched upon in this study. Also, the reader should bear in mind that this study employed a rating scale as the criterion measure, and, consequently, the problem of the halo effect cannot be ignored. To what extent it entered into the results is uncertain, although the raters were quite knowledgeable about the subjects, rating scales, and the halo effect problem.

Psychology Department
Hofstra University
Hempstead, NY 11550

---

[2] The correlation matrix used for the factor analysis and the zero-order correlation matrix have been deposited with the National Auxiliary Publications Service, Order Document No. 02731 from the National Auxiliary Publications Service, c/o Microfiche Publications, 305 E. 46th St., New York, NY 10017. Remit in advance $5.00 for photocopies or $1.50 for microfiche and make checks payable to Microfiche Publications.

Gleaning, harvesting and similar activities may provide employment for retarded workers in rural areas. This paper delineates the economic parameters of a variety of such activities. A model for providing extended sheltered employment for severely retarded adults in rural areas is suggested and the advantages of the proposed model over more traditional approaches are discussed.

Gleaning: Sheltered Employment for Retarded Adults in Rural Areas

J. Walter Jacobs

Underpinning the proposed model for providing sheltered employment for retarded persons in rural areas are several premises. First it is maintained that within the retarded population there are individuals who are poor candidates for competitive employment but are, nevertheless, capable of productive work. For such individuals placement in extended sheltered employment would be called for. The primary goal of such employment should be to maximize the income to the worker while reducing administrative overhead to the state. This is not to maintain that social, emotional, and intellectual development goals be abandoned, but simply to stress the need for economically viable work programs. Finally it is asserted that industrial contract based sheltered workshop programs, the primary traditional approach to sheltered employment, are often difficult to implement in rural areas. The chief limitation of such programs from an economic perspective is the availability of contract work. Such programs are favored in highly industrialized areas. In areas in which contract work is less readily available because of a paucity of industry, a contract procurement agent soliciting over a wide geographical area may be able to procure sufficient contract work. However, the fact that the agent must work large areas to procure sufficient work would argue against the likelihood of numerous contract based programs being economically successful. This, basically, is the dilemma faced by rural based sheltered work pro-grams. Seldom do workers from such programs generate enough income to be or even to approach economic self-sufficiency.

In many rural areas farming is often the major industry. However, for some years now farm labor as a vocational goal for the retarded person has been in disfavor. Wolfensberger (1967) states:

> One still hears the traditional contention that farm work is a good activity for the retardate and one for which he is well suited. This misconception is usually held by those ignorant of the contemporary farm situation and those that have difficult to discard commitments to agricultural or horticultural training.

Contrary to Wolfensberger's assertion, there is a need for manual labor in many areas which the retarded adult might meet. For the most part, this labor is needed for harvesting various crops in season. Thus, a frequently voiced criticism of the employment of retarded workers in farm labor is that such employment is temporary and seasonal in nature.

This paper reports the initial development of an alternative model for sheltered work activities for retarded persons in rural areas. This project is currently exploring the economic parameters of a variety of farm-based activities in which retarded adults might be employed. We are testing the feasibility of employing profoundly and severely retarded persons year round in such activities. By exploring a variety of farm-based activities, the program is attempting to surmount the seasonal nature of farming.

An Alternative Model

One might, for the sake of clarity, think of the proposed alternative as simply an "out of house" sheltered work program. Again, the program is

[1] This research was funded by the Georgia Department of Human Resources (DHR contract #901117) and the Charles L. Mix Memorial Fund, Georgia Southwestern College, Americus, Georgia.
[2] Gleaning refers to the practice of collecting the remainder of a crop left during normal harvesting. Ancient Hebrew law required the landowner to leave this portion of his crop for use by widows, orphans, and handicapped persons.

conceived and primarily intended to provide extended employment for those clients who are poor candidates for competitive employment.

The program is administered by a work supervisor and an aide who have broad responsibilities for effectively implementing the program. These responsibilities include procuring work for the group, providing transportation, teaching required work skills, and generally supervising the work. Careful logs must be kept on rate of production, time worked, weather conditions, *etc*. Where necessary, problems of production and adjustment problems must be rectified. Since the primary objective of the program is to generate substantial income for the workers, a major concern of the administrative personnel is the development of an efficient and proficient work group. Finally, the supervisor is charged with the task of negotiating and administering the monetary compensation to the workers.

The basic work unit consists of a supervisor, his aide and ten workers. The supervisor and aide are compensated by the administering agency. The workers, of course, derive their compensation directly from their labors. In addition, the administering agency provided for transportation costs, maintenance, and equipment costs. No facility is required to house such a program. The major equipment costs are for the purchase of a van and pick-up truck.

Clients in the present program are ten retarded adult males. The ages of workers range between 18 years and 55 years with the mean age being 34 years. The average IQ is 32.2 with a range between 19 and 38. Half of the workers have been institutionalized for periods ranging from 10 to 28 years. All workers now reside in a small southwest Georgia community, either in foster care homes or in their natural homes. With the one exception, none of the workers have any functional academic skills (*i.e.*, number concepts, reading, writing). In the excepted case, the worker can sign his name. No worker has ever been gainfully employed and by traditional criteria would be "unemployable."

The abbreviated title of this program is the Gleaners Project[3], a designation based on early efforts to glean various crops in which substantial wastage occurs due to mechanical harvesting. From the outset, it had been clear that considerable demand for labor existed during the harvesting seasons. The southwest Georgia community in which the program is based is known for its vegetable crops. For the most part, this labor need is met by highly efficient migrant farm laborers. Understandably, the author felt considerable trepidation toward the task of attempting to harvest very valuable and highly perishable vegetable crops with an untested group of profoundly and severely retarded adults. Thus, the project turned initially to gleaning wasted crops while maintaining the long range goal of competing with migrant labor for the very lucrative job of harvesting perishable vegetables and fruits.

Gleaning. While gleaning crops wasted during mechanical harvesting may have been a second choice in terms of economic potential, this is not to say that substantial income cannot be derived from such activity. An earlier study (Jacobs, 1976) has already demonstrated that significant income might be derived from corn gleaning. How one goes about the task of gleaning corn and economic parameters of that activity are detailed in the aforementioned article. At this juncture, it appears that the earlier study may have overestimated the economic potential of corn gleaning. Nevertheless, it remains clear that if one is fairly judicious in selecting fields to be worked, the activity has the potential of providing a minimum wage or better. The success of corn gleaning is particularly significant for two reasons. First, the retarded worker has little competition from other workers. More importantly, it is an activity which might engage the worker for nearly six months of the year, from August through January.

It is not possible within the scope of this paper to detail the mechanics of gleaning the wide variety of crops which were studied. Therefore, it must suffice to mention those crops which were discovered to have a significant economic potential.

Substantial wastage occurs in both the manual and mechanical harvesting of many vegetables. Certain types of string beans, for instance, are picked mechanically with considerable loss in the process. Workers might go behind the pickers and retrieve beans left on the vine or dropped to the ground. Individual workers in this program were able, in this way, to pick three to five bushels per day. Depending on the market, these beans brought between $5 and $8 per bushel. There is substantial wastage in numerous other vegetables and fruits. However, these crops are perishable and difficult marketing obstacles are encountered. Nuts, on the other hand, are much less perishable. In our area, pecan orchards are numerous. Primary harvesting is usually mechanical. In some instances, however, nuts are still harvested by hand and the retarded worker, of course, might be employed. More lucrative, however, is the gleaning of pecans left by mechanical harvesting. In this case, one can typically negotiate for fifty percent of the value of the nuts for retrieving what remains. This has been a particularly lucrative venture for the Gleaners' Project with individual earnings frequently ranging between $100 and $200 per week. Importantly, harvesting of pecans is an activity of the fall and winter months (*i.e.*, October through February). Finally, it should be pointed out that certain crops, such as cotton and peanuts, are not feasible for gleaning.

Primary harvesting. Retarded workers have traditionally been employed in direct harvesting, an activity at which they are often quite adept. For a variety of reasons (*i.e.*, the seasonal nature of harvesting, mechanization, urbanization, and prejudice directed toward farm laborers), this type of employment of retarded workers has been largely abandoned. Clearly, there is considerable potential for employment of the retarded worker in direct harvesting. The gleaning of certain crops, combined with various other winter and spring activities, could extend this employment to the entire year.

Throughout the summer and early fall many rural areas have crops that might be harvested by retarded workers. In our area, there is a myriad of vegetables, fruits and melons which retarded workers might harvest. Often this labor entails substantial economic potential.

Other activities. To ensure year round employment, a number of activities which might engage the worker during the winter and spring months were studied. In many rural areas, the forest products industry comprises a major portion of economic base of the region. In the Southeast, the forest products industry is based primarily in the cultivation of pine forests. There are several aspects of this industry in which retarded workers might be employed. Throughout the winter and early spring, retarded workers might be employed in pine tree planting. Economic returns, of course, depend on the proficiency of the worker. The land owner will typically contract for the service on a per acre basis. The fee ranges between $15 and $18 per acre. While there was great variability among our workers, the best workers could plant approximately 2 acres per day. Another seldom considered activity is the harvesting of pine cones for seeds. This is done in the fall of the year, and the cones bring about $2.75 per bushel. In portions of the South, resins from pine trees are suitable for use in the naval stores industry. Refined resins are used in a variety of industrial products. Workers employed in the Gleaners' Project, with the aid and support of the Georgia Forestry Commission, are currently involved with a pilot program directed toward the redevelopment of a naval stores industry in this region. Data from this pilot program are at this juncture preliminary. Nevertheless, indications are that the development of such a program for retarded workers holds considerable potential both in terms of employment opportunities and in monetary returns from this employment. Hypothetically, six hundred people could be employed full time in the naval stores industry in Sumter County, Georgia. At present, no one is employed in the industry.

The basic proce·, involves slashing the trunk of certain varieties of pine trees and collecting the resins that run out. The owner of the trees will typically receive 20 percent of the gross return from resins sold. A substantial portion of the initial equipment outlays are returned by Federal subsidies in the industry. Net returns per tree presently range between $1.40 and $2.00. An upper limit for the number of trees a person might work would be approximately 10,000.

Two other small business ventures were developed in farm employment during the spring lag. The Gleaners' Project markets to the public used railroad cross ties, cow manure for garden fertilizer, peanut hulls and saw dust for mulch, and pine straw and pine bark for ground cover. Cow manure is purchased from dairy farmers for five dollars per pick-up truck load and marketed at $15 per load. Other products are obtained at no cost and marketed at $12 per truck load. Expansion of this activity in the coming year will involve packaging these products and marketing them in urban areas.

Another activity of the Gleaners' Project involves waste recycling. Scrap metals are collected from farmers. In many instances, the market value of these commodities can be treated as a gift to a charitable organization with the donator receiving a tax credit. The commodities are then marketed with the income generated going equally to the workers.

The naval stores program, waste recycling, and garden products businesses were developed to provide employment and income during a period in the spring when there are few farm employment opportunities. However, each of these businesses has demonstrated substantial economic potential and will be continued throughout the year.

Finally, it should be noted that workers in the program have also been employed to remove rocks and other debris from newly cleared land, to pick up limbs after the pruning of orchards, to clear fence rows, and to sprig-plant bermuda grass. For these activities, workers were compensated at an hourly rate commensurate with the minimum wage.

Advantages of Proposed Model

Economic. Contrary to our early misgivings, the Gleaners' Project at no time encountered difficulty in obtaining employment for the workers. Indeed, throughout most of the year several alternative work activities were continuously available. While some activities (*i.e.*, gleaning peanuts and cotton) proved not to be economically feasible, others proved to have considerable economic potential for the retarded worker. Given the ready availability of work that was encountered, such a program clearly is a viable alternative in some areas to the extended sheltered workshop. Further, the farm-based program would seem to have several advantages over traditional programs. The initial projection of a potential income of $4000 to $5000 per year for the workers seems now to be a realistic one. Additionally, there were few programming difficulties in teaching the retarded worker the skills required in the various activities. Given the penchant for complex assembly tasks now in evidence in sheltered workshops, one might conclude that there is a linear relationship between the technology involved and the economic potential for retarded workers. This may or may not be the case. Certainly it is enlightning and impressive that rehabilitation professionals can program the assembly by retarded workers of intricate electronic or mechanical apparatus. However, given the need for gainful employment among large numbers of retarded persons, demonstrations of complex assembly amount largely to academic exercises. The ease and simplicity involved in teaching the task to retarded workers must remain an important consideration.

Administrative costs of providing sheltered employment for retarded workers under proposed model are substantially below traditional sheltered workshop costs. Basic costs are for supervisory personnel, vehicles, maintenance and transportation costs. Although in this program workers bear no portion of these costs, it is conceivable that in the future a portion of their earnings might go toward this end. At present, these basic costs are fifty to eighty percent below those costs typically encountered in traditional programs. Further, since the workers are earning relatively substantial incomes, the costs of Social Security and Supplemental Security Income are eliminated or significantly diminished.

Humanitarian. Perhaps the most compelling arguments for the proposed model are humanitarian ones. In spite of the rhetoric one hears about the demise of the work ethic, this is still a society in which one is largely what one does. For the first time these retarded adults are gainfully employed in productive work. Many of the humanitarian ends desired for these persons derive from the fact of their employment. While the data are largely anecdotal, it is evident that self-concept and self-esteem have markedly improved. Further, the attitudes of family members toward these retarded persons appear to have improved significantly. No longer are they a financial burden. To the contrary, the added income has a significant economic impact on the family.

Among the urban middle class, manual farm labor tends to carry demeaning connotations. While this prejudice may be borne by some, it certainly is not common in the community from which this sample of workers is drawn. If anything, the workers' employment is frequently envied. Parents, relatives, and normal workers have on several occasions asked to work in the program.

Although the Gleaners' Project was met initially with sympathetic support in the farming community, this support now seems to derive more from self-interest. That is, farmers are already trying to schedule workers for the coming season. This certainly argues that the workers offer a needed service to the farmer. However, initial overtures to area farmers were met with considerable skepti-cism. All the typical myths and prejudices (e.g., physical ineptness, lethargy, criminality) deriving from stereotypes of retarded persons were encountered. It is the author's feeling that the demise of such prejudices lies in the presentation of contrary evidence. The strong support now enjoyed in the farming community would argue that these prejudices are substantially altered. In summary, it can be concluded that the employment of these retarded adults has directly enhanced their self-concept, their esteem within the family and their image in the larger community.

Other direct and indirect benefits also appear to have accrued as a result of employment. For example, observation of the development of friendships among the workers is enlightening. Efforts to develop social contacts for retarded persons are often contrived and "unnatural." Retarded persons might, for example, be brought together for a dance with the expectation that friendships will flourish. If readers will reflect for a moment on their own friendships, it should be apparent that many of these developed through job associations. Likewise, workers in the Gleaners' Project have developed friendships among themselves. Indeed, a strong comraderie has developed among the workers. These friendships, in turn, are carried to leisure time activities and interests. Together they attend movies, wrestling matches and other activities of their choosing. This leisure time is now zealously guarded so that Saturday work is virtually impossible.

In this work-oriented society, the primary habilitative goal for retarded adults must be gainful employment. Toward this end, a model for providing extended sheltered employment for retarded adults in rural areas has been proposed. Within the context of this program, heretofore unemployable retarded adults have approached economic self-sufficiency. The farm related activities have proven to be a source of employment for which the retarded adult is suited and in which there is considerable economic potential. Development of the required skills even in very low functioning individuals was accomplished with relative ease. Finally, a substantial need for the type of labor service offered by the retarded worker was discovered. The purposed model can be implemented at substantial economic savings over traditional approaches. More importantly, however, a broad range of humanitarian ends are served indirectly. The gainfully employed retarded person has a better self-concept and higher esteem in his family and the community. In short, he is happier, healthier, and better adjusted than his unemployed counterpart.

Ankers Capitol Photographers

194

Horticulture:
Job Training For
Mentally Retarded

Paula D. Relf, Ph.D.

Traditionally, institutions for the mentally retarded have been located on large acreage and have included agricultural activities as an integral part of their program. Many state institutions phased out their agricultural programs over the years.

However, today, as urban sprawl brings the city closer to many of the once isolated institutions, there is an increased interest in using the agricultural land for programs which will provide training for jobs in the community. The many varied aspects of horticulture, from vegetable and fruit production to nursery and floral work, make it an ideal area for job training.

There is distinct need for people trained to work in horticulture. Such areas as grounds maintenance, home landscaping, and greenhouse crop production all have jobs which can be handled quite satisfactorily by mentally handicapped people. These jobs typically require a minimal level of decision making (*i.e.*, does the fruit look like the others that were ready to be picked? Or is the hole large enough to hold the plant?). These are skills in decisionmaking that mentally retarded people have demonstrated the ability to acquire. Often the tasks are repetitive in nature, providing greater opportunity for development of the skills involved in the particular task. Some of the jobs require that the person be able to deal with the public; however, the majority would not require contact with more than a small group of people.

The facilities needed for training people for jobs in horticulture vary as greatly as the jobs themselves. Some

institutions for the mentally retarded use the maintenance of the grounds as the starting point in establishing their program, while others set up more elaborate facilities, such as greenhouses and nurseries. Orchards and vegetable gardens are also frequently included in the program. The sale of items from these areas is often enough to make the program self-supporting.

Many different centers, such as the Ellisville State School (Ellisville, Mississippi), the Sunland Training Center (Miami, Florida), and the Marbridge Ranch (Austin, Texas), include training in horticultural techniques in their vocational rehabilitation programs. One of the most extensive programs using horticulture as a means of vocational training for mentally retarded men and women is Melwood Horticultural Training Center in Upper Marlboro, Maryland. Started in 1962 with a tent and seven acres, Melwood has grown until today it includes four greenhouses, a retail nursery and florist, an administrative office building, several activity buildings, and a 108-acre farm. At first, Melwood's program consisted primarily of on-the-job training programs for developing social and vocational skills. A part-time, special education teacher was then hired to supplement academic skills. Eventually academics were integrated with daily vocational duties and functions. This system was found to be quite effective as classroom concepts found meaning in the concrete tasks of daily work.

Graduates of Melwood have been placed in local florist, nurseries, and

landscaping businesses, as well as on the grounds maintenance crews at the University of Maryland, the National Park Service, and local government facilities.

Dr. Henry T. Skinner, past Director of the National Arboretum, where several mentally retarded young people from Melwood have been hired, has been very pleased with their work and has indicated that there is opportunity for the placement of large numbedicapped people in horticulture—to the benefit of both the vocation and the person.

However, training in horticulture does not necessarily lead to job placement within the community. For the severely retarded, there is potential for group employment contracted on a "finished job" basis. Thus, a group of severely retarded people, who may or may not reside in an institution, work together in a semisheltered situation to complete a task. Harvesting fruit and cleaning park grounds have both proved to be successful group jobs.[2][3]

In work reported by Dr. Carl E. Hansen,[4] trainable mentally retarded with IQ's of 50 or less developed into skilled work crews able to contract for such jobs as lawn work, ditch cleaning, weed pulling, brush removal, and numerous other gardening jobs. The crew situation provided the degree of competition which encouraged each member to work his hardest. The competition was on an equal basis, that of striving against someone on one's own ability level and did not create the feeling of inferiority often encountered in other

ables than their specific job capacities and skills. In general, the assessment of any person's ability to do well in a horticultural rehabilitation program has been rather subjective. The person expressed through words or action some personal interest in working around plants or a staff member in the institution thought he might be capable. However, a new test developed by Ralph L. Becker, Columbus Institute, known as the Reading-Free Vocational Interest Inventory [5] specifically includes horticulture as a work area of interest.

As a result of increased interest in the use of horticulture in programs for the handicapped, a new organization, The National Council for Therapy and Rehabilitation through Horticulture, has been formed. Information regarding this group can be obtained by writing NCTRH, Mt. Vernon, Virginia 22121.

Dr. Relf is Assistant Professor, Department of Horticulture, Virginia Polytechnic Institute and State University, Blacksburg, Virginia.

References
[1] Brubeck, Thomas. "Growing." *American Rehabilitation.* 1975. Nov-Dec. pp.26-29.
[2] Chigier, E. *The Use of a Group Approach in Rehabilitating of Severely Retarded Adolescents in Agriculture in Israel.* HEW Research Project Report VRA--ISR--23--65. 1970.
[3] Hansen, Carl E. "The Work Crew Approach to Job Placement for the Severely Retarded." *Journal of Rehabilitation.* 1969. May-June. pp. 26–27.
[4] *Ibid.*
[5] AAMD-Becker. Reading-Free Vocational Interest Inventory. American Association of Mental Deficiency, 5201 Connecticut Ave., Washington, D. C. 22015.

competitive situations. The use of trainable mentally retarded work crews in county, state, or federal recreational areas as well as in private lawn and yard work, was recommended.

Regardless of the facilities available or the approach to training the individual, it must be pointed out that for the job placement to be successful, the training must not only provide the basic horticultural skills, but must include "work readiness" development. As in any other job area, there are certain expectations of how an employee will behave—he will report to work on time, he will dress in a reasonable clean and neat fashion, etc. In addition to horticultural skills and job readiness skills, the prospective employee needs to be aided in developing social skills—the ability to fulfill, to some degree, societies expectations of his relationship with his employer and fellow workers; also, the ability to find activities to fill his nonwork hours.

When considering individuals for placement in such a program, it should be remembered that studies concerned with the vocational training of the educable retarded youth indicate that work interest, habits, and motivation are far more critical vari-

New Horizons For The Mentally Handicapped

LOUISE DURBIN

Louise Durbin is a Washington-based free-lance writer.

The rolling, fertile Maryland countryside near Upper Marlboro seems an ideal site for a horticultural center, and so it is. But at the Melwood Horticultural Training Center, plants are really the by-products, for the most important things that take root and grow here are the self-reliance, sense of responsibility, and job skills that are being carefully nurtured in the mentally retarded trainees.

Melwood was founded nine years ago on seven acres of surplus land from Andrews Air Force Base, when parents in the Prince George's (Maryland) County Association for Retarded Children, Inc., pitched a tent on the untilled acreage to start a center that would provide vocational training in horticulture for youths with mental retardation. Samuel L. Scheinberg, a geneticist at the U.S. Department of Agriculture's research station at Beltsville, Maryland, had proposed to the parents that training in horticulture, where workers were in demand, would be ideally suited for the mentally handicapped. Not only could horticultural work be carried on at a slow pace, he pointed out, but the therapeutic benefits of working with one's hands in the soil were well recognized by psychiatrists and green-thumb amateurs alike.

But when the new arrivals, 15 years of age and up, come to Melwood it's cash, not cold-frames, that interests them. This is an opportunity for them to earn while they learn, and though few of them have ever had a job before, most of them

Photo: Melwood Training Center

Co-ed trainees specialize in floral design.

do anticipate, with pleasure, having money to spend as they please. Their "pay," which ranges from $2 to $20 a week, depending on the attendance record and effort—not production—the individual puts out, is actually work incentive. The interest in horticulture and career opportunities develops later.

Now a sprawling complex consisting of greenhouses, a vocational education building and florist shop, portable classrooms, and rows of beds of nursery stock for use in landscaping jobs, Melwood provides day training for about 65 to 70 youths at a time. Of the trainees, whose average I.Q. is in the 60 to 70 range, 25 are teen-age girls who concentrate on doing floral designs and corsages, making change in the florist shop, learning how to help customers pick out plants, wreaths or floral arrangements, and wrapping the selections. The co-eds, who have been at Melwood only three years, have become such an integral part of the center that not only do they maintain the florist shop from 8 a.m. to 4 p.m.—in regular training hours—during the five days a week when it is open to the public, but they also give workshops for members of women's organizations who come to Melwood to learn how to make their own floral and ever-green table and door decorations.

The core of the center is the horticultural vocational training program for young men which includes greenhouse, nursery, and on-the-job training in the community. Landscaping and grounds maintenance work—frequently small jobs which commercial companies cannot handle—are carried on throughout the area by work crews from Melwood. A second work experience program, geared for trainees with more limited capabilities, is structured along lines similar to the vocational training program but focuses on basic personal development within a narrower training program.

Complementing all of the vocational programs is an educational and recreational program that stresses "survival academics." Part-time instructors, paid by the Prince George's County public schools, come to Melwood several days a week to teach remedial "3 R's." Many of the trainees who arrive at Melwood cannot read or write; others need practical training in counting, making change, telling time, and preparing and managing a simple budget. Training is also given in safety, recreation, working with money, and socialization—which includes how to operate a pay telephone, how to read traffic signs, and how to travel independently by public transportation to the specific

pick-up points where a battered old bus meets them to take them the last lap of the way to Melwood.

Under its energetic young director, Earl Copus, Jr., Melwood offers a rounded training program aimed to prepare the trainees not only to be employable and to have a sense of job responsibility but also to become self-supporting adults with social and recreational activities they can enjoy in the community. Student enrichment classes are given two evenings a week in driver education, crafts, cooking, photography, and other subjects for both Melwood trainees and alumni who now hold jobs in the community. One alumnus, now employed by the U.S. Department of Agriculture's showcase for horticultural research, the National Arboretum, returned to present a movie about the Arboretum one evening and created quite a flap among his female colleagues when he arrived driving a new car he had purchased, for cash, with his earnings.

Copus, who graduated in forestry and sociology from the University of Georgia before serving a stint with the Peace Corps in Brazil, heads a dedicated and enthusiastic staff that now numbers about 20, including a job placement officer and evaluator, a director of training, supervisors and instructors.

Fieldwork on the seven-acre site, where over 5,000 plants are being cultivated, is an important part of basic training.

The Division of Vocational Rehabilitation of the Prince George's County Department of Education refers prospective trainees to Melwood, which always has a waiting list.

"We hate to have to turn anyone away," says Copus, but he points out that "you can't really reach people in groups as large as 30, particularly if they are handicapped." The maximum counselor-trainee ratio at Melwood would be six to one, he said.

Training fees, which are channeled from HEW's Social and Re-

habilitation Service (SRS) through the State Government of Maryland, are received by Melwood, which also receives an allocation from the United Givers Fund (UGF). However, some 40 percent of Melwood's annual income is generated from the center's own earning power, Copus stressed. In addition to the center's year-round sale of trees, shrubs, house plants, and floral decorations and arrangements, Melwood has a special sales promotion at Christmas and Easter when floral and evergreen wreaths, ropes, and other decorations made by the trainees

are sold. Other earnings come from the trainees' services rendered in landscaping public and private grounds, in erecting playground equipment, and in working in community cleanup drives. Melwood has also received an HEW research and demonstration grant and, through SRS, a grant to set up an information and in-service training unit for HEW's Region III (which includes the States of Pennsylvania, Maryland, Delaware, Virginia, and the District of Columbia) so that other communities will be able to follow Melwood procedures if they

In the greenhouse, trainees learn fundamentals of growing and caring for hothouse plants.

and responsibility in carrying out job assignments are all emphasized.

The training program is divided into three phases, with the first four weeks at Melwood used as a period of evaluation for each trainee to determine his or her vocational potential, personal adjustment needs, demonstrated abilities, and special interests. One of the teachers also assesses the trainee's competence in the "3 R's" during this period.

"We try to keep the newer boys close to the center until they get to know a little about working with the plants and learn some self-sufficiency," says Copus, who added that the new boys were always eager to go out on the trucks with the experienced boys who were working on maintenance contracts or in the fields.

The final phase of the training may vary from a few months to approximately a year, when each trainee acquires, according to his ability, various job skills. The trainee spends the majority of his time outdoors, doing field work on the seven-acre site on which over 5,000 plants are being cultivated. He also trains in the greenhouse, where he learns the fundamentals of growing and caring for hothouse material, of transplanting, spraying, watering and fertilizing various species of plants. As the plants grow, so does the pride of the trainee, who can then enjoy seeing the proof that he is doing his job well. In the workshop, the trainee also acquires basic carpentry and painting skills and learns the proper use of hand tools and other equipment. As he progresses, the trainee is given additional responsibilities, such as keeping the tool room in order.

Throughout their stay at Melwood, trainees are not only put in a learning environment but also placed in positions where they can learn to cope with being in normal community situations. Two of the girls took part in a holiday plant sale in the Department of Agriculture patio, most of the trainees are on hand for Melwood Open Houses, and all learn to travel by public transportation—a function that few training centers or parents expect of retarded individuals!

Once the trainee has acquired the

choose to establish similar programs in their areas.

But funding is only one of the ways that Melwood receives help from its friends. The Lions Clubs of Suitland, Southgate, and Clinton, Maryland, have each recruited manpower, money and materials to help construct some of the buildings, including the "little red schoolhouse" on the grounds. The Lawyers' Wives Club of Prince George's County, the Officers' Wives Club of Andrews Air Force Base and several garden clubs are among the others who have contributed help and support. The Crescent City, Maryland, Jaycees are now trying to help raise money to sponsor a home economics unit, where Melwood trainees would be able to make jams, jellies, and baked goods both as vocational training and as items for sale.

There are, of course, adjustment problems in some cases. One boy hid in the woods among the tall pines for several days, another sat shyly behind the file cabinet in the office. But newcomers to Melwood are treated as young men, not little boys, and usually they soon respond by acting in a manner that is expected of them. One trainee, who was showing a visitor around Melwood, explained: "I used to be retarded myself."

During the next phase of the training, consisting of 16 weeks of personal vocational adjustment, the trainee learns what daily requirements will be made of him in the work-a-day world. His personal appearance, adjustment to working alone or within a group structure,

Landscaping and grounds maintenance work on public and private property provides both on-the-job training for work crews and income for Melwood.

skills, stability, and know-how to work in a competitive situation, every effort is made to place him in a job. Some 20 to 30 Melwood trainees gain employment in the community each year—with nurseries, florists' shops, and government agencies such as the National Arboretum. Their earnings usually are between $2.25 and $3.00 an hour, and one young woman was hired at $3.41 per hour to do floral design work in the garden shop of a Washington, D.C., store. Some trainees who prefer other work are placed in vocations that are not related to horticulture—one young woman is a nurse's aide, and a young man is working as a dietitian's aide. The most important thing that Melwood can teach its trainees, Copus points out, is job responsibility; the specific job skills are secondary.

The most recent addition to the Melwood complex is a 108-acre farm in Charles County, Maryland, near Nanjemoy, which will, in time, be developed as a residential ranch setting for social and recreational as well as vocational opportunities for Melwood trainees and their families.

"At Melwood, new ground is being broken in the lives of the mentally retarded—in the green-houses, potting sheds, and classrooms—to provide career opportunities that most of the handicapped, and their families, had never dreamed possible," Earl Copus has said. At the same time, Melwood has proven itself as a training center for potential employees for the floral and nursery industries, in which there has long been a national shortage of trained workers.

"We are here at this farm to work," wrote Joe, a trainee, in the Melwood monthly newsletter. "Not to listen to radio or watch T.V. or sit around. As we are, we are working to make money." And so they are.

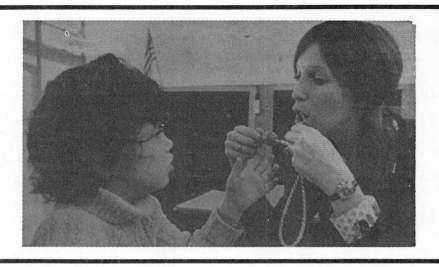

ELWYN INSTITUTE A CHANGING ROLE FOR A RESIDENTIAL FACILITY

Marvin S. Kivitz

MARVIN S. KIVITZ, PH.D., Vice President for Programs at Elwyn Institute, Elwyn, Pennsylvania, received an M.A. in Vocational Counselling from Teachers College, Columbia University, and his Doctorate in Clinical Psychology from the University of Pennsylvania. He has served as Vice President (Vocational Rehabilitation Division) of the American Association on Mental Deficiency. He has been consultant to the Rehabilitation Services Administration of the Department of Health, Education and Welfare, as well as consultant to the Delaware County Association for Retarded Citizens and the Philadelphia Board of Education.

Abstract. Recently large institutions have been characterized as dehumanizing, inflexible, self-serving facilities. In sharp contrast, Elwyn Institute provides an impressive progression of comprehensive education, training and rehabilitation services designed to meet the needs of a large residential and day population. The Institute works closely with local agencies in filling gaps in existing community services and making its programs and expertise available to fill these needs. Elwyn has pioneered the development of work activity centers, sheltered workshops, community work programs and group homes. The Elwyn model has been employed in developing comprehensive satellite rehabilitation facilities which are helping to meet community needs in several states.

"Large" institutions for the retarded have been depicted as being archaic, dehumanizing and inflexible facilities. Recent studies in Canada, England and the United States have indicated that many small facilities and group homes can be dehumanizing and devoid of services if not properly operated and supervised. Thus, it is not the size of a facility that determines its value, but rather its organizational structure, staff and basic philosophy.

Elwyn Institute is dedicated to providing education, training and rehabilitation programs which permit each individual to progress to the limits of his capabilities. An attempt is made to have each student feel productive and worthwhile regardless of his limitations. A graduated progression of programs has been developed. The programs are self-evaluating in nature and without time limits. As the individual matures, develops and displays increasing competency, he is moved to the next higher level in the progression. All students below the age of 21 are provided with a comprehensive education program five full days a week. As the individual matures, increasing emphasis is placed on vocationally oriented activities.

People are referred to Elwyn Institute from all over the world by physicians, educators, organizations and agencies. Locally, Elwyn receives referrals from community schools and intermediate units, as well as pediatricians and mental health/mental retardation centers. Elwyn now serves over 800 residents and approximately 475 day students. The satellite programs provide community services for an additional 700 people.

At the time of admission, a comprehensive evaluation including psychological testing, audiologic screening, and neurological examination, is provided so that appropriate educational programs may be prescribed. Over 30% of the referrals have significant hearing losses which have to be taken into consideration in rehabilitation planning. Many of these individuals have been in programs where this defect has been undetected. Psychological testing is done in order to gain a picture of the current functioning level of the individual so that individualized program plans can be developed. Experience has indicated that diagnostic labels have relatively little relevance to rehabilitation planning for the individual.

For those students requiring residential care, Elwyn provides an attractive, stimulating physical environment. A full range of recreational services enrich the lives of residential students. Special education classes are available for both residential students and day students who are transported from every school district in Delaware County. Children below the age of three are enrolled in Elwyn's infant stimulation program and receive vital sensory, perceptual-motor and language stimulation. A preschool language acquisition classroom for 3-, 4- and 5-year-olds focuses on language stimulation and enrichment. In the language classroom daily individual language training and parent counselling are used to teach non-verbal children a functional language. The Davidson Program consists of special education classes for children with multiple handicaps including mental retardation, brain damage, emotional disturbance, and visual and hearing impairment. Children are grouped into a variety of individually designed programs to provide prescriptive teaching and training. Academic foundations, career training, and pre-vocational classrooms are equipped to deal with children at all levels of mental handicap. A full complement of ancillary service specialists supplements classroom instruction with manual language training, physical therapy, remedial reading, speech therapy, library services, home economics, adaptive physical education and swimming. Elwyn's audio-visual department allows students the opportunity to participate in the taping of TV broadcasts and provides needed feedback for help in improving personal appearance and social adjustment. Elwyn students participate in scouting programs, as well as religious services for all major denominations.

Students between the ages of 16 and 21 years attend a Work-Study Program which emphasizes community living skills, and also receive work training within the community or school setting. The program allows the students to begin the process of career preparation and occupational choice while still in school and ensures that classroom instruction is relevant to the needs, interests and abilities of each individual. Conscious effort is made to involve the individual in decision making processes involving program choices. Student motivation is maintained by participation in sports, community trips, driver education, social events, and recrea-

tional activities. Work-Study students participate in a formal graduation upon completion of the program and receive diplomas from their home schools or from Elwyn Institute.

Upon graduation students enter the vocational training and rehabilitation phase of their program. Again, assessment is a key factor in prescribing needed remedial programs. Part of the evaluation process includes an exploratory work experience. During this period, students rotate among various vocational assignments in order to familiarize themselves with available training opportunities and to form job preferences. A hierarchy of vocational training opportunities is provided with increasing demands and responsibility required in step-wise fashion as the individual progresses through the training program. For students with minimal work ability, an Adult Adjustment Program is available for instruction in pre-vocational skills. The aim of the Adult Adjustment Program is to prepare the individual to graduate into work activities or sheltered work shop programs, which Elwyn maintains on the Campus.

A sheltered contract workshop is used to teach basic work habits and knowledge. Elwyn Industries, as the workshop is labeled, secures packaging, sub-assembly and other non-skilled jobs on a contract basis from local businesses and industry. The workshop is operated on a non-profit basis. Money derived from contracts is paid to workers on a piece-work basis in conformance with standards established by the United States Wage and Hours Commission. Elwyn Industries provides gainful employment for many persons who require sheltered employment opportunities. The use of specialized equipment, such as the skin packager, and individualized teaching techniques allow Elwyn Industries to maintain a factory atmosphere and high levels of production. In addition to the contract workshop program, Elwyn provides vocational training in a number of occupations suitable for the handicapped. Courses available include business education, janitorial services, dietary and food services, power sewing, printing, hospital aide training, baking, and laundry services. While the students receive vocational training, they are also enrolled in adult education classes for instruction in basic social competencies requisite for community living. Individual and group counselling, or Personal Adjustment Training, helps students in dealing with social and emotional problems associated with mental handicap or institutionalization.

After completion of vocational training, an individual may be enrolled in the community work program. This permits an individual to be employed in the community at regular going community rates, while he continues to reside at the school, receiving the required and individual counselling and adult education necessary for community adjustment. At the completion of his vocational training and habilitation program at the main campus, a student is eligible to enter Elwyn's halfway house program. One floor of Chestnut Hall, a residential hotel in West Philadelphia, is used for this purpose. Chestnut Hall provides a transitional experience for Elwyn students being trained for independent living and competitive employment in the community. Students share apartments and are provided with an opportunity to apply skills learned during their training program. They commute to jobs using public transportation facilities. They also continue to receive adult education and counselling during this phase of the program. Success in the transitional program leads to discharge. Many Elwyn graduates now live independently in the community and work at competitive jobs in business and industry. Others may continue to require some degree of supervision while residing and working in the community. An Alumni Club provides social and recreation opportunities for graduates and provides informal support and guidance.

The success of Elwyn's programs has created a demand

for application of the training methods at other settings. Community need has resulted in the establishment of a variety of satellite programs. A comprehensive rehabilitation program has been established at the Elwyn-West Philadelphia Rehabilitation Center. Elwyn community workshop programs have been developed in Media, Pennsylvania; Wilmington, Delaware; and Fountain Valley, California. In Upper Darby, Pennsylvania, an Elwyn vocational program offers rehabilitation services to individuals with social and emotional problems. A variety of halfway house and after-care services have been developed in Delaware County and Philadelphia to serve individuals coming from other institutions or who have resided in the community until parents are no longer able to care for them. These services not only form a transitional bridge to the community but serve as alternatives to institutional placement.

In each of these settings, as on the main campus in Media, Pennsylvania, Elwyn continues the tradition of providing quality programs to help the mentally handicapped individual function at his highest potential.

Assistential Model on the Philosophy of Respect for the Human Dignity of the Mentally Retarded Person (AZUPANE) in Venezuela

Gregorio J. Finol

Abstract. The philosophy and methods of the Association Zuliana de Padres y Amigos de Ninos Excepcionales (AZUPANE) are detailed. The treatment, care, and development of the mentally retarded are conducted through programs in sensorial stimulation, motor coordination, corporal expression, social conduct, recreation, an academic program, and remunerative work, emphasizing mobility, language, and interpersonal relationship skills. The total program allows the development of full potential in the mentally retarded.

AZUPANE, a private non-profitmaking Association, was founded on July 13, 1968; its services were open to eight children in the Instituto Educacional AZUPANE. The activities of the Institute are oriented toward the model school. On May 7, 1973, a new orientation in the activities of AZUPANE began, and at the present time in the "Centro de Desarrollo Humano" there are 92 children and adolescents with moderate or serious mental retardation.

In this world of constant and continous change in which modern man lives, AZUPANE affirms its aim of service to the exceptional child in the philosophy of respect for the human dignity of the child. The limiting aspect of the child with mental retardation is taken into account, but from a positive point of view. It is not the limitation as such that is important; it is the human potentiality in evolution that exists in each human being, in spite of certain organic or psycho-affective limitations. A child with mental retardation, however grotesque he may appear to our eyes, however limited he may be in his activities as a free and independent human being, is, and will always be, a human being worthy of admiration and respect and equal to any other person, even to one with superior endowments. His dignity as a human being is never diminished nor altered because of organic malformation or cerebral lesions.

His dignity remains unaltered and he may enter into a dialogue with the world, although his world is limited in space, time and interpersonal relationship. His dialogue is rich in symbolism, and full of human warmth. The dialogue of the individual with mental retardation is a challenge to "normal" man accustomed to a dialogue of linear communication, either in verbal or written language. The language of the person with mental retardation is more global, personalized, visual, totalizing, in which the gestures of the body and each visual reaction are more significant than words of guttural sounds, which probably have no real meaning, but which are full of context in a personal contact and as the expression of a body which vibrates in its communication with the object or the human being with whom he is communicating. We are unaccustomed to this dialogue of the person with mental retardation and instead of accepting and recognizing our own limitations, we ignore the person and take refuge in labels that are nothing more than the expression of our own ignorance. The aim in AZUPANE is to look for the meaning and content of the dialogue with a person with mental retardation, but we have to start by recognizing in all its amplitude the human dignity of the person with mental retardation, without making of the limitation, "the fact of mental retardation," the essence of the human being who is retarded.

The respect for the human dignity of the person with

4. MANPOWER

mental retardation implies the recognition and acceptance of his own limitations, his real limitations, but not of those limitations imposed upon him by a discriminatory society which does not accept any deviation from what has been determined as normal, and that supposes a greater emphasis on the limitations rather than on the potential of development. We have to recognize that the right to be himself, to realize his human potential, intrinsic in every human being, is not a favor or a privilege that an elite few concede to the many. The creation of an environment in which this potentiality, scarce though it may be, may reach its maturity, is the true expression of a real respect for the human dignity of a person with mental retardation. This is the task of AZUPANE.

The person with mental retardation has a right to live in the community and enjoy all of its benefits and privileges. There is a sense of urgency to make the community aware of its obligation to provide all the help necessary so that the mentally retarded persons may take part in all the advantages and opportunities that society provides for its members without discrimination or limitation. To take full advantage of these possibilities will depend on the personal choice of the individual, the freedom to choose between alternatives, freely and independently, and finding no barriers in his aspirations that have been imposed upon him by the conscious or unconscious rejection of the community.

The actual objectives of AZUPANE are precise: the scientific study of the problem of mental retardation, the training of personnel to work directly in the specialized field of mental retardation, and the care of the individual with mental retardation.

The scientific study of the problem of mental retardation leads to the investigation of its causes and methods of treatment. This investigation is oriented more toward the prevention than to the treatment and care of the mentally retarded; however, new methods are being found that will make it easier for the individual to realize his potential and easier to integrate the mentally retarded into the community. This method must be analyzed concretely. The realities of communities with different cultural development and socio-economic conditions cannot be put aside in the aspiration to incorporate into that community the person with mental retardation. We cannot adopt the standards of North America or Europe, although we may use their methods and programs of stimulation and work; for the underdeveloped countries, the adoption of these standards would not only be inconvenient but also alienating for the person with mental retardation, for in addition to this bio-psycho-social problem, he will also face the complexity of transculturization, having to live in his own environment with frames of reference entirely different from his own.

The direct action of AZUPANE as a Center of Training and Assistance implies the technical training of the personnel who will work in the field of mental retardation; this personnel is chosen more for the human qualities and abilities in profound and significant interpersonal relationship rather than on actual knowledge of the subject. This training is concerned with the personal action of each one in relation to the mentally retarded person. They must be conscious at all times of "what" is being done, "why" it is being done and "how" it must be done, which is the first level of training equivalent to a Bachelor's Degree. The second level, besides incorporating all the characteristics previously described, must have as a requisite the supervision of groups of students of the first level; Level Two is the equivalent of a Master's Degree. Finally, the creation of new models of learning, and the fulfillment of certain academic requirements at the level of Universities will earn the Doctorate.

The aims of AZUPANE are definite: to actualize the potential of the individual with mental retardation, slight as it

may be. We do not pretend that miracles will take place, but in accepting the reality of the limitations of the individual, we employ all the means available so that the child will reach the degree of personal independence which is possible for him. If the level of independence which he can reach is to smile happily and to express himself through bodily movement or facial expression, that is good, but the assistant must not be satisfied with less than that. There are persons with mental retardation who become economically independent, and that is an important aim, for it means the personal realization of those individuals.

In our institutions the emphasis is the following: to create a feeling of confidence, physical in the sense of personal safety, and spiritual in the sense of emotional balance. Confidence in himself, in the external world, will be the result of a stimulating environment of creativity where all basic necessities, physical and emotional, are satisfied in order to use the internal expression in all of its forms.

There are three aspects of human activity which have priority in the methodology of AZUPANE: mobility, language and interpersonal relationship.

Mobility — movement is the manifestation of life. The repetition of movement internalizes the action, which becomes spontaneous and organized. Motor coordination supposes personal integration and better functional organization of the cerebral centers, in which the sensitive current is transformed into motor current. Every movement has value in itself: the child's fixed glance on an object which he follows with his eyes, his smile, the flexions of his arms and legs, creeping, taking one step, walking, until he reaches more global movements such as swimming, athletics and gymnastics. To move from one place to another independently is the synonym of spatial independence and is the axis of AZUPANE's programs.

Language — means of communication. The spoken word is communication, the spoken word which is personalized in the dialogue-meeting between two human beings who are enriched in their communication and affirmed in their reality of being. Language is the total expression of man's being: language, which is not only a word correctly pronounced, not only an elegant phrase, but the language of total man: gestures, glances, movements of the body, vibrations of the internal ego. This language is charged with the personal contents of man who wants to listen and to be heard. Language is not a repeated mechanization or a therapeutic form, but rather an ambient of trust in an attitude of attention, which understands the internal communication of the individual who is communicating. Language makes the human being a part of all mankind and allows him to communicate with another human being. Through language, the human being structures his personality and is linked with the personality of the others with whom he communicates.

Interpersonal relationship — the individual with mental retardation, by the mere reality of his retardation, is isolated, ignored; his efforts to communicate are misunderstood. The individual with mental retardation has an expression of boredom, a vague look; he is inexpressive. The search for interpersonal relationship is almost an obsession with him, and his infantilism is nothing more than a way of attracting attention and to satisfy superficially his wish to relate to others. Frequently the relationship with a mentally retarded person is functional. He is looked upon as an object that is either cherished or ignored, as an object to scientists who study the causes of mental retardation, as an object to professionals who work with the mentally retarded, as an object to his family who overprotect or reject him, as an object to the community which ignores him or neglects him.

The individual with mental retardation has the same need as any other individual for personal relationship. He needs a personal relationship that makes him feel like a human being and understand himself. He needs a relationship that allows his development and valorization in all of his human dimension. He needs a relationship in which his "I" is confronted with the "I" of the other in a game of intimate approach and moving away a certain distance to see himself reflected in the other, who makes it easier for him to find himself, discovering himself as a human being capable of loving and being loved.

Interpersonal relationship is the natural environment of the activities of AZUPANE in its "Center for Human Development." The most important activity is "how" these activities take place and the total acceptance of the person with mental retardation, looking at him, accepting him as a person in a personal encounter which causes his internal ego to vibrate, in a profound dialogue that needs no words. There he is accepted and confronted in his behavior as a person worthy of appreciation and admiration, as a person who not only in his external appearance, but also in his actions and personal interchange, influences and changes the ego of the other person with whom he is communicating in a totalizing dialogue.

A group of technicians integrates the "Center for Human Development" of AZUPANE. Doctors, psychologists, neuropediatricians, psychopedagogues, social workers and child psychiatrists constitute the Technical Team. This Team periodically evaluates the children at the Center, meets with their parents in case of necessity, and is the most important factor in the professional improvement of the assistants. This Team analyzes the applications for admission, makes the necessary studies, and plans an individual program for each student.

Every application for admission is studied by a social worker who examines all previous evaluations and medical and psychopedagogic diagnoses, besides making a case history of the applicant. The psychologist evaluates the applicant's functioning at the level of mental retardation, using the Gessell Tests, the Hungarian Scale of Development (AZUPANE adaptation) WISC and interviews with the applicant's family. The neuropediatrician makes a clinical examination of the applicant and all the information obtained is analyzed in a general meeting of the Technical Team. According to this initial analysis, the applicant is admitted in the areas judged most convenient for him. In area activities, the psychopedagogue observes the pupil's abilities, and together with the attending assistants a report is elaborated and the P.A.C. Test of Abilities is given to the child, and in certain cases the Reel Language Scale. After two or three months, the placement of the child is reconsidered, and the elaborated programs are confirmed. In certain cases, psychiatric interviews, both individual and in family groups, take place, or complimentary tests are required from the medical services of the community.

There is a periodic reevaluation of the child, at least every 2 years, emphasizing his actual problems and the progress of the program. For these reevaluations, we take into account the opinion of the attendant, who brings a human dimension into the problems of the pupils.

Once the proper environment has been created, both physical and human, AZUPANE elaborates the program of action for the children. We are not concerned merely with "teaching" habits but rather we attempt to structure intelligent human conduct, and this on the level possible for each child. We do not try to teach mechanical behavior, which at best offers a repertory of doubtful value to the pupil, and which finds justification only in the illusory satisfaction of parents or teacher. We do stress the development of the mentally retarded individual and the participation with him in the discovery of new abilities in intimate·relation with the world which surrounds and stimulates him.

For this reason, we call the assistential practices "activities." These activities are physical and intellectual but always have real meaning, inserted into human reality, not locked up in experimental cubicles.

In AZUPANE we have no classrooms, nor teachers, although there are rooms set apart for special activities which require a definite setting. The activities take place mostly in the open air, taking full advantage of the luxuriant vegetation offered by our tropical climate — greenery of all shades, flowers and fruit, which give us a feast of colors and savors. We do not turn our backs to this natural spring of stimuli but rather we choose to submerge into it.

The attention of the child is the result of his internal motivation and his interest in the activity presented to him rather than on imposed activity. Thus, the gates of AZUPANE are always wide open.

We work in a circle, face to face, adults and children at the same level, using grass to sit on and natural elements as didactic materials.

Areas of Activity

Sensorial Stimulation. The youngest children from 0 to 5 years, are initiated in the area of sensorial stimulation. We are fully convinced that the earlier a child begins a specially structured program which motivates him, the greater will the opportunities be for the development of his cognitive and behavioral potential.

In the evolution of the child who is initiated in the area of sensorial stimulation, we are always conscious and stress in a special manner the three aims which AZUPANE seeks: mobility (control of the body), language (affirmation of the person who recognizes himself as a human being in a human environment), and interpersonal relationship (the capacity to express himself and to be understood on the plane of affection and intellectuality).

The program is one of attention to the individual child's needs for language, sensorial perception, and motor stimulation. The process of learning perception and representation during the development of the child takes place on a field of interpersonal and social affection of great importance in the formation of psychic structures. The affective field is the cement which synthesizes and joins the perceptive network, the representation and the corporal plan.

The child who is handled correctly from an emotional point of view learns to love himself and accept his body, his vibrations and the world around him. If his mother and others around him accept him as a total person, he will create his own stable and integrated corporal plan.

Motor Coordination. In the area of motor coordination we stress mobility and bodily coordination. The understanding of the corporal plan is not reduced to recognizing the parts of his body; rather, the corporal plan must be the realization of movement as a total entity, and that understanding must be used to integrate oneself to collective activities.

The program includes formation of a corporal plan for conscious control and balance and economical management of the body and breathing exercise. Motor perceptive behavior is taught as training in perception, spatial organization and time structuring. For motor behavior, balance in general and eye-hand coordination are taught. Differentiated psycho-motor training includes training of the hands and preparation for learning and better physical shaping of the child.

Corporal Expression. The area of expression helps the child to understand his development in communication, verbal and non-verbal. Even though the child is well-stimulated verbally in all areas, it is an expression where he

"WE WANT TO BE"
is the motto of AZUPANE

"hears himself" at the level possible for him, and understands the demands that are always present, and which will give way to language on more complex levels. This stage is reached through four basic activities: story telling and dramatics, painting and modelling, games, and music. All children between 5 and 10 years of age attend these sessions, and also the "dependent" children who are older.

Painting and drawing enhance attention, concentration and good habits. They lead to an increase in vocabulary and develop self-confidence by means of activities such as the games which precede drawing and painting, with arms, hands, fingers, drawing lines in various directions, passing from the controlled or uncontrolled scrawl to description, matching colors and forms, and later expressing feelings in drawing.

Music gives the child security and self-confidence, helps in his integration with others, and develops auditory perception. It stimulates energy, motor activity, attention and memory through activities such as listening to loud or soft music, vocalizing sounds, singing simple melodies, and eventually taking part in performing groups.

Modelling develops perceptive, tactile and visual capacity and spatial perception, motor coordination and attention, increasing the experiences of the child, giving him security and self-confidence through these activities.

Dramatics and story telling awaken the imagination and experience and depict situations common in daily life, bringing to the child greater self-confidence, expressed through play acting, experiences which he then teaches to younger children.

Social Conduct. The area of social conduct has as its objective the development of interpersonal relationships in the children, who, not having acquired routine habits, see the difficulties beyond the limitations imposed on them by their retardation, such as their integration to society. Therefore, prime importance is given to table manners, personal cleanliness, personal appearance and control of their bodily functions. Each of these activities is considered in its total aspect, which depends on various elements, among which the psychological and psychoemotional are not the least important. We do not aim at mechanized conduct, but rather at the result of acquiring these abilities from the interplay of environment-person, without submitting the child to veritable torture to obtain results.

We provide the child with stimuli through contact with colors, tastes, sounds, noises, forms and sizes. We allow the child to touch, use, manipulate and see all kinds of objects of common usage and help him understand their functions. Understanding his body will allow the child to have a full consciousness of himself, of others, of space and of time. This understanding is realized through rhythmic activities connected with the natural movements of walking, running, jumping, flexing the body, clapping, etc. We aim to stimulate the memory, attention, conceptualization, consciousness of external objects and internal understanding, such as dreams, thoughts, ideas. For each habit we have elaborated a scale of increasingly difficult behavior related with habits, and the form of learning is explained. The habits are: dressing, eating, personal hygiene and discipline.

Recreation. All the children attend activities in the Recreational Area. The program of games combines physical activity with entertainment. Each week all the children go to a swimming pool; providing them with swimming instruction has been one of our most satisfactory programs for water gives the child a different dimension in which to manage his body. Basketball and recently, dancing, complete their activities in this area.

Academic Program. After 5 years of age, and until their departure from the Center, all of the children who show potential for learning are enrolled in academic classes. Perceptual education, perception for reading and writing, and teaching these skills to some of the children are part of the programs. General information is given and the children are encouraged to work in groups, as a preparation for their future incorporation into the community.

We aim to help the group acquire skills and develop their senses through observation, discrimination, classification of forms, sizes and colors, and sounds, representing more and more complicated stimuli; the program includes visits to libraries and art centers. The program is subdivided into: visual discrimination, auditive discrimination, olfactory discrimination and gustative discrimination. Another object is to improve the quality of fine motor coordination, the balance of the body, fine movements; we begin by reaffirming the understanding of the corporal plan in the activities of daily living. It is subdivided into: pre-writing, pre-reading, pre-calculus, reading, writing, and calculus.

The general knowledge program includes a wide spectrum of activities: recognition of patriotic symbols, national holidays, historical sites, cities, the community in which they live, sex education and orientation, and understanding religion and spiritual experiences which may help the individual to serve the community better and to have a happy and full life.

Remunerative Work. The area of remunerative work is the culmination of the process of development which began theoretically in the area of sensorial stimulation. In this process of human development work must be present. The manipulation of objects, their proper use, and the transformation of natural objects are essential characteristics of man's occupation. For the person with mental retardation, work cannot be mechanized or automatized, because of the special characteristics of the mentally retarded person. No one must regard the hiring of mentally retarded persons as a reason for giving them mechanized and routine tasks; on the contrary, this attitude would contribute to their personal alienation. We feel that any task which can be performed by a mentally retarded person must be very simple, within his

potential, but total. By this we mean that the person must be able to see and feel the results of his work.

We have included here all the possible tasks which provide learning experiences for the children, beginning with the most simple (cutting with scissors) and advancing as far as possible within the initiative and creativity of the child and of the assistant in accord with the personal interest of the child in the task or activity. This program includes the following tasks: cutting, pasting, mosaic, beading, open work, threading, modelling, assembling, making mats, wood carving, tatting, embroidery, carving, engraving, and knitting.

Manual tasks are oriented to everyday living. The children learn gardening, cleaning, washing cars, plumbing, selling, carpentry, farm labor. The girls also learn cooking, sewing, housekeeping arts, housecleaning, maintenance and care of clothing.

In all the activities the children are both observers and participants; we insist that they not only learn how to do a task but also to acquire basic aptitudes fundamental in a responsible working person: order, cleanliness, safety, honesty, and loyalty. We always have in mind the integrated formation of the child in the development of his personality.

"WE WANT TO BE" is the motto of AZUPANE. This is the cry of liberation of children, adolescents, adults who have the right to live in a society which stresses their REALITY OF BEING and not the limitation of their potentialities.

GREGORIO J. FINOL received two bachelors degrees and the license in Philosophy in Spain, Masters in Divinity at Montreal, Canada, Masters in Education at Duquesne University and Ph.D. in counseling psychology at the University of Pittsburgh. He has been professor of Biology, Spanish, and Graduate Assistant at the University of Pittsburgh counseling program. He was the first Catholic Chaplain at Western State School and Hospital in Canonsburg, Pennsylvania, organizing religious programs for all residents of Catholic, Protestant and Jewish faiths. Dr. Finol is a man who blends in easily in different cultures and human situations. He is a man with many hats but only with one concern: the respect of human dignity of man regardless of man's inadequacies.

Presently, Dr. Finol is the Executive Director of AZUPANE, The Zulian Association for Parents and Friends of Exceptional Children at Maracaibo, Venezuela.

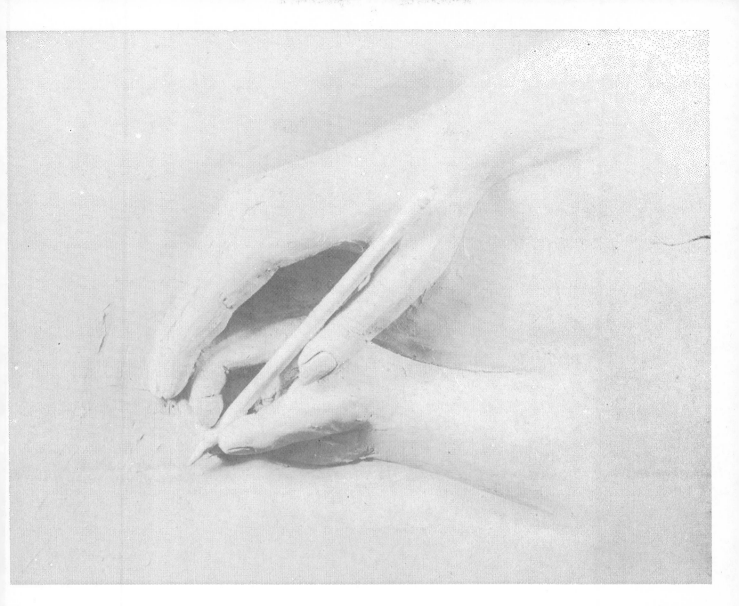

STAFF

Publisher	John Quirk
Editor	Roberta Garland
Editorial Ass't.	Carol Carr
Permissions Editor	Audrey Weber
Director of Production	Richard Pawlikowski
Director of Design	Donald Burns
Customer Service	Cindy Finocchio
Sales Service	Dianne Hubbard
Administration	Linda Calano

Cover Design   Donald Burns
Cover Photo   Richard Pawlikowski

LIST OF STATE CHAPTERS OF THE NATIONAL ASSOCIATION FOR RETARDED CITIZENS

ALABAMA
4301 Norman Bridge Rd.
Montgomery 36101

ALASKA
Star Route A, Box 23H
Anchorage 99507

ARIZONA
5610 S. Central
Phoenix 75040

ARKANSAS
University Shopping Center
Little Rock 72204

CALIFORNIA
1225 Eighth St., Suite 312
Sacramento 95314

COLORADO
643 S. Broadway
Denver 80209

CONNECTICUT
410 Asylum St.
Hartford 06103

DELAWARE
Box 1896
Wilmington 19899

DISTRICST OF COLUMBIA
405 Riggs Rd., N.E.
Washington D.C. 20011

FLORIDA
P.O. Box 1542
Tallahassee 32302

GEORGIA
1575 Phoenix Blvd., Suite 8
Atlanta 30349

HAWAII
245 N. Kukui St.
Honolulu 96817

IDAHO
P.O. Box 816
Boise 83701

ILLINOIS
#6 N. Michigan Ave.
Chicago 60602

INDIANA
752 E. Market Street
Indianapolis 46202

IOWA
1707 High St.
Des Moines 50309

KANSAS
6100 Martway, Suite 1
Mission 66202

KENTUCKY
P.O. Box 275
Frankfort 40601

LOUISIANA
7465 Exchange Pl.
Baton Rouge 70806

MAINE
269 1/2 Water St.
Augusta 04330

MARYLAND
55 Gwynns Mill Ct.
Owings Mills 21117

MASSACHUSETTS
381 Elliot St.
Newton Upper Falls 02164

MICHIGAN
416 Michigan National Tower
Lansing 48933

MINNESOTA
3225 Lyndale Ave.
Minneapolis 55408

MISSISSIPPI
Box 1363
Jackson 39205

MISSOURI
230 W. Dunklin
Jefferson City 65101

MONTANA
P.O. Box 625
Helena 59601

NEBRASKA
620 N. 48th S-318
Lincoln 68504

NEVADA
1800 E. Sahara Ave., Suite 102
Las Vegas 89104

NEW HAMPSHIRE
52 Pleasant St.
Concord 03301

NEW JERSEY
97 Bayard St.
New Brunswick 08901

NEW MEXICO
8200 1/2 Menaul Blvd. NE, Suite 3,
Albuquerque 87110

NORTH CAROLINA
P.O. Box 18551
Raleigh 27609

NORTH DAKOTA

207 E. Broadway
Bismarck 58501

OHIO
61 E. Gay St.
Columbus 43215

OKLAHOMA
P.O. Box 14250
Oklahoma City 173114

OREGON
3085 River Rd.
N. Salem 97303

PENNSYLVANIA
1500 N. Second
Harrisburg 17102

RHODE ISLAND
Snow Bldg. 2845 Post Rd.
Warwick 02886

SOUTH CAROLINA
P.O. Box 1564
Columbia 29202

SOUTH DAKOTA
P.O. Box 502 111 W. Capitol
Pierre 57501

TENNESSEE
2121 Belcourt Ave.
Nashville 37212

TEXAS
833 W. Houston
Austin 78756

UTAH
2952 S. 7th East
Salt Lake City 84106

VERMONT
323 Pearl St.
Burlington 05401

VIRGINIA
827 E. Main St., Suite 1801
Richmond 23219

WASHINGTON
213 1/2 E. 4th, Suite 10
Olympia 98501

WEST VIRGINIA
Union Trust Bldg., Rm 614
Parkersburg 26101

WISCONSIN
351 W. Washington Ave.
Madison 53703

WYOMING
Box C.
Buffalo 82834

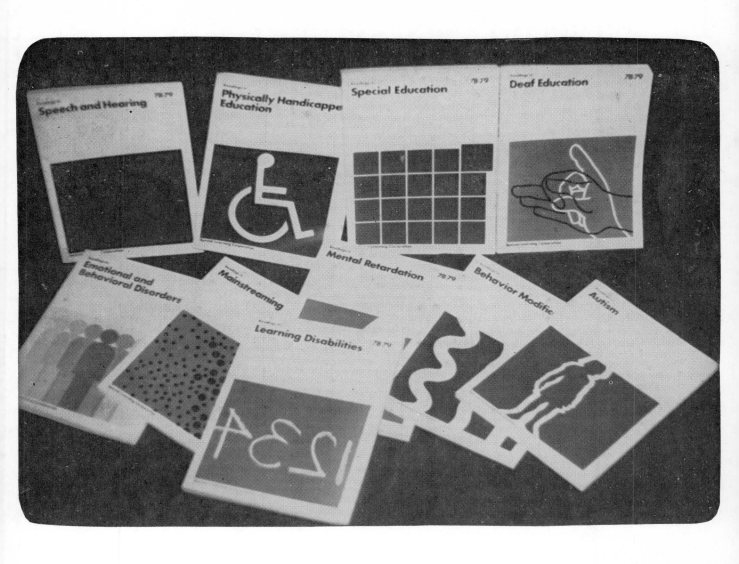

SPECIAL LEARNING CORPORATION
COMMENTS PLEASE:

Does this book fit your course of study?

Why? (Why not?)

Is this book useable for other courses of study? Please list.

What other areas would you like us to publish in using this format?

What type of exceptional child are you interested in learning more about?

Would you use this as a basic text?

How many students are enrolled in these course areas?

_____ Special Education _____ Mental Retardation _____ Psychology _____ Emotional Disorders
_____ Exceptional Children _____ Learning Disabilities   Other _____

Do you want to be sent a copy of our elementary student materials catalog?

Do you want a copy of our college catalog?

Would you like a copy of our next edition? ☐ yes ☐ no

Are you a ☐ student or an ☐ instructor?

Your name _____ school _____

Term used _____ Date _____

address _____

city _____ state _____ zip _____

telephone number _____

CUT HERE ● SEAL AND MAIL

V/T